MANAGING DIVERSITY THROUGH NON-TERRITORIAL AUTONOMY

Managing Diversity Through Non-Territorial Autonomy

Assessing Advantages, Deficiencies, and Risks

Edited by
TOVE H. MALLOY
ALEXANDER OSIPOV
and
BALÁZS VIZI

OXFORD
UNIVERSITY PRESS

OXFORD

UNIVERSITY PRESS

Great Clarendon Street, Oxford, OX2 6DP,
United Kingdom

Oxford University Press is a department of the University of Oxford.
It furthers the University's objective of excellence in research, scholarship,
and education by publishing worldwide. Oxford is a registered trade mark of
Oxford University Press in the UK and in certain other countries

Published in the United States of America by Oxford University Press
198 Madison Avenue, New York, NY 10016, United States of America

British Library Cataloguing in Publication Data
Data available

Library of Congress Control Number: 2015933280

ISBN 978–0–19–873845–9

Printed and bound by
CPI Group (UK) Ltd, Croydon, CR0 4YY

Acknowledgements

This volume is the first in a series of books constituting the output of a major programme that the European Centre for Minority Issues (ECMI) has initiated with the aim of exploring, understanding, and developing the concept of non-territorial autonomy (NTA) together with a number of partners. The series is expected to consist of five volumes that will address the status quo, the tensions within the concept, alternative approaches, theoretical and conceptual challenges, and new modes of application. The series will be elaborated from the perspectives of law and political science; it will be policy-oriented, and it will be global in scope. Authors and partners are members of the ECMI's general network, and the series editor is Tove Malloy. The ECMI would like to thank the Board of Oxford University Press for its interest in the topic and willingness to enter into this working relationship.

This first volume incorporates papers developed during a workshop organized by the ECMI in June 2011 and read during a workshop organized by the Tom Lantos Institute in May 2012. The final editorial work and revisions were prepared in cooperation with the Hungarian Academy of Sciences, Institute for Minority Studies (with the support of OTKA, K105432 project). Particular thanks go to the directors of the three institutions—Tove Malloy in Flensburg, Rita Izsák (and later Anna-Maria Bíró), and Attila Z. Papp in Budapest—for their generous support in securing funding for the project. The editors are also thankful to the numerous staff of the three institutions who have contributed to making the workshops and meetings happen.

The editors are deeply grateful to the contributors to this volume. They were very patient with us both in the search for a publisher and in the editorial process. Special thanks are due to Levente Salat who has shepherded the editorial team skilfully and with superior advice throughout the process. We also thank Oana Buta for providing copy-editing support and preparing the index and, to Jenő Böszörményi for preparing the front matter. At Oxford University Press, the editors would like to thank Alex Flach for his support in bringing our work to the Board of the publisher, Cathy Keable-Elliott for excellent copy-editing, Saipriya Kannan for patiently guiding us through the editing process, as well as Elinor Shields and Natasha Flemming for assisting us with relations with OUP.

The editors wish to dedicate this particular volume to the memory of Gáspár Bíró, Professor at the Institute of Political Science of the Faculty of Law, Eötvös Loránd University (Budapest) and a member of the Advisory Committee to the Framework Convention for the Protection of National Minorities in respect of Hungary for many years. Gáspár was himself an 'automomist' who championed the NTA model for Hungary in the early years after democratization. He remained, however, very critical of the 1993 Law which provisioned autonomy for the first time in Hungary. Gáspár was part of our project from the very beginning and was due to deliver the concluding analysis of the volume. His untimely passing in February 2014 deprived us all of a dear colleague and friend as well as a sharp and insightful mind and mentor in the studies of national minority rights.

Tove H. Malloy
Series Editor
Flensburg

Contents

III. SYMBOLIC PARTICIPATION

Table of Cases

CANADA

CROATIA

HUNGARY

RUSSIA

SERBIA

SLOVENIA

Table of Legislation

Table of International Treaties

Table of Documents

List of Abbreviations

ACFC	Advisory Committee on the Framework Convention
APK	The Assembly of People of Kazakhstan
APR	Assembly of the Peoples of Russia
BDN	Bund Deutscher Nordschleswiger
BNA	Act British North America Act
CEE	Central and Eastern Europe
CIEC	The Belarusian Consultative Inter-Ethnic Council
CLNM	Constitutional Law on Rights of National Minorities
CoE	Council of Europe
CSCE	Conference on Security and Co-operation in Europe
DE	Germany
DK	Denmark
DOS	Democratic Opposition of Serbia
EBLUL	European Bureau for Lesser-Used Languages
EC	European Commission
ECMI	European Centre for Minority Issues
EU	European Union
FCA	functional collective autonomy
FCNM	Framework Convention for the Protection of National Minorities
FIDESZ	Fiatal Demokraták Szövetsége
FUEN	Federal Union of European Nationalities
GONGO	governmental non-governmental organizations
ICCPR	International Covenant on Civil and Political Rights
ICESCR	International Covenant on Economic, Social and Cultural Rights
ILO 169	International Labour Organization Convention No. 169
INTERREG	European Territorial Cooperation
LHN	Landwirtschaftlicher Hauptverein für Nordschleswig
NATO	North Atlantic Treaty Organization
NCA	National-cultural autonomy
NGOs	non-governmental organizations
NMC	national minority councils
NTA	non-territorial autonomy
OLMCs	Official Language Minority Communities
OSCE	Organization for Security and Co-operation in Europe
OTKA	Országos Tudományos Kutatási Alapprogramok (in English: The Hungarian Scientific Research Fund)
PEI	Prince Edward Island
RAIPON	Russian Association of Small Indigenous Peoples of the North, Siberia and Far East
RFL	Radio Free Europe
RK	Republic of Kazakhstan
RL	Radio Liberty
RTV	Radio Television Slovenia

SP	Slesvigske Parti
SSF	Sydslesvigske Forening
SSV	Sydslesvigske Vælgerforening
SWOT analyses	Strengths, Weaknesses, Opportunities and Threats analyses
TA	territorial autonomy
UNDP	United Nations Development Programme
UNDRIP	UN Declaration on the Rights of Indigenous Peoples
UNESCO	United Nations Educational, Scientific and Cultural Organization
UNPFII	United Nations Permanent Forum on Indigenous Issues
VAH	Alliance of Vojvodina Hungarians
WCIP	World Council of Indigenous Peoples
WWII	Second World War

List of Contributors

Daniel Bourgeois is Executive Director of the Beaubassin Research Institute in Moncton, New Brunswick, Canada.

Timo Koivurova is Research Professor and Director of the Northern Institute for Environmental and Minority Law at the Arctic Centre, University of Lapland. He is also Docent of International Law in the Faculty of Law, Economics and Business Administration, University of Eastern Finland, and in the University of Turku.

Miran Komac is an Associate Professor at the University of Ljubljana and a Senior Researcher at the Institute for Ethnic Studies in Ljubljana.

Tamás Korhecz is Professor at the Union University Belgrade, Faculty for Legal and Business Studies, Novi Sad, and former President of the Hungarian National Council in Serbia.

Tove H. Malloy is Director of the European Centre for Minority Issues in Flensburg, Germany and Professor at the Europa-University, Flensburg.

Alexander Osipov is a Senior Research Associate of the European Centre for Minority Issues in Flensburg, Germany, and the head of ECMI's Justice and Governance Cluster.

Anna Petrétei is a Researcher and PhD student in the Northern Institute for Environmental and Minority Law at the Arctic Centre, University of Lapland.

Antonija Petričušić is a Lecturer in the Department of Sociology at the Faculty of Law at the University of Zagreb.

Vadim Poleshchuk was a Legal Advisor and Analyst at the Legal Information Centre for Human Rights in Tallinn, Estonia, from December 1999 until July 2014.

Detlev Rein was (until his retirement) Head of Division for National Minorities and Regional Languages in Germany, European Policy on Minorities, at the German Federal Ministry of the Interior.

Petra Roter is an Associate Professor of International Relations at the University of Ljubljana, and Co-ordinator of the MA Programme in International Relations at the Faculty of Social Sciences, University of Ljubljana.

Levente Salat is Professor of Political Science at Babes-Bolyai University in Cluj, Romania.

Adam Stępień is a Researcher and PhD student at the Arctic Centre, University of Lapland.

Sherrill Stroschein is Senior Lecturer in Politics at University College London.

Balázs Vizi is Researcher at the Centre for Social Science of the Hungarian Academy of Sciences, Senior Researcher at the European Centre for Minority Issues in Flensburg, Germany, and an Associate Professor at the Department of International and European Law of the National University of Public Service, Budapest.

Introduction

Tove H. Malloy

Non-territorial autonomy (NTA) is one policy tool of a greater family of state-craft tools that aim to accommodate ethno-cultural diversity in situations where states must either cope with division due to irreconcilable differences or wish to develop society through promoting diversity as an added value. In either case, NTA aims to consolidate the state and promote social unity through accommodating ethno-cultural demands and requirements. As such, the viability of NTA as a state policy is vital not only to enhancing social unity but also to ensuring justice. Moreover, as a diversity management tool, NTA can contribute to social cohesion. However, the conceptual and functional features of NTA are poorly defined. Conceptually, NTA lives in the shadow of the much broader toolkit available for territorial autonomy (TA) regions. Both notions imply autonomy for ethno-cultural groups, but they are tools with distinct, separate aims. Moreover, the functions of NTA are rarely described comprehensively due to the concept's conflation with the very broad regime of human and minority rights. True, NTA needs to be normatively underpinned, but its institutional functions must be in place in order to speak of and implement autonomy. This volume seeks to describe and analyse the various functions of NTA through a number of case studies of existing NTA arrangements in Europe and Canada. The aim is twofold. On the one hand, we wish to contribute to sharpening the conceptual contours of NTA. On the other, we hope to provide informed contextual knowledge on the basis of which decision-makers and policymakers may determine the viability of NTA as a diversity management tool for policymaking in multicultural and multi-ethnic states.

1. The NTA Research Profile

This is not to argue that there is a shortage of research in the field of autonomy studies. Heretofore, a broad field of autonomy research has collected and analysed examples of autonomy arrangements. One need only refer to the seminal works of Hurst Hannum,[1] Ruth Lapidoth,[2] Markku Suksi,[3] Yash Ghai,[4] Weller and Wolff,[5] as well as Zelim Skurbaty.[6] This research has focused on TA in federal and centralized states from the perspective of law and conflict studies in political science and international relations.[7] With very few exceptions, this body of research has focused mainly on the macro perspective of policymaking.[8] However, unlike this established field of research, NTA research has not developed into a separate field; at best, it has attained a sub-field status within autonomy research, and even that is an over-statement. Very few works dedicated solely to NTA exist in Anglo-American academic literature. These may be divided into several sub-fields of research, such as nationalism studies,[9] conflict studies,[10] and diversity management studies.[11] And like most TA research, these NTA studies focus on the macro perspective.[12]

---

[1] Hurst Hannum, *Autonomy, Sovereignty, and Self-Determination. The Accommodation of Conflicting Rights* (Philadelphia: University of Pennsylvania Press, 1990).

[2] Ruth Lapidoth, *Autonomy. Flexible Solutions to Ethnic Conflicts* (Washington, D.C.: United States Institute of Peace, 1996).

[3] Markuu Suksi, ed., *Autonomy, Applications and Implications* (The Hague: Kluwer Law International, 1998). See also André Légaré and Markku Suksi, 'Introduction: Rethinking Forms of Autonomy at the Dawn of the 21st Century', *International Journal on Minority and Group Rights* vol. 15, nos 2–3 (2008): pp. 195–225.

[4] Yash Ghai, ed., *Autonomy and Ethnicity: Negotiating Competing Claims* (Cambridge: Cambridge University Press, 2000).

[5] Marc Weller and Stefan Wolff, eds, *Autonomy, Self-Governance and Conflict Resolution. Innovative Approaches to Institutional Design in Divided Societies* (London: Routledge, 2005).

[6] Zelim A. Skurbaty, ed., *Beyond a One-Dimensional State: An Emerging Right to Autonomy?* (Leiden/Boston: Martinus Nijhoff Publishers, 2005).

[7] See also Javaid Rehman, 'The Concept of Autonomy and Minority Rights in Europe', in *Minority Rights in the 'New' Europe*, edited by Peter Cumper and Steven Wheatley (The Hague: Martinus Nijhoff Publishers, 1999), pp. 217–32; and more recently, Zoltan Kantor, ed., *Autonomies in Europe: Solutions and Challenges* (Budapest: L'Harmattan, 2014).

[8] For a good example of a legal description of TA, see Jens Woelk, Francesco Palermo, and Joseph Marko, eds, *Tolerance through Law: Self-Governance and Group Rights in South Tyrol* (Leiden: Martinus Nijhoff Publishers, 2008).

[9] Ephraim J. Nimni, ed., *Otto Bauer: The Question of Nationalities and Social Democracy* (Minneapolis: University of Minnesota Press, 2000); Ephraim Nimni, Alexander Osipov, and David J. Smith, eds, *The Challenge of Non-Territorial Autonomy. Theory and Practice* (Oxford: Peter Lang, 2013).

[10] John Coakley, 'Approaches to the Resolution of Ethnic Conflict: The Strategy of Non-Territorial Autonomy', *International Political Science Review* vol. 15, no. 3 (1994): pp. 297–314. See also Steven C. Roach, *Cultural Autonomy, Minority Rights and Globalization* (Aldershot: Ashgate, 2005).

[11] David J. Smith and Karl Kordell, eds, *Cultural Autonomy in Contemporary Europe* (London: Routledge, 2008); see also André Légaré and Markku Suksi, 'Introduction: Rethinking Forms of Autonomy at the Dawn of the 21st Century', *International Journal on Minority and Group Rights* vol. 15, nos 2–3 (2008): pp. 195–225; *Ethnopolitics* vol. 6, no. 3 (2007): Kinga Gal, ed., *Minority Governance in Europe* (Budapest: Local Government and Public Service Reform Initiative, 2002).

[12] A few individual papers have focused on the implementation of NTA models. See for instance, D. Christopher Decker, 'The Use of Cultural Autonomy to Prevent Conflict and Meet the Copenhagen Criteria: The Case of Romania', *Ethnopolitics* vol. 6, no. 3 (2007): pp. 437–50; Balázs Dobos, 'The Development and Functioning of Cultural Autonomy in Hungary', *Ethnopolitics* vol. 6, no. 3 (2007): pp. 451–69; and Bill Bowring, 'The Tatars of the Russian Federation and National-Cultural Autonomy: A Contradiction in Terms?', *Ethnopolitics* vol. 6, no. 3 (2007): pp. 417–36.

There are reasons for the hegemony of TA studies, most notably the direction taken by contemporary discourses on European history, but also conceptual ones. With regard to contemporary discourses, TA research speaks to the security paradigm defining both European and global history of interstate relations over the last 400–500 years whereas NTA was seen as a religious accommodation tool in contemporary statecraft. With regard to the conceptual perspective, TA speaks to the security paradigm in terms of the diffusion of power to collectivities that are fairly easy to define as well as in terms of the nationalism discourse, whereas NTA diffuses power to individuals expressing group identities but living dispersed among the majority populations and thus very difficult to define. As such, NTA as a concept may overlap with the human and minority rights paradigm after World War II that emancipates the individual as opposed to the group. Because NTA as a distinct research field, and more importantly as a policy tool, has not been excavated from the TA research field, it is difficult to determine its value as a statecraft tool for multicultural and multi-ethnic societies. This volume aims to fill this gap.

2. The Aims of the Book

As noted, the main aim of this volume is to begin carving out a space for knowledge production on NTA in law and the social and political sciences. While the super goal is to produce open-ended knowledge, the specific purpose with regard to this volume is to produce contextualized knowledge on NTA arrangements in Europe and Canada. Contextual knowledge is particularly relevant for decision-making and policymaking. Contextual knowledge on NTA arrangements involves the description of institutions and their functionality as well as of the institutional and legal frames protecting them. It also involves critical assessment and risk analyses as well as penetrating insights as to the unintended consequences and hidden agendas behind NTA policies. All knowledge is of course theoretically informed, and this is also the case with contextualized NTA research. However, theoretical underpinnings of research are often not clearly delineated; often concepts float around in a sea of mist or are borrowed from one context to the next without logical or coherent explanations. As a result, the concept of NTA is at best opaque as to the differences between applications, at worst incorrectly analysed. In order to begin overcoming this problem, this volume will address three key approaches of NTA functions that devolve power to ethno-cultural groups living dispersed within multicultural states: (1) voice, (2) *quasi*-voice, and (3) non-voice.

With regard to *voice*, we will focus on self-governing policies for ethno-cultural minorities. We will ask, what self-governing institutions ethno-cultural groups have that enable them to take decisions or participate in decision-making about affairs relevant to their existence as distinct groups? Not all forms of representation and participation provide for autonomous decision-making. Thus, we ask, are these institutions really exercising diffusion of powers, and do they provide the freedom of choice and thought to the organizations representing ethno-cultural groups seeking protection and promotion of their culture? With regard to *quasi-voice* we will focus on minority organizations established under public and private law. We will ask what self-management institutions exist that assist minorities in preserving and promoting their minority culture. Specifically, we try to ascertain if self-management involves self-governance, that is, do minority organizations decide on how to manage their institutions, or do they take directions from dominant groups imposing their ideological views through regulations and legal provisions? And with regard to *non-voice* we will focus on symbolic policies. We will ask whether there are NTA arrangements that purport to promote ethno-cultural autonomy without fulfilling the general aims of NTA as a right to make decisions or to co-decision. Basically, we wonder whether NTA has been used in manners that go against the core tenets of the notion of autonomy.

As such, our approach is conceptual and problem-oriented in its focus. We have sought to be systematic and comprehensive in the analysis of NTA examples. The chapters in this volume aim to describe the ideological backgrounds to NTA examples by analysing terminology, objectives, justifications, formal and informal practice, as well as legal frameworks. In other words, how are NTA arrangements presented in the broader narratives and discourses of diversity management in the particular state? The main aim of the chapters is to provide a mapping of the institutions and functionality of NTA examples. Do the NTA arrangements create and facilitate institutions, do they provide for resource distribution and accumulation, do they promote the acquisition and fulfillment of public competences, or perhaps local authority, do they provide for service delivery, and finally, what diffusion of power functions do they provide in terms of representation with decision-making powers? Moving from the descriptive to the analytical, the chapters will also discuss dynamics and outcomes of NTA arrangements. What achievements and failures are there, and what about unintended consequences? To fortify this discussion and enable analysis of the legitimacy of NTA examples, we also seek to bring in the beneficiaries by describing their reactions and views. Finally, the chapters will, where feasible, offer recommendations to policymakers with regard to strategic value and to ethno-cultural organizations with regard to legitimacy. A major ambition of this volume is thus to create a new methodological platform for NTA research through the institutional approach, since such has not been attempted systematically in the academic literature so far.

3. Defining NTA

The lack of clarity and accuracy in defining NTA derives, we believe, from the lack of institutional descriptions. References to institutions such as consultative bodies and reserved seats in local assemblies or parliaments are at times used as evidence of ethno-cultural groups holding the right to self-government even if in fact they have representation rights without autonomous powers. Elections to school boards may mean a say over educational issues but it needs to be established how such school boards actually function: are they defining their own governance, or do they have to follow regulations set by the majority? It is clearly not easy to penetrate the many layers of governance and legislation to properly unearth the functioning of all institutions of NTA. However, lack of institutional description creates a gulf between theory and practice: what is observed is likely to be erroneously analysed as NTA, and what is perceived as theoretically valid is perhaps not reality. It is not feasible to determine the reasons for such scholarly stretches here. We know that the notion of autonomy is used in several academic disciplines and derives from the ancient Greek idea of the right or ability to make one's own laws.[13] In law and the social and political sciences, the notion takes guidance from the philosophical notion of self-mastery and positive liberty through one's own rational will. Specifically with regard to positive liberty, it is important to stress the idea of being free from dominance and coercion.[14] But to gain conceptual clarity, institutional knowledge and functional precision are vital. And more importantly, to provide advice in policymaking, it is essential.

Ironically, the reason why institutional knowledge is important has been pointed out early in the history of developing autonomy research and in the quest for a conceptual definition. Ruth Lapidoth, who in 1997 offered one of the most systematic accounts of the phenomenon of autonomy in statecraft, summarizes the academic consensus on the concept of autonomy into five main categories: (1) the right to act on one's own discretion; (2) independence; (3) decentralization; (4) exclusive powers of legislation; administration, and adjudication in specific areas; and (5) limited self-rule seen mainly as part of the minority rights regime.[15] She concludes that this typology requires that one distinguish between administrative autonomy and political autonomy.[16] Lapidoth elaborated her study in terms of specific TA arrangements, such as federalism, decentralization, self-government, associate statehood, and self-administration backed up by a number of case studies, all of which pertain to TA. With regard to NTA, Lapidoth offers a brief discussion of what she calls personal or cultural autonomy.[17] This notion, she argues, emerged with the view to protect minorities living dispersed among the majority population. Specific historical examples according to Lapidoth are the Jews in Europe and non-Muslims in the Ottoman Empire. After World War I, certain countries adopted minority protection schemes that provisioned self-rule institutions in cultural areas, such as language, religion, and education. It follows, according to Lapidoth, that the difference between personal (cultural) autonomy and minority rights is mainly institutional; without self-regulating institutions, personal (cultural) autonomy does not exist.

---

[13] *Auto* = self, *nomos* = law or rule.

[14] Philip Pettit, *Republicanism. A Theory of Freedom and Government* (Oxford: Clarendon Press, 1997).

[15] Ruth Lapidoth, *Autonomy*, ch 3.

[16] Lapidoth offers her own definition of political autonomy for territorial units: 'a territorial political autonomy is an arrangement aimed at granting to a group that differs from the majority of the population in the state, but that constitutes the majority in a specific region, a means by which it can express its distinct identity'. Lapidoth, *Autonomy*, ch 3.

[17] Lapidoth, *Autonomy*, ch 4.

Lapidoth further notices that personal (cultural) autonomy might be extended to other areas of societal issues, such as national questions of foreign affairs and security, through the notion of national cultural autonomy (NCA) developed by Karl Renner.[18] Renner's approach basically promoted a matrix-type organization of public administration in culturally diverse states allowing for self-rule to ethno-cultural groups in (local) cultural and educational affairs while consociational institutions would rule the (national) central affairs, such as security and foreign affairs. The beneficiaries of NCA were identified on the basis of the 'personality principle', that is, the declaration of allegiance and belonging to a certain ethno-cultural group at the age of voting.[19] Of course, the 'personality principle' has since lost all legitimacy in light of the singling out of minorities by the National Socialists during World War II, and in fact resulted in the emergence of the freedom of choice to belong or not belong after that war.[20] Lapidoth also notes that TA and NTA are not mutually exclusive; they can well be applied in parallel in the same region or country. However, she argues that ethno-cultural groups, like minorities, often seek TA powers because these are stronger than personal (cultural) autonomy powers, for instance with regard to self-rule in socio-economic areas. She argues, therefore, that the scope of personal (cultural) autonomy should perhaps be extended to these areas as long as it does not regulate any territorial issues.

One might question whether Renner and Lapidoth were not consumed by the conceptual mist that engulfs NTA research when seeking to extend powers to national (central) affairs. Today, almost twenty years after Lapidoth's excellent account, it remains questionable whether the scope of personal (cultural) autonomy is seeing an extension to these levels. None of the examples described in this volume attest to this. However, in terms of the diffusion of personal (cultural) autonomy powers exercised through institutions and institutional frameworks, as defined above, Lapidoth's argument guides this volume. The institutional approach will allow not only policymakers but also beneficiaries a set of options from which to choose when seeking to accommodate ethno-cultural diversity. Moreover, given that Lapidoth foresees the target group as members of ethno-cultural groups who live dispersed in society, her argument speaks to the non-territorial notion assumed in NTA. Beneficiaries of NTA need not live together in one area or region; they may benefit from the diffusion of powers anywhere within the territory of the

---

[18] Karl Renner, *Das Selbstbestimmungsrecht der Nationen in besonderer Anwendung aug Österreich* (Leipzig/Vienna: Franz Deuticke, 1918).

[19] See Ephraim Nimni, 'National-Cultural Autonomy as an Alternative to Minority Territorial Nationalism', *Ethnopolitics* vol. 6, no. 3 (2007): pp. 345–64.

[20] For an example of the freedom of choice in minority rights, see the European Framework Convention for the Protection of National Minorities, art 3, available online, accessed 24 September 2014, <http://conventions.coe.int/Treaty/en/Treaties/Html/157.htm>. For an example of the 'personality principle' still in use, see the Autonomy Statute for the Province of Bozen/Bolzano and Emma Lantschner and Poggeschi Giovanni, 'Quota System, Census and Declaration of Affiliation to a Linguistic Group', in *Tolerance through Law: Self-Governance and Group Rights in South Tyrol*, edited by Jens Woelk, Francesco Palermo, and Joseph Marko (Leiden: Martinus Nijhoff Publishers, 2008).

state. Whether this is implemented is another question. This would be dependent on the individual claiming such powers; often this does not happen. Therefore, the most important factor is Lapidoth's insistence on the existence of institutions; without institutions, NTA is not autonomy.

We might in fact speak of 'institutional NTA' in order to underline the difference between NTA and the broader regime of human and minority rights. The question is which institutions are relevant as NTA institutions? When can we argue that NTA exists? More importantly, how do we determine that these institutions allow ethno-cultural groups a degree of self-rule? To answer these questions, we need to unpack institutional NTA further.

4. Merits and Problems of Institutional NTA

Following Lapidoth, NTA institutions may address administrative issues and/or political issues, and they may address only certain sectors, such as culture, religion, and education, as opposed to addressing the broad spectrum of societal sectors, from the administrative issues of culture to the socio-economic sectors, and foreign policy and security. There is thus clearly a menu of sectors from which to choose, just as there is a scope for devolving degrees of self-rule administratively or politically, that is, weak self-rule versus strong self-rule. The fewer sectors, the weaker the self-rule arrangement; the more sectors included in the NTA arrangement, the stronger the self-rule. Moreover, the nature of the institutions also will determine the strength of the NTA arrangement. Strong institutions may provide co-decision power at all political levels, whereas very weak institutions may provide a mere consultative function, formal or informal. Some strong institutions may provide self-government or self-governing and perhaps degrees of self-determination, whereas weaker institutions concentrate on providing the individual members of minorities with certain freedoms of choice. Medium-strong institutions may provide degrees of self-management or self-governing in areas of ethno-cultural minority identity, including education and language, religion, and folklore activities as well as social care for the elderly. Thus, one can place institutional NTA on a continuum from the very weak to the very strong in terms of self-rule decision power.[21] Or, one can think of NTA as less onerous to very onerous ('expensive' or burdensome) in terms of both legal strength and political burdens.

The political burden may be defined further depending on specific and unique historical and regional aspects. One example is language policies. Linguistic rights may be addressed at the political and cultural levels, or only at the cultural level. Strong institutions tend to be underpinned by national political decisions on

---

[21] See Andreea Cârstocea, and Mindaugas Kuklys, 'Contemporary Accommodation of Minority Groups: A Continuum of Institutional Approaches', *ECMI Handbook* (2015, forthcoming). See also Michael Tkacik, 'Characteristics of Forms of Autonomy', *International Journal on Minority and Group Rights* vol. 15 (2008): pp. 369–401.

language policies of bilingualism or multilingualism, depending on the situation. Weaker institutions tend to handle linguistic rights as a cultural matter. Thus, political rights emanating from language policies involve linguistic rights in both the private and the public spheres, whereas linguistic rights aimed at cultural protection involve mainly the educational and private spheres.

The degree of funding to back up approaches and instruments is also a variable. No matter how beautiful the law text, and even if NTA is adopted by consensus, NTA without financial support and sustainability is inherently weak, if not non-existent. Moreover, at times financial support is extended but without autonomous powers to decide how the funds are used, thus putting in question the degree of autonomy. Finally, the degree to which institutions are anchored in law also determines the strength and degree of self-rule. Institutions may be either constitutionally entrenched or they may be adopted as statutes. A mixture of public and private law approaches exist in some countries while most countries prefer public law instruments. In some cases, private law institutions and a degree of trust can allow ethno-cultural groups self-management.

The questions to answer with regard to institutions are daunting, to say the least, but must be attempted. What follows in the rest of this section is a brief line-up of ethno-cultural institutions and institutional frames that may or may not provide NTA powers but which could be seen as relevant for ascertaining degrees of self-rule, either individually or in conjunction with other institutions.

4.1 Consultative bodies

Consultation with ethno-cultural groups is particularly important in countries where there are no arrangements to enable participation of minorities in parliament or other elected bodies. As such, states can establish advisory or consultative bodies within appropriate institutional frameworks to serve as channels for dialogue between governmental authorities and minorities.[22] In order to ensure the legitimacy of consultative bodies, it is essential that their appointment procedures be transparent and inclusive allowing for members of ethno-cultural groups to maintain their independence. Specific types of consultative bodies that include ad hoc consultations can be useful to address particular issues while special purpose committees may be useful for addressing issues such as housing, land, education, language, and culture. It is essential that the legal status, role, duties, membership, and institutional position of consultative bodies be clearly defined just as it is important to ensure that consultative bodies have a legal personality (lack of this may undermine their effectiveness and their capacity to fulfil their mission). Publicity of the work of consultative bodies should be promoted to enhance transparency. Most importantly, the effective functioning of these bodies will require that they have adequate resources.

---

[22] Marc Weller and Katherine Nobbs, eds, *Political Participation of Minorities: A Commentary on International Standards and Practice* (Oxford: Oxford University Press, 2010).

Consultative bodies should be duly consulted in the process of drafting new legislation, including constitutional reforms that directly or indirectly affect minorities. They should be able to raise issues with decision-makers, to formulate legislative and other proposals, as well as to prepare recommendations. Furthermore, they should be empowered to monitor developments and to provide views on proposed governmental decisions that may directly or indirectly affect minorities. While the system of consultative bodies may sound onerous to governments due to the need to ensure it through law and resource allocation, it is usually the least costly for governments to implement. Consultative bodies exist in numerous countries across Europe, including but not exclusively in Belarus, Czech Republic, Denmark, Finland, Germany, Moldova, the Netherlands, and Romania.

4.2 Service institutions

Public–private service institutions formed by ethno-cultural groups, who are not territorially defined, provide services to these minority groups. They usually take a variety of shapes. The issues most susceptible to regulation by these arrangements include education, culture, use of minority language, religion, and other matters crucial to the identity and way of life of minorities. Individuals and groups have the right to choose to use their names in the minority language and obtain official recognition of their names. Taking into account the responsibility of the state authorities to set educational standards, ethno-cultural minority institutions can usually determine curricula for teaching of their minority languages, cultures, or both. Ethno-cultural minorities can also determine and enjoy their own symbols and other forms of cultural expression. For this reason, service institutions are found as medium-strong on the continuum. The cost of such approaches varies from country to country and according to the development of social models. Service institutions may be established in private law both with and without government subsidies, or they may be established in public law with funding on an equal basis with majority institutions. The more autonomy the institutions have, the stronger the degree of NTA power. Service institutions thus leave a large amount of discretion to governments and policymakers as to the level of burden carried by public programmes. Many countries have opted for this approach as it provides for adjustment to specific circumstances, including for instance Austria, Canada, Denmark, Germany, the Netherlands, and Ukraine.

4.3 Political representation

Having representation in the political sphere means being heard, and depending on the nature of the representation it may also mean participating in decision-making. There are numerous ways to have representation; consultative bodies are also a type of representation. But where consultative bodies do not provide for voting rights, political representation usually does. At the political level representation tends to be more formal and usually enshrined in law, at either the national or local level. For this reason, it is a stronger institution than consultative bodies. However, governments may consider it onerous, not only because allowing political representation usually requires subsidies to office holders and party secretariats, but also because it cements the relationship into law.

Reserved seats in parliamentary assemblies are a way to recognize the right of ethno-cultural groups to participate in the political decision-making process. Opinions vary as to the effectiveness of reserved seats, and critics warn that they may only have token value. Many countries, however, practise the system, for instance when ethno-cultural minorities are too small to be able to compete in the regular political party system. Countries also combine reserved seats with other institutions of accommodation, including consultative bodies. While reserving seats in parliamentary assemblies must be formalized, there is also an option to reserve seats in terms of cabinet positions, seats on the supreme or constitutional court or lower courts, and positions on nominated advisory bodies or other high-level organs.[23] Many countries provide for reserved seats, mostly in parliaments. These include Belgium, Denmark, Croatia, Finland, Italy, Kazakhstan, and Slovenia.

Most countries in Europe permit ethno-cultural minority parties. The right to form political parties is based on several human rights standards, such as the freedom of expression, the freedom of thought, and the freedom of assembly. It is therefore a core democratic institution that should be available to all. Ethno-cultural parties usually form on the basis of ethnic or religious identities.[24] For ethno-cultural groups to be able to form political parties and to compete in the public sphere for opinions and claims is a major tool of access to the decision-making process in democratic societies. Even though ethno-cultural parties are likely to get out-voted by the majority, they nevertheless provide ethno-cultural groups with a voice. In that sense, ethno-cultural parties range higher on the scale of institutions, or on the continuum they are stronger institutions than consultative bodies. For governments ethno-cultural parties may be seen as onerous in the sense that they will require subsidies on an equal footing with other parties. Funding ethno-cultural parties equally with majority parties is however a democratic right.

Experience in Europe demonstrates the importance of the electoral process for facilitating the participation of ethno-cultural groups in the political sphere. States are supposed to guarantee the right of ethno-cultural minorities to take part in the

---

[23] See for instance, Florian Bieber, 'Power-Sharing at the Governmental Level', in *Political Participation of Minorities: A Commentary on International Standards and Practice*, edited by Marc Weller and Katherine Nobbs (Oxford: Oxford University Press, 2010), pp. 414–33; and Francesco Palermo, 'At the Heart of Participation and of its Dilemmas: Minorities in the Executive Structures', in *Political Participation of Minorities: A Commentary on International Standards and Practice*, edited by Marc Weller and Katherine Nobbs (Oxford: Oxford University Press, 2010), pp. 434–52.
[24] For a definition of ethnic minority parties, see Janusz Bugajski, *Ethnic Politics in Eastern Europe: A Guide to Nationality Policies, Organizations, and Parties* (New York: Sharpe Armonk, 1993); Janusz Bugajski, *Political Parties of Eastern Europe. A Guide to Politics in the Post-Communist Era* (Armonk, NY/London: M. E. Sharpe, 2002); Karl Cordell, ed., *Ethnicity and Democratisation in the New Europe* (New York: Routledge, 1999); Levente Salat and Monica Robotin, eds, *A New Balance: Democracy and Minorities in Post-Communist Europe* (Budapest: Local Government and Public Reform Initiative, 2003); Lieven De Winter and Huri Türsan, eds, *Regionalist Parties in Western Europe* (London: Routledge, 1998).

political debate and process. International law prescribes the principle of freedom of association through the right to form political parties, including the freedom to establish political parties based on collective identities, such as culture, language, religion, or ethnicity. Where ethno-cultural groups are concentrated territorially, districts may provide sufficient minority representation. However, it might be necessary to allow for lower numerical thresholds for representation in the legislature to enhance the inclusion of ethno-cultural minorities in the political process. In that sense geographic boundaries of electoral districts should facilitate equitable representation of minorities. Systems of reduced thresholds do raise controversy in countries where they exist as well as in countries that have not adopted the approach. The notion is often raised that ethno-cultural minorities get a 'discount' and thus may not represent proportionally as many voters as ordinary parties while nevertheless holding the same degree of power. For this reason, securing the right to be exempt from thresholds at the constitutional level is often necessary, so that it may not be contested in courts. As such, it provides for a stronger measure from the perspective of diffusion of powers. Governments may see constitutionalization as a high 'price' to pay. Perhaps for that reason, threshold exemptions do not exist in many European countries; but Italy, Germany, Poland, and Romania provide for such.

A strong form of institutional, political accommodation is participation in coalition governments.[25] This presumes, however, a consistent participatory pattern in politics, not only through representation but also through effective participation in public affairs across the board. In other words, ethno-cultural minorities will need to be represented in a broad spectrum of society's institutions. It requires for the minorities to have a platform for the future of the shared nation in terms of all aspects of society management, including foreign and security policy. Not many ethno-cultural groups achieve this strong presence in mainstream society. In Europe, examples of coalition governments that included ethno-cultural parties have existed at the national level in Belgium, Croatia, Finland, Lithuania, the Netherlands, Romania, Slovakia, and Switzerland. At the local level, ethno-cultural minorities have been in coalition in Germany, Italy, Lithuania, Romania, and Switzerland.

4.4 Self-governing

Self-governing institutions hover between administrative autonomy and political autonomy. Often self-governing institutions are a combination of the institutions mentioned above. Usually this approach is referred to as self-government, although the institutions do not provide for government-type tasks. They may, however, be devolved powers in terms of self-government in certain competence areas, such as political decisions about these institutions. For this reason, self-governing

---

[25] For a good discussion on coalition building, see Giovanni Sartori, *Parties and Party Systems: A Framework for Analysis* (Cambridge: Cambridge University Press, 1976).

institutions provide a greater degree of autonomy than the public–private institutions. Basically, self-governing allows ethno-cultural minorities the ability to consent or dissent on the issues relevant to their community. Self-governing institutions are, therefore, placed high on the scale of the continuum. Self-governing institutions are, by the nature of the stronger NTA powers, also more onerous to sustain. Systems of self-governing exist, among others, in Belgium, Finland, Hungary, Norway, and Slovenia.

5. Trends in NTA Research

There is no doubt that ethno-cultural minority institutions exist across Europe, East and West, as well as in Canada. Usually, ethno-cultural minority groups seek NTA powers because they object to assimilative strategies of governments and wish to preserve and promote their culture and identity. Governments, on the other hand, will usually have country-specific reasons for choosing NTA as a tool of accommodation. Country-specific reasons are often determined by historical legacies and events. Depending on the nature of the country-specific reasons, governments may choose instrumental and/or normative approaches. Distinguishing between instrumental and normative approaches is not always possible in determining a government strategy. A crude analysis would hold that instrumental approaches usually have the overall aim of holding control over territory and populations, whereas normative approaches aim to provide justice. A more sophisticated analysis would reveal that normative approaches may also have instrumental aims, especially if providing justice secures control over territory and populations. A common denominator is, therefore, control.

Control in the political and social sciences usually refers to the hegemony of one dominant group, often a particular ethno-cultural group, over state ideology and institutions held through manipulative methods.[26] If a dominant group is to relinquish any control, it will depend on the depth of the divide between dominant and non-dominant groups as well as on the prospects of maintaining hegemony. Surrendering some control while maintaining hegemony is only possible if territorial borders remain intact, and in so far as that power over all important institutions servicing the dominant group remains unchallenged. Thus, any diffusion of powers to non-dominant groups will have to be measured carefully, and most likely be weak and controllable in nature. Autonomy as a concept signifying restricted diffusion of power fits into this scenario of maintaining control through devolution.

Government strategies with regard to maintaining control of ethno-cultural groups have taken two main paths over the twentieth century. Most dominant has

---

[26] Ian Lustick, 'Stability in Deeply Divided Societies: Consociationalism versus Control', *World Politics* vol. 31, no. 3 (1979): pp. 325–44; Eric Kaufmann, ed., *Rethinking Ethnicity: Majority Groups and Dominant Minorities* (London: Routledge, 2004).

been the security approach, which aims to control non-dominant groups without diluting state power. This approach is the legacy of several hundred years of wars in the European continent; wars that often were fought over territory and thus over population groups living in these territories. These population groups were often minorities either in terms of religious or linguistic differences or in terms of national allegiances. Especially, national allegiances of such groups to their mother group have been the cause for conflict and strife. Hence, the securitization of issues related to accommodation has contributed to the overpowering position that the security approach has held and still holds in contemporary research on TA. The other approach is the minority rights approach, or the protection approach, which is considered a normative strategy and an approach that seeks to accommodate non-dominant groups based on good faith rather than control. The aim here is to implement some positive measures for non-dominant groups because they are seen as representing an intrinsic cultural value, be it a culture, a nation, a religion, or some other. The minority rights regime developed in Europe after 1990 includes a few positive measures all of which are cast nevertheless in very cautious state-centred language. Thus, it could be argued that minority protection in terms of the paternalistic normative framework also belongs in the category of control.[27] As noted, instrumental approaches can also have normative aims. This may be a reason why NTA research lacks clarity as to the concept's position and aim as a statecraft instrument.

A important reason why studies of the two strategy approaches do not provide a full picture of the strategic role that institutional NTA plays in the statecraft of multicultural and multi-ethnic societies is the predominant focus on the macro-level perspective. Both strategies are top-down, and both provision primarily formal measures and instruments through legal frameworks. They both see the power relations between dominant and non-dominant groups as hegemonic in a traditional paternalistic and controlling sense, meaning the dominant group decides to which fraction of power the non-dominant group is entitled. Thus, studies analyse the macro level of the state or of international cooperation; hence, overlooking meso- and micro-level action and actors. And in so doing, they overlook the functions of NTA institutions as a diversity management and statecraft tool.

6. Plan of the Book

As already hinted in section 2, this volume is divided into three parts, each devoted to analysing different degrees of power devolution in terms of the strength of voice that ethno-cultural groups have in their own affairs and in the community. For each part we have identified relevant case studies that aim to support the specific purpose of producing contextualized knowledge on institutional NTA in Europe

---

[27] Jennifer Jackson Preece, *National Minorities and the European Nation-States System* (Oxford: Oxford University Press, 1998).

and Canada. Thus, a mapping of NTA arrangements in a number of countries will lay the foundation for the conclusive analysis on the concept of NTA as well as the final statecraft analysis. The authors of the individual chapters are associating themselves with the theories of their choice but have been asked to apply the institutional approach to the description and analysis of the relevant NTA models adopted within the country they have been assigned. The chapters are structured according to a stylized description of the ethno-cultural institutions and the dynamics of these, including brief analyses of the outcomes of the implementation of NTA powers.

In order to set the stage for the micro-level discussions, Chapter 1 starts out at the macro level with a discussion that interrogates the political issues that states may face when seeking to decide on a strategy to accommodate ethno-cultural groups, including the possibility of choosing between TA and NTA (Sherrill Stroschein). Unlike most works on autonomy that praise the model of TA as the superior model of accommodation and minority–majority relations as a zero-sum game, the discussion in Chapter 1 highlights the advantages of NTA as a peaceful solution to inter-ethnic and inter-cultural settlement.

Part I focuses on the aspect of voice through institutions of self-governing. Five country cases have been identified to represent the idea that NTA institutions enable ethno-cultural groups to take decisions or participate in decision-making about affairs relevant to their existence. The discussion in this part begins with Chapter 2 detailing the system of 'self-government' in Hungary (Balázs Vizi) and continues in Chapters 3 and 4 with two examples of NTA through national minority councils in Croatia and Serbia (Antonija Petričušić and Tamás Korhecz). Chapter 5 discusses NTA arrangements for Hungarians and Italians in Slovenia (Miran Komac and Petra Roter), and finally Chapter 6 provides an analysis of the institutionalization of the Sami Parliaments in Finland (Adam Stępień, Anna Petrétei, and Timo Koivurova).

Part II continues to deal with voice, however, in a weaker sense in terms of the delegation of public functions to ethno-cultural minorities. To recall, we term this *quasi*-voice as it is questionable how autonomous such institutions are. Three examples have been selected to discuss this phenomenon. The discussion starts in Chapter 7 with a description of the self-management of minority education in Canada (Daniel Bourgeois). Chapter 8 discusses the institutional framework for the Sorbs in Germany and asks whether this is in fact a case of NTA (Detlev Rein), and Chapter 9 takes a cross-national perspective and discusses functional NTA in a reciprocal setting, namely between Denmark and Northern Germany (Tove Malloy).

Part III focuses on the weakest form of autonomy. Basically, the two selected cases in this part represent what we have termed non-voice following the arguments made in the two chapters. This is because they do not constitute a say over own affairs or any co-decision power. Thus, Chapter 10 discusses the situation in a number of countries in the post-Soviet space, all of which have adopted NTA legislation without devolving any self-governing or self-management power to ethno-cultural groups (Alexander Osipov), and Chapter 11 recounts the situation of the Estonian approach to NCA, a clear example of empty promises of purely symbolic value (Vadim Poleshchuk).

Finally, the Conclusion (Levente Salat) takes stock of the institutional approaches introduced by the authors and provides a typology of weak-to-strong NTA institutions, which may function as a toolkit for future policymaking in the area of ethno-cultural accommodation. On this basis, the Conclusion also assesses the conceptual revision of NTA in order to direct toward further research, which we pursue in future volumes.

PART I

MINORITY SELF-GOVERNANCE

1

Reconfiguring State–Minority Negotiations for Better Outcomes

Sherrill Stroschein

1.1 Introduction

The governance of states that are home to several different identity groups can become a focus of struggle between those groups. Most states in the world contain a variety of ethnic and religious groups that produce identity-based majorities and minorities. In democracies, majority groups will have strong governance advantages over minorities, unless these advantages are mitigated by electoral systems accommodating minorities as well as minority rights protection schemes.[1] Scholars and policymakers have considered which of these options might be best for resolving the day-to-day disagreements between majorities and minorities in democracies, without simply resorting to majority tyranny. These considerations tend to be framed as rights or as institutions for minority protection.

Majorities and minorities will frequently disagree on policies relating to their different identities. The nature of such disputes tend to focus on matters such as language use and education, religious practice, the public display of group symbols, and group holidays and commemorations. In theory, policy, and law, some advocate approaching these questions in terms of individual human rights. From this perspective, identity groups are a collection of individuals with individual rights. While minority practices regarding language use or religion might be infringed upon, these harms take place on an individual, rather than a collective basis. Thus, some theorists argue they must be addressed using remedies that are based on individual rights.[2] In this individualist or egalitarian view, individual rights protection regarding language and culture should be sufficient to address these dilemmas. For strict egalitarians, based on these premises a just society does not require special

---

[1] However, even proportional representation electoral systems (or ranked systems) cannot completely eliminate the fact that minorities will be outnumbered by majorities in voting.

[2] Brian Barry, *Culture and Equality* (Cambridge, MA: Harvard University Press, 2001).

attention to groups or group rights.[3] Reflecting the predominance of this view, most minority rights treaties are based on individual rights.

This individualist position is disputed by a range of others who argue that in theory, law, and policy, individual rights are not sufficient to address these questions, because they are inherently group-based. This viewpoint is reflected in the communitarian and multiculturalist perspectives in political theory.[4] From this perspective, group or collective rights must be applied to ensure minority protections against majorities in democracies. Language use, religious practices, and symbolic matters including holidays and commemorations are areas that should be preserved via group-based collective rights, rather than simply via individual rights.[5]

Some thinkers have tried to merge these views with the notions of justice for individuals in liberalism. As argued by Will Kymlicka, the full exercise of individual rights requires an acknowledgement of a status for collectives and collective rights. For Kymlicka, such thinking can be consistent with liberalism due to its enhancement of the status of minority individuals through collective rights for their identity groups.[6] This perspective is called liberal pluralism (or sometimes liberal nationalism),[7] and represents an attempt to combine both individualist and collective views on rights.

How might these rights questions be addressed by institutions in practice? From the liberal egalitarian view, human rights as individual rights provide

---

[3] It should be noted that the concept group or collective rights is used in its generic form here, acknowledging that the notion has several conceptualizations in theory and practice. In international law, it is used only in reference to the right of peoples to self-determination in Article 1 of the United Nations Charter, with peoples referring to populations of well-defined sovereign jurisdictions with boundaries, such as states or indigenous people within reserved territories. In international human rights law, it is used in reference to the right to enjoy jointly specific individual human rights that require joint exercise, such as language rights. In private law, it refers to physical entities whose membership is distinctly defined according to known criteria, including states but most often corporations and associations. In domestic public law, some states have adopted collective home-rule rights for specific cultural groups, including indigenous groups, usually inhabiting traditional home regions. In political and social science, it is often used interchangeably with group rights indicating a right of specific groups to enjoy jointly certain freedoms and entitlements but without strong definition of the nature of such rights. The use in this chapter falls within the last category.

[4] Charles Taylor, *Multiculturalism and the Politics of Recognition* (Princeton: Princeton University Press, 1992); Will Kymlicka, *Multicultural Citizenship* (Oxford: Oxford University Press, 1995); Jacob Levy, 'Classifying Cultural Rights', in *Ethnicity and Group Rights*, edited by Ian Shapiro and Will Kymlicka (New York: New York University Press, 2000).

[5] This dispute is not simply a theoretical one—efforts by Hungary (though unsuccessful) to get collective rights represented in the EU constitution soon after its admission to the Union demonstrate the importance of this view in Hungarian discourse. These efforts relate to the fact that ethnic Hungarians in Hungary's neighbouring states comprise one of Europe's largest ethnic minorities: 'Hungary Seeks Collective Rights in European Constitution', Radio Free Europe/Radio Liberty (RFE/RL) Newsline, 30 September 2003, accessed 5 October 2014, <http://www.minelres.lv/mailing_archive/2003-October/002968.html>.

[6] Kymlicka, *Multicultural Citizenship*.

[7] Yael Tamir, *Liberal Nationalism* (Princeton: Princeton University Press, 1995).

sufficient remedies for those individuals who engage in practices such as the use of a minority language. International law and some domestic courts reflect this insistence on an individual basis for rights. However, collective rights approaches have also become more recognized in law and policy over time,[8] as with the Lund Recommendations discussed in this chapter. Collective or group rights take a variety of forms in practice. For example, globally some countries recognize exemptions for religious group practices, such as the Canadian state's approach that the headdress of Sikh men allows them an exemption from the legal requirement of motorcycle helmets. In the United States, the use of the peyote drug, a controlled substance, is allowed for members of the Native American Church.[9] Other forms of collective rights might be positive measures, such as affirmative action/positive discrimination for employment and in school admissions.[10]

Collective rights might also establish a foundation for minorities to govern themselves, providing a means for them to protect their identity-based practices with a minimum of majority influence. Such institutions take the form of autonomy structures for minorities. Autonomous structures have become recognized in international documents such as the Lund Recommendations as a useful means to preserve minority identity against majority pressures in democracies. As the Lund Recommendations are the most widely accepted (including outside Europe), this document will be emphasized here.[11]

The argument of this chapter begins from this orientation around collective remedies for minorities, in the form of autonomy as advocated by the Lund Recommendations. I first provide an overview of the territorial and non-territorial autonomy structures proposed in the Lund Recommendations. I then outline the ways in which majority–minority disputes are framed within an institutional framework of territorial autonomy (TA), and I contrast this with the framing of majority-minority disagreements and accommodation in terms of non-territorial autonomy (NTA). I demonstrate how NTA removes the zero-sum nature of disputes between majorities and minorities, such that better outcomes become possible for each than under conditions of TA.

---

[8] See note 3.   [9] Levy, 'Classifying Cultural Rights', pp. 25–9.
[10] Levy, 'Classifying Cultural Rights', pp. 29–32. It should be noted that affirmative action as a positive measure to overcome discrimination is applied to the individual beneficiary and a right cast as an individual right.
[11] The Lund Recommendations on the Effective Participation of National Minorities in Public Life & Explanatory Note (adopted 1 September 1999), accessed 5 October 2014, <http://www.osce.org/hcnm/32240?download=true>. It is worth mentioning that this document is wide reaching but not legally binding. Within the context of Europe, other important documents include the Framework Convention for the Protection of National Minorities (adopted 1 February 1995) (FCNM) and the European Charter for Regional or Minority Languages (adopted 5 May 1992, entry into force 1 March 1998) CETS No.: 148 (ECRML).

1.2 Collective and Individual Rights, and the Lund Recommendations

The Lund Recommendations on the Effective Participation of National Minorities in Public Life, produced by the OSCE's High Commissioner on National Minorities, outline two areas of emphasis with regard to a state's treatment of its minorities. The first emphasis involves the participation of minorities in the decision-making processes of the home state, or 'participation in governance of the State as a whole'.[12] The second emphasis is on the minorities' control over matters of importance to group identity, or 'self-governance over certain local and internal affairs'.[13]

This dual desire for integration and for increased minority self-governance presents a configuration that resonates with some of the literature on ideal types of democracies more generally. As outlined by Robert Dahl in his work on democracy, favourable institutions involve two factors: inclusiveness or participation, and open contestation between different views. Inclusiveness requires broad participation in state institutions, while contestation is about the presence of different viewpoints or identities in the polity—rather than simply a homogeneous configuration of identities.[14] Dahl presents a graphic depiction of how these two factors relate to each other, with favourable levels of democracy representing high levels of each factor. A similar graphic depiction was later used by Charles Tilly to present a breakdown of democratic factors into civil liberties and political rights.[15]

The two aspects of state interaction with minorities as endorsed by the Lund Recommendations can be represented in a similar graphic fashion. The graphic depiction inspired by Dahl allows us to logically consider how the two factors might relate to each other, when high levels of each are endorsed by the Lund Recommendations. This depiction appears in Figure 1.1.

In this figure, the horizontal axis represents the aspect of the effective participation of minorities in mainstream public life. High levels of their participation in state affairs would be represented by points closer to the arrow. The vertical axis represents levels of minority internal self-government—or governance over their own affairs. As with the horizontal axis, high levels of self-government would be represented by points closer to the arrow of this axis. Minority participation within the main state is a function of their representation in state institutions. State recognition and representation of minorities, as well as their participation in state institutions, thus differ greatly from minority participation in their own internal self-governments. If a minority focuses efforts on its own internal self-government institutions, this focus will tend to imply a reduced focus on participation and

---

[12] Lund Recommendations, 'Introduction'.   [13] Lund Recommendations, 'Introduction'.
[14] Robert Dahl, *Polyarchy: Participation and Opposition* (New Haven: Yale University Press, 1971), p. 7.
[15] Charles Tilly, *Democracy* (New York: Cambridge University Press, 2007), p. 47.

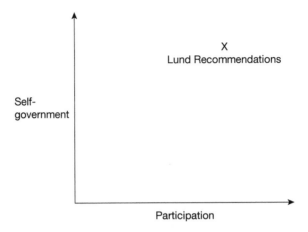

Figure 1.1 Aspects of the Lund Recommendations: self-government and state participation for minorities—higher levels of each represented by proximity to arrows on each line.

integration in the institutions of the main state.[16] These two strategies of focus thus exist in a trade-off relationship.[17] As outlined by these premises of the Lund Recommendations, minorities should have both high levels of participation in the main state *and* high levels of internal self-government. An ideal application of the Lund Recommendations would thus lie around point X in Figure 1.1, where there are high levels of each factor present.

What institutions might facilitate this ideal point? A great deal of literature has considered various means to represent minorities in the decision-making processes of the state, in the form of consociationalism[18] and electoral structures.[19] Less consideration has been given to the aspects of autonomy that are also included in the Lund Recommendations—thus the analysis in this chapter.[20]

1.3 State–Minority Relations with Territorial Autonomy

TA involves the allocation of governance powers to more local levels of government, on a geographic/territorial basis. The position taken by minorities toward

[16] This trade-off is represented in the everyday choices made by minority members and their elites with regard to how they will spend their time, and in which institutions they will invest.

[17] Some exceptions exist, most notably the power held by Scottish MPs in Westminster allowing them to vote on matters pertaining to English constituencies. Other examples are self-rule entities, such as the Faroe Islands and Greenland, South Tyrol and the Åland Islands, all of which are represented in both legislatures and public services, and whose representatives at times have the deciding votes in matters of national interest.

[18] Arend Lijphart, *Democracy in Plural Societies: A Comparative Exploration* (New Haven: Yale University Press, 1977).

[19] Benjamin Reilly, *Democracy in Divided Societies* (New York: Cambridge University Press, 2001).

[20] Indeed, this relative imbalance with regard to the literature on NTA is one reason for this volume.

TA will often relate to their demographic concentrations. Minorities in enclaves, or regions where their numbers constitute a local majority, tend to favour TA as a means for them to govern their own affairs within that TA territory—as is the case of the German-speaking minority in Alto Adige (South Tyrol) in northern Italy. Interestingly, this goal often differs from the goals of minorities who are dispersed throughout the state, because TA for the enclave does not address the situation of those living outside that enclave.[21] For minorities who live in enclave areas, the establishment of TA for these areas can allow them to create a type of 'mini-state', one that reproduces state administrative duties at a local level that is under the political control of the minority group.[22]

The creation of such 'mini-states' via autonomous territorial structures can foster the break-up of states. As some observers have argued, TAs can provide an institutional foundation that can become a platform for those minorities that might wish to secede from the state.[23] Thus, in this view the federations of Yugoslavia, Czechoslovakia, and the Soviet Union met their demise when autonomous structures made efforts to exit the main states. A number of states that are experiencing increased demands for secession are seeing those claims being made from within TAs, as in the case of Quebec–Canada, Catalonia–Spain, and Scotland–UK (as well as perhaps Crimea in 2014). TAs are intended to mitigate minority claims for secession, by allowing minorities a degree of self-governance.[24] But why is it that so many do not satisfy the minorities they are intended to assist?

As envisioned by theorists, TA transfers governmental powers to minorities on a territorial basis. In doing so, it adheres to the principle of subsidiarity, which is the 'notion that responsibilities should be assigned to the lowest level government that can adequately perform them'.[25] The Lund Recommendations also invoke subsidiarity as a reason for TA, 'particularly where it would improve the opportunities of minorities to exercise authority over matters affecting them'.[26] TA increases the self-governance powers available to minorities, which in the Lund

---

[21] This is the case for Hungarians in Romania, where there have been some Hungarian claims for autonomy with the Hungarian enclave region, but these claims are less relevant for Hungarians living elsewhere in Romania. Jóhanna Kristín Birnir, *Ethnicity and Electoral Politics* (New York: Cambridge University Press, 2007); Sherrill Stroschein, 'Demography in Ethnic Party Fragmentation: Hungarian Local Voting in Romania', *Party Politics* vol. 17 (2011): pp. 189–204.

[22] This statement holds under conditions of democracy in which there are institutions governed by local elections. In some cases, local demographic realities also imply local control of the police.

[23] Shaheen Mozaffar and James Scarritt, 'Why Territorial Autonomy is Not a Viable Option for Managing Ethnic Conflict in African Plural Societies', *Nationalism and Ethnic Politics* vol. 5 (1999): pp. 230–53; Dimitry Gorenburg, *Minority Ethnic Mobilization in the Russian Federation* (New York: Cambridge University Press, 2003); Henry Hale, 'Divided we Stand: Institutional Sources of Ethnofederal State Survival and Collapse', *World Politics* vol. 56 (2004): pp. 165–93; Philip Roeder, *Where Nation-States Come From: Institutional Change in the Age of Nationalism* (Princeton: Princeton University Press, 2007).

[24] Donald Rothchild and Caroline Hartzell, 'Security in Deeply Divided Societies: The Role of Territorial Autonomy', *Nationalism and Ethnic Politics* vol. 5 (1999): pp. 254–71.

[25] Ronald Watts, 'Federalism, Federal Political Systems, and Federations', *Annual Review of Political Science* vol. 1 (1998): p. 124.

[26] Lund Recommendations on the Effective Participation of National Minorities in Public Life, 'Territorial Arrangements', art 19.

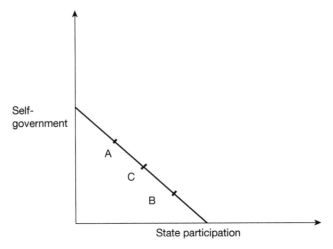

Figure 1.2 Minorities, TA, and the Lund factors. Territory presents a trade-off structure that limits options for minority governance to the line. Negotiations between states and minorities are limited to points along these lines such as A, B, and C. However, full potential is not reached.

Recommendations document is envisioned as compatible with increasing their broader participation in the state. Both of these 'prongs' are understood to support the effective engagement of minorities in the public life of the state. *In theory*, both of these prongs should be able to work together.

In practice, however, the 'mini-states' that are created through TA tend to present a trade-off for minorities. As has emerged in practice, minorities often tend to focus on building the self-government institutions of these 'mini-states' at the expense of their participation in the main federal or union state—as has taken place in Quebec, Catalonia, and Scotland.[27] The territorial aspect of such autonomies means that many of the aspects of state authority, such as control over the local economy,[28] can be conducted by the minority groups to some degree *without* participation with the main state. The 'mini-states' produced by TA can thus favour self-governance at the expense of minority participation in the main state.

This trade-off for the focus of minorities, between self-government and main state participation, is represented in Figure 1.2.

This graph represents the fact that under circumstances of TA, the 'mini-states' created by these structures in practice can draw minority attention away from

---

[27] With the exceptions listed in note 17.
[28] Local demographics also imply that a large number of those working for the local police force will be members of the ethnic group dominant in the enclave. For states that have some decentralization of the police force, there can be some local ethnic de facto control of policing as well.

participation in the main state.[29] Negotiations between states and minorities are
limited to discussions of the potential strength of the 'mini-state' relative to state
governance. These negotiations tend to be unstable. The minority will prefer point
A, in which most governance processes are focused through self-government institutions. The state will prefer point B, where there could be TA but where most
governance processes take place via institutions of the main state. At point C,
states and minorities can reach a balance between their demands along these lines.
However, the incentives for each to push toward their more favoured outcome
of A or B renders the settlement rather unstable. The institutions of TA establish
the foundations for a 'mini-state' that provides an ongoing temptation for some
voices within the minority to withdraw from main state participation entirely.[30]
For example, Quebec has held two referenda on withdrawal; Catalonia continues
to negotiate for a referendum on separation from Spain; and Scotland held such
a referendum (though unsuccessful) in September 2014.[31] Even when unsuccessful, such referenda reinforce identity lines between the autonomous unit and the
main state. In addition, TA can easily foster strong disputes between minorities
and state authorities, due to the fact that the populations of those territories that
are targeted for autonomy are almost never homogenous. These problems can be
removed by institutions that do not produce 'mini-states', but that instead produce
entirely new configurations for governance: the institutions of NTA discussed in
section 1.4.

1.4 State–Minority Relations and the Promise
of Non-Territorial Autonomy

The potential trade-off outlined in section 1.3 illustrates how the 'mini-state' features of TA can produce a dynamic that is difficult for states and minorities to
resolve. Transforming these potential disputes to facilitate state–minority reconciliation requires a reconfiguration of available governance structures. The principle of subsidiarity has typically been taken to imply that local-level governance
takes place at the level of a geographic locality. However, for matters such as language use and education for minorities, the placement of government at its closest
proximity to those governed may require a non-territorial structure, based upon a
personal principle.

---

[29] A consideration of the day-to-day allocation of time by an elite would reveal decisions to focus
on one or the other institution. Further research into the time spent by elites would be useful to reveal
how they think about this time allocation and institutional investment.
[30] The potential likelihood for some of these voices to succeed in making a case for withdrawal
will vary across different contexts and will also depend on the particular structures of the territorial
autonomies in question. The degree of power devolution may determine whether mobilization occurs.
[31] Examples from Eastern Europe include Gagauzia in Moldova and Crimea in Ukraine before
Russian annexation.

The linguistic communities, or institutional councils, that serve as the non-territorial units of the Belgian federation provide an example of how such non-territorial structures work in practice. The Belgian federal structure that has developed since 1993 has produced a state that is quite weak at the centre. Much of the work of governance takes place within the six units of the Belgian federation. There are three territorial units: Flanders, Wallonia, and Brussels capital. There are also three non-territorial units, or the linguistic communities: the Francophones, the Flemish community, and the Germans. The territorial units tend to focus on functions linked to territory, such as economic policy and infrastructure matters such as transport. The non-territorial units control matters similar to those outlined in the Lund Recommendations for non-territorial units: education, language, and culture—as well as health care, as the latter has a strong linguistic element. To further complicate matters, the Flemish territorial and non-territorial units are fused.[32] The primary result of this structure is a reduction of potential disputes over linguistic matters in the Brussels capital region, which is home to both Francophone and Flemish speakers. Instead, linguistic matters that could easily become group disputes in Brussels are removed from the arena of inter-group debates and placed within each linguistic community.[33] The Belgian structures thus include aspects of representation and governance.[34] As such, they could provide a model for states that face complex governance problems, such as Bosnia, Kosovo, or Ukraine,[35] especially in places in which one ethnic group refuses to be governed by another. The presence of NTA allows for debates to be concentrated within those groups affected, rather than requiring debates over identity issues to take place between groups.

NTA thus allocates certain functions of governance according to a personal principle, rather than a territorial principle. The notion that groups need not all be subject to the same rule is an old concept originating in the *millet* system of the Ottoman Empire. In this system, the Muslim Empire allowed non-Muslims to have some control over their own affairs, delegating powers to Jewish and Christian religious leaders to adjudicate over areas such as family law. Individuals of one of these groups could access the rules of their own community even if they were

[32] Dirk Jacobs and Marc Swyngedouw, 'Territorial and Non-Territorial Federalism in Belgium: Reform of the Brussels Capital Region, 2001', *Regional and Federal Studies* vol. 13 (2003): pp. 127–39.

[33] Philippe Van Parijs, 'Power Sharing versus Border-Crossing in Ethnically Divided Societies', in *Designing Democratic Institutions*, edited by Ian Shapiro and Steven Macedo (New York: New York University Press, 2000), pp. 296–320.

[34] An overview of these structures and their specific powers appears in Jacobs and Swyngedouw, 'Territorial and Non-Territorial Federalism in Belgium'.

[35] Sherrill Stroschein, 'What Belgium Can Teach Bosnia: The Uses of Autonomy in "Divided House" States', *Journal on Ethnopolitics and Minority Issues in Europe (JEMIE)* no. 3 (2003), accessed 5 October 2014, <http://www.ecmi.de/jemie/>; Sherrill Stroschein, 'Making or Breaking Kosovo: Applications of Dispersed State Control', *Perspectives on Politics* vol. 6 (2003): pp. 655–74. It should be noted that with the 2008 Constitution, Kosovo has begun the path towards a dual lingual state. Ukraine, on the other hand, is in a state of flux, and the language communities are far less distinct and therefore more difficult to identify.

scattered throughout a particular territory—because these rules adhered to individuals on a personal, rather than a territorial, principle.[36] This notion that identity issues might be governed according to a personal principle was also taken up by Otto Bauer and Karl Renner as the Austro-Hungarian Empire began to unravel in the late 1800s, due to similar problems of minority governance.[37] Although these ideas were not put into practice in Austro-Hungary, they continue to provide a foundation for potential governance options that might eschew direct conflicts between ethnic groups over identity issues and governance.[38]

The non-territorial linguistic communities in Belgium provide and administer education to those French and Flemish families who may not live in geographical proximity to others who speak their language. Their children can attend schools in their own language without being forced to move to other geographic locations, at least where such schools are provided. As noted by the Lund Recommendations, non-territorial arrangements might provide remedies in instances in which 'a group is geographically dispersed'.[39] From a justice perspective, a group member living outside an enclave should have the same rights as one living within a group enclave. Non-territorial structures enable this possibility, and do so in a way that reduces potential tense exchanges between groups over the matter of language education for children. Rather than requiring homogenous populations for the purpose of education provision, these structures *redefine* the means of provision instead—transforming the zero-sum nature of potential disputes between groups. As outlined in more general terms in the Lund Recommendations, non-territorial arrangements may perform 'functions', which need not be linked to territory: 'education, culture, use of minority language, religion, and other matters crucial to the identity and way of life of national minorities'.[40] In practice, most examples of non-territorial units generally seem to limit themselves to these applications, though health care can also be considered a linguistic matter for many individuals.

In removing the territorial and demographic aspects of these linguistic, religious, or cultural practices, NTA allows for a potential transformation of the negotiations between states and minorities. TA focuses minority attention on self-government and the strengthening of 'mini-states', as outlined in section 1.3, whereas NTA allows for minorities to engage in self-governance on these matters of identity, while leaving non-identity matters within the structure of the main

---

[36] Uri Ra'anan, 'The Nation-State Fallacy', in *Conflict and Peacemaking in Multiethnic Societies*, edited by Joseph Montville (New York: Lexington Books/Macmillan, 1991), pp. 12–15; Ephraim Nimni, 'Introduction: The National Cultural Autonomy Model Revisited', in *National Cultural Autonomy and its Contemporary Critics*, edited by Ephriam Nimni (New York: Routledge, 2005).

[37] Karl Renner, 'State and Nation', in *National Cultural Autonomy and its Contemporary Critics*, edited by Ephraim Nimni (New York: Routledge, 2005). The original was written in 1899 and is reproduced in the book.

[38] For more on the historical trajectory of this concept within a particular context, see Alexander Osipov, 'Non-Territorial Autonomy in the Post-Soviet Space', in this volume.

[39] Explanatory Note to the Lund Recommendations on the Effective Participation of National Minorities in Public Life, 'Non-Territorial Arrangements', art 17.

[40] Lund Recommendations on the Effective Participation of National Minorities in Public Life, 'Non-Territorial Arrangements', art 18.

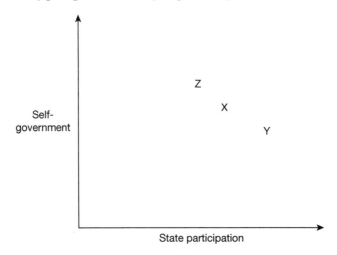

Figure 1.3 Minorities, NTA, and the Lund factors. Non-territorial aspects remove the trade-off effects of territoriality with regard to minority questions. Negotiations between states and minorities can result in points X, Y, or Z, maximizing potential.

state. Governance functions requiring a territorial focus, such as commerce, agriculture, and transport, could be addressed within the main state structure, while non-territorial units would allow for their self-governance on identity matters. In contrast, the structure of TA does not distinguish between issue functions, and requires all matters to lie within the administration of the 'mini-state' unit, with the exception of security and foreign policy matters.[41] TA produces a trade-off that NTA eliminates. NTA is thus a useful policy option for places with complex governance problems.

This reconfiguration of state–minority disputes under NTA produces an outcome displayed in Figure 1.3.

This graph illustrates how conditions of self-governance and state participation for minorities can remove the territorial constraints illustrated in Figure 1.2. Without the trade-off between self-government and state participation that is posed for minorities under TA, higher points can be reached on each axis. Negotiations between states and minorities are not forced into the zero-sum constraints of TA. By breaking down the notion of governance into specific functional competences, it is possible to reframe these potential disputes for better outcomes for each.

These functional competences might be either formal or informal in practice.[42] Formal competences might be represented in a constitution or in formal procedures,

---

[41] Although in Belgium, some linguistic matters such as educational treaties may also lie with the non-territorial units.

[42] Gretchen Helmke and Steve Levitsky, 'Informal Institutions and Comparative Politics: A Research Agenda', *Perspectives on Politics* vol. 2 (2004): pp. 725–40.

as is the case with Hungary's minority governments and in Belgium's non-territorial federative units. Informal competences might take several forms, including societal organizations or non-governmental organizations (NGOs), such as the organizations that exist on the German–Danish border to provide resources for the members of each community. In addition, informal non-territorial practices and procedures might develop in a state vacuum, as was perhaps the case with Kosovo's pre-1999 shadow government. The discussions in this book provide examples from both formal and informal contexts. They share a focus on a personal, rather than a territorial, principle for allocating governance functions.

1.5 Conclusions

In this chapter, I have provided an outline of the way in which NTA can evade some of the problems of TA by reconfiguring disputes between states and minorities. In removing the 'mini-state' nature of governance structures for minorities, non-territorial solutions facilitate minority strength in both areas of self-governance and in broader state participation. NTA emphasizes governance as a menu of functional competences. Territorial functions such as the regulation of commerce and transport can remain within the realm of the main state, while non-territorial functions such as linguistic matters and education can be allocated to the minority without the creation of 'mini-states'.

NTA is grounded on a personal principal for governance, and is thus similar to the personal principle that lies behind the application of rights and rules in legal pluralism. The fact of the existence of different group identities within the legal systems of diverse states has prompted more conversation about the way in which the individual members of different groups might access different legal rights within the state.[43] Like NTA, the differential application of laws might also provide a means to address potential governance disputes between groups, because laws can be applied on a personal, rather than a territorial, principle. The potential avoidance of territorial restrictions shows great promise for transforming negotiations between states and minorities by eliminating trade-offs on identity questions. The chapters in this book provide examples of how some of these current arrangements work in practice.

---

[43] Levy, 'Classifying Cultural Rights'.

2

Minority Self-Governments in Hungary— a Special Model of NTA?

Balázs Vizi

2.1 Introduction

The collapse of communist regimes in Central and Eastern Europe (CEE) raised concerns about the emergence of a visible and often deep political cleavage along ethnic lines in the transition countries.[1] Post-socialist countries faced the challenges of democratic transition parallel with divergent nation-building endeavours, which resulted in many cases in secessionist movements or violent ethnic conflicts (see, e.g. the dissolution of former socialist federations, the Soviet Union, Yugoslavia). These countries needed to answer simultaneously, in a brief and politically often hectic period, the questions of building democracy, defining citizenship, and also reformulating their national identity. In this context, in the early 1990s most CEE states were characterized by increasing national and nationalist tensions between minorities and majorities and the incorporation of strong minority rights in the legal system was usually off the agenda. Against this background Hungary has often been seen as an exception among post-socialist countries, offering a new model to diversity management, by including a clear formulation of collective minority rights and minority self-government[2] in the 1989 Constitution and by adopting a specific law on minority rights in 1993. Hungary was obviously in a specific situation: in comparison to other states in the region, it is an ethnically rather homogeneous country. Except for the Roma, small, dispersed, linguistically assimilated minority communities live in Hungary and show a strong loyalty to the Hungarian state. On the other hand—as a result of border changes following the dismemberment of historical Hungary

---

[1] Marijke Breuning and John T. Ishiyama, *Ethnopolitics in the 'New Europe'* (Boulder, CO: Lynne Rienner, 1998). Most recently from a global perspective, Jacques Bertrand and Oded Haklai, eds, *Democratization and Ethnic Minorities* (London–New York: Routledge, 2014).

[2] The term minority self-government is used here as it appears in Hungarian legislation ('kisebbségi önkormányzat')—this term can be debated, but in this chapter it is used exclusively in reference to Hungarian legal terminology.

(Austria–Hungary) after World War I under the Paris Peace Treaties—large and politically active Hungarian minority communities live in neighbouring countries.[3] Despite their dynamic demographic decrease since 1990, even today there are almost 2.5 million people declaring themselves Hungarians. Hungarian minority communities form regional majorities in certain parts of Romania (Szeklerland), Serbia (Northern Vojvodina), Slovakia (South Slovakia), and Ukraine (Beregovo/Beregszász). After 1989, these communities also nurtured a strong desire for obtaining some form of territorial autonomy in their state—despite a rather hostile political environment which characterizes all these countries in this respect.

Taking into consideration the demographic structure, the territorial settlement, and the degree of social integration of most minority groups in Hungary, there was neither an irresistible political pressure on the Parliament nor an urgent need to offer specific group rights for minorities in the 1990s. It can be argued that with the introduction of minority self-governments, the declarative acknowledgement of minority groups' right to autonomy was largely inspired by foreign policy commitments Hungary made in the field of minority protection (i.e. its responsibility expressed for Hungarian minorities living abroad). Some authors argued that in this way, the legislation adopted for domestic minorities was intended to serve as a 'model' to neighbouring countries as well—especially at a time, when a more articulated international codification of minority rights standards had just started.[4] Even if this direct link can be debated,[5] the arguments on the standard-setting ambitions of the Hungarian legislator regularly return.[6]

Irrespective of the actual political considerations of that time, the conceptual foundations of minority policy in Hungary remained stable and long lasting. Although the legal regulation has substantially changed since 1993—through the modification of the original law in 2005, and especially by the adoption of a new law in 2011—it is firmly anchored in the collectivist concepts of minority rights. This may need a deeper, historical explanation.

---

[3] See more on that: Nándor Bárdi, Csilla Fedinec, and László Szarka, eds, *Minority Hungarian Communities in the Twentieth Century* (Boulder, CO: Atlantic Research and Publication Inc., 2011).

[4] Among others see George Schöpflin, *Nations, Identity, Power: The New Politics of Europe* (London: Hurst, 2000), p. 375.

[5] See the reminiscences of Gáspár Bíró and Jenő Kaltenbach—two influential experts who were involved in the drafting process—at the Conference on Nationalities in the Hungarian Legal System—twenty years on, published in *Barátság* 2014. Gáspár Bíró, 'Az 1993. évi törvény létrejöttének körülményei' [The Circumstances of the Creation of the 1993 Act], *Barátság* vol. 21, no. 1 (2014): pp. 7765–87; Jenő Kaltenbach, 'Esély vagy illúzió, a kisebbségi törvény a valóságban?' [Is the Minority Law a Chance or an Illusion in Reality?], *Barátság* vol. 21, no. 1 (2014): pp. 7765–87.

[6] E.g. Balázs Dobos, 'The Development and Functioning of Cultural Autonomy in Hungary', *Ethnopolitics* vol. 6, no. 3 (2007): p. 456.

2.2 Historical Background and Minority Communities Living in Hungary

Before World War I, Hungary was traditionally a multi-ethnic state. The question of accommodating minority rights had already emerged in the nineteenth century, and the first law on minorities was adopted during the 1849 revolution. But this law could never be implemented, since it was cancelled after the defeat of the Hungarian liberation movement against Austrian rule. Later, the need to regulate minority (at that time called nationality) rights emerged after the stipulation of the Compromise between Austria and Hungary in 1867. Primarily based on the ideas and works of József Eötvös, the Act on Nationalities was adopted in 1868,[7] which instead of collective rights formulated a more liberal individualist approach. First of all, it declared the norm of equality of all citizens irrespective of their national origin, reflected in the unity of the Hungarian 'political nation' and provided a wide set of rights in the cultural field and in education in their mother tongue. After the dissolution of Austria–Hungary, defeated in World War I, the new, independent Hungary, which had lost two-thirds of its territory and one-third of its (mostly non-Hungarian, but also affecting large groups of its ethnic Hungarian) population, emerged as an ethnically rather homogenous country. In the interwar period minority language education remained an important element of minority protection. During the communist decades, under the ideology of internationalism, minorities enjoyed rather limited cultural rights, while the governments portrayed them as supporters of the regime, having their national umbrella organizations and enjoying limited rights to preserve their language and culture.[8] Between 1989 and 1990, during the democratic transition, the substantial modification of the Constitution (Act 20/1949) was on the agenda, and there was a wide consensus both within the reformer elites of the ruling Socialist Workers' Party as well as among the emerging opposition movements on the need to transform minority rights legislation as well.

The intention behind the 1989 constitutional regulations on minorities, and behind the subsequent Minority Law adopted in 1993, was to find a solution for the particular situation of a large number of small, scattered, and in large part assimilated national minorities as well as the significant Roma community

---

[7] Act XLIV 1868. On the 1868 legislation on minority rights in Hungary, see Mikó Imre, *Nemzetiségi jog és nemzetiségi politika* [Nationality Law and Nationality Policies] (Kolozsvár: Minerva, 1944), pp. 89–243. On Eötvös see also Judy Batt, '"Fuzzy Statehood" versus Hard Borders: The Impact of EU Enlargement on Romania and Yugoslavia. "One Europe or Several?"', *Working Paper*, no. 46 (2002): pp. 4–10. His political ideas on the role of state are best reflected in József Eötvös, *The Dominant Ideas of the Nineteenth Century and their Impact on the State. Vol. I–II.*, translated, edited, and annotated by D. Mervyn Jones (New York: Columbia University Press, 1996).

[8] Balogh Sándor, ed., *A magyar állam és a nemzetiségek. A magyarországi nemzetiségi kérdés történetének jogforrásai 1848–1993* [The Hungarian State and Nationalities. Legal Resources of the History of Nationality Question 1848–1993] (Budapest: Napvilág, 2002).

that is dispersed throughout the territory of the country and is itself a divided community.[9] Furthermore while all other minorities are well integrated into society, the Roma often live in socially marginalized communities, in suburban areas, and often face discrimination in different areas of everyday life. The primary goal of the legislator was not to offer a general remedy to all problems related to minorities, but rather to establish appropriate institutional structures for guaranteeing the survival of minority identities, cultures, languages, and assuring the political participation of minority communities.[10] The leading principle was to offer a chance to these weak communities to revive their identity, to organize themselves, and to preserve their culture and language. The aim of minority policy in the new democratic Hungary was adjusting assimilation processes characterizing previous periods. This policy can be seen as a 'cultural differentiation' or a dissimilatory policy.

To evaluate the effects of the 1993 Minority Law, it may be instructive to examine how the number of persons belonging to minorities has changed in the past decades (see Table 2.1).

Although at the census declaration of national or ethnic identity was optional, the statistical data in 2011 revealed that 15 per cent of the total population did not give any answer to the question on national identity. This confirms to a certain extent the success of this 'pro-minority' strategy: while in 1990 there were 232,751 people declaring their minority belonging, in 2011, among those who responded to the nationality question of the questionnaire, their number increased to 555,507 (in large part thanks to the increased number of Roma declaring their identity), while the total population of the country is decreasing.[11] The percentage of people declaring their minority identity has risen from approximately 5 per cent to 6.5 per cent between 2001 and 2011, which could be seen as an indicator of the positive effects of the minority rights system. Minority organizations tend to estimate the number of the members of their minority community even higher than the census results (they seem to take less into account the assimilation processes of the past decades).[12] Behind these numbers, however, there is a highly problematic understanding of minority identity in Hungary. For example, most

---

[9] The Roma community in Hungary is composed of three main groups, according to their mother tongue: the Hungarian-speaking Romungro (89.6 per cent), the Romani-speaking Gypsy (4.7 per cent), and the Romanian-speaking Boyash (5.7 per cent) groups (Ernő Kállai, 'The Hungarian Roma Population During the Last Half-Century', in *The Gypsies/the Roma in Hungarian Society*, edited by Ernő Kállai (Budapest: Teleki László Foundation, 2002), pp. 35–51; István Kemény, 'Linguistic Groups and Usage among the Hungarian Gypsies/Roma', in *The Gypsies/the Roma in Hungarian Society*, edited by Ernő Kállai (Budapest: Teleki László Foundation, 2002), pp. 28–34. It should be stressed that besides such linguistic divisions, the Roma are also politically divided; they cannot be seen as forming a true political community.

[10] Report submitted by Hungary pursuant to art 25, para 1 of the Framework Convention for the Protection of Minorities (1999) ACFC/SR (1999) 010, Part One—Introduction.

[11] See the official data of the Hungarian Central Statistical Office, accessed 10 September 2014, <http://www.nepszamlalas.hu>.

[12] Balázs Dobos, 'The Hungarian Minority Policy—Ten Years after EU-enlargement'. Paper presented at the ASN Conference 'Nationalist Responses to Economic and Political Crisis', Central European University, Budapest, 12–14 June 2014.

Table 2.1 Minorities living in Hungary (2001 and 2011)[1]

Minority	Mother tongue (2001)	Nationality (2001)	Mother tongue (2011)	Nationality (2011)
Armenians	294	620	444	3,293
Bulgarians	1,299	1,358	2,899	3,556
Croats	14,345	15,620	13,716	23,561
Germans	33,792	62,233	38,248	131,951
Greeks	1,921	2,509	1,872	3,916
Poles	2,580	2,962	3,049	5,730
Roma	48,685	190,046	54,339	308,957
Romanians	8,482	7,995	13,886	26,345
Rusyns	1,113	1,098	999	3,323
Serbs	3,388	3,816	3,708	7,210
Slovaks	11,816	17,692	9,888	29,647
Slovenes	3,187	3,040	1,723	2,385
Ukrainians	4,885	5,070	3,384	5,633
All together	135,787	314,059	148,155	555,507
Total population of Hungary		10,349,808	9,938,000	

[1] Official Census 2001 and 2011, accessed 12 September 2014, <http://www.nepszamlalas.hu>.

people declaring their minority identity at the census declared themselves also to be Hungarians. Taking a look at the number of minority language speakers—with the exception of Roma and Germans—any dissimilation process is questionable in itself. In any case, there is great uncertainty with regard to minority identities in Hungary and there is strong, traditional affiliation among people belonging to minorities both with Hungary and with the Hungarian nation as a political community. Minority communities can be classified into three groups:

i) Traditional minorities which were recognized as such even before 1989 and mostly live in their traditional—though usually scattered—areas, forming at times a local majority in some villages (Croats, Germans, Romanians, Serbs, Slovaks, and Slovenes). These minorities have also a broad network of cultural and educational institutions, NGOs.

ii) Armenians, Bulgarians, Greeks, Poles, Rusyns, and Ukrainians form another groups; they are dispersed and primarily the descendants of migrants who settled in the twentieth century in Hungary. They live mostly in the capital and in larger cities. These groups were recognized as minorities only in 1989.

iii) And the third group are the Roma, who live throughout the country in various sized communities, and—despite the declared efforts of Hungarian governments—many times face serious problems with housing, access to health care, employment, etc. In the case of the Roma, often identity is not a question of individual choice but a question of the majority's judgement. Another important phenomenon of the last decades is the increasing proportion of persons who belong to a specific minority group but who were born abroad and do not always possess Hungarian citizenship either.[13] In this context the Minority Law could only offer one possible legal framework—which could not perfectly fit all minority communities in Hungary.

2.3 The Legal Framework of Minority Protection after 1989

The substantial modification of the Constitution in 1989 specified local and national minority self-governments as the future organizational framework for minorities. At the same time, it admitted the—not precisely circumscribed—right of national and ethnic minorities living in Hungary to political representation, and it declared the need for a law concerning minority rights. These basic provisions have then been implemented and specified in Act 77/1993 on the Rights of National and Ethnic Minorities (Minority Law).

The preparatory work for the 1993 Minority Law lasted three years and involved the government, different ministries, the representatives of political parties, the governmental Office for National and Ethnic Minorities, the minorities' representatives, and several Hungarian and international experts on minority issues.[14] During the preparatory work on the bill, the two principal concepts of minority protection were confronted: many experts and politicians promoted a 'liberalist' or 'individualist' concept of minority rights, while others argued for an 'autonomist' approach. Liberalists argued that the stable institutions of democracy and the respect for human rights would offer a favourable political and legal environment for minorities to organize themselves, to create their own civil associations, etc. Advocates for this opinion also underlined that, perhaps with the exception of the Germans and the Roma, there was no need to offer broad collective rights to the minorities living in Hungary, since they might not even ask for them, and given their dwindling numbers, they might not be able to benefit from them. On the other hand, autonomists warned that without appropriate, legally defined self-government structures, minorities would be too weak and divided to establish the effective institutional structures for running minority institutions and representing their interests. They argued that since minority communities need strong governmental help to maintain their language and culture, their representatives

---

[13] Ágnes Tóth and János Vékás, 'Borders and Identity', *Hungarian Statistical Review*, Special no. 13. (2009): pp. 3–31.

[14] The Government Secretary for National and Ethnic Minorities organized an international conference on the concept and legislation of the Hungarian Minority Law in Dobogókő, in April 1990. Among the participants were internationally acclaimed experts and politicians (e.g. legal experts including Prof. Felix Ermacora, Prof. Georg Brunner, and also members of the Parliamentary Assembly of the CoE). See in detail Róbert Győri Szabó, *Kisebbségpolitikai rendszerváltás Magyarországon* [Transformation of Regime in Minority Policy in Hungary] (Budapest: Osiris, 1998), pp. 277–301.

would have to negotiate regularly with the government and would need to have influence on and legal structures to run minority institutions (schools, cultural institutions, etc.).[15] In this sense the best solution would be to offer autonomy structures for minorities enabling them to establish their legitimate representative bodies which could control and administer minority institutions as well. Due to the great number of conceptual differences, the negotiations between the Office for National and Ethnic Minorities in Hungary, the respective Ministries and the Minority Roundtable[16] did not conclude until the summer of 1993. In the end, the 'autonomist' concept received stronger political support, though it was substantially changed as a result of various compromises between the different actors involved in the process.[17] The Act, defining the legal framework of cultural autonomy, was adopted by the Parliament on 7 July 1993 with a majority of 96.5 per cent. The Constitution and the Minority Law framed the minority protection system mainly upon the definition of the policy target and the institution of the system of minority self-governments. The term 'minority self-government' was introduced by the law as a reference to the elected autonomous representative bodies of minorities both at the local and national level. Even if the competences of minority self-governments are limited to representation, participation in decision-making (on issues affecting them), and to the optional administration and control over minority institutions, this term is used here in coherence with Hungarian legal terminology.

In 2011 a new constitution and a new law was adopted on minority rights. The new legislation introduced new measures and new wording, but it essentially preserved the main elements of minority rights protection instruments, including the privileged role of minority self-governments.

2.4 The Theoretical Background of the Minority Law

In the 1990s the main arguments on minority rights protection developed focusing on the extension of individualist human rights and on security concerns closely attached to minority issues at the international level. At the same time, minority policy and minority rights legislation was dominantly influenced by communitarian domestic political and legal traditions. According to Krizsán,[18] the Hungarian minority protection framework in general and the system of minority

---

[15] Gáspár Bíró, *Az identitásválasztás szabadsága* [Free Choice of Identity] (Budapest: Századvég, 1995), pp. 36–43.

[16] This was a non-governmental, civil forum of minority representatives. On its role, see, e.g. Doncsev Toso, 'A magyarországi kisebbségi törvény' [The Minority Law of Hungary], *Kisebbségkutatás* 1 (2004): pp. 94–101.

[17] On this see Bíró, 'Az 1993. évi törvény létrejöttének körülményei' and Kaltenbach, 'Esély vagy illúzió, a kisebbségi törvény a valóságban?'.

[18] Andrea Kirzsán, 'The Hungarian Minority Protection System: A Flexible Approach to the Adjudication of Ethnic Claims', *Journal of Ethnic and Migration Studies* vol. 26, no. 2 (2000): pp. 247–62.

self-government (see also section 2.5) in particular clearly revealed a resemblence to the model of personal cultural autonomy developed in theory at the beginning of the twentieth century by Austro-Marxists and modified by Hungarian Oszkár Jászi.[19] From the historical perspective, the 1993 Minority Law in large part and the system of minority self-governments it introduced can be seen as a modern practical implementation of the ideas of Renner and Jászi.[20] Any form of autonomy can be seen at the highest level in the hierarchy of minority rights.[21] Today cultural autonomy is understood as a form of non-territorial autonomy, and it is seen 'as promising [an] alternative that … offers minorities the option of substantive cultural self-determination without linking it to territorial autonomy, with all the centrifugal tendencies the latter may awaken'.[22] However, within the context of European integration and as the contours of state sovereignty have become more blurred, minority claims for autonomy—and especially for cultural autonomy—should neither be seen as a security issue nor as a challenge to state sovereignty. The focus of minority autonomy claims is more about creating better structures for representation, for control over cultural, social, and economic development than about issues of sovereignty and statehood. Cultural autonomy may be seen as an institution which may help minority communities fully expand their social resources, through preserving their identity. The main feature of cultural autonomy in this regard is unaltered: the minority is entitled to exercise some form

---

[19] In a short reflection Jászi recalls especially the Rennerian heritage as strongly shaping his own ideas on minority policy. See Oszkár Jászi, *Magyar kálvária, magyar feltámadás* [Hungarian Calvary, Hungarian Resurrection] (Budapest: Magyar Hírlap Kiadó, 1989), pp. 183–191, at 185.

[20] The idea of the Austrian social democrats was to localize ethno-cultural issues, so that in national politics there would be class or ideological parties. According to Karl Renner there are two ways to tackle the issue of ethnocultural diversity, one following the principle of territorial autonomy and the other that he defined as 'personal' cultural autonomy. If there is no objective possibility of offering autonomy to territories resulting in a federation or confederation, the legal structure should follow the 'personal' principle. It implies that a community of individuals living anywhere in the country, joined together in an autonomous organization on the basis of their common ethnic belonging, is recognized as an intermediate legal entity, namely nations on the basis of association, nations having cultural (and only cultural) sovereignty. This entails a sharp separation of the state and nation, in which the state takes care of the material culture whereas nations take care of the spiritual culture. All nations participate in the governing of the country. At the local level the Rennerian solution is rather a hybrid of the territorial and personal view. The idea is that if a group is a majority within an administrative unit, the principles of the territorial view apply and it has territorial authority. This authority is checked, however, by the ethnic authority of the minority groups within the administrative unit. Most groups will exercise territorial and personal ethnic authority at the same time in the different administrative units of the country. This solution was elaborated with the aim of avoiding the disadvantages of the territorial approach, namely its contradiction with the prerogatives of the modern state (the need for some centralization and homogenization of codes of behaviour and penalties). It also represented a way of overcoming the pitfalls of the territorial principle for ethnic groups not residing within the compact settlement. A practical example could be Estonian cultural autonomy. In the interwar period, Estonia established a well-elaborated cultural autonomy structure for its minorities. In fact this could be considered as the only similar precedence implemented by law in Europe.

[21] Georg Brunner and Herbert Küpper, 'European Options of Autonomy—A Typology of Autonomy Models of Minority Self-Governance', in *Minority Governance in Europe*, edited by Kinga Gál (Budapest: LGI-ECMI, 2002), pp.11–36.

[22] David J. Smith and Karl Cordell, 'Introduction: The Theory and Practice of Cultural Autonomy in Central and Eastern Europe', *Ethnopolitics* vol. 6, no. 3 (2007): p. 342.

of institutional control over issues relevant to the preservation of its minority identity. In Hungary the situation of minorities could not raise any security issue in the political discourse—in this sense the Hungarian legislation on minority rights was motivated by an ideological approach (securing the survival of minorities in Hungary and designing a progressive model of minority rights protection—with an eye on the Hungarian minorities living in neighbouring countries).

The 1989 modification of the Constitution, stating that national and ethnic minorities represent a constituent part of the State,[23] offered a broad perspective for minority rights: the inapplicability of territorial autonomy made clear that the most extensive arrangement could be fully developed cultural–personal autonomy. The Constitution also declared that the State guarantees the collective participation of minorities in public life and the enjoyment of cultural and linguistic rights.[24] The primary goal of the 1993 Minority Law was to establish institutional structures for guaranteeing the survival of minority identities, cultures, and languages and for assuring their political participation. The Law was built on three main pillars: a) the principle of non-discrimination and the free choice of identity; b) a set of individual rights (on language use, on the use of personal names, etc.); and c) collective rights (minority self-governments). Moreover the Minority Law established the institution of a special Parliamentary Commissioner (Ombudsman) for the Rights of National and Ethnic Minorities.

The legislative ambitions of this law were well reflected in the opinion of the CSCE High Commissioner on National Minorities, Max van der Stoel. Following the visit of his expert team to Hungary in November 1993, he underlined that the 'Act on the Rights of National and Ethnic Minorities, … is of special relevance. If its potential is used to the full, this Act could have a great beneficial effect for the minorities'.[25] As a matter of fact the implementation of the Act regularly posed the main question for all observers, whether the Minority Law's potential is really 'used to the full'.

2.5 Main Elements of the 1993 Minority Law

The explicit aim of the Minority Law was the establishment of personal cultural autonomy (arts 21–54).[26] The organizational consequence of this—and thus the essence of the entire regulation—is a system of minority self-governments endowed with legal status. In principle minority self-governments are designed by law as legitimate representative bodies of minority communities, elected by the members

---

[23] The Constitution (Act 20/1949 as modified by the Act 31/1989), art 68(1).

[24] Including the right to use their mother tongue, especially in education, and to use their names in their mother tongue. The Constitution, art 68(2).

[25] CSCE Communication no. 307 (adopted 29 November 1993, Rome), 1331/93/L.

[26] Personal cultural autonomy is understood here as based on the principle of free choice of identity and the autonomous representative bodies are elected by the members of minority community at national level irrepsective of their territorial settlement.

of that community. They are invested with administrative and political powers to run minority institutions, to consult with state authorities, and to participate in decision-making on issues relevant for minorities. Minority self-governments were established at the local level in villages, towns, and at the national level with a nationwide competence. There is no hierarchal relation between local and national minority self-governments, their competences are neatly separated by the law.

The minority self-governments with nationwide competence could establish and maintain different types of institutions (libraries, theatres, museums, publishing companies, and secondary and higher education institutions) with a national scope. The minority self-governments at the national level were also entitled to voice opinions on bills concerning the minority that they represented. They had a right of veto in the course of preparing legislation on the preservation and conservation of the historical settlements and architectural monuments of the minority as well as in regard to the development of the core curriculum of minority education (arts 35–9). As far as the financial conditions of the operation of minority self-governments are concerned, they received annually adjusted, standard financial assistance from the central budget. At the local level, however, minority self-governments needed to cooperate closely with local governments—the technical and material conditions of the work of the minority self-governments depended largely on the relationship with the local government. The minority self-governments both at the local and national level were also expected to form the legitimate representation of the minority communities. Since the election process could not be truly representative, in certain cases the minority self-governments were not accepted by their partners as politically legitimate actors. Nevertheless in general the creation of a system of minority self-governments was an inspiration and motivation for minority communities to better organize themselves. In regard to the Roma community, the self-governments also helped the emergence of political elites both at the local and the national level.[27]

One of the main deficiencies of the Minority Law was the so-called 'trap of free identity choice' causing representation problems in the functioning of minority self-government institutions.[28] The procedure defined by the Minority Law[29] built on the following main elements: active and passive voting rights were not limited; the elections of minority self-governments were attached to the elections of the local governments and took place in the same place and at the same time; for candidacy only five recommendations were required; only a minimum number of valid votes was required for the establishment of minority self-governments; national minority self-governments were elected by local representatives of the

---

[27] Kállai Ernő, *Helyi cigány kisebbségi önkormányzatok Magyarországon* [Local Roma Minority Self-Governments in Hungary] (Budapest: MTA Etnikai-nemzetiségi Kisebbségkutató Intézet—Gondolat Kiadói Kör, 2005).

[28] Report of the Parliamentary Commissioner for National and Ethnic Minority Rights, 12 April 1995, s 4(2).

[29] Art 64 of the Minority Law modified the relevant articles of the Law LXIV of 1990 on the election of local self-governments and mayors.

local minority self-governments; and candidates running at the elections representing minorities were favoured/facilitated in getting a seat in the local council. In fact—independently of their ethnic belonging—all Hungarian citizens had a right to vote and a right to stand for candidacy at the minority self-government elections. This led to the sporadic but problematic practice of 'ethno-business'[30]: without any possibility of a legal control many people, who were neither members nor had any links to the minority community they were supposed to represent, ran at the minority self-government elections and gained seats. The Parliamentary Commissioner for Minority Rights called the attention of the Parliament and the broader public to this 'business-like' phenomenon from 1998.[31]

Until 2005, the guiding principle of the law was respect for an absolute free choice of identity. Tragic historical experiences, like the expulsion of Germans during 1946–7, and the forced exchange of Hungarian and Slovak populations between Hungary and Czechoslovakia during 1945–8 were still living memories in minority communities. So in the early 1990s, minority representatives strongly opposed any form of registration of persons belonging to minorities. Later, having experienced the problems arising from 'ethno-business', the Minority Law was modified in 2005. To repair the negative consequences of the 'identity-blind' voting rights, the modification established a registry of voters entitled to participate in the elections of minority self-governments. The request for registration was optional and was based on self-declaration, without any further objective requirement. On the other hand, passive voting rights could be exercised exclusively on the recommendation of a minority organization. Moreover, the Parliament decided to integrate minority self-governments into the system of local/regional governments and modelled minority representation on the regulations for local governments. After 2005 minority self-governments could be formed at three levels: the local, the regional (i.e. in the counties and in Budapest), and the national.

Nevertheless the changes could not heal all the problems of the minority self-government system: the registry of minority voters was formal (based on the individual's self-declaration without any objective criteria) and the financial constraints limited the potential of minority self-governments in creating or maintaining their own institutions.[32] In addition, one of the crucial elements of the law was the presumption that minority self-governments and local governments

---

[30] Árpád Rátkai, 'Az intézményesülő etnobiznisz' [The Institutionalization of Ethnobusiness], 2003, accessed 15 September 2014, <http://www.nemzetisegek.hu/etnonet/ratbiz.htm>.

[31] Annual Report of the Parliamentary Commissioner for National and Ethnic Minority Rights 1998, s 2(1)(3).

[32] Among others see the annual reports of the Parliamentary Commissioner for National and Ethnic Minority Rights submitted to the Parliament; Ferenc Eiler and Nóra Kovács, 'Minority Self-Governments in Hungary', in *Minority Governance—Concepts at the Threshold of the 21st Century*, edited by Kinga Gál (Budapest: LGI-ECMI, 2002): pp. 171–97; Orsolya Szabó, 'Reform vagy módosítás?' [Reform of Modification?], in *Tér és terep III* [Third Yearbook of the Institute for Minority Studies of the Hungarian Academy of Sciences], edited by L. Szarka et al. (Budapest: Akadémiai Kiadó, 2004), pp. 191–208.

will cooperate smoothly in the interest of the minority community. This was regularly—primarily due to financial issues—not the case.[33]

2.6 The New Constitutional Framework— the New Law on Minority Rights

Following the landslide victory of the right-wing FIDESZ at the 2010 parliamentary elections, the new government obtained a solid two-thirds (i.e. constitutional) majority in Parliament. The new parliamentary majority had great ambitions to change the post-transition political structures of the country and adopted a new constitution—the Fundamental Law.[34] The new Constitution introduced significant symbolic changes affecting also the position of minorities in Hungary. The term 'minority' was replaced by the historical expression 'nationality', and the preamble attached to the law (National Avowal) was overloaded with symbolic and historical references. Many experts criticized the new constitution as changing the previous 'civic state' concept into an 'ethnic national state'.[35] In coherence with the new constitutional framework, the 1993 Minority Law was replaced by the end of 2011 by the Act on the Rights of Nationalities (hereafter Law on Nationalities).[36] The return to the use of the term 'nationality' (as it appeared in the first legislation on minority rights in the nineteenth century) instead of 'minority' was justified by the government as departing from the numerical differentiation between majority–minority and as recognizing the equality of non-Hungarian communities in Hungarian society.[37] Others welcomed this terminological shift as leaving behind the meaningless distinction between national and ethnic minorities (as it appeared in the 1993 Minority Law).[38]

The preamble of the Law on Nationalities 'relying on the most noble traditions of Hungarian history' reinforces with a declarative scope the inclusive approach to diversity, when it states, among other things: 'nationalities form a constituent part of the Hungarian political community and the State ... cultural diversity and the diversity of languages are not a source of division but of enrichment; the cultural values created by nationalities form an integral part of Hungary's cultural heritage ...'. In the same way, the preamble strengthens the post-1989 commitment

---

[33] Ernő Kállai, 'Működési tapasztalatok és változási igények a helyi cigány kisebbségi önkormányzatoknál' [Experiences and Claims for Changes Among Local Roma Minority Self-Governments], in *Tér és terep III* [Third Yearbook of the Institute for Minority Studies of the Hungarian Academy of Sciences], edited by L. Szarka et al. (Budapest: Akadémiai Kiadó, 2004), pp. 227–51.

[34] The Fundamental Law of Hungary 2011.

[35] See, e.g. the criticisms formulated by liberalist constitutional lawyers in the special issues of *Fundamentum* dedicated to the new constitution: *Fundamentum* 2011/1 and 2011/2.

[36] Act 179 on the Rights of Nationalities 2011.

[37] Csaba Latorcai, Under-Secretary of State interviewed by Kossuth Radio, 21 November 2011.

[38] Balázs Szabolcs Gerencsér, 'Gondolatok az új nemzetiségi törvényről' [Thoughts on the New Law on Nationalities], *Pázmány Law Working Papers*, no. 34 (2012), accessed 15 September 2014, <http://plwp.jak.ppke.hu/images/files/2012/2012-34-Gerencser.pdf>.

to recognize and safeguard minorities as living communities promoting their cultural autonomy and guaranteeing 'the right of their actual communities to self-administration and self-government'.

Although the new law maintained the principle characteristics of the former legislation (like cultural autonomy, individual and collective rights) it provoked heavy debates both among politicians and in academia. The main criticism formulated by a group of experts was that the Fundamental Law and even the Law on Nationalities reflects a conceptual turn in minority–majority relations. Majtényi argued that the new constitutional setting creates a hierarchy between ethnic Hungarian and non-Hungarian segments of the population and does not meet the Rawlsian requirement of moral equality.[39] From the legal text it would be hard to arrive at this conclusion, because the new provisions are more confusing than signalling a clear U-turn in this respect. The Fundamental Law maintains an inclusive tradition and its preamble almost copies the former provision when it declares 'nationalities ... form part of the Hungarian political community and are constituent parts of the State'; it also states that 'We [the members of the Hungarian nation] commit to promoting and safeguarding our heritage, our unique language, Hungarian culture, *the languages and cultures of nationalities living in Hungary*' (emphasis added). The detailed provisions on minority rights under Article XXIX preserved substantially the previous constitutional provisions.[40] In this way the constitutional status of minorities has not changed. The Fundamental Law also keeps the Ombudsman's control over minority issues; even if the position of a special ombudsman for minority rights was abolished, Article 30(3) states that the deputies of the Commissioner for Fundamental Rights (who are also elected by a two-thirds majority in Parliament) 'shall protect the interests of future generations and the rights of nationalities living in Hungary'. From this perspective, the new constitutional arrangements continue the existing collectivist and inclusive approach to minorities. Nevertheless, other elements of the Fundamental Law may raise concerns about the primacy of the Hungarian nation over other national communities. With the explicit recognition of the need to protect the Hungarian language as an official language, the historical–symbolic preamble of the law formed a departure from the previous ethnically almost 'neutral' constitutional terminology. By changing the structure and wording of the constitution, the Fundamental Law now follows the constitutional traditions of neighbouring countries developed in the early 1990s, which contain similar provisions on state language,[41] national unity,[42] and the privileged position of the ethnic majority,[43] and by making preambular references exclusively to the majority's historical

---

[39] Balázs Majtényi, 'Történelmünk hagyománya' [Tradition of Our History], *Fundamentum*, no. 2 (2011).

[40] It repeatedly declares that nationalities are constituent parts of the State, it recognizes their special linguistic, educational, and cultural rights. It also confirms their right to establish self-governments at local and national levels.

[41] Constitution of Romania 1991, art 13; Constitution of the Slovak Republic 1992, art 6(1).

[42] Constitution of Romania, art 1(1).   [43] Constitution of Romania, art 4(1).

traditions.[44] The question is how does the Fundamental Law define the political community, does it offer a multicultural image of society or does it codify the dominance of the majority nation?[45] Apparently the drafters of the Fundamental Law made an attempt to codify simultaneously a more symbolic national–ethnic character to the Constitution while maintaining the existing special status and rights of minorities. But this attempt is more confusing than clarifying the real character of the political community: these two approaches can hardly be coherent under the same legal roof. So, instead of offering a new conceptual framework, the Fundamental Law just confused opposing images of the political community.

Against this background, the adoption of the Law on the Rights of Nationalities in 2011 was of particular importance. The Law on Nationalities was adopted as a cardinal act (i.e. requiring a two-thirds majority in Parliament) which maintains the traditional importance of minority issues in the Hungarian constitutional structure. The new law drew great attention both in Hungary and at the international level. The Venice Commission[46] started to investigate it during 2011–12, and the Parliamentary Commissioner for Fundamental Rights submitted a complaint to the Hungarian Constitutional Court concerning some provisions of the law that he evaluated as unconstitutional. The Constitutional Court however repelled the initiative in its decision, stating that the law was in conformity with the Fundamental Law.[47] Although the Law on Nationalities did not change the fundamental principles of minority rights protection of the 1993 Minority Law, it is a more complex, more detailed—in some parts even chaotic[48]—piece of legislation.

The first and very important feature of the Hungarian minority protection system is the way the Act on Nationalities defines minorities, which is almost identical to the former definition of the 1993 Minority Law. Article 1 offers the following definition:

> Pursuant to this Act, all ethnic groups resident in Hungary for at least one century are nationalities which are in numerical minority amongst the population of the State,

[44] See the preamble of the Slovak Constitution and in a more detailed form the 'Historical Foundations' of the Constitution of Croatia.
[45] While there are more ethno-symbolic references in the Fundamental Law, it starts as 'we the members of the Hungarian nation…' and later declares that nationalities constitute parts of the State: this seems to express a merely political character of the nation, especially taking into consideration that minority representatives and the minority self-governments were actively involved in drafting the new Constitution. Ernő Kállai, 'A nemzetiségi jogok helyzete Magyarországon a jogszabályváltozások tükrében' [The Situation of Nationality Rights in Hungary in the Light of Legislative Changes], accessed 15 September 2014, <http://www.uni-miskolc.hu/~wwwdeak/Collegium%20Doctorum%20Publikaciok/K%E1llai%20Ern%F5%20.pdf>.
[46] The European Commission for Democracy through Law (also known as the Venice Commission, since it meets in Venice) is the Council of Europe's advisory body on constitutional matters. The Venice Commission is composed of legal experts delegated by member states and its role is to provide legal advice to its member states in line with European standards and international experience in the fields of democracy, human rights, and the rule of law. The European Commission for Democracy through Law, accessed 20 October 2014, <http://www.venice.coe.int>.
[47] Decision of the Constitutional Court, 41/2012.
[48] Taking a look at the Provisions of Entry into Force (art 157) it lists seven (!) different dates for entering into force of the different articles of the law.

are distinguished from the rest of the population by their own language, culture and traditions and manifest a sense of cohesion that is aimed at the preservation of these and at the expression and protection of the interests of their historically established communities.

In fact, the subjects of the law are determined by a definition that builds a great deal on Capotorti's definition;[49] it uses the main elements of the definition applied in Article 1 of the Council of Europe 1201 (1993) PA Resolution.[50] However, the requirement of residence for one hundred years remains problematic.[51] Another basic principle of the Law and of the entire protection of minorities is that each individual is granted the inalienable right to declare his/her national identity and to refuse to do so.[52] The same article adds also a definition of a person belonging to a nationality as a person 'who resides in Hungary, regards himself as part of a nationality and declares his affiliation with that nationality in the cases and manner determined in this Act'.[53] The distinction between 'nationality' and the individual who belongs to a nationality clarifies the distinction between collective and individual rights: the nationality communities are entitled to collective rights (such as the right to cultural autonomy) and the individuals to individual rights (e.g. right to use one's name in her/his mother tongue). Appendix 1 of the law lists the thirteen nationalities which *ex lege* are entitled to collective rights, while for enjoying individual rights the law requires a subjective self-identification with one of these nationalities. The nationality communities recognized by law are the same as before: Bulgarian, Gypsy, Greek, Croatian, Polish, German, Armenian, Romanian, Ruthenian, Serbian, Slovakian, Slovenian, and Ukrainian.[54] The most important change introduced by the new law in this regard is an apparent opening towards new immigrants belonging to these recognized minorities: all people who reside in Hungary are entitled to enjoy minority rights if they wish so, although they do not have passive voting rights at the elections of nationality self-governments. Considering the particular situation of smaller nationalities in Hungary, this new approach was welcomed, even though it may pose some dangers in special cases: for example, immigrants may outnumber some small communities

---

[49] Francesco Capotorti, 'Study on the Rights of Persons Belonging to Ethnic, Religious and Linguistic Minorities', (1979) UN Doc E/CN.4/Sub.2/384/Rev.1, pp. 5–12.

[50] Council of Europe Parliamentary Assembly Recommendation 1201 on an additional Protocol on the Rights of National Minorities to the European Convention on Human Rights 1993.

[51] CoE European Commission for Democracy through Law (Venice Commission), Opinion on the Act on the Rights of Nationalities of Hungary (adopted 19 June 2012) CDL-AD (2012) 011.

[52] The emphasis on the privacy of one's ethnic or national self-identification is further reinforced by the Law on the Freedom of Information (Act CXII On Informational Self-Determination and Freedom of Information 2011—in the same way as in the previous law Act LXIII on Data Protection 1992) which deemed to be sensitive data any information on national or ethnic origin and introduced strict regulations on the processing of such data.

[53] Act 179 on the Rights of Nationalities 2011. (The text quoted here is the official translation of the Act, submitted to the Council of Europe Venice Commission, CDL-REF (2012) 014.)

[54] But this enumeration is not exclusive: the Act allows—in the same way as in the previous law—for any other minority group to apply for recognition as a minority if it fulfils the conditions under art 1(2) and is supported by at least 1,000 citizens who profess to belong to it (art 148(3)).

in certain municipalities or localities. The extension of the legal definition to all residents, however, could hardly be seen as recognition of immigrant communities, as such.[55]

2.7 Cultural Autonomy and Self-Government

While the 1993 Minority Law referred only to minority self-governments, the Law on Nationalities puts a strong emphasis on the concept of cultural autonomy.[56] The Law recognizes collective rights and also autonomy as a manifestation of collective rights.[57] In this sense the law distinguishes cultural autonomy from nationality self-government; it embodies a great variety of collective rights—including the establishment of nationality self-government. The self-government, as an elected body, is rather the materialization of cultural autonomy, a representative forum, and an administrative tool to realize cultural autonomy. Let us take a look at how this autonomy is translated in the competences of nationality self-governments.

Nationality self-governments are elected directly at the local, regional (in the counties and in Budapest), and national level. This keeps to the new system introduced in 2005, and it fully conforms to the territorial administrative levels in Hungary (local governments, counties, and national level). Like the regional governments, the regional nationality self-governments do not play an important role. Most of the competences are attributed to the local and national level. The law gives detailed provisions on the internal structure of nationality self-governments, on their function and on their competences. While the first issues do not necessarily require a legislative regulation in every detail, the 'public duties'—to use the legal term—of nationality self-governments are of great importance.

According to Article 115 of the Law the 'mandatory public duties' of local nationality self-governments cover: i) duties related to the maintenance of institutions fulfilling national duties (e.g. schools or cultural institutions); ii) at own initiative, fulfilment of other responsibilities and competence delegated by other local governments, including duties related to the maintenance of transferred institutions; iii) duties related to the maintenance of institutions taken over from other organization; iv) duties related to the interest representation of the community represented and creating equal opportunities, with special regard to the duties of local municipalities related to the enforcement of nationality rights; v) exercising decision-making and cooperation rights serving to reinforce the cultural autonomy

---

[55] Moreover in Hungary, we cannot really talk about immigration as a tangible phenomenon. Immigrants arriving with a goal to stay and live in Hungary are still today overwhelmingly Hungarians from neighbouring countries.

[56] In this sense it is similar to the approach of the Croatian law on minorities.

[57] Art 2(3): 'nationality cultural autonomy: a collective nationality right that is embodied in the independence of the totality of the institutions and nationality self-organisations under this Act through the operation thereof by nationality communities by way of self-governance'.

of nationality communities in connection with the operation and responsibilities of institutions operated by state, local governments, or other agencies in the nationality self-government's jurisdiction; vi) in the interest of the reinforcement of the cultural autonomy of the community represented, supporting community initiatives with organizational and operational services, liaison with the local nationality civil organizations and initiatives of the community represented and local church organizations; vii) initiation of the measures necessary for the preservation of cultural assets associated with the nationality community in the jurisdiction of the nationality self-government; viii) participation in the preparation of development plans; and ix) assessment of demand for education and training in nationality languages. The local nationality self-governments are also entitled to fulfil voluntary responsibilities—if this does not affect the duties of state authorities—in particular in the field of nationality education, culture, social inclusion, public employment, social, youth, and cultural administration.[58]

The Act on Nationalities gives on different policy issues the right of consultation or the right of agreement to nationality self-governments; such rights are granted in relation to public education and cultural self-government affecting the nationality concerned (arts 27 and 33–49).[59] The nationality self-governments with nationwide competence are expected: a) to fulfil the duties of interest representation and interest protection of the nationality in those localities where there is no nationality self-government; b) to engage in the interest representation at county level; c) to represent and protect the interests of the nationality represented by it on a national level; and d) to maintain a national network of nationality institutions in the interest of the development of nationality cultural autonomy.[60] Moreover the nationality self-government with nationwide competence shall be consulted on bilateral and multilateral international agreements related to the protection of nationalities, may request information relevant to the nationality from public authorities and agencies, shall exercise the right of consent on issues directly affecting the nationality in connection with development plans. The government is obliged to consult nationality self-governments with nationwide competence with respect to issues concerning the educational self-administration of people belonging to that nationality. This is a new element of the law, that it brings back the possibility of creating territorial minority self-government—an option that was abolished by the 2005 modification of the previous law. A local nationality self-government may declare itself a transformed nationality self-government if on the day of the election more than half of the citizens recorded in the register of franchised citizens in the locality are recorded in the given nationality's electoral register, and where more than half

[58] Art 116 also states that 'within the boundaries of the available resources' local nationality self-governments may take as voluntary public duties: i) the establishment of nationality institutions; ii) establishment of decorations, establishment of the conditions and rules of awarding; iii) invitation of nationality tenders, establishment of scholarships.

[59] However this is not an absolute veto right; according to the law each of the parties have thirty days to issue their opinion which may be postponed for another thirty days, after which, if the nationality self-government does not declare its position, the court may take a decision in substitution.

[60] Law on Nationalities, art 117(2).

of the elected members ran as the given nationality's candidates at the local government elections.[61] This option—in theory at least—offers to those nationality
communities which live in majority in a village or locality, the possibility of creating a special form of limited territorial autonomy. In this way the local government and the local minority self-government are merged in the locality concerned.
Nevertheless the Law asks very strict requirements for that: meeting both criteria
(majority of local voters should be registered as nationality voters and half of the
members of the local council should be elected on nationality lists) seems almost
impossible for most local minority communities. The previous experiences of territorial minority self-governments were not really positive either: the central state
budget allocations did not take into consideration the different character and the
increased responsibilities of a nationality self-government in a locality with respect
to an ordinary local government. In this way it is doubtful if there will be any local
governments able and willing to transform to nationality self-government.

2.8 The Enduring Challenge of 'Ethno-Business'?

One of the main criticisms formulated against the previous Minority Law was
that it opened the door to any 'ethnic entrepreneur' willing to run at the minority
self-government elections: it was a regularly recurring problem after the elections
that minority self-governments were also established in localities where there had
never been registered at the census any members of that minority community, and
often the representatives of the minority community concerned protested as well.
Seeing the troubling impact of 'ethno-business' on the credibility and legitimacy of
the system of minority self-governments, the 2005 modification of the law introduced the register of minority voters, which required registration by citizens both
for active and passive voting rights. However, as it turns out from the Ombudsman's
reports, the number of 'problematic' minority self-governments did not decrease.[62]
Here again the greatest problem was the pure formality of registration—no one
was entitled to examine the identity, knowledge of minority language, or even just
cultural affiliation (criteria required by the law for registration) of people declaring that they belong to the minority community concerned and registering either
as voters or as candidates. This situation was particularly worrying in light of the
indirect election of minority self-governments with nationwide competence. At
the national level, the electors of the local minority self-governments had voting
rights. This situation needed to be changed, and indeed the 2011 Act introduced
the direct election of nationality self-governments with nationwide competence.

---

[61] Law on Nationalities, art 71.

[62] *Beszámoló a nemzeti és etnikai kisebbségi jogok országgyűlési biztosának tevékenységéről* [Report
on the Activities of the Parliamentary Commissioner for National and Ethnic Minority Rights]
(Budapest, 2006), pp. 16–25; *Beszámoló a nemzeti és etnikai kisebbségi jogok országgyűlési biztosának
tevékenységéről* [Report on the Activities of the Parliamentary Commissioner for National and Ethnic
Minority Rights] (Budapest, 2010), pp. 11–27.

However, as it also turned out from the Ombudsman's reports, this is only one part of the problem: the Ombudsman warned that if registration is to be governed by the unlimited freedom of choice of identity, the registered voters who do not belong to that minority could easily influence the personal composition of the nationality self-government with nationwide competence.[63] The guarantees introduced by the 2011 law are too weak to prevent misuse of voting rights. The definition of minorities or the identification of the members of a minority is always problematic: usually the mixture of objective and subjective criteria[64] applied by the law will always be an authoritarian delimitation of identity. The drafters of the law apparently tried to escape this trap by making reference to the results of national censuses. However this solution raises a number of serious concerns: the declaration of national identity was optional in the 2011 census (just as in the previous census), and at the time of data collection no one was informed that later, under a new law, these data would be used for the election of nationality self-governments. According to the law, local nationality self-government elections can be held only in those localities where at the latest census at least thirty people declared that they belonged to that particular nationality. There are a number of localities where according to the data of the census relatively large nationality communities live (or at least thirty people) while the factual basis of this data was questioned by the interested nationality self-government with nationwide competence. On the other hand, there are other localities where fewer than thirty people declared their nationality identity in the census, but where Slovaks, Slovenes, or Roma live traditionally, and they will not be able to establish their self-government. In accordance with the recommendations of the Venice Commission, the Ombudsman proposed a modification: if the facts contradict the results of the census, then, for example, in cooperation with nationality self-governments with nationwide competence, the lawmaker could adopt a list of 'historical settlements' where certain minority rights could be guaranteed by law.[65] Unfortunately the new law has not changed the criteria for registration—even if it was visible in the previous elections that practically any citizen could register in the elections of minority self-governments. The new element introduced by the law is that any elector registered on the list will be able to exercise his/her voting rights until he/she asks to cancel his/her data from the registry. Otherwise all the objective criteria prescribed by law[66] are exclusively based on the individual's declaration. As from 2014, refugees and residents without

---

[63] Kállai Ernő, 'Vélemény a készülő nemzetiségi törvény tervezetéről' [Opinion on the Draft Law on Nationalities], 14 November 2011, accessed 15 September 2014, <http://kisebbsegiombudsman. hu/hir-706-velemeny-keszulo-nemzetisegi-torveny.html>.

[64] See, e.g. the definition used in the Act on Sami Parliament of Finland 1995. In general, Balázs Vizi, 'Protection without Definition—Notes on the Concept of "Minority Rights" in Europe', *Minority Studies*, no. 15 (2013): pp. 7–26.

[65] Erzsébet Szalayné Sándor, 'A 2014. évi választások a magyarországi nemzetiségekért felelős biztoshelyettes szemszögéből' [The 2014 Elections from the Persepctive of the Deputy Commissioner Responsible for the Nationalities Living in Hungary], *Kisebbségkutatás*, no. 1 (2014).

[66] For passive voting rights declaration on belonging to that nationality, and for becoming a candidate, the elector is required to declare that he/she is willing to represent that nationality and speaks the nationality language, and knows its traditions and culture (arts 53–4 as modified by the Act 89/2013).

citizenship may also participate at the elections; they may also ask for registration at the nationality self-government elections. Another guarantee introduced by the law is that the only electors allowed to run as candidates at the elections are those who have not been a candidate of another nationality at the previous two nation- ality self-government elections. However this will be applicable only after 2019. Based on these provisions the Parliamentary Deputy Commissioner (Deputy Ombudsman) for the rights of nationalities formulated concerns about the legal guarantees of representation at the nationality self-government elections.[67] The greatest challenge in this regard is that the law keeps open the door for 'ethnic entrepreneurs' who only want to influence or establish nationality self-government for financial reasons or to gain representation at the local government.

2.9 Conclusions

Nationality self-governments are designated by the Law on Nationalities as poten- tially providing an institutional framework for cultural autonomy. That is why the law formulates a public entity status for nationality self-governments, that is, they are entitled to fulfil public duties by law. However, the real opportunities for developing a functioning cultural autonomy are rather weak. Cultural autonomy is usually understood as a form of autonomy where the members of a minority community—without territorial limitation—can establish a representative body, which can carry out cultural and other activities relevant for the minority at both local and national levels. Tkacik adds to this that cultural autonomy typically implies some regulatory power as well.[68] In this sense the experiences of the past decades show that in Hungary important elements of the development of a fully fledged cultural autonomy are missing in practice. Competences given to the nationality self-governments cannot be effective without the stable cooperation of other state entities, but neither central state authorities nor local governments are constrained by law to support their activities in these fields. In fact, there are only two areas where nationality self-governments could have stronger powers. Local governments need the explicit consent of the nationality self-government for any decision which would affect the nationality population in the field of public education, language use, media, culture, social inclusion policies, and social services (art 81(1)). But here again there is no real motivation for or constraint on local governments to cooperate.[69]

What is more, the law recognizes Hungarian as a nationality language of the Roma and Armenians, so anyone willing to register as a Roma or Armenian elector may also speak only Hungarian.

[67] Sándor, 'A 2014. évi választások a magyarországi nemzetiségekért felelős biztoshelyettes szemszögéből'.

[68] Micheal Tkacik, 'Characteristics of Forms of Autonomy', *International Journal on Minority and Group Rights* 15 (2008): p. 371; Asbjørn Eide, 'Cultural Autonomy: Concept, Content, History and Role in the World Order', in *Autonomy: Applications and Implications*, edited by Marku Suksi (The Hague: Kluwer Law International, 1998).

[69] Moreover this co-decision right binds the local government if it adopts an order; if the decision is taken in the form of a resolution the consent of the nationality self-government is not needed. This

Furthermore, nationality self-governments have a vital interest in keeping good relations with the local authorities, because of their strong political and financial dependency; thus they often feel too weak to veto even a disadvantageous decision of the local government, which could risk the otherwise harmonious cooperation with, and additional financial support offered by, the local government. The Law on Nationalities made an attempt to ease this dependency of nationality self-governments from local governments by prescribing that local governments have to provide the necessary personal and material conditions for the local nationality self-governments to enable them to fulfil their tasks, but still it may easily lead local governments to limit this opportunity exclusively to the time limit set up by law.[70]

In principle the other strong element of cultural autonomy would be minorities' right to take over public institutions from the State or from the local government, for example, minority schools or other state-financed minority institutions (a theatre, etc.). In practice, however, there are only very few examples for such an undertaking, because neither the specific legal conditions of passing the administrative and owner responsibilities to nationality self-governments nor the financial details were clarified. In these circumstances the nationality self-government would have faced serious financial risks by taking over these institutions. As a result, minority schools are usually operated by the local governments and the nationality self-governments exercise only their consultative rights. To give an example, according to a survey conducted by the Minority Ombudsman in 2011, there were 900 kindergartens in Hungary offering some form of minority education, but only nine of them were directly run by the minority self-governments.[71] Most of the minority cultural institutions are also operated by minority NGOs or are affiliated with other public cultural institutions.

Recent research on the introduction of cultural or non-territorial autonomy arrangements in CEE suggest that these structures were likely created by governments imposing politically irrelevant competences to minorities (e.g. in the area of education and culture) in this way preventing any potential territorial claims.[72] In regard to Hungary it seems to be clear that there was a different rationale behind the introduction of cultural autonomous self-governments. It was surely the result of a top-down process, and the Hungarian political elites could have different

---

provision as such questions the nationality's right to consent—since many issues affecting them are by law required to be decided in the form of a resolution.

[70] The new provision that local governments are required to offer a suitable and appropriately equipped office for sixteen hours per month for the local nationality self-government for free.

[71] 'A nemzeti és etnikai kisebbségi jogok országgyűlési biztosának jelentése a nemzeti és etnikai kisebbségi óvodai nevelés helyzetéről (2011)' [Report of the Parliamentary Commissioner for National and Ethnic Minority Rights on the Situation of National and Ethnic Minority Kindergarten Education], accessed 20 October 2014, <http://kisebbsegiombudsman.hu/data/files/205104474.pdf>.

[72] David J. Smith, 'Challenges of Non-Territorial Autonomy in Contemporary Central and Eastern Europe', in *The Challenge of Non-Territorial Autonomy*, edited by Ephraim Nimni and Alexander Osipov (Oxford-Bern: Peter Land, 2013), pp. 117–32; Alexander Osipov, 'Non-Territorial Autonomy as a Way to Frame Diversity Policies: The Case of Russia', in *The Challenge of Non-Territorial Autonomy*, edited by Ephraim Nimni and Alexander Osipov (Oxford-Bern: Peter Land, 2013), pp. 133–48.

motivations arriving at the same solution of autonomy (either motivated by setting a minority protection model in the region, or by adjusting former injustices suffered by minorities in Hungary). But the institution of self-government was apparently internalized by the minority communities and by wider public opinion as well: the continuous discussion about its competences, about accommodating minority claims to more resources and about solving problems of institutional legitimacy, etc., show a general interest in operationalizing the idea of minority autonomy.

The experiences of the past twenty years of minority self-governments show the enormous challenge in the revitalization of largely assimilated minority communities. The adopted autonomist structure may be useful for some minorities; it could help traditional minorities in forming their representative bodies, and it could create a legal structure for their cultural, educational institutions. Among traditional minority communities, Slovaks, Slovenians, Serbs, Croats, Romanians, and Germans are well organized to be able to operate a complex system of cultural and education institutions—even if not *by* nationality self-governments, but with their active involvement. But the system of self-governments cannot answer the most challenging issues affecting the Roma (social marginalization, discrimination) and cannot be really effective in creating or maintaining real communities of the members of dispersed minorities (such as Polish, Armenian, or Greek). Even if the new constitutional settings suggest a less inclusive, more ethnocentric turn in the legal system, both the Fundamental Law and the 2011 Law on Nationalities build on the recognition of minorities' right to autonomy and to effective self-government. In regard to parliamentary representation the new legislation even improved conditions.[73] Nevertheless, it remains doubtful if the new system of nationality self-governments will be better able to help the revival of minority identities than the previous law. And it will surely need some changes to make the system more representative, more effective, and more functional.

---

[73] The new constitutional setting also makes an attempt to remedy the problem of minorities' parliamentary representation: it reformulates the former promise to representation, by saying instead, 'The participation of nationalities living in Hungary in the work of the National Assembly shall be regulated by a cardinal Act' (art 2(2) of the Fundamental Law). Indeed, the 2011/203 Act on the election of the members of parliament offers a preferential procedure for the election of the minority candidates; each nationality is entitled to set up its list and run at the elections. Even if one nationality's list does not get enough votes to send an MP, it is entitled to delegate a parliamentary spokesperson who, having consultative rights, may participate in the work of the Parliament.

3

Non-Territorial Autonomy in Croatia

Antonija Petričušić

3.1 Introduction

Although the Croatian ethnic picture has noticeably changed in comparison to the early 1990s, it is an ethnically heterogeneous country.[1] Croatia is 'a nation state of the Croatian nation and the state of the members of autochthonous national minorities: Serbs, Czechs, Slovaks, Italians, Hungarians, Jews, Germans, Austrians, Ukrainians, Ruthenians, Bosniaks, Slovenians, Montenegrins, Macedonians, Russians, Bulgarians, Poles, Roma, Romanians, Turks, Vlachs, and its other citizens'.[2] With 7.67 per cent of its population made of minority ethnic communities, and bearing the burden of 1990s ethnic conflict consequences, Croatia was conditioned by the international organizations with a human rights mandate, primarily the Council of Europe and the European Union, to develop its minority legislative framework and to align it with the European standards of minority protection. After a decade of inappropriate and partial implementation of the minority legislation that was originally passed in 1992, the new minority law, the Constitutional Law on Rights of National Minorities (hereinafter the Constitutional Law) was passed in 2002, incorporating all contemporary minority protection standards as set by the Council of Europe's Framework Convention for the Protection of National Minorities (FCNM) and the European Charter for Regional or Minority Languages.[3]

Among an array of instruments that aimed to suppress secessionist claims and to manage diversity in ethnically heterogeneous states, the autonomy and self-government of national minorities at the sub-national level sometimes emerges

---

[1] Croatian Bureau of Statistics, '2011 Census Results', accessed September 2014, <http://www.dzs.hr/Eng/censuses/census2011/results/htm/E01_01_05/E01_01_05.html>.

[2] Preamble of the Constitution of the Republic of Croatia (consolidated text), Official Gazette 85/2010.

[3] See the Constitutional Law on the Rights of National Minorities 155/02, 47/10, 80/10 (hereinafter CLNM). See also Antonija Petričušić, 'Croatian Constitutional Law on the Rights of National Minorities', *European Yearbook of Minority Issues* vol. 2 (2004): pp. 607–29; Siniša Tatalović, *Nacionalne u Hrvatskoj* [National Minorities in Croatia] (Split: Stina, 2005).

as a solution.[4] Scholarly legalistic analyses on autonomy distinguish between several types of autonomy that apply to members of national minorities. Michael Tachnik recognizes, for example, a distinction between personal, cultural, administrative, and territorial autonomy.[5] Steven C. Roach opts for a binary distinction between regional and cultural autonomy. Whereas the first presupposes 'the right to exercise limited sovereignty over provincial territorial borders', the second can be characterized as 'a non-territorial and self-administered form of local governance (e.g. councils and trade unions) in regard to matters which affect the maintenance and reproduction of a group's culture'.[6] The terms non-territorial and cultural autonomy are interchangeably used in the literature. Asbjørn Eide defines cultural as the 'right to self-rule, by a culturally defined group, in regard to matters which affect the maintenance and reproduction of its culture'.[7] Ephraim Nimni argues that cultural autonomy implies that '[m]embers of each national community, whatever their territory of residence, would form a single public body or association endowed with constitutionally enshrined collective rights, a legal personality, and sovereignty to deal with all national-cultural affairs'.[8] In the case that cultural autonomy is assured in a country inhabited by national minorities, members of a certain national minority should jointly exercise regulatory powers over issues important for the preservation and maintenance of their culture and identity even if they are not necessarily territorial concentrated but dispersed across the territory of the country. Alexander Osipov defines institutions of non-territorial autonomy as 'ethnicity-based, self-governing institutions which are not part of a territorially defined public authority and which are in regular possession of certain allocative (material) or authoritative (pertaining to power and authority) public resources'.[9] However, he argues that norms prescribing minority autonomy might often fall into a trap of 'fictitious norms', being not more than 'a verbal formula that has the shape of a legal norm, but cannot be deemed as such because the supposed right holders and/or duty bearers are non-existent and/or the envisaged legal relationship lacks content'.[10] Though cultural autonomy of national minorities in

[4] Ephraim Nimni, 'National-Cultural Autonomy as an Alternative to Minority Territorial Nationalism', *Ethnopolitics* vol. 6, no. 3 (2007): pp. 345–64.

[5] Michael Tkacik, 'Characteristics of Forms of Autonomy', *International Journal on Minority and Group Rights* vol. 15 (2008): pp. 369–401. See also Markku Suksi, ed., *Autonomy: Applications and Implications* (The Hague: Kluwer Law International, 1998) and Yash Ghai, ed., *Autonomy and Ethnicity: Negotiating Competing Claims* (Cambridge: Cambridge University Press, 2000).

[6] Steven C. Roach, 'Minority Rights and an Emergent International Right to Autonomy: A Historical and Normative Assessment', *International Journal on Minority and Group Rights* vol. 11 (2004): pp. 411–32.

[7] Asbjørn Eide, 'Cultural Autonomy: Concept, Content, History and Role in the World Order', in *Autonomy: Applications and Implications*, edited by Markku Suksi (The Hague: Kluwer Law International, 1998), p. 252.

[8] Ephraim Nimni, 'National-Cultural Autonomy', p. 347.

[9] Alexander Osipov, 'Non-Territorial Autonomy and International Law', *International Community Law Review* vol. 13 (2011): pp. 393–411, 396.

[10] Alexander Osipov quotes the Russian legal theorist Alexander Ushakov who coined the term. See Alexander A. Ushakov, 'Zakonodatelnaya Tekhnika' [Legislative Technique], *Gosudarstvo, Pravo, Zakonnost: Uchenye Zapiski* vol. 2 (1970): pp. 214–25. Quoted in Alexander Osipov, 'Non-Territorial Autonomy', p. 411.

Croatia is foreseen by the 1991 Constitution and the 2002 Constitutional Law on Rights of National Minorities (CLNM), the present chapter will demonstrate it is not more than a 'fictitious norm' since none of the institutions through which the cultural autonomy is being implemented is given an autonomous competence.

The Croatian Constitution guarantees protection of the rights of national minorities as well as the freedom of national minorities to express their national belonging, to freely use their language and script, and to exercise cultural autonomy.[11] The Constitutional Law guarantees a set of rights that should contribute to the preservation, development, and expression of minority cultures, and to the preservation and protection of their cultural heritage and tradition.[12] The realization of cultural autonomy is split between the governmental institutions, which control the spending of the state budget funds assigned for cultural autonomy, and the minority associations, and institutions that implement various projects and programmes to preserve, develop, promote, and express their national and cultural identity. The Constitutional Law, in addition, foresaw a new model of minority representation that should contribute to inter-ethnic cooperation at the local and regional level: national minority councils. Although they are directly elected by members of a single national minority when it makes up more than 1.5 per cent of the local population and in so far as the territory of a local unit is home to at least 200 national minority members, minority councils are merely consultative bodies. The idea behind putting forward those bodies was to consolidate further the right of national minorities to effectively participate in the public life of regional and local self-government units (i.e. counties and cities). The legislators were inspired by the Hungarian minority self-governance model that emerged in 1990s; replicating only part of the characteristics with which those institutions of minority self-governance are endowed.[13] Cultural self-government of minorities apart from Hungary can be found in Estonia, Russian Federation, Serbia, and Slovenia.[14] However, unlike other minority self-government systems that allow establishment of local, regional, and national minority self-governments, the Croatian institutional counterpart lacks autonomous competences to manage education in minority languages, administer printed and electronic media in minority languages, and pursue a wide range of other activities that aim at the protection of

---

[11] Constitution of the Republic of Croatia, art 15.   [12] CLNM, art 7, para 4.

[13] Niamh Walsh, 'Minority Self-Government in Hungary: Legislation and Practice', *Journal on Ethnopolitics and Minority Issues in Europe* vol. 4 (2000): pp. 1–73. See also Balázs Dobos, 'The Development and Functioning of Cultural Autonomy in Hungary', in *Cultural Autonomy in Contemporary Europe*, edited by David J. Smith and Karl Cordell (London/New York: Routledge, 2008): pp. 115–34. See also Katinaka Beretka, 'National Councils of National Minorities in Serbia: Pros and Contras of an Ethnic Self-Governance', in *Challenge of Non-Territorial Autonomy: Theory and Practice*, edited by Ephraim Nimni, Alexander Osipov, and David J. Smith (Oxford: Peter Lang, 2013).

[14] For comparative insights into different forms of non-territorial autonomy solutions across Europe, see André Légaré and Markku Suksi, 'Introduction: Rethinking the Forms of Autonomy at the Dawn of the 21st Century', *International Journal on Minority and Group Rights* vol. 15 (2008): pp. 143–55. See also David J. Smith, 'Challenges of Non-Territorial Autonomy in Contemporary Central and Eastern Europe', in *Challenge of Non-Territorial Autonomy: Theory and Practice*, edited by Ephraim Nimni, Alexander Osipov, and David J. Smith (Oxford: Peter Lang, 2013), pp. 117–32.

minority tradition and culture. This chapter will, therefore, argue that the degree of non-territorial autonomy that national minority councils are entitled to exercise is negligible since the vast part of cultural autonomy is exercised by the national minority associations, which are, moreover, financially independent. If councils are to be endowed with non-territorial autonomy competence, they should be given more prominent executive and legislative powers with respect to culture and education.

3.2 Guaranteed Cultural Autonomy for National Minorities

The Croatian Constitutional Law lists a set of rights described as cultural autonomy: the right to private, public, and official use of their language and script, the right to the use of symbols and insignia, the right to observe events and commemorate persons of importance to the historical and cultural identity of the national minority, the right to education in the national minority language and script, the right to religion, expression of a religious world view, the right to form religious communities, the right to association, and the right to access to public media.[15] The cultural autonomy programmes of national minority organizations and institutions at the state level are financed by the Council for National Minorities, the Ministry of Culture, and the Ministry of Science, Education, and Sports. In the following paragraphs the realization of the right of national minorities will be elaborated with regard to their rights to maintain their identities by providing adequate opportunities to develop their culture, to use their language, and to practise their religion. Though the distribution of financial means for the realization of minority cultural autonomy is split between different state institutions, with little or no control by the national minority associations, institutions, and councils, the Croatian system of minority protection has widely conceptualized cultural autonomy and endows minority associations and institutions to participate actively in realization of minority cultural autonomy.

The right to form minority associations enhances the right of minorities to maintain and develop their culture and to preserve the essential elements of their identity, such as their religion, language, tradition, and cultural heritage. Indeed, the chief part of cultural autonomy in Croatia is being executed by minority associations. However, the intermediary institution which makes the realization of cultural autonomy possible is the Council for National Minorities (*Savijet za nacionalne manjine*). This is a government-financed institution that was established in 2003 with a mission to cooperate with government and self-government bodies, councils of national minorities, national minority organizations, and legal entities engaged in activities related to the exercise of minority rights and freedoms.[16] It has the right to propose to the Parliament and the government issues significant for the implementation of the Constitutional Law, as well as other legislative

---

[15] CLNM, arts 15–16.   [16] CLNM, arts 35–6.

pieces establishing national minority rights. The Council for National Minorities is in addition entitled to evaluate public media programming from the standpoint of national minority interests and to provide suggestions and opinions to media outlets on how to promote minority rights. However, the most important competence of the Council for National Minorities is the allocation of state budget funds assigned for the cultural autonomy of national minority associations and institutions. It allocates a majority of the funds for programmes and projects of national minority associations dealing with cultural amateur activities, safeguarding of minority identities, and performing media-related activities. Examination of a list of approved project grants suggests that the promotion of cultural autonomy supports predominantly traditional, not contemporary culture.[17] In addition, the distribution of the state budget assigned for minority cultural autonomy is done in a way that funds are (almost) proportionally allocated to each minority community. This results in splitting the overall budget into many small grants, which, in turn, prevents significant capital investment for the maintenance of minority cultural autonomy.[18] In addition, currently applied financing schemes for cultural autonomy have therefore necessarily resulted in a mushrooming of the minority civil society scene. As a result, national minority associations implement projects that deal predominantly with folkloristic activities, publishing newspapers and books in minority languages, or maintaining contacts with their kin-states. In pursuing these projects, minorities are rarely spreading their impact to the wider (majority) community, but often subscribe to a ghettoization within their own minority community. Apart from the state budget's share assured for national minority cultural autonomy, the remaining funding of minority associations comes from kin-states funding or, on a smaller scale, from the funds of local governments.[19]

National minorities may, in order to preserve, develop, promote, and express their national and cultural identity, establish organizations, trusts, and foundations as well as institutions for the performance of public information, cultural, publishing, museum, archival, library, and scientific activities.[20] Several national minorities have established minority central libraries. These libraries are, as a rule, established in one of the city libraries outside the capital, in those cities where a national minority traditionally dwells. The Ministry of Culture provides funding for the salaries of employees in the central libraries of national minorities and assures funds for the programmes of these libraries. Along with the Council for

---

[17] Decisions of the Council for National Minorities, accessed September 2014, <http://www.savjet.nacionalne-manjine.info/odluke.php>. See also Government of the Republic of Croatia, State Report in respect of the Fourth Monitoring Cycle under the Framework Convention (ACFC/SR/IV(2014)012), accessed September 2014, <http://www.coe.int/t/dghl/monitoring/minorities/3_FCNMdocs/PDF_4th_SR_Croatia_hr.pdf>.

[18] Tihomila Jovanović, 'Kako nacionalne manjine troše proračunske kune' [How National Minorities Spend Budget Money], *T-Portal*, 12 October 2014, <http://www.tportal.hr/vijesti/hrvatska/354011/Kako-nacionalne-manjine-trose-proracunske-kune.html>. See also Antonija Petričušić, 'Lice i naličje brige o 'vlastitoj' manjini' [Both Sides of the Coin of the Care for 'Their Own' Minority], *Nezavisni magazin Identitet* vol. 185 (2013): pp. 32–3.

[19] CLNM, art 15, para 2.   [20] CLNM, art 15, para 1.

National Minorities, the Ministry of Culture on a yearly basis provides grants for programmes of national minorities in the field of culture. Finally, the sacral heritage (i.e. churches) of national minorities is also financed from the sources of the Ministry of Culture.

The maintenance of minority collective identity through education is assured in the text of the Constitutional Law, the Law on Education in the Language and Script of National Minorities, and the Law on Upbringing and Education in Primary and Secondary Schools.[21] There is a long tradition of education in the languages of national minorities in the Croatian educational system. For that reason, members of Hungarian, Italian, Czech, Slovak, Serb, Ukrainian, and Ruthenian communities who are being educated in minority languages and scripts generally do not criticize existing educational models for minorities. The inclusion of the Roma minority into the educational system has been steadily improving over the course of the last fifteen years, particularly after a special policy for the inclusion of the Roma minority was introduced. However, neither minority associations nor national minority councils have competences over educational matters, as will be explained. This segment of minority rights protection is managed by the Ministry of Science, Education, and Sports.

The Law on the Use of Languages and Scripts of National Minorities prescribes conditions under which minority languages and scripts might become official along with the Croatian language and Latin script in the administrative and legislative procedures at the local and regional level.[22] There are three different criteria for the introduction of regional or minority languages into official use in the units of regional and local self-governments (i.e. municipalities, cities, and counties): speakers of the minority language must constitute at least one-third of the population of the municipality, city, or county; or it might result from an international agreement; or a municipality, city, or county has prescribed the use of a minority language and script in their statutes.[23]

3.3 Councils of National Minorities: Competences and Coordination

National minority councils (*vijeća nacionalnih manjina*) are minority-specific consultative bodies that exist at local and regional levels of government in Croatia (i.e.

---

[21] See also the Law on Education in the Language and Script of National Minorities 2000; Law on Upbringing and Education in Primary and Secondary School 87/08, 86/09, 92/10, 105/10, 90/11, 5/12, 16/12, 86/12, art 7.

[22] Law on the Use of Languages and Scripts of National Minorities 2000. See also art 12 of the CLNM.

[23] Antonija Petričušić, 'Ravnopravna službena uporaba jezika i pisma nacionalnih manjina: Izvori domaćeg i međunarodnog prava' [Equal Official Use of the Language and Script of National Minorities: Sources of National and International Law], *Zagrebačka pravna revija* vol. 2, no. 1 (2013): pp. 11–39.

in municipalities, cities, and counties), with the principal mission to coordinate and promote common interests of national minorities in the administrative unit where they are established and operate. A council is a body elected for one particular minority within the given area, and there might be several councils elected for each national minority residing in a municipality, city, or county. If the number of minority members in a single unit of self-government is small, they elect not a council but representatives.

The councils can be formed in self-government units (i.e. municipality, city, or county) through elections, if members of a particular minority of a local unit constitute not less than 1.5 per cent, and if in that unit there live at least 200 (in towns and municipalities) or 500 (in counties and in the City of Zagreb) minority members. If one of the above enumerated requirements is met in the unit of local or regional self-government, members of such a national minority community may elect a national minority council for that city or county.[24] The voting right (either to vote or to be elected) pertains to those Croatian citizens who have permanent residence in the particular municipality, city, or county where the elections for national minority councils or representatives is being held. The voters in those special elections need moreover to be registered in the electoral register as members of national minorities at the state administration offices in the county where they reside. The members of national minority councils and representatives of national minorities are elected directly, in secret ballots, for a period of four years, in accordance with the provisions of the Law on the Election of Members of the Representative Bodies of Local and Regional Self-Government.[25] They can be nominated by minority organizations or a group of minority members from a municipality, city, or county. Political parties are not entitled to put forward candidates for the councils, but that does not mean, in practice, however, that councillors are not members of (minority) political parties.

The councils are non-profit legal entities that acquire legal personality upon registration in the Register of national minority councils run by the Ministry of Administration.[26] The president and vice-president of a council are elected by secret ballot by all the council's members. The president represents the council, calls its sessions, and has various other rights and duties determined by the statute of the council. The council must adopt a working programme, financial plans, final statements of account, and the statutes by a majority vote of all its members. The documents must be published in a local or regional Official Gazette. The

---

[24] Whenever none of the conditions specified for the election of the national minority council have been fulfilled, but at least one hundred members of a national minority live in the territory of the self-government unit, a representative of the national minorities can be elected for the territory of that self-government unit.

[25] Law on the Election of Members of the Representative Bodies of Local and Regional Self-Government 33/01, 10/02, 155/02, 45/03, 43/04, 40/05, 44/05, consolidated text 109/07 and 24/11.

[26] Ordinance on Forms and Manner of Keeping the Register of the Councils of National Minorities 120/03 and 24/04; Law on the Register of the Councils, Coordination Units of the Councils and Representatives of National Minorities 80/11 and 34/12.

council members perform their tasks, as a rule, on a voluntary basis.[27] From the resources that are assured to the councils by counties and cities, they are only entitled to receive the reimbursement of accrued costs related to their work and the award pursuant to the Rulebook on the Compensation of Expenses and Awards for the Work to the Council Members and the National Minority Representatives.[28] Such a practice hinders the professionalism of the councillors, since they are put in the position of performing the duty of minority council members exclusively as a part-time activity.

Although members of the national minority councils often in public refer to the institution they participate in as 'minority self-government', the councils' primary competences are consultative. That is, they have a right to propose to the self-government units measures for the improvement of the position of a national minority in the state or parts thereof, including submission of proposals of general acts which regulate issues of significance for a national minority. They also have the right to propose candidates for duties in state administrative bodies and bodies of self-government units; to be informed about issues, which the working bodies of the representative body of a self-government unit will discuss, and which pertains to the position of a national minority; and to provide opinions and proposals with regards to the programmes of radio and television stations intended for national minorities or programmes which deal with minority issues at the local and regional level.[29] Thus, while directly elected, the councils are not governing bodies which bear autonomous public functions and competences, but are merely endowed with the right to provide opinions and proposals concerning the issues related to the position and rights of national minorities in local and regional communities.

Local or regional self-government units must secure resources for the work of national minority councils.[30] They might also ensure funds for the implementation of certain activities determined by the working programmes of the councils.[31] The councils may realize other funds from property, donations, gifts, inheritances, or other sources, and these shall also be exclusively used for the councils' activities.[32] Since national minorities often live in economically deprived areas, where revenues of local governments are insufficient, the councils are often excluded from the funding to which they are entitled in accordance with the Constitutional Law. The Constitutional Law has not provided for a remedy in the case of insufficient self-governments' funds or sanctions to be applied to local self-government units which do not implement the Law. The Constitutional Law, though, has foreseen that the financial means for the implementation of certain programmes of national minority councils can be ensured from the state budget. Exactly this provision was applied to justify the

---

[27] CLNM, art 30.
[28] Rulebook on the Compensation of Expenses and Awards for the Work to the Council Members and the National Minority Representatives 24/2006.
[29] CLNM, art 31, para 1.   [30] CLNM, art 31, para 2.   [31] CLNM, art 28.
[32] CLNM, art 29.

government's intervention on national minority council financing. However, it took place too late, only in 2009, when the government provided alternative funding for the local councils operational in those municipalities and cities that were not financially strong enough to assure resources for the work of national minority councils.[33] Such intervention, however, has not been constant since it was introduced in 2009; it was replicated only in 2012 and 2013.[34]

When preparing minority-related legislation, the self-government unit authority is obliged to request the opinion of the national minority councils in its jurisdiction. The councils are thus expected to deliver their views on intended legislative amendments that concern minority rights. If the national minority councils consider that the self-government unit legislative act or some of its provisions are violating the Constitution, the Constitutional Law, or any bi-law regulating the rights and freedoms of national minorities, they must immediately inform the Central State Office for Administration, the self-government unit authorities, and the Council for National Minorities. Eventually, the Central State Office for Administration might forward its decision on local legislation that violates prescribed minority rights to the government, with a proposal to start a constitutional review before the Constitutional Court, and it is expected to inform the self-government unit about the undertaken procedure. The councils, along with the Council for National Minorities, the Central State Office for Administration, and the government are also allowed to initiate a constitutional review of the implementation of national minority legislation.[35]

The Constitutional Law prescribes that several national minority councils are entitled to establish a coordination unit of national minority councils at the local, regional, and national level. The coordination unit might be a mono- or multi-ethnic body, since the legislation does not restrict the creation of a single ethnic group.[36] Three coordination units are supposed to harmonize and promote joint interests and to enable the minorities to agree on the positions referring to the issues within their scope of activities. The councils are entitled to authorize their coordination units to establish certain measures which may be implemented by the councils, such as undertaking initiatives related to the use of the language and script of national minorities as well as regarding the preservation of traditional toponyms in minority languages in areas traditionally or predominantly inhabited by members of national minorities. If more than half of the national minority councils at the regional level form a coordination unit, it would be considered that a coordination unit of national minority councils for the territory of the Republic of Croatia has been established.[37] This, however, has not yet taken place.

---

[33] Decision of the Croatian Government on the Financing of the Programs of the National Minority Councils and Representatives 2009.

[34] Decision of the Croatian Government on the Financing of the Programs of the National Minority Councils and Representatives 2013; Decision of the Croatian Government on the Financing of the Programs of the National Minority Councils and Representatives 2012.

[35] CLNM, art 38.   [36] CLNM, art 33.   [37] CLNM, art 33.

Coordination units, unlike the councils, do not have a legal personality, and therefore it is difficult to institutionalize their efforts. In addition, they do not receive financial support either from the budget of self-government units or from the state budget, since this was not prescribed by the Constitutional Law. In order to tackle some of the coordination units' shortcomings, provisions of the Constitutional Law dealing with coordination units were amended in 2011. Firstly, it was prescribed that a national coordination unit of national minority councils may be established once more than half of the national minority councils elected in all Croatian counties (i.e. units of regional self-government) agree to this. The national coordination unit should serve as a non-profit legal entity, acquiring a legal personality by enrolment in the register kept by the Ministry of Administration.[38] Although there were attempts to regulate the manner of work and financing of the coordination units in a separate law, this was incorporated into the amended Constitutional Law. Second, and peculiarly, the amended Constitutional Law foresaw a provision that favoured one political faction of the Serb national minority. Being a coalition partner in the former government, under which the amendments of the Constitutional Law were passed, the Independent Serbian Democratic Party was able to influence significantly (and condition) the changes of the Constitutional Law. The amendments to the Constitutional Law were predominantly serving the (political) interests of this Serb party, but were not assuring equality of all members of the Serb national minority. Therefore it does not come as a surprise that several non-governmental organizations, not merely those advocating minority rights, requested a judicial review of the CLNM.[39]

The amendment provided that the umbrella association of the Serb minority should be the Serb National Council which was given the capacity to act as the Coordination Unit of the Councils of the Serb National Minority in Croatia. In this way, the members of the Serb national minority were put in an advantageous position compared to other national minority communities. Indeed, the Constitutional Court ruled that such a legal situation is not in accordance with the values of equality and pluralism in a democratic society based on the rule of law since the cause lies in the impermissible degree of legalized preference for one of several associations of the Serb national minority in Croatia, which at the same time—with regard to the Serb national minority—infringed on the

---

[38] CLNM, art 3, para 5.

[39] Though one might be persuaded by its name, the Constitutional Court does not have competence to undertake a judicial review of the CLNM content with the Constitution. The Constitutional Court does not have the jurisdiction to review the conformity of the Constitutional Law amendments with the Constitution since '[t]he fact that some acts are called constitutional does not change the legal nature of these acts, does not make them legally different from what they are under the Constitution and according to their content, and the Constitutional Court does not review them according to their name but according to their legal nature'. See the Constitutional Court's Judicial Review of the Constitutional Law on Amendments to the Constitutional Law on the Rights of National Minorities, Decision of the Constitutional Court U-I/3786/2010, Official Gazette 93/11.

legal purpose for introducing coordination units of national minority councils.[40] In other words, if the Constitutional Court had not abolished the provisions related to the Serb coordination unit, the members of the Serb national minority would have been discriminated against in setting up the national coordination unit, clearly breaching the constitutional provisions on equality and the right to association.[41] This is because the other national minorities were allowed to freely set up the national coordination of their national minority councils through such a provision. The Constitutional Court repealed this provision, establishing that the equal legal position of all the registered associations of one national minority, and also the equal chances they must be ensured in a democratic society to express their programmes and views, belong to the highest constitutional values.[42]

Partially due to an unclear mandate of the councils, but also due to unwillingness and the inability of local authorities to back the functioning of minority councils financially, the councils' capacities and actual results remain generally invisible to members of national minorities who in turn show little interest in participating in the general elections for national minority councils. So far, three electoral cycles for national minority councils have been held, in 2003, followed by by-elections and repeated elections in early 2004,[43] 2007,[44] and 2011.[45] The general observation of previous voting cycles is that the voter turnout was very low and in general merely 10 per cent of the minority electorate cast their votes.[46] Such persistently small turnouts of voters in the national minority council elections raises a question of legitimacy of the institutions that should assure

---

[40] Point 29 of the Decision of the Constitutional Court U-I/3786/2010.

[41] Art 15 of the Constitution prescribes that members of all national minorities shall have equal rights in the Republic of Croatia. In addition, art 43 of the Constitution states that 'everyone shall be guaranteed the right to freedom of association for the purposes of protection of their interests or promotion of their social, economic, political, national, cultural and other convictions and objectives. For this purpose, everyone may freely form … associations, join them or leave them, in conformity with law'. See Constitution of the Republic of Croatia 2001 (consolidated version). In addition, such a provision infringes art 17, para 2 of the Framework Convention for the Protection of National Minorities of the Council of Europe and art 11 of the Convention for the Protection of Human Rights and Fundamental Freedoms, both being legally enforceable in Croatia.

[42] Point 33 of the Decision of the Constitutional Court U-I/3786/2010.

[43] See the Decision of the Government of the Republic of Croatia on Announcing Elections for National Minority Councils in Units of Local and Regional Self-Government 97/03, 44/04.

[44] See the Decision of the Government of the Republic of Croatia on Announcing Elections for National Minority Councils in Units of Local and Regional Self-Government 73/07, 82/07.

[45] See the Decision of the Government of the Republic of Croatia on Announcing Elections for National Minority Councils in Units of Local and Regional Self-Government 56/11 and 58/11.

[46] State Election Commission of the Republic of Croatia, 'Information on the Results of the Elections for the National Minority Council and Representatives of National Minorities', 28 May 2003; State Election Commission of the Republic of Croatia, 'Information on the Results of the Elections for the National Minority Council and Representatives of National Minorities', 26 February 2004; State Election Commission of the Republic of Croatia, 'Information on the Results of the Elections for the National Minority Council and Representatives of National Minorities', 9 July 2007; State Election Commission of the Republic of Croatia, 'Report on the Results of Elections for Members of the Councils and Representatives of National Minorities 2011', 10 July 2011.

more effective minority participation at regional and local levels of governance.[47]
All elections for national minority councils had taken place separately from the
elections for local and regional self-government and from the parliamentary elections. That means that voting for national minority councils takes place in a
significantly limited number of polling stations. At the last minority council elections, voting took place at 736 polling stations, in comparison with more than
6,000 polling stations at regular elections.[48] This probably discourages some
voters from casting their ballot, because they might feel uncomfortable about
publicly declaring themselves as members of national minorities. Moreover, such
elections are undervalued by national minority voters because of the weak capacity of the institution. They abstain from voting because the councils cannot produce change to their everyday lives in the community where they are elected.
Harmonization of future elections for national minority councils to coincide with
the election date for representatives of local self-government units could happen
only if a change in the Constitutional Law and electoral legislation were to take
place. The number of polling stations would increase if the minority councils'
elections were held together with local elections. Such a practice would not only
be less costly for the state, but would increase the number of minority members elected to minority councils, thus strengthening the legitimacy of elected
minority representatives.

3.4 Ways to Make National Minority Cultural Autonomy
more Efficient

Research on councils of national minorities undertaken so far has detected a
number of issues which hamper the effectiveness of the local national minority
councils.[49] For instance, inadequate implementation of minority right provisions
by local and regional government mostly demonstrated insufficient recognition of local national minority councils as relevant factors and partners in the
decision-making processes at the local level; weak logistical support and inadequate capacity-building provided by the local government for institutions was
further evidence; persistent problems of adequate financing, and chronically low

[47] Antonija Petričušić, 'Izbori za vijeća i predstavnike nacionalnih manjina—legalitet bez legitimiteta' [The Elections for the Councils and Representatives of National Minorities—Legality without
Legitimacy], *Informator* vols 6004–5 (2011): pp. 17–18. See also Antonija Petričušić, 'Vijeća nacionalnih manjina—institucija upitnog legitimiteta i uglavnom neostvarene nadležnosti' [National Minority
Councils: Institution of Questionable Legitimacy and Predominantly Unachieved Competences],
Revus—Revija za evropsko ustavnost vol. 17 (2012): pp. 91–104.
[48] State Election Commission of the Republic of Croatia, 'Report on the Results of Elections for
Members of the Councils and Representatives of National Minorities 2011'.
[49] Siniša Tatalović, Ružica Jakešević, Tomislav Lacović, 'Funkcioniranje vijeća i predstavnika
nacionalnih manjina u Republici Hrvatskoj' [The Functioning of the Councils and Representatives
of National Minorities in the Republic of Croatia], *Međunarodne studije* vol. 10, nos 3–4
(2010): pp. 40–56.

voter turnout at the elections for the national minority councils and representatives furthermore underlines the inefficiency.[50] Capacity-building of the national minority councils was one of the fundamental conditions of the accession of Croatia to the European Union. The European Commission (EC) noted in its 2006 Progress Report that

> the capacity of councils of national minorities to advise local government in relation to minority issues [...] continues to go unrecognised by the majority of local authorities. Councils of national minorities [...] lack a clear understanding of their role and struggle to obtain premises and basic funding. It was noted that the local authorities need to institutionalise their relations with councils of national minorities.[51]

This problem has been tackled by numerous training sessions organized for both minority council members and for local officials. These training sessions were conducted and organized by the government's Office for National Minorities and local non-governmental organizations, often funded by international donors, with the aim of acquainting both members of national minority councils as well as representatives of local authorities with the scope of rights to which the national minority councils are entitled according to Constitutional Law. The EC acknowledged in 2008 that the capacity of the local councils of national minorities has improved and that most of the councils have been provided with premises and funding.[52] A year later, the EC negatively assessed the government's efforts to make local and regional authorities understand the role of the national minority councils. The government was criticized because it had not sufficiently ensured that the councils were recognized as advisory bodies by the majority of local authorities, despite increased financial support for their work. Moreover, the EC reckoned that the independence and influence of the councils is affected by the fact that they depend on the budget of the town authority or council.[53] In 2011 the EC acknowledged that financial support to the local councils for national minorities had increased and training was provided for local authorities, making them aware of the extent of rights stemming from the Constitutional Law.[54] The Committee of Ministers in the Resolution on the implementation of the FCNM by Croatia adopted on 6 July 2011 found that

> [t]he functioning of the councils of national minorities is, in many self-government units, unsatisfactory. In particular, co-operation between the councils of national minorities and local authorities is lacking. In addition, the low turnout at elections to the councils of national minorities undermined the democratic legitimacy of the

[50] Tatalović, Jakešević, and Lacović, 'The Functioning of the Councils'.
[51] Progress Report of the European Commission of 8 November 2006 on the Progress made by the Republic of Croatia in Respect of the Preparation Process for the EU Membership.
[52] See Commission of the European Communities, 'Croatia 2008 Progress Report' (SEC (2008) 2694), p. 13.
[53] See Commission of the European Communities, 'Croatia 2009 Progress Report' (COM (2009) 533), p. 15.
[54] Commission of the European Communities, 'Croatia 2011 Progress Report' (SEC (2011) 1200 final), p. 12.

electoral process. The funding for the councils, which should be secured through the local self-government units and the state budget, remains inadequate, seriously limiting their capacity to function effectively.[55]

The weak and unclearly prescribed competences and the illegitimacy of the institutions due to low voter turnout means that minority councils have not so far contributed significantly to the improvement of the position of national minorities at the regional or local level. To address the enduring problems the national minority councils are facing, a set of amendments to the existing legislation should be introduced. Two possible solutions to the problem of institutional incapacity are possible. The first solution is less costly, since it would imply the abolishment of the institution and the transfer of its competences to the elected representatives of the national minorities in representative and executive bodies of the counties and cities. Since minorities are guaranteed proportional representation in those bodies anyway, their elected representatives could easily perform the competences of the councils and at the same time have legitimacy to pursue rights and interests related to minority language, tradition, and culture at the regional and local level. The second solution is less radical, but would require a systemic restructuring of the minority council competences. Similar to the competences of the minority self-governments of, for example, Serbia and Hungary, those institutions might become endowed with the authority to take action well beyond presently very limited competences. For example, if they became entitled to manage cultural and educational issues for national minorities at the level of governance directly elected by minority voters, they would be in charge of the distribution of financial resources for minority cultural autonomy activities, presently being managed by the Council for National Minorities, the Ministry of Culture, and the Ministry of Science, Education, and Sports. Granting financial autonomy to national minority councils would not only help to develop and expand their mandate but also would enhance institutional relevance among minority voters, persuading them to take part in elections for national minority councils in more substantive numbers.

3.5 Conclusions and Recommendations

None of the above analysed institutions demonstrates the clear features of non-territorial autonomy: minority associations which implement programmes and projects that foster cultural autonomy lack financial independence, and the national minority councils, though constituted through direct popular vote, lack executive and legislative powers in respect to culture and education. However, this does not mean that cultural autonomy of Croatian national minorities is not being fostered. Although cultural autonomy is not being executed by national minorities themselves, but is being managed through the financial means approved by the

[55] See Committee of Ministers, 'Resolution on the Implementation of the FCNM by Croatia' (CM/ResCMN (2011)12).

Council for National Minorities and several ministries, it encompasses a number of rights that allow for the preservation of the cultural identity of national minorities (the right to education in the national minority languages and scripts, the right to use minority languages and scripts, the right to form minority associations, the right to maintain minority religion, the right to access to public media, the right to use minority symbols and insignia, as well as to commemorate important persons and historical events). The practice of the Council for National Minorities in distributing the state budget funds for national minority cultural autonomy shows it prefers financing a wide number of projects and programmes of national minorities, instead of focusing resources on infrastructural projects (e.g. schools, cultural institutions such as museums, etc.) that would more likely keep minority communities in the areas where they traditionally live. The existing financial model for minority cultural autonomy has resulted instead in a mushrooming of national minority associations that are implementing a number of small-scale projects, serving principally as a source of income and employment for some national minority members. On the other hand, the educational system for minorities managed by the Ministry of Education is an example of a fairly successful maintenance of minority identities and cultures.

National minority councils are a relatively novel institution of minority participation, which appeared in the Croatian minority legislation in late 2002 as an attempt to increase the participation of national minorities in public life and management of local affairs. The above analysis shows, however, that the national minority councils in Croatia are rather an example of symbolic representation than a model of participation in decision-making or a realistic form of non-territorial autonomy. Unlike in other countries that have introduced this institution of minority participation, national minority councils in Croatia are given a purely consultative role, and, being financially dependent on the budget of often insolvent local governments, they cannot often exercise even narrow competences pertaining to non-territorial autonomy. Moreover, since three electoral cycles for national minority councils and representatives of national minorities at the local and regional self-administration units mobilized worryingly low numbers of the minority electorate, it is reasonable to question if this institution is at all perceived by national minority members as an empowerment tool for non-territorial autonomy. Even the international organizations that oversee implementation of minority rights have repeatedly assessed the functioning of the national minority councils in Croatia as poor and inadequate. The manifestations of institutional weakness indicate that the 'fictitious norms' on minority non-territorial autonomy through minority councils are not significantly contributing to the preservation of minority cultures and identities.

This above analysis demonstrates that the introduction of a new institution of national minority protection does not necessarily produce novel and enhanced impact on the life of national minority communities in those areas where institutional competences are supposed to be executed. Given that national minority councils with the presently assigned competences have a worryingly limited mandate, enjoying no autonomy in decision-making, and given that this institution of minority participation is not able to appeal to relevant numbers of voters to direct elections, the Croatian government might reconsider if other options could substitute this minority institution. Whether this means abolishing the institution, moving its competences to national minority representatives in the assemblies of cities and counties, or a considerable reform that would endow minority councils with competences to manage culture and education at the level of governance where the councils have been elected, the time for change has come.

4

National Minority Councils in Serbia

Tamás Korhecz

4.1 Introduction

Even without Kosovo, the Republic of Serbia (hereinafter Serbia) is a multi-ethnic state, in which more than 15 per cent of the total population belongs to various national minorities traditionally living in the current territory of Serbia.[1] The largest national minority in Serbia are the Hungarians living almost exclusively in the Autonomous Province of Vojvodina concentrated in the region bordering Hungary and numbering 253,000 (3.53 per cent of the total population).[2] The second largest national minority are the Roma who are living dispersed throughout Serbia and numbering 147,000 (2.05 per cent), while the third largest national minority are the Bosniaks concentrated in the Sandžak/Raška region in south-west Serbia and numbering 145,000 (2.02 per cent).[3] Beside these three national minorities, Serbia is also populated by large number of Croats, Slovaks, Albanians, Montenegrins, Vlachs, Romanians, Macedonians, Bulgarians, Bunjevci, and Ruthenians, primarily living in Vojvodina.[4] Although, for example, the legal status of the large Hungarian minority is formally equal with the status of the much smaller Macedonian or Bunjevci minorities, there are substantial and relevant differences, not only demographic but also historical, legal, social, political, and cultural, between the various national minorities living in Serbia. Some national minorities like the Hungarians, the Croatians, the Montenegrins, and the Bulgarians became minorities after historical events. Prior to these, they had the status of titular nation (majority) in the regions where they lived,[5] while others, such

[1] Statistical Office of the Republic of Serbia, 'Population, Ethnicity, Data by Municipalities and Cities', *2011 Census of Population, Housholds and Dwellings in the Republic of Serbia* (2012): p. 15.
[2] Statistical Office of the Republic of Serbia, 'Population', pp. 14–15.
[3] Statistical Office of the Republic of Serbia, 'Population', pp. 14–15.
[4] The number of Croats is 57,000, Slovaks 52,000, Albanians 61,000 (census 2002, in 2011 Albanians boycotted the census), Montenegrins 38,000, Vlachs 35,000, Romanians 29,000, Macedonians 22,000, Bulgarians 18,000, Bunjevci 16,000, Ruthenians 14,000. Statistical Office of the Republic of Serbia, 'Population', pp. 14–15.
[5] The current territory of Vojvodina, together with the substantial ethnic Hungarian population, was part of the Hungarian Kingdom (Austro-Hungary) till the end of World War I and 1920 Paris Peace Treaty. Bulgarians in eastern Serbia live mainly in two municipalities, Bosilegrad and Dimitrovgrad, which were part of Bulgaria until the end of World War I. Croats and Montenegrins

as, for example, the Roma, the Slovaks, and the Ruthenians always had a minority status since they have lived in the current territory of Serbia.[6] Furthermore, some national minorities are well organized politically, represented at all levels of government (Hungarians, Bosniaks, and Albanians) while others are not and have no authentic (ethnic) political representation.[7] Some national minorities have culture and languages substantially different and distinct from the culture and language of the Serb majority (Hungarians, Slovaks, Albanians, and Romanians) while others share very similar languages and culture with the Serbs (Croats, Montenegrins, Bunjevci, Macedonians, and Bulgarians). The above-mentioned differences are often relevant; they influence social and political positions, integration and assimilation, political demands, interests, and the overall influence of these groups in Serbia, such as the sentiments of the Serb majority towards these minorities.

These different national minorities enjoy formally equal minority protection guaranteed by the Serbian Constitution and by a large number of laws. This protection includes the collective right to self-governance in the areas of education, culture, information, and official language use, which can be utilized through elected national councils. The national council of a national minority is a representative body, elected by persons belonging to a national minority (living anywhere in Serbia) conducting various competences conferred by law in the areas of education, culture, media, and language use and financed primarily by the Serbian budget. National councils are most often officially defined as (the highest) institutions of cultural autonomy of national minorities in Serbia.[8] They were gradually introduced into the legal and political system of Serbia from 2002 onwards. First, members of national councils were elected by the assembly of electors in accordance with provisional electoral rules established by the Yugoslav Law on the

---

were titular nations during the era of socialist Yugoslavia, and became national minorities only after the break-up of Yugoslavia.

[6] These ethnic communities settled in the current territory in several waves and in different historical periods during and after the Ottoman rule, but evidently they have populated their homeland for centuries.

[7] UNDP Country Office in Serbia, *Human Development Report 2005—Serbia—Strength of Diversity* (Belgrade: UNDP, 2005), p. 62; Third Report Submitted by Serbia Pursuant to Article 25, Paragraph 2 of the Framework Convention for the Protection of National Minorities (received on 14 March 2013) ACFC/SR/III(2013)001, pp. 344–5, accessed September 2014, <http://www.coe.int/t/dghl/monitoring/minorities/3_FCNMdocs/PDF_3rd_SR_Serbia_en.pdf>.

[8] National councils are also defined as institutions of cultural autonomy in the following official documents: Second Report Submitted by Serbia Pursuant to Article 25, Paragraph 1 of the Framework Convention for the Protection of National Minorities (received on 4 March 2008) ACFC/SR/II(2008)001, p. 363, accessed September 2014, <http://www.coe.int/t/dghl/monitoring/minorities/3_fcnmdocs/PDF_2nd_SR_Serbia_en.pdf>; Third Report Submitted by Serbia Pursuant to Article 25, Paragraph 2 of the Framework Convention for the Protection of National Minorities (received on 14 March 2013) ACFC/SR/III(2013)001, p. 349, accessed September 2014, <http://www.coe.int/t/dghl/monitoring/minorities/3_FCNMdocs/PDF_3rd_SR_Serbia_en.pdf>; Pokrajinski Ombudsman Autonomne pokrajine Vojvodine, *Dve godine nacionalnih saveta—Istraživanje Pokrajinskog Ombudsmana* [Two Years of National Councils—Research of the Provincial Ombudsman] (2012): p. 4, accessed September 2014, <http://www.ombudsmanapv.org/riv/index.php/istrazivanja/741-dve-godine-nacionalnih-sveta-ii-deo>; UNDP Country Office in Serbia, *Human Development Report 2005*, p. 63.

Protection of Rights and Freedoms of National Minorities (hereinafter Yugoslav Law on Minority Rights)[9] and a ministerial decree on the functioning of assemblies of electors for the election of national councils.[10] In this way twelve national councils were established between 2002 and 2004 under provisional rules,[11] but their status, financing, and competences were not regulated until late 2009, when, after long bargaining between Hungarian political representatives and the ruling Serbian political parties, the Serbian National Assembly enacted a Law on National Councils of National Minorities (hereinafter Law on National Councils).[12] This complex law regulated in detail the status, registration, and competences, as well as the financing of national councils, thus opening the door to direct democratic elections of members of national councils upon separate voting registers of persons belonging to each national minority. In addition, the collective rights of national minorities to self-governance and national councils were recognized and guaranteed by the Constitution. The relevant provisions on collective rights and national councils of the Yugoslav Law on Minority Rights were almost literally copied-and-pasted into the 2003 Constitution of Serbia and Montenegro,[13] while after the secession of Montenegro into the new 2006 Constitution of Serbia.[14] Between 2002 and 2014 provisions of laws regulating national councils were subject to constitutional reviews first before the Yugoslav[15] and later before the Serbian Constitutional Court,[16] while in 2014 the Law on National Councils was substantially amended. By October 2014, when the general re-election of national councils took place, nineteen Serbian national minorities established national councils and in this way realized their collective constitutional rights to self-governance.[17]

---

[9] Zakon o zaštiti prava i sloboda nacionalnih manjina, Službeni List SRJ Broj 11/2002 [Law on the Protection of Rights and Freedoms of National Minorities 2002].

[10] Pravilnik o načinu rada skupštine elektora za izbor saveta nacionalnih manjina, Službeni List SRJ Broj 41/2002 [Rules on the Work of the Assembly of Electors for the Election of Councils of National Minorities 2002].

[11] UNDP Country Office in Serbia, *Human Development Report 2005*, p. 63.

[12] Zakon o nacionalnim savetima nacionalnih manjina, Službeni glasnik Republike Srbije Broj 72/2009, 20/2014 and 55/2014 [Law on National Councils of National Minorities 2009, 2014, and 2014].

[13] Povelja o Ljudskim i manjinskim pravima i građanskim slobodama, Službeni list SCG Broj 6/2003 [Charter on Human and Minority Rights and Civil Freedoms 2003], art 47.

[14] Ustav Republike Srbije, Službeni glasnik RS Broj 98/2006 [The Constitution of the Republic of Serbia 2006], art 75, para 2. Unofficial English translation of the Constitution of the Republic of Serbia is available on the following website, accessed September 2014, <http://www.srbija.gov.rs/cinjenice_o_srbiji/ustav.php?change_lang=en>.

[15] Odluka Ustavnog suda Savezne Republike Jugoslavije, Broj IU 181/2002, 193/2002, 197/2002, Službeni List SRJ Broj 66/2002 [The Decision of the Constitutional Court of the Federal Republic of Yugoslavia, Number IU 181/2002, 193/2002, 197/2002].

[16] Odluka Ustavnog suda Republike Srbije Broj, Iuz-882/2010, Službeni glasnik RS Broj 20/2014 [The Decision of the Constitutional Court of the Republic of Serbia, IUZ-882/2010].

[17] In accordance with the 2009 Law, sixteen national minorities elected directly, upon separate voting register their national councils in June 2010 (Albanians, Aškalije, Bosniaks, Bunjevci, Bulgarians, Czechs, Egyptians, Germans, Greeks, Hungarians, Roma, Romanians, Ruthenians, Slovaks, Vlachs, and Ukrainians), while three national minorities elected their national councils by electors (Croats, Macedonians, and Slovenians). The competences of the Jewish national councils are conducted in accordance with the Law on National Councils by the Alliance of Jewish municipalities.

The main aim of this chapter is to introduce the reader to the Serbian model of non-territorial autonomy (NTA) exercised by national councils of national minorities. We particularly wish to identify the relevant ideology, political circumstances, and policy issues influencing the emergence and development of the NTA arrangement, such as to describe the relevant legal framework and functionality of national councils in Serbia. We will make some observations concerning the results and benefits of the Serbian model of NTA from several perspectives, including the Serbian state, national minorities, and minority protection in general.

4.2 Ideology and Circumstances that Led to the Establishment of NTA

As noted earlier, national councils in Serbia were introduced at the beginning of 2002 with the Yugoslav Law on Minority Rights as a completely new institution.[18] Since then, the legal framework and the practice of national councils have substantially evolved. One can reasonably ask: what led to the decision to introduce national councils, did it have a solid ideological background, or was it a logical result of the Serbian policy of diversity management? Was a wide public debate organized before the decision, or was public consensus reached before the legal introduction of national councils? Answers to all these questions are mainly in the negative. From 1990 onwards, after the collapse of socialist Yugoslavia and one-party communist rule, Serbia has continuously lacked a government policy of ethnic diversity management, at least a codified, written, and transparent government policy with clearly defined principles based on public consensus.[19] Even after the political changes in October 2000, the legislative framework of minority protection and the implementation of minority rights have not usually been the result of a clear and transparent government policy, but rather the result of a mixture of various political circumstances, pressure from the international community or minority political leaders, and various compromises.[20] This is also true in the case of the establishment of national councils and the legal recognition of collective minority rights. The introduction of national councils in 2002 was governed by three main political circumstances; these circumstances together led to the legal recognition of the collective minority right to self-governance and to the establishment of national councils in Serbia. First, it was the continued influence

---

[18] Zakon o zaštiti prava i sloboda nacionalnih manjina.

[19] Vojislav Stanovčić, 'Predgovor: Pregled istraživanja položaja manjina' [Introduction: Overview of Researches on the Situation of Minorities], in *Položaj nacionalnih manjina u Srbiji*, edited by Vojislav Stanovčić (Beograd: Srpska akademija nauka i umetnosti, 2007), p. 35.

[20] Nenad Đurđević, 'Minority Policy in Serbia—Fostering Integration—Analyses and Recommendations for Improving Minority Policy and Integration Process in the Republic of Serbia', *Forum—Forum for Ethnic Relations, Policy Paper* vol. 4, no. 1 (2014): p. 8, accessed September 2014, <http://www.fer.org.rs/uploads/sr/dokumenti/publikacije/analiza-i-preporuke-za-unapredjenje-manjinske-politike-i-procesa-integracije-u-republici-srbiji/Forum-1-2014-ENG-web.pdf>.

of Yugoslavian heritage in the area of diversity management and minority protection. Second, the specific political situation in post-Milošević Serbia (Federal Republic of Yugoslavia) resulted in the Yugoslavian and the Serbian states making genuine efforts to establish high standards of human and minority rights in the course of European integration. Finally, the political influence and capacities of the Hungarian ethnic political parties in Serbia made it possible to partially realize their autonomy demands in legislation.

4.2.1 The Yugoslav socialist heritage of diversity management

Serbia was part of Yugoslavian state formation between 1918 and 2006. For the longest period (between 1945 and 1990) Serbia was part of socialist federal Yugoslavia, forming its largest federal unit. Although socialist federal Yugoslavia was a state directed by the autocratic rule of the Communist Party, it had an authentic and developed policy for managing ethnic diversity.[21] The federal state organization, with six republics and two autonomous provinces, was constructed to maintain and support ethnic equality and multi-ethnic coexistence, to prevent ethnic domination by the majority in this truly multi-ethnic and diverse state.[22] The constitutional and legal framework guaranteed the national equality of Yugoslav nations and nationalities, and many constitutional and legal provisions protected minority rights. Ethnic diversity was maintained through public institutions (schools, cultural institutions, media), protecting the identity, language, and culture of nations and national minorities.[23] Ethnic diversity and peace were also maintained by the policy of proportional ethnic representation in state institutions (the so-called policy of ethnic keys or ethnic quotas), for example by the official use of various languages.[24] The Yugoslav socialist federal state broke up under the pressure of rising nationalism in the early 1990s. Under the leadership of Slobodan Milošević, Serbia almost eliminated the Yugoslavian way of diversity management, fighting for the establishment of an enlarged, strong nation–state under Serb domination.

However, besides rising nationalism and nationalist policies, Milošević's Serbia preserved much of Tito's Yugoslavia. After the break-up of socialist Yugoslavia, Serbia established, with Montenegro, the Federal Republic of Yugoslavia and declared it the legal and political successor to socialist Yugoslavia. The Milošević-led socialist party was legally and also in merit a successor to the Serbian Communist Party, and the laws of the previous state continued to be in force in the new. Thus,

---

[21] Boris Krivokapić, *Zaštita manjina u međunarodnom i uporednom pravu—Knjiga III—Zaštita manjina u nacionalnim porecima država* [The Protection of Minorities in the International and Comparative Law, Volume III, Protection of Minorities in National Orders of State] (Beograd: Ministarstvo za ljudska i manjinska prava Srbije i Crne Gore, 2004), p. 27.

[22] Tibor Várady, 'Minorities, Majorities, Law, and Ethnicity: Reflections of the Yugoslav Case', *Human Rights Quarterly* vol. 19 (1997): pp. 17–18; UNDP Country Office in Serbia, *Human Development Report 2005*, p. 12.

[23] Várady, 'Minorities, Majorities, Law', p. 18.

[24] UNDP Country Office in Serbia, *Human Development Report 2005*, p. 12.

although Serb ethnic nationalist rhetoric dominated Serbian politics of the 1990s, the legal and institutional framework for the protection of national minorities was not abolished, and it served as a standard for new legislation. In this way, even in the 1990s, formal legal standards of minority protection remained relatively high in comparison with other post-socialist multi-ethnic states. The Serbian state was simply not ready and not motivated to sharply and openly break with Yugoslavian standards of minority protection; rather it rarely chose to implement minority rights and legal standards in many areas. The relatively high standard of minority rights served as propaganda arguments for internal and external use by the Milošević regime as evidence that Serbian policy was not exclusivist and nationalist. On the other hand, these former, relatively high standards of minority rights persuaded Serb political elites and the population to be relatively tolerant towards the demands of national minorities seeking the preservation of diversity. The above-described influence of socialist Yugoslavia's standards on minority rights protection was one of the elements that made possible the establishment of NTAs with national councils after the changes in 2000.

4.2.2 Post-Milošević Serbia and European integration

Besides the influence of Yugoslavian heritage, the recognition of collective rights and the establishment of national councils in 2002 by the Yugoslav Law on Minority Rights were also a result of the authentic efforts of the post-Milošević Yugoslavian and Serbian governments[25] to guarantee high standards of human and minority rights and to cooperate with the international community and with neighbouring countries. After international isolation and sanctions, the new Yugoslavian and Serbian governments wished to clear the problematic human rights record by accepting European standards of human and minority rights. The accession to the Council of Europe (CoE) and potentially the European Union (EU) was an important priority, while a Yugoslav Law on Minority Rights, together with bilateral agreements with neighbouring countries on minority protection were strong tools for this end, serving as strong evidence of good faith in this process. The 2002 Yugoslav Law on Minority Rights mainly accepted the standards of the CoE Framework Convention for the Protection of National Minorities, while national councils were conceptualized as a realization of the obligations rising out of Article 15 of the Framework Convention.[26] The international community, the

---

[25] After the break-up of socialist (large) Yugoslavia, tiny Montenegro and Serbia formed the Federal Republic of Yugoslavia in 1992. Despite the federal state structure the new state formation was under the decisive domination of Serbia and Milošević, who was first the President of Serbia, later the President of the Federal Republic of Yugoslavia. With this in mind it is not incorrect to use Serbia and Yugoslavia as almost synonymous in the period between 1992 and 2003.

[26] Art 15 of the Framework Convention facilitates various policies for the effective participation of national minorities in decision-making. See more in Asbjørn Eide, 'The Council of Europe Framework Convention for the Protection of National Minorities', in *Synergies in Minority Protection—European and International Law Perspective*, edited by Kristin Henrard and Robert Dunbar (Cambridge: Cambridge University Press, 2009), pp.139–41.

Organization for Security and Co-operation in Europe (OSCE), the EU, and the CoE made no direct demands on Yugoslavia or Serbia to establish national councils or other minority self-governments, but they required and welcomed positive steps, including legislative efforts in the area of minority rights protection.[27] Such steps would be authentic and convincing only if those concerned (national minorities) were satisfied with such legislative and other measures. Moreover, high standards of minority protection and legislative efforts in this area might strengthen the position of Yugoslavia and Serbia in respect of the Kosovo province, then under international supervision and rule. Serbia's efforts to protect the Serb population in Kosovo would be more convincing with a respectable record on minority protection in Serbia.[28]

The Law on Minority Rights, including the collective right to self-governance, was presented to the public mainly as a tool for the smooth European integration of the Federal Republic of Yugoslavia and later the successor state Serbia, and as genuine proof of high human rights standards. Although the issue was not an important focus for the Serbian public during 2001–2, the legislative step was generally supported by almost all parliamentary parties. Moreover, the majority of the Serbian population also supported it, especially those supporting the policy of European integration, and the opening of and break-up with the Milošević era. Despite relative support for the improvement of minority rights in Serbia within the population, one can claim that the average Serb in Serbia had little or no knowledge of what national council or minority self-governance was.

4.2.3 Political influence of Hungarian political parties

Apart from Albanians in Kosovo, Hungarians in Vojvodina form the largest national minority living in Serbia. Ethnic Hungarians for more than a millennium populated the current territory of Vojvodina and became a national minority less than a century ago, when Hungary lost huge territories after World War I. Even after turbulent historical events, Hungarians are still a local majority of the population in the north-central part of Vojvodina, on the right bank of the river Tisa, in eight municipalities.[29] However, around 30 to 40 per cent of Hungarians in Vojvodina live in settlements, mainly as a local minority outside this 'Hungarian-dominated' sub-region. The Hungarian minority has a strong Hungarian ethnic identity, language, culture, and religious affiliation that are very distinct from the Serbs'. The Hungarians in Vojvodina have continued to manifest a strong will to preserve their language, culture, and distinctiveness when they found themselves outside the

---

[27] János Vékás, 'Serbia', in *Minority Hungarian Communities in the Twentieth Century*, edited by Nándor Bárdi, Csilla Fedinec, and László Szarka (Boulder, CO: Atlantic Research and Publications, Inc., 2011), p. 544.

[28] Đurđević, 'Minority Policy in Serbia', p. 9.

[29] Subotica (Szabadka), Kanjiža (Magyarkanizsa), Senta (Zenta), Čoka (Csoka), Ada, Bečej (Óbecse), Mali Iđoš (Kishegyes), Topola (Topolya). Statistical Office of the Republic of Serbia, 'Population', p. 18.

borders of Hungary after 1920. They soon organized Hungarian ethnic political parties and demanded self-governance. After the socialist, one-party rule period in Yugoslavia (1945–90), the Hungarians in Vojvodina organized themselves politically on the eve of the multi-party system in Serbia and formulated autonomy claims.

In the last twenty to twenty-five years, ethnic Hungarian political parties have had three main characteristics: first, they rejected violence as a means of realizing their political goals; second, they openly advocated various autonomy arrangements, territorial or non-territorial, and third, they tried to realize their political goals within the legal and political system of Serbia, never advocating revision of the border between Serbia and Hungary.[30] Various Hungarian autonomy proposals were drafted in the decade between 1990 and 2000, which incorporated ethnic territorial autonomy for Hungarian-dominated municipalities, non-territorial (cultural) autonomy for all Hungarians, primarily in the area of education, culture, and media, and wide political autonomy for Vojvodina, as a traditional autonomy within Serbia, yet mainly populated by Serbs. During the 1990s, Hungarian autonomy proposals were entirely neglected by Milošević-led Yugoslav and Serbian governments. Hungarian politicians during this period were not able to convince the Serbian leadership to negotiate autonomy proposals. The political situation dramatically changed in October 2000 when the twelve-year-long rule of Slobodan Milošević and his Serbian Socialist Party collapsed instantly and the Democratic Opposition of Serbia (DOS) came to power. The coalition of eighteen opposition parties, including the largest Hungarian political party, the Alliance of Vojvodina Hungarians (VAH) soon acquired a majority in the Parliaments of the Federal Republic of Yugoslavia, and in Serbia as well as in Vojvodina province; Hungarians in this way became part of the ruling majority. The new political situation made it possible for the VAH to actively influence legislation in post-Milošević Serbia, primarily in the area of human and minority rights. In 2001, when the Federal Ministry for Human and Minority Rights established a working group for the preparation of the bill for the law on the protection of rights and freedoms of national minorities, experts delegated by the VAH were appointed. The initiatives of VAH experts concerning NTA were finally incorporated into the bill, and the bill was passed by the Yugoslav Parliament almost unanimously in February 2002. The relevant provisions of the Yugoslav law on national minorities were far from the original autonomy proposals of the Hungarian political parties; however, the law recognized the collective right of national minorities to self-governance and the establishment of the Hungarian National Council, thus laying the foundations for NTA. From the current perspective, it seems that the political majority within DOS weighed up the situation and decided that by formally accepting the Hungarian claim for non-territorial self-governance, they could prevent more radical claims by the Hungarians and other national minorities including territorial

---

[30] Tamás Korhecz, 'Vojvodina—The Next Stage of the Dismantling Process?', *Cambridge Review of International Affairs* vol. 12, no. 2 (1999): p. 158.

autonomy claims. Political representatives of other national minorities were mainly passive on the whole issue, but moderately supportive of this process, being more or less aware of the potential benefits arising from the establishment of national councils.

With the 2002 Yugoslav Law on Minority Rights, the establishment of national councils as bodies of national minorities, with undefined competences in areas of education, culture, information, and language use, was legally guaranteed. However, for seven years they remained symbolic institutions without rules for the democratic election of their members or clearly defined competences for financing. In 2009, again with the active and deep involvement of the VAH and Hungarian legal experts, the Law on National Councils was drafted and enacted in the Serbian National Assembly. This Act in its complexity regulates the status, election, competences, and financing of national councils.[31]

The above-mentioned facts are evidence that the Serbian model of NTA is deeply entrenched in Serbian constitutional and public law and as such is a formal arrangement within the legal and political system of Serbia. This establishment as well as the development of the NTA arrangement was influenced by a variety of political factors and pressures. It is hard to claim that the Serbian state introduced this NTA arrangement within the framework of a state policy of ethnic diversity management, with defined objectives and public support, although some state objectives by NTA might be identified indirectly. The first objective of the Serbian state with NTA was to demonstrate its determination to protect national minorities by guaranteeing them the highest standards of minority rights, including collective rights.[32] In this way Serbia tried to strengthen its international position during the course of European integration, for example through its endeavours to protect Serbs in neighbourhoods in Kosovo, Bosnia, and Herzegovina, Croatia, Macedonia, Montenegro, and Hungary, etc.[33] The second objective of the Serbian state with NTA was to integrate national minorities in Serbia into its legal and political system so that they accepted Serbia as their state.[34] National councils are institutions of the Serbian legal system and their competences are constructed in a way that they are expected to cooperate with various local and state authorities

---

[31] Tamás Korhecz, 'Non-Territorial Autonomy in Practice: The Hungarian National Council in Serbia', in *Autonomies in Europe: Solutions and Challenges*, edited by Zoltán Kántor (Budapest: L'Harmattan, 2009), pp. 152–3.

[32] Serbian President Boris Tadić declared that Serbia, with the 2009 Law on National Councils, guaranteed rights for national minorities that did not exist in the majority of EU countries. See Mladen Đorđević, 'Nacionalni saveti—Problem umesto rešenja' [National Councils—A Problem instead of a Solution], *Nova Srpska Politička Misao* (2010), accessed September 2014, <http://www.nspm.rs/politicki-zivot/nacionalni-saveti—problem-umesto-resenja.html>.

[33] Đurđević, 'Minority Policy in Serbia', p. 9.

[34] This objective was clearly recognized in the recent landmark decision of the Serbian Constitutional Court: Odluka Ustavnog suda Republike Srbije Broj, Iuz-882/2010, Službeni glasnik RS Broj 20/2014 [The Decision of the Constitutional Court of the Republic of Serbia IUZ-882/2010], pp. 47–8. See also: Minoritynews.rs, 'Intrvju Dr Suzana Paunović Direktorka Kancelarije za ljudska i manjinska prava' [Interview with Dr Suzana Paunovic, Director of the Office for Human and Minority Rights], April/May 2013, p. 5, accessed September 2014, <http://www.minoritynews.rs>.

and institutions. It is hoped that this cooperation will integrate more national minorities into Serbian society, and vice versa, making various authorities more open and sensitive to the issues relevant to national minorities. This cooperation and integration might also make easier the implementation of minority rights and prevent potential conflicts between the authorities and the representatives of national minorities. National councils are representative, democratically elected bodies, thus authorities will always have adequate address, if they wish to solve a question related to a national minority.

The third objective of the Serbian model of the NTA arrangement is to neutralize more radical claims of national minorities. If the majority of people belonging to a national minority as well as the major political parties accept national councils and policy-making through them, radical claims outside the legal system are likely to be neutralized. This objective is of primary importance in the case of large, concentrated minorities with a strong political identity, such as the Hungarians, the Albanians, and the Bosniaks. Although NTA cannot substitute completely the territorial claims of these large and territorially concentrated minorities, it can still ease tensions and integrate minorities to some extent.[35]

4.3 The Current Legal Framework of the Serbian Model of NTA

The Serbian model of NTA is deeply entrenched in Serbian public law. The Constitution of the Republic of Serbia guarantees the collective right of persons belonging to national minorities to participate in decision-making concerning their identity and stipulates that '[p]ersons belonging to national minorities may elect their national councils in order to exercise the right to self-governance in the field of culture, education, information and official use of their language and script, in accordance with the law'.[36] The constitutional provisions on national councils are now specified primarily in the Law on National Councils; however the remit of national councils is also partially regulated by other legislative acts in the Serbian legal system.[37] Sometimes the provisions on the competences of national councils

---

[35] David J. Smith, 'Minority Territorial and Non-Territorial Autonomy in Europe: Theoretical Perspectives and Practical Challenges', in *Autonomies in Europe: Solutions and Challenges*, edited by Zoltán Kántor (Budapest: L'Harmattan, 2009), p. 22.

[36] Ustav Republike Srbije, Službeni glasnik RS Broj 98/2006 [The Constitution of the Republic of Serbia 2006], art 75, para 2.

[37] Various laws regulating culture, information, and the educational system contain some provisions on the competences of national councils. Zakon o Kulturi, Službeni glasnik Republike Srbije Broj 72/2009 [Law on Culture 2009]; Zakon o javnom informisanju i medijima, Službeni Glasnik RS, Broj 83/2014 [Law on Public Information and Media 2014]; Zakon o elektronskim medijim, Službeni glasnik RS, Broj 83/2014 [Law on Electronic Media 2014]; Zakon o osnovama sistema obrazovanja i vaspitanja, Službeni glasnik Republike Srbije Broj 72/2009, 52/2011, 55/2013 [Law on the Basis of the System of Education and Training 72/2009, 52/2011, 55/2013]; Zakon o učeničkom i studentskom standardu, Službeni glasnik RS, Broj 18/2010, 55/2013 [Law on the Students and Pupils Standards 18/2010, 55/2013].

are not regulated uniformly in the Law on National Councils and laws regulating the areas of education, culture, information/media etc.[38] In presenting the legal framework of national councils in Serbia, the focus is primarily on the provisions of the Law on National Councils, since this Act regulates the main issues related to national councils. The Law on National Councils[39] consists of 139 articles divided into ten chapters, from basic provisions to provisions detailing violations.[40] In the following the provisions on the status and election, competences, and financing of national councils will be briefly elaborated.

4.3.1 Provisions on status, organization, and election of national councils

National councils have fifteen to thirty-five elected members depending on the size of the represented national minority.[41] They are registered in the register of national councils kept by the Ministry responsible for human and minority rights (the Ministry).[42] National councils have a president, an executive committee, and working committees for education, culture, information, and official language use.[43] The Law regulates in detail (in almost eighty articles) the procedure for the election of national councils. There are two systems for the election of national councils, direct by members of the national minority or indirect by the assembly of electors. If at least 40 per cent of all persons belonging to a national minority according to the latest census voluntarily register with the voting registers, direct elections for the national council take place; if not, national council members are elected by electors, indirectly.[44] Bearing in mind that almost all national minorities fulfil the necessary requirement for direct elections, including the most numerous and politically most influential national minorities, one can argue that as a rule, national councils are directly elected by adult members of the national minority who voluntarily enrol onto the voting registers kept by the Ministry.[45] Elections are organized for all national minorities in one day throughout Serbia.[46] The main

[38] Advisory Committee on the Framework Convention for the Protection of National Minorities, Third Opinion on Serbia, p. 47.

[39] Zakon o nacionalnim savetima nacionalnih manjina.

[40] The titles of the chapters are: I. Basic provisions (arts 1–6.); II. Issues related to the status of national councils (arts 7–9a.); III. The competences of the national councils (arts 10–22); IV. Relationship of the national councils with the authorities of the Republic, the autonomous province, and local self-governments (arts 25–6); V. International and regional cooperation (arts 27–8); VI. Election of national councils (arts 29–109); VII. Financing the national councils (arts 112–19), VIII. Supervision (arts 120–2), IX. Provisions on offences (arts 123–8); X. Transitional and concluding provisions (arts 129–39).

[41] Zakon o nacionalnim savetima nacionalnih manjina, art 9.

[42] Zakon o nacionalnim savetima nacionalnih manjina, art 3.

[43] Zakon o nacionalnim savetima nacionalnih manjina, art 7.

[44] Zakon o nacionalnim savetima nacionalnih manjina, art 29.

[45] 'A person will be registered as a minority voter if he/she has a general voting right in Serbia and if he/she declares his/her affiliation to the respective national minority in written application form.' Zakon o nacionalnim savetima nacionalnih manjina, art 52.

[46] Zakon o nacionalnim savetima nacionalnih manjina, art 36.

authority organizing the elections is (according to the latest amendments of the Law on National Councils in 2014) the Republican Electoral Committee, which is responsible for the organization of parliamentary and presidential elections.[47] According to the relevant provisions, members of national councils are elected through a proportional electoral system with nominated lists of candidates.[48] Lists of candidates can be proposed by the organizations of national minorities (political parties and non-governmental organizations (NGOs)) and groups of citizens (belonging to the respective national minority) on condition that their nomination is supported by 1 per cent of the voters registered with the voting register for the respective national minority.[49] After voting, all lists receive seats in national councils proportionate to the number of votes they gathered.[50] In cases where a sufficient number of voters are not registered twenty-four hours before the date declared by the Ministry, national council members are elected indirectly by electors.[51] Electors are persons formally supported by at least twenty to one hundred persons listed with the voting register depending on the size of the respective national minority.[52] In cases where the minimal legal requirements are fulfilled, the assembly of electors elects national councils members by the proportional electoral system.[53]

4.3.2 Remits and competences of national councils

Probably the most significant issue related to the Serbian model of NTA is the issue of competences, that is the delegated public powers enabling national councils to self-govern in the areas of education, culture, information, and official language use. The Law on National Councils regulates various competences of national councils in thirteen expansive articles.[54] All competences (according to some experts there are eighty different competences)[55] of national councils could be divided into three groups: (1) autonomous decision-making powers; (2) consent and proposing powers; as well as (3) powers to express opinions regarding almost all administrative decisions in conjunction with culture, education, information, and language use of national minorities. In the case of the competences of national councils, the concept of the law is not to delegate (mainly administrative) decision-making powers to national councils, but to involve them in the decision-making process of

---

[47] Zakon o nacionalnim savetima nacionalnih manjina, arts 60 and 62.
[48] Zakon o nacionalnim savetima nacionalnih manjina, art 98.
[49] Zakon o nacionalnim savetima nacionalnih manjina, art 71.
[50] Zakon o nacionalnim savetima nacionalnih manjina, art 98.
[51] Zakon o nacionalnim savetima nacionalnih manjina, art 29.
[52] Zakon o nacionalnim savetima nacionalnih manjina, art 101.
[53] Zakon o nacionalnim savetima nacionalnih manjina, arts 105–9.
[54] Zakon o nacionalnim savetima nacionalnih manjina, arts 10–22.
[55] Third Report Submitted by Serbia Pursuant to Article 25, Paragraph 2 of the Framework Convention for the Protection of National Minorities, received on 14 March 2013, ACFC/SR/III(2013)001, p. 351 accessed September 2014, <http://www.coe.int/t/dghl/monitoring/minorities/3_FCNMdocs/PDF_3rd_SR_Serbia_en.pdf>.

central, provincial, or local authorities. Most often this involvement is in the form of giving opinions (authorities are obliged to ask opinions of national councils prior to the decision but they are not obliged to accept them). In many other cases the involvement of national councils in decision-making is more effective, such as when national councils are solely empowered to propose a draft decision or they have consent (veto) power concerning a decision. In a few cases, national councils are empowered to decide autonomously with authorities in matters related to the identity of the national minority.[56] In this way, the Law on National Councils guarantees that almost no decision of central administrative authorities or the authorities of an autonomous province of local self-government can be made without the participation of national councils (by proposing a draft decision, providing consent, or giving an opinion).

The majority of these competences are related to the management of public educational and cultural institutions that are vital for the identity of the respective national minority. In the case of public educational (kindergartens, elementary and secondary schools, grammar and vocational training schools) and cultural institutions (theatres, libraries, museums etc.), which are linked to a national minority (e.g. the language of instruction is exclusively or predominantly a minority language), national councils are entitled to propose some of the executive board members.[57] When considering the competences of national councils, it is important to note the stipulations which permit the founding rights of the most important state, provincial, and local public educational and cultural institutions to be partly or completely transferred to the national council in cases where a national council so requests.[58] In such cases, the Law on National Councils also guarantees that budgetary subsidies of these institutions transferred to national councils remain consistent.[59] These provisions open the door to the gradual establishment of a system of public institutions under the umbrella and management of national councils.

4.3.3 Provisions on the financing of national councils

Provisions on finances constitute the third important group of provisions in the Law on National Councils. The provisions stipulate that activities of national councils are financed by the budget of the Republic, the budget of the autonomous province, the budget of local self-governments, donations, and other incomes.[60] The budget of the autonomous province finances those national councils whose seats are allocated to the autonomous province, while the unit of local government

---

[56] e.g. national councils determine the traditional names of settlements and other geographic names in the language of the national minority if the minority language is in official use in that area. Zakon o nacionalnim savetima nacionalnih manjina, art 22.

[57] Zakon o nacionalnim savetima nacionalnih manjina, art 12.

[58] Zakon o nacionalnim savetima nacionalnih manjina, arts 11 and 16.

[59] Zakon o nacionalnim savetima nacionalnih manjina, art 116.

[60] Zakon o nacionalnim savetima nacionalnih manjina, art 114.

finances those national councils that represent national minorities whose members constitute at least 10 per cent of the local population, or whose language is in official use in the territory of the local self-government.[61] The annual sum assigned to national councils from the Serbian budget has to be specified each year in the budget of the Republic.[62] This sum has to be divided among national councils in the following way: 30 per cent of the sum has to be divided proportionally between national councils, while the remaining 70 per cent has to be divided in proportion to the size of the given community, the development and number of institutions, and the frequency of cultural and other activities.[63] Councils should enact detailed yearly financial plans and final accounts, and they must spend their incomes in accordance with the law.[64] Yearly amounts and criteria for budgetary subsidies from the provincial and local budgets should be determined by the regulations of these authorities.[65]

4.4 The Functionality of the Serbian Model of NTA

National councils in Serbia have functioned since the end of 2002. However, they have only been performing competences with full democratic legitimacy and within relatively precise legal frameworks since 2010. To what extent have they used their competences, and how have they contributed to the protection and effective implementation of minority rights in Serbia? Have they created a network of public institutions and ensured their functioning? What programmes have they launched, financed, and managed for the benefit of the respective national minority? Have Serbian authorities financed and accepted national councils as their partners in decision-making concerning education, culture, information, and official language use of national minorities? Were they representative and transparent enough to democratically perform their duties? These are the questions this part will try to answer at least briefly. It should be noted that it is not easy to analyse the functioning of national councils generally. Although all national councils function in the same legal environment, the actual circumstances in which they function are substantially different. The national minorities they represent are different not only in their numbers and territorial concentration, but also in their history, political organization, institutional framework, and social and economic positions. All of these directly influence available budgetary resources, administrative capacities, plans and programmes, political weight, and the influence of national councils as well.

It is problematic to compare the functioning of Hungarian councils with their Egyptian or Greek counterparts. Not only is the Hungarian population in Serbia

---

[61] Zakon o nacionalnim savetima nacionalnih manjina, art 115.
[62] Zakon o nacionalnim savetima nacionalnih manjina, art 115.
[63] Zakon o nacionalnim savetima nacionalnih manjina, art 115.
[64] Zakon o nacionalnim savetima nacionalnih manjina, art 117.
[65] Zakon o nacionalnim savetima nacionalnih manjina, art 115.

several hundred times greater than these communities, but the number of public institutions towards which these national councils execute their competences is simply incomparable.[66] It has already been noted that the Serbian model of NTA was very much developed under the influence of Hungarian political parties (primarily VAH) and their concept of NTA. The legal framework was tailored to fit the Hungarian minority, the institutional system, and actual needs and plans. In this way it was mainly those national minorities whose actual positions, needs, and plans were and are similar to the Hungarians who were able to benefit from the Serbian model of NTA. These are primarily those national minorities in Serbia which had a relatively developed public institutional framework for the implementation of minority rights, and the preservation of language, culture, and identity at the end of the twentieth century. While Hungarians, Slovaks, Romanians, and Ruthenians in the Autonomous Province of Vojvodina, and to a lesser extent Albanians and Bulgarians in south and east Serbia, had a relatively developed network of public educational, cultural, and media institutions, and language traditionally recognized as the local official language, other national minorities had no public institutional framework protecting their culture and identity. Thus, the first group of national councils was able, at least partially, to use competences related to the transfer of founding rights and the management rights of public educational, cultural, and media institutions, and competences in the area of official language use.

Other national councils, on the other hand, in the absence of public institutional frameworks (instruction in the native language, official language use, etc.) were practically denied the use of a majority of the competences stipulated by the Law on National Councils.[67] In this situation, the national councils of so-called *new minorities* acted as representatives, and state-financed NGOs with democratic legitimacy formulated plans, initiatives, and demands towards authorities while protesting against the violations of rights on behalf of the national minority they represented. Their efforts were primarily directed towards the establishment of educational, cultural, and informational public institutions, the recognition of their language, the development of their administrative capacities, and the practical implementation of their minority rights as guaranteed by the Constitution and laws. Bearing in mind this dichotomy, the functioning of national councils is presented primarily through the functioning of national councils which have had the opportunity to use competences stipulated by the Law on National Councils in areas important for the operation of the Serbian model of NTA.

---

[66] There are no public kindergartens or schools with instruction in Greek or Egyptian in Serbia, while there are more than 150 such public institutions with instruction in the Hungarian language, towards which the Hungarian National Council has competences. Magyar Nemzeti Tanács, 'A Magyar Nemzeti Tanács Négy Éve—2010. Június 30.—2014 Június 30' [Four Years of the Hungarian National Council—30 June 2010–30 June 2014], *Subotica* (2014): p. 45.
[67] Pokrajinski Ombudsman Autonomne pokrajine Vojvodine, *Dve godine nacionalnih saveta*, p. 29; Centar Za Regionalizam, 'Evaluacija Rada Pet Nacionalnih Saveta U Srbiji—Analize I Preporuke' [Evaluation of the Work of Five National Councils in Serbia—Analysis and Recommendations] (2011): p. 8.

4.4.1 Institutionalization and the transfer of powers

The essence of minority self-governance, such as cultural autonomy, is to administer certain affairs essential to national minorities by representatives of national minorities or at least to ensure effective participation in the decision-making process.[68] The logical consequence of this principle is that various public institutions linked to a national minority play a key role in the preservation of the language, culture, and tradition of the minority and allow them to govern and manage their activities. The Law on Minority Rights and later the Law on National Councils made it possible for the founding rights of the most important state, provincial, and local self-governmental public educational, cultural, and media institutions to be partly or completely transferred to the respective national council if the national council had so requested. In the last twelve years, the process of partial or complete transfer of founding rights has begun but is still not complete. While the authorities of the Autonomous Province of Vojvodina were cooperative in this respect,[69] local self-governments were seldom cooperative,[70] while central authorities were reluctant to implement these legal stipulations.[71] The opposition to the transfer of founding rights was sometimes explained by the lack of objective criteria of the minority cultural or educational institution's founding documents.[72] The available data and records prove that the functioning and performance of institutions transferred to national councils remain stable. Furthermore in some cases progress is even evident.[73] Critics emphasized that political parties with the most influence in national councils used it to politicize public institutions.[74]

---

[68] Georg Brunner and Herbert Küpper, 'European Options of Autonomy: A Typology of Autonomy Models of Minority Self-Governance', in *Minority Governance in Europe*, edited by Kinga Gál (Budapest: Local Government and Public Service Reform Initiative, 2002), p. 13.

[69] The Assembly of the Autonomous Province of Vojvodina in the period between 2003 and 2012 transferred completely or partially to the national councils the founding rights of: traditional newspapers and periodicals in the Hungarian, Slovak, Romanian, Croat, and Ruthenian languages; Hungarian, Slovak, Romanian, Croat, and Ruthenian provincial cultural institutes; the Hungarian language Forum publisher; eight grammar schools and vocational training schools with instruction exclusively or predominantly in Hungarian; one grammar school with instruction in Slovak; and one grammar school with instruction in Ruthenian.

[70] e.g. the National Council of Hungarians partially took over the founding rights of the Kosztolanyi Dezso theatre in Subotica, Zentai Kamaraszinhaz in Senta, libraries in Kanjiža, Bačka Topola, and Senta; however in some cases the local self-government did not cooperate in the transfer of founding rights to the Hungarian National Council (some cultural institutions in Novi Sad, Ada, and Subotica).

[71] e.g. the Hungarian National Council initiated the partial transfer of twenty elementary schools with instruction in the Hungarian language in 2011, whose founder was the Republic of Serbia. Despite the declared consent of the Ministry for Education, the government responsible for the decision on transfer never discussed the issue; in fact the government prevented the transfer of founding rights. Magyar Nemzeti Tanács, 'A Magyar Nemzeti Tanács Négy Éve', p. 46.

[72] Advisory Committee on the Framework Convention for the Protection of National Minorities, Third Opinion on Serbia, p. 49.

[73] Centar za regionalizam, 'Evaluacija Rada Pet Nacionalnih Saveta U Srbiji', p. 53; Magyar Nemzeti Tanács, 'A Magyar Nemzeti Tanács Négy Éve'.

[74] Pokrajinski Ombudsman Autonomne pokrajine Vojvodine, 'Dve godine nacionalnih saveta', p. 30; Advisory Committee on the Framework Convention for the Protection of National Minorities, Third Opinion on Serbia, p. 48.

The influence of party politics through national councils was emphasized mainly in the case of media institutions whose founding rights were transferred to national councils.[75]

4.4.2 Management of educational and cultural issues

Apart from public institutions whose founding rights are transferred to national councils, there are a larger number of educational and cultural public institutions for which national councils have some competences. These competences are mainly related to the election and appointment of managing boards and directors of educational institutions of all levels, dormitories, museums, theatres, libraries, and cultural centres whose activities are closely linked to the language, culture, and traditions of the respective national minority.[76] The competences include voicing an opinion on candidates, proposing candidates to the managing board or to the directors or the appointment of some members of the managing boards as well as consent rights during appointment, etc. Based on the evidence of actual practice, the conclusion is that these competences are mainly respected by public institutions and various authorities; however, sometimes serious obstruction and opposition towards these competences of national councils were reported as well.[77] Moreover, some national councils have sought court protection in these cases by launching lawsuits. The Administrative Court of Serbia has in several cases protected the rights and competences of national councils.[78] It could be concluded that after four years of functioning it is now the rule that the representatives proposed or delegated by the respective national councils are present on the boards of almost all public cultural, educational, and media institutions which serve the preservation of the identity of national minorities; even more, these institutions are regularly communicating and cooperating with national councils in performing their public duties.

4.4.3 Political and constitutional issues

Since 2010, when democratically elected national councils began to use their competences with public institutions guaranteed by the Law on National Councils, opposition to national councils (primarily the most active and influential Hungarian National Council) and NTA became more and more pronounced, mainly from some Serbian politicians, authorities, and parts of the media, as well as from some NGOs and public opinion.[79] In some ways, when national councils were bodies

---

[75] Centar za regionalizam, 'Evaluacija Rada Pet Nacionalnih Saveta U Srbiji', pp. 64–5.

[76] These competences are in conjunction with more than 200 different schools and dozens of various public cultural institutions mainly in the Autonomous Province of Vojvodina.

[77] Among others it was the conclusion of the Provincial Ombudsman's report. Pokrajinski Ombudsman Autonomne pokrajine Vojvodine, 'Dve godine nacionalnih saveta', pp. 29–30.

[78] Magyar Nemzeti Tanács, 'A Magyar Nemzeti Tanács Négy Éve', p. 162.

[79] Tamás Korhecz, 'Non-Territorial Autonomy in Practice', pp. 159–60.

without practical influence, money, or power, they were largely neglected, but when they began to use and implement their competences, they became a target for fierce critics and obstruction from various sides. Altogether eight initiatives were launched before the Serbian Constitutional Court in 2010 and 2011, asking the Court to review the constitutionality of provisions in thirty-six articles of the Law on National Councils.[80] Various initiators (individuals and NGOs linked to Serbian opposition parties) questioned the electoral rules based on separate voting registers, and the 'too wide' competences of national councils primarily towards public institutions which should 'serve all citizens and should not be governed by the representatives of a particular national minority through a national council'.[81] The Serbian academic community was divided on the issue of the constitutionality of national councils; some raised arguments in favour of the initiators,[82] others claimed that the competences of national councils were not violating the constitutional framework of NTA stipulated by Article 75, arguing that 'the competences are mainly reaching only the minimal threshold of participation in decision-making'.[83]

The Constitutional Court dismissed all objections concerning the electoral procedure but struck down some provisions concerning the obligatory transfer of powers of some public institutions and some competences of national councils towards educational institutions and media. The Constitutional Court ruled two articles completely unconstitutional and several paragraphs in eight other articles, while it rejected declaring unconstitutional various provisions in twenty-six articles of the Law on National Councils.[84] The Constitutional Court upheld the general position of the Serbian political public towards the NTA. This position could be

---

[80] See Rešenje Ustavnog suda Republike Srbije Broj Iuz-882/2010 from 17 January 2013 [The Warrant of the Constitutional Court of the Republic of Serbia No. IUZ-882/2010], accessed September 2014, <http://www.ustavni.sud.rs>.

[81] Tamás Korhecz, 'Nemzetiségi Autonómia Az Alkotmánybíróság Szorításában—A Szerbiai Alkotmánybíróság A Nemzeti Tanácsokat Szabályozó Törvénnyel Kapcsolatos Döntésének Kritikus Elemzése' [Ethnic Autonomy in the Wring of the Constitutional Court—Critical Analyses of the Decision of the Serbian Constitutional Court on the Law Regulating the National Councils], *Jog—Állam—Politika* vol. 6, no. 3 (2014): p. 7; Minoritynews.rs, 'Ustavni sud o Nacionalnim savetima nacionalnih manjina' [The Constitutional Court of the National Councils of National Minorities] no. 3, July 2013, pp. 4–5, accessed September 2014, <http://www.minoritynews.rs>.

[82] Vladimir Đurić, 'Javna ovlašćenja neteritorijalne autonomije u pravnom sistemu Republike Srbije' [Public Competences of Non-Territorial Autonomy in the Legal System of the Republic of Serbia], *Pravna Riječ* vol. 10, no. 35 (2013): p. 197.

[83] Tibor Varady, 'Mišljenje o ustavnopravnim pitanjima koja se postavljaju povodom osporenih odredaba zakona o nacionalnim savetima—Izneto na javnoj raspravi rred Ustavnim sudom 2. Jula 2013. Godine' [Opinion on Constitutional Law Issues Raised regarding the Disputed Provisions of the Law on National Councils—A View Elaborated at the Public Hearing before the Constitutional Court on 2 July 2013], *Pravni Zapisi* vol. 4, no. 2 (2013): pp. 427–8.

[84] See Rešenje Ustavnog suda Republike Srbije Broj Iuz-882/2010 [The Warrant of the Constitutional Court of the Republic of Serbia No. IUZ-882/2010] from 17 January 2013 and Odluka Ustavnog suda Republike Srbije Broj Iuz-882/2010, Službeni glasnik RS Br. 20/2014 [The Decision of the Constitutional Court of the Republic of Serbia No. IUZ-882/2010], from 16 January 2014, accessed January 2014, <http://www.ustavni.sud.rs>.

summarized as a readiness to formally accept high standards of minority rights but much less openness to implementing obligations, sharing powers with representatives of national minorities, and accepting ethnic diversity.

4.4.4 Strategic planning and development programmes managed by national councils

As well as activities related to public institutions and their involvement in administrative decision-making, national councils also began to act as specific policymakers. The Law on National Councils stipulates that national councils 'issue statement, undertake initiatives and undertake measures concerning all issues directly linked to the position, identity and rights of national minority'[85] and also enact the cultural and information strategies of national minorities.[86] Based on these provisions, the Hungarian National Council, as well as the Slovak and Bulgarian national councils, began to prepare mid-term development strategies and plans in four main areas (education, culture, information, and official language use).[87] These development plans were primarily formed in accordance with the rules of strategic planning, with SWOT analyses of the current situation, vision and strategic goals, programmes, monitoring, etc. The positive effects of these development plans were dependent on certain factors, among others the capacities of national councils, the budget available for the implementation of development programmes, and the cooperation of respective public institutions and authorities.

The most ambitious development programmes were launched by the Hungarian National Council in the area of education, with substantial donations from Hungary. The sophisticated stipend system currently involves more than a thousand Hungarian minority students studying in Serbian universities with the aim of tackling the massive under-representation of Hungarians in the academic community of Serbia.[88] A school bus programme of the Hungarian National Council has made it possible for pupils living far from schools teaching Hungarian to reach these schools and in this way to preserve their language and identity.[89] The annual budget for these programmes is over two million euros, but they have already generated positive changes within the Hungarian population in Serbia.[90] Strategic planning by national councils is a new dimension in minority protection; however, the positive effects of these efforts depend mainly on the support of institutions beyond national councils, such as the state administration.

---

[85] Zakon o nacionalnim savetima nacionalnih manjina, art 10, para 1(14).
[86] Zakon o nacionalnim savetima nacionalnih manjina, art 18, para 1(2) and art 21, para 1(1).
[87] Centar Za Regionalizam, 'Evaluacija Rada Pet Nacionalnih Saveta U Srbiji', pp. 37, 56, 118.
[88] Magyar Nemzeti Tanács, 'A Magyar Nemzeti Tanács Négy Éve', pp. 66–7.
[89] Magyar Nemzeti Tanács, 'A Magyar Nemzeti Tanács Négy Éve', pp. 51–3.
[90] Magyar Nemzeti Tanács, 'A Magyar Nemzeti Tanács Négy Éve', pp. 78–83.

4.4.5 Representation and transparency

A challenging issue for all NTAs is representation.[91] Clearly, democratic representation needs democratic, plural, and free elections, and equal and secret ballots, but in the case of minority self-governments it additionally needs to ensure that members of the respective national minority vote.[92] In Serbia, as in Hungary and Croatia, the separate voting registers should ensure the realization of this principle. Bearing in mind that the only two conditions for enrolment in separate voting registers are the general voting right and a written statement that the citizen is a member of the particular national minority, many thought that this system might be open to various problems, manipulation, and misuse. Others feared that members of national minorities would be too afraid to declare their national affiliation. Separate voting registers were formatted in late 2009 and by August 2014 more than 457,000 voters were registered as members of twenty-one different national minorities.[93] Although various misuses were reported in 2009 and 2010 concerning the enrolment in the voting register of some national minorities, the majority of individuals enrolled voluntarily, reflecting their genuine national affiliation.[94]

The first direct democratic elections were organized in June 2010, and a majority of the enrolled voters did vote. The first direct elections for national councils revealed several administrative weaknesses as well as the unacceptable intrusion of the authorities in the establishment of the Bosniak national council; however, the elections were within the minimum/basic standards of democratic elections.[95] National councils were accepted by both members of national minorities and the authorities as bodies democratically representing national minorities in the field of education, culture, information, and official language use. National councils, especially those representing large national minorities, had some presence in the public sphere within their community as well as with the Serb public. However critics pointed out that more efforts should be made to present the activities of national councils to the Serb general public and in the Serb language.[96]

[91] Brunner and Küpper, 'European Options of Autonomy', pp. 27–8.

[92] Tamás Korhecz, 'Democratic Legitimacy and Election Rules of National Ethnic Minority Bodies and Representatives—Reflections on Legal Solutions in Hungary and Slovenia', *International Journal on Minority and Group Rights* vol. 9, no. 2 (2002): pp. 179–81.

[93] Data is from the Decision of the Ministry for State Administration and Local Self-Governments, No: 90-00-00047/2014-17, available on the following website, accessed January 2014, <http://www.mdls.gov.rs/doc/Izbori0000.pdf>.

[94] Centar Za Regionalizam, 'Evaluacija Rada Pet Nacionalnih Saveta U Srbiji', pp. 9–13.

[95] Advisory Committee on the Framework Convention for the Protection of National Minorities, Third Opinion on Serbia, pp. 46–7.

[96] Centar za Regionalizam Novi Sad, 'Monitoring transparentnosti u radu nacionalnih saveta nacionalnih manjina—Analize i preporuke' [Monitoring Transparency in the Work of National Councils of National Minorities—Analysis and Recommendations] (2014): pp. 17, 22, 37, accessed September 2014, <http://www.centarzaregionalizam.org.rs/prilozi/monitoring/Monitoring_transparentnosti_u_radu_nacionalnih_saveta_nacionalnih_manjina.pdf>; Centar za regionalizam, 'Evaluacija Rada Pet Nacionalnih Saveta U Srbiji', pp. 51, 57, 71.

4.5 Achievements and Failures

After twelve years, the Serbian model of NTA has proved to be viable. The gradual development of the legal framework as well as its implementation has improved the position of national minorities in Serbia, contributed to the development and democratization of the institutional framework protecting national minorities, and has also served as a tool for the integration of national minorities into Serbian society. However, national councils have been unable to fulfil certain unrealistic expectations. They have been unable to solve many problems faced by members of national minorities, primarily demographic, economic, and social problems. The Serbian model of NTA in particular, but NTA generally, is by default a limited autonomy with a limited range of functions in comparison to territorial autonomy arrangements.[97]

The beneficiaries of the Serbian model of NTA are mainly those national minorities in Vojvodina which had developed institutional frameworks as well as political and administrative capacities to use the competences stipulated by the Law on National Councils. Some programmes run by national councils positively influenced the position of national minorities in Serbia. Moreover, *new minorities* also benefited from NTA, mainly because their national councils became professional institutions which advocated and protected the interests of national minorities more strongly than any other organization had previously. Furthermore, the Serbian state also benefited from NTA because the latter has created representative institutions which helped channel minority issues into the legal and administrative framework of the State.

4.6 Conclusions and Recommendations

The Serbian model of NTA through democratically elected national councils has become a legal, political, and social reality in Serbia. As the Advisory Committee on the Framework for the Protection of National Minorities has observed, national councils play a dominant role in the realization of minority rights and generally have become the main channel for the participation of national minorities in decision-making.[98] Today, almost no serious political force denies the viability and usefulness of national councils. However, while political representatives of national minorities demand more money and competences for national councils, political representatives of the Serb majority usually prefer weaker and more light-weight national councils. The legal framework of NTA has developed and become more sophisticated in several phases from 2002; however, the recent decision of

---

[97] Brunner and Küpper, 'European Options of Autonomy', pp. 30–1.
[98] Advisory Committee on the Framework Convention for the Protection of National Minorities, Third Opinion on Serbia, p. 47.

the Serbian Constitutional Court indicates that Serbian authorities and political decision-makers are far from a consensus on the issue of NTA. Furthermore, the current legal framework and competences of national councils are tailored primarily to fit traditional national minorities with a strong network of public institutions. Despite various problems, today very few political actors deny the legality and the representativeness of national councils. The fact that almost half a million adult members of various national minorities enrolled voluntarily in the voting registers is evidence that these communities need national councils as self-governments protecting their rights and interests. Unfortunately, in spite of the evident progress, national councils are still not accepted and recognized as serious partners by all Serbian authorities.

After the recent decision of the Serbian Constitutional Court, some amendments to the Law on National Councils are to be expected. It is desirable to find solutions in accordance with the decision of the Court but without cutting back the competences of national councils. Future amendments should also in some way respect the large differences among existing national councils and their capacities to use their competences.[99] Furthermore, future amendments should equalize the status and position of national councils and units of local self-governments; namely they are both tools for decentralization of state powers and democratically elected public bodies with competences. It is not acceptable that several legal rules and principles applied to units of local self-governments are not applied to national councils.[100] Furthermore, it is important to remove the contradictions between the Law on National Councils and various laws on education and culture, which have often provided an excuse for authorities not to implement the rights of national councils.[101] The legal framework should also be improved in respect of implementation mechanisms. Evidence proves that authorities ignore and violate the competences of national councils; thus, new procedures and legal mechanisms should be stipulated in order to ensure law enforcement in the case of law violations.

Beyond the improvement of the legal framework and its proper implementation, communication and cooperation between national councils and primarily central state authorities should be improved. National councils are often ignored by the Serbian government and ministries, and contacts are usually sporadic and formal. In the period between 2009 and 2014 the presidents of national councils and the Council for National Minorities (established by the government,[102] and whose members are the President and members of the government) had no

---

[99] Pokrajinski Ombudsman Autonomne pokrajine Vojvodine, 'Dve godine nacionalnih saveta', pp. 29–30; Đurđević, 'Minority Policy in Serbia', p. 52.

[100] Among others these rules concern financing and expenditure, employment rules and procedures, and the prohibition on accumulating public functions and property, etc.

[101] Advisory Committee on the Framework Convention for the Protection of National Minorities, Third Opinion on Serbia, p. 47.

[102] Odluka o obrazovanju Saveta za nacionalne manjine, Službeni Glasnik RS Broj 46/2013, 98/2013 [The Decision on the Establishment of the Council for National Minorities, Official Gazette of RS No. 46/2013, 98/2013].

meetings. Furthermore, the minister in charge of national councils met the presidents of national councils only twice during this period. In October 2014, members of twenty-one national councils were elected and a new four-year mandate of national councils began. This provides a new opportunity to improve the legislative framework and the functioning of the Serbian model of NTA. Some authors argue that it is crucial to definitively define the vision of the Serbian state and society of multiculturalism: to foster integration by the inclusion and acceptance of minority identities, or to accept that Serbia is a linguistically and culturally fragmented State where national minorities should autonomously implement their rights through their own self-governments.[103] A third option is to establish a differentiated policy of diversity management, a policy which will take into account substantial demographical, historical, political, and cultural differences between national minorities in Serbia. The Serbian model of NTA may evolve and function effectively, if this differentiation is observed in future.

[103] Goran Bašić, 'Društveni identitet i etnokulturalna politika' [Social Identity and Ethno-Cultural Policy], in *Položaj nacionalnih manjina u Srbiji*, edited by Vojislav Stanovčić (Beograd: Srpska akademija nauka i umetnosti, 2007), p. 98.

5

The Autonomy Arrangement in Slovenia

An Established Institutional Framework Dependent on Implementation of Minority Protection

Miran Komac and Petra Roter

5.1 Introduction

Like other European states, Slovenia has always been an ethnically heterogeneous state, although the number of its ethno-national minorities, their numerical strength, or their economic and political power have changed over time. The declaration of independence in 1991 has left Slovenia with a diverse group of non-Slovenian minorities. These can be divided into two categories: historical, traditional, territorial, or 'autochthonous national communities' (the term used in the 1991 Constitution[1]); and the constitutionally non-recognized so-called territorially dispersed ethnic communities or 'new minorities'.[2] The latter category, numerically some twenty times bigger (see Table 5.1) than the three autochthonous minorities mentioned in the Constitution (the Italian, Hungarian, and Roma), consists predominantly of persons belonging to former Yugoslav nations and nationalities (Croatian, Serbian, Bosniak/Muslim, Montenegrin, Macedonian, and Albanian) who migrated to Slovenia from the 1960s onwards, mainly for employment.[3] Slovenia's German-speaking group cannot be easily classified into one of the two categories: it is not constitutionally recognized but it enjoys some cultural rights based on a bilateral agreement between Slovenia and Austria.[4]

[1] Constitution 1991 (No. 33/91-I, 42/97, 66/2000, 24/03, 69/04, 68/06, and 47/13), hereafter '1991 Constitution'.

[2] Miran Komac, 'Varstvo "novih" narodnih skupnosti v Sloveniji' [Protection of the 'New' National Communities in Slovenia], *Razprave in gradivo/Treatises and Documents* 43 (2003): pp. 6–33; Miran Komac, ed., *Priseljenci. Študije o priseljevanju in vključevanju v slovensko družbo* [Immigrants. Studies on Immigration and Integration into Slovenian Society] (Ljubljana, INV: 2007), pp. 69–102.

[3] Danilo Dolenc, 'Priseljevanje v Slovenijo z območja nekdanje Jugoslavije po drugi svetovni vojni' [Immigration to Slovenia from the Former Yugoslavia after the Second World War], in *Priseljenci. Študije o priseljevanju in vključevanju v slovensko družbo*, edited by Miran Komac (Ljubljana, INV: 2007), pp. 69–102.

[4] This undoubtedly long-established community almost disappeared in the wake of World War II, and it was only before Slovenia's independence when the German community began to show some

Table 5.1 Slovenia's population by ethnic affiliation in the territory at census times, selected data, census 1953, 1961, 1971, 1981, 1991, 2002*

Census—year**	1953	1961	1971	1981	1991	2002
Ethnic affiliation	Number and percentage (of the total population)					
TOTAL	1,466,425	1,591,523	1,679,051	1,838,381	1,913,355	1,964,036
Ethnically declared	1,466,214	1,587,585	1,664,093	1,800,680	1,845,022	1,766,982
%	99.99	99.75	99.11	97.95	96.43	89.97
Slovenes	1,415,448	1,522,248	1,578,963	1,668,623	1,689,657	1,631,363
%	96.52	95.65	94.04	90.77	88.31	83.06
Italians	854	3,072	2,987	2,138	2,959	2,258
%	0.06	0.19	0.18	0.12	0.15	0.11
Hungarians	11,019	10,498	8,943	8,777	8,000	6,243
%	0.75	0.66	0.53	0.48	0.42	0.32
Roma	1,663	158	951	1,393	2,259	3,246
%	0.12	0.01	0.06	0.08	0.12	0.17
Albanians	169	282	1,266	1,933	3,534	6,186
%	0.01	0.02	0.08	0.11	0.18	0.31
Austrians	289	254	266	146	126	181
%	0.02	0.02	0.02	0.01	0.01	0.01
Bosniaks	–	–	–	–	–	21,542
%						1.10
Montenegrins	1,356	1,384	1,950	3,175	4,339	2,667
%	0.09	0.09	0.12	0.17	0.23	0.14
Croats	17,978	31,429	41,556	53,882	52,876	35,642
%	1.23	1.97	2.47	2.93	2.76	1.81
Macedonians	640	1,009	1,572	3,227	4,371	3,972
%	0.04	0.06	0.09	0.18	0.23	0.20
Muslims (ethnically)	1,617	465	3,197	13,339	26,577	10,467
%	0.11	0.03	0.19	0.73	1.39	0.53
Germans	1,617	732	400	309	298	499
%	0.11	0.05	0.02	0.02	0.02	0.03
Serbs	11,225	13,609	20,209	41,695	47,401	38,964
%	0.77	0.86	1.20	2.27	2.48	1.98
Ethnically undeclared	–	2,784	12,280	32,400	25,978	22,141
%		0.17	0.73	1.76	1.36	1.13
Yugoslavs	–	2,784	6,616	25,615	12,075	527
%		0.18	0.39	1.39	0.63	0.03
Bosnians (regional affiliation before 2002)	–	–	–	–	–	8,062
%						0.41
Did not wish to reply	–	–	–	–	–	48,588
%						2.47
Unknown	211	1,154	2,678	5,301	42,355	126,325
%	0.01	0.07	0.16	0.29	2.21	6.43

* Statistical Office of the Republic of Slovenia.
** The census in 2012 was only a statistical census, and no data on ethnicity or identity markers such as language is available for 2012.

The differences between minorities in Slovenia correspond with the approach to, and the level of, their protection as well as with minority autonomy arrangements in Slovenia. Indeed, the prevailing minority arrangement in Slovenia—a mixed non-territorial self-government (autonomy arrangement), applies solely to the two constitutionally recognized autochthonous Hungarian and Italian national communities. It is based on relatively broad constitutional provisions (and a legislative framework of some sixty laws), which stipulate (art 5) that the state 'shall protect and guarantee the rights of the autochthonous Italian and Hungarian national communities'; that in addition to Slovene as the official language in Slovenia, '[i]n those municipalities where Italian or Hungarian national communities reside, Italian or Hungarian shall also be official languages' (art 11); and the scope of the autonomy arrangement for these two communities. According to the 1991 Constitution (art 64), 'Special Rights of the Autochthonous Italian and Hungarian National Communities in Slovenia' include

> the right to use their national symbols freely and, in order to preserve their national identity, the right to establish organizations and develop economic, cultural, scientific, and research activities, as well as activities in the field of public media and publishing. [...] the right to education and schooling in their own languages, as well as the right to establish and develop such education and schooling. [...] the right to foster relations with their nations of origin and their respective countries. The state shall provide material and moral support for the exercise of these rights.
>
> In order to exercise their rights, the members of these communities shall establish their own self-governing communities in the geographic areas where they live. On the proposal of these self-governing national communities, the state may authorize them to perform certain functions [...] and shall provide funds for the performing of such functions.
>
> The two national communities shall be directly represented in representative bodies of local self-government and in the National Assembly.
>
> [...] The rights of both national communities and their members shall be guaranteed irrespective of the number of members of these communities.
>
> Laws, regulations, and other general acts that concern the exercise of the constitutionally provided rights and the position of the national communities exclusively, may not be adopted without the consent of representatives of these national communities.

For the Roma, the 1991 Constitution only establishes (art 65) that '[t]he status and special rights of the Romany community living in Slovenia shall be regulated by law'. The law was adopted only in 2007,[5] and the Roma community enjoys fewer rights than the Italian and Hungarian communities. The Roma are both a national minority (though internally diverse) and a social minority, faced with

---

signs of its revitalization—too late for it to be included in Slovenia's constitutional minority protection (Miran Komac, ed., 'Narodnost—manjšina ali skupnost. Urejanje, uresničevanje in varstvo pravic narodnosti (narodnih manjšin) v Republiki Sloveniji' [Nationality—A Minority or a Community. Managing, Implementation and Protection of the Rights of Nationalities (National Minorities) in the Republic of Slovenia], *Razprave in gradivo/Treatises and Documents* 24 (1990): p. 133).

[5] Law on the Roma Community 2007.

discrimination, negative stereotypes, prejudice, and lack of equal access to employment, education, health care, and living conditions. Their options for managing their own affairs autonomously are very limited: they participate in decision-making locally (in twenty municipalities where they live autochthonously, according to the legislator, they elect one Roma representative to each municipality council), but cannot form national self-governing communities (as legal persons), which is the basic building block of Slovenia's minority autonomy arrangement. Still, the Roma community has managed to establish itself as a national actor in the past decade or so, and this has been reflected in the formation of a Roma Council (a national consultative body) with elected (only seven out of fourteen members) and appointed (by the Association of the Roma) Roma members.[6]

For all other communities, the possibilities of becoming organized as actors who decide on their affairs are more limited as their 'legitimate interests' can only be realized through individual rights. When seeking to preserve their distinct identity, they can rely on two modest constitutional provisions on expression of national affiliation,[7] and on the right to use one's language and script.[8] They have preserved their identity in a bottom-up manner—by themselves, in the absence of any notable state support to this effect, with the exception of funding for various cultural activities through their cultural associations.

Slovenia's approach to diversity management, including its autonomy arrangement, has resulted from the processes of nation-building and state-formation. Both constitutionally recognized national communities are historically long-established groups who inhabit the legally defined 'ethnically mixed areas' close to Hungary and Italy; whose members are citizens of Slovenia; who distinguish themselves from ethnic Slovenians primarily by language. Both communities became national minorities with border changes in the process of state-formation and both are considered autochthonous. Both communities have a kin-state where Slovenian national minorities reside (a more sizable community in Italy). Those 'mutual' minorities have affected the development of Slovenia's comprehensive autonomy arrangement: the latter is directly related to reciprocal expectations with regards to protection of Slovenian minorities in neighbouring states (particularly in Italy and in Austria), also kin-states to Slovenia's national minorities.

Slovenia's autonomy arrangement is decades old and it has been preserved after independence. The legal arrangement is comprehensive and it extends to every aspect of societal organization, with guaranteed seats for national minorities in the National Assembly (Parliament), dual voting rights of persons belonging to these

---

[6] Miran Komac, 'Konstrukcija romskega političnega predstavništva' [The Construction of Roma Political Representation], _Razprave in gradivo/Treaties and Documents_ 53–4 (2007): pp. 6–26.

[7] 'Everyone has the right to freely express affiliation with his nation or national community, to foster and give expression to his culture, and to use his language and script' (art 61 of the 1991 Constitution).

[8] 'Everyone has the right to use his language and script in a manner provided by law in the exercise of his rights and duties and in procedures before state and other authorities performing a public function' (art 62 of the 1991 Constitution).

communities (who cast two votes at national and local elections: one as members of a national minority, and another as Slovenia's citizens), and official bilingualism in ethnically mixed areas. Minority protection extends to individual and collective rights of national communities, organized as legal entities in the form of self-governing national communities. The latter provide the central element of Slovenia's autonomy arrangement for both autochthonous national minorities. The very noticeable absence of any minority arrangement for the most sizable 'new minorities' is also related to state-formation and nation-building: persons belonging to the former Yugoslav nations and nationalities, rather than minorities, enjoyed no special protection as minorities in the Socialist Republic of Slovenia (as one of Yugoslavia's republics). This legacy, however, appears no longer to match their expectations of being recognized as collective actors.

This chapter focuses on an in-depth analysis of the comprehensive arrangement for Hungarian and Italian communities and unveils some of its shortcomings, as minorities are increasingly disappointed with how this ambitious model works in practice. Furthermore, this model has unintentionally affected minority arrangements, or the lack thereof, for Slovenia's other minorities. We argue that the arrangement for Italians and Hungarians is difficult to sustain because both communities are small (with their numbers most likely decreasing), because the model is largely limited to the demographically dynamic ethnically mixed areas and because the arrangement has been faced with practical limits. Furthermore, with a growing need to address the expectations of 'Yugoslav' communities living in Slovenia, the existing autonomy arrangement will necessarily serve as a point of reference (with minority representation in the National Assembly being its particularly desirable aspect). However, Slovenia appears unwilling to extend its minority protection to national minorities other than Italians and Hungarians and the Roma (who enjoy a limited set of rights in comparison with the Italians and Hungarians). But the very presence of such requests, coupled with the overwhelming perception that minority protection in Slovenia can be given as a role model, blurs the need to address any problems and obstacles towards a more effective autonomy arrangement for the Italians and Hungarians.

5.2 Ideology and the Autonomy Arrangement

As the present autonomy arrangement predates the 1991 Constitution by some three decades, its ideological foundations need to be analysed in the Yugoslav context, involving intra-state diversity management and expectations with regards to diversity management applicable to Yugoslav nations' kin-minorities in other states. During the Cold War, such kin-states' interests risked being interpreted as interference in the internal affairs of states and/or blocks of states. The only alternatives at times of East–West confrontation were multilateral minority protection (Yugoslavia was among the most active protagonists of minority protection in the United Nations) and minority protection nationally, with a hope that the 'favour' was going to be reciprocated in neighbouring states. It was such expectations that were behind the establishment of Yugoslavia's/Slovenia's minority rights (autonomy) in the 1960s. The arrangement applied to the Italians and the Hungarians whose kin-state's lack of interest resulted in slightly different characteristics in the arrangement for the Hungarian minority. Of course, the legislation has changed in independent Slovenia, its substance has not been significantly modified.

Indeed, the Constitution of 1991 continues the approach to minority protection, which was already established by the Constitution of 1963 and elaborated in more detail in the Constitution of 1974. Throughout these years, the autonomy arrangement has been largely internalized by the Slovenian public, with the help of education, the media, and political elites. Slovenia's model of minority protection has remained largely unchallenged, and unaffected by the few and occasional nationalist criticisms.[9] Importantly, this relative absence of any severe criticism of the broad set of minority rights and the autonomy arrangement needs to be understood in the context of Slovenia's role as a kin-state.[10]

5.2.1 Characteristics and basic principles of the autonomy arrangement

The basic elements of the autonomy arrangement are the concept of 'ethnically mixed areas' and the system of collective (group) rights. The latter are provided in those areas, irrespective of the numerical strength or proportion of both communities. Individual statutes of municipalities define the relevant ethnically mixed area, composed of those settlements in municipalities where members of the Italian/Hungarian minority live autochthonously. Hungarian settlements exist in the municipalities of Hodoš/Hodos,[11] Šalovci,[12] Dobrovnik/Dobronak,[13] Lendava/Lendva,[14] and Moravske Toplice,[15] and Italian in the municipalities of Koper/Capodistria,[16] Izola/Isola,[17] and Piran/Pirano,[18] and in the newly constituting municipality of Ankaran/Ancarano. The statutes follow the same pattern of minority organization and functioning (competences).

Furthermore, the minority arrangement applies to all inhabitants of both ethnically mixed areas, regardless of minorities' numerical strength. This model is based on the idea that the cultural and spiritual inheritance of an ethnically mixed area is the common property of all its inhabitants, irrespective of their ethnic affiliation and/or the status they possessed in different historical periods. Given

---

[9] See Constitutional Court U-I-283/94, no. 20/98 and OdlUS VII, 26.

[10] The 1991 Constitution leaves no doubt about this (see art 5). See also a special Law on Regulating Relations between the RS and Slovenians Abroad 2006 and 2010.

[11] Statute of the Municipality Hodoš 2011.

[12] Statute of the Municipality Šalovci 2011.

[13] Statute of the Municipality Dobrovnik 2007.

[14] Statute of the Municipality Lendava 2010.

[15] Statute of the Municipality Moravske Toplice 2014.

[16] Statute of Municipality of Koper/Capodistria 2000.

[17] Statute of the Municipality of Izola/Isola 1999.

[18] Statute of the Municipality of Piran/Pirano 1999.

their small size, this is an essential element of the autonomy arrangement for national minorities, but it is also one of its problems as the territorial framework for minority protection is not always in accordance with the living habits of individuals who migrate for work or education, for example. Only some rights can be enjoyed by minority members living outside those areas, including the right to be listed on a special minority electoral register for elections of a minority deputy to the National Assembly, and the right to learn the language of the national community.[19]

In sum, the mixed autonomy arrangement in Slovenia is composed of territorial, personal, and functional autonomy,[20] whereby the territorial autonomy presents the basic principle of minority protection in Slovenia—this despite the fact that persons belonging to national communities are exceptionally in the numerical majority in their municipalities (this is only the case in some predominantly Hungarian settlements). Special minority rights are implemented only in ethnically mixed areas. However, in the context of local self-government in Slovenia, the 'ethnically mixed area' has no autonomous status. This status is reserved for municipalities, which can be formed with their entire area being defined as an ethnically mixed area, or only with some settlements falling in the ethnically mixed area of a national community[21]—that is, in a manner that will secure protection of minority interests.[22] Where national minorities live, they can establish their self-governing national communities with a view to managing their affairs and securing protection of their interest.[23] But some minority rights can also be enjoyed elsewhere, not only within ethnically mixed areas, as provided by the 1991 Constitution (art 64).

This personal autonomy applies to the right to receive minority language instruction if at least five pupils outside the ethnically mixed area so require, and the right of individuals to be included on a special minority voting registry for the election of a minority member of the Parliament. Additionally, Slovenia's autonomy arrangement is also characterized by functional autonomy, following Heintze's definition of the latter as a transfer of 'selected State functions and rights to private minority group organizations', whereby the minority 'obtains the competence for culture, the media, education and religion, insofar as they are essential for the group's identity. Functional autonomy requires that the minority is organized in a private form, that is, collectively and without State influence'.[24] All this is met by Slovenia's model of the autonomy arrangement, with the establishment of self-governing national communities.

---

[19] Law on the Voting Rights Register 2013, art 27; Law on Regulating Special Rights of Members of the Italian and Hungarian National Communities in the Field of Education 2001, art 9.

[20] Hans-Joachim Heintze, 'On the Legal Understanding of Autonomy', in *Autonomy: Applications and Implications*, edited by Markku Suksi (The Hague: Kluwer Law International, 1998), pp. 7–32.

[21] According to the Law on the Establishment of Municipalities and Municipal Boundaries 2011, art 5, the boundaries are defined in municipal statutes.

[22] Law on Local Self-Government 2007, art 5.   [23] 1991 Constitution, art 64.

[24] Heintze, 'On the Legal Understanding', pp. 23–4.

5.2.2 The way of minority self-organization

Slovenia's autonomy arrangement is based on protection of minorities as objectively existing social entities, whereas persons belonging to them can choose to exercise individual rights. The most important element of the autonomy arrangement is the constitutionally guaranteed collective right to form their self-governing national communities,[25] as legal entities with political and representative functions at the municipal level and at the level of the community as a whole (in the ethnically mixed area).[26] A special Law on Self-Governing National Communities[27] specifies their competences (art 3), including their autonomous decision-making, agreeing on matters of special interest to national communities on which they co-decide with local self-government authorities, analysing minority-related issues and adopting initiatives for the responsible authorities, and establishing activities with a view to preserving national minority identity. The Law further defines (art 4) the manner in which those competences can be realized: to this effect, self-governing national communities promote and organize cultural, scientific, informational, and publishing activities, they establish organizations and public institutions, monitor and promote minority education and participate in its realization, develop relations with their kin-states and kin-nations and carry out different tasks as set up by national legislation and municipality statutes. The Law also defines their organization and competences in relation to state authorities, and ways of financing them: they are organized in every municipality with an autochthonous Italian or Hungarian population, whereas all municipal self-governing communities form a self-governing community for the entire national minority. Municipalities provide sufficient space and finances for the functioning of municipal self-governing communities, whereas the functioning of the 'umbrella' self-governing communities is financed by the state budget. Some half of those finances are spent on their own expenses, and the other half on programme-related activities of the self-governing community.[28] Importantly, not only can those 'umbrella' self-governing national communities initiate proposals before the National Assembly, the government, and other state organs, but those organs have to seek the opinion of self-governing communities prior to deciding on matters that concern persons belonging to national communities.[29] A similar arrangement applies at the local (municipal) level: when a municipal organ, such as a municipality council, decides on minority-related matters, minority representatives in the council (the dual voting right of minority members applies also to local elections at which the national communities elect their representatives to the municipal councils) are obliged to seek prior agreement from the municipal self-governing

---

[25] Miran Komac, 'Minority Self-Government in Slovenia', *Südosteuropa* vol. 40, nos 7–8 (2000): pp. 358–74.

[26] Law on Self-Governing National Communities 1994.

[27] Law on Self-Governing National Communities 1994.

[28] Personal interview with a minority representative, Ljubljana, September 2014.

[29] Law on Self-Governing National Communities 1994, art 15.

national communities.[30] Representatives of self-governing national communities also participate in inter-state bilateral (Slovenia and a minority's kin-state) initiatives on minority protection.[31] This completes the range of their competences in managing their own affairs and status locally, nationally, and internationally. The self-governing national communities are also vested with functional autonomy in the form of their competences to establish (with municipalities) kindergartens, primary schools, and secondary schools in ethnically mixed areas, and their own cultural, scientific, or media institutions.

Self-managing national communities are not the only possible form of minority (political) organization. However, if established, such other organizations could not replace the self-governing national communities as the only legal actors vested with the authority to represent national minorities in relations with the state. Their competences are significant according to law, but in practice, they tend to be seen as very limited by minority representatives.

5.2.2.1 Italian and Hungarian self-governing national communities

In every municipality with an ethnically mixed area with either an Italian or Hungarian national minority, the minority establishes a self-governing national community as a legal person, governed by a council that is composed of directly elected minority representatives. Further, each national community manages its affairs through an 'umbrella' self-governing national community—also a legal person, established by municipal self-governing national communities and governed by a council that is indirectly elected (each council of municipal self-governing national communities elects among themselves a certain number of councillors as members of the council of the 'umbrella' self-governing national community). All self-governing national communities determine their organizational structure; they act and adopt decisions independently. A national community determines the number of councillors of the municipal council of their respective self-governing communities, their elections, and the formation of the national minority electoral registry. Each municipal self-governing national community acts independently, based on its statute. The 'umbrella' self-governing community acts as a political representative body in relation to the local communities, and it represents the national community before state organs (in practice, this is carried out by the president of the council, elected by the councillors).

The Hungarian national community has formed municipal self-governing communities in the municipalities of Lendava/Lendva, Dobrovnik/Dobronak, Moravske Toplice, Hodoš/Hodos, and Šalovci. The 'umbrella' Pomurje Hungarian self-governing national community (based in Lendava) has been established by the five municipal self-governing Hungarian national communities. Its council (as the highest decision-making body) comprises twenty-one members: ten from

---

[30] Law on Self-Governing National Communities 1994, art 13.
[31] Law on Self-Governing National Communities 1994, art 17.

the municipal council of the Lendava/Lendva self-governing national community, four from the Dobrovnik/Dobronak council, three from the Moravske Toplice council, and two from the Hodoš/Hodos and the Šalovci councils (all councillors are appointed for the duration of four years).

The Italian national community manages its affairs and seeks to protect its interests through the municipal self-governing communities in Koper/Capodistria (where its council has nine elected members,[32] three of whom are appointed as councillors to the 'umbrella' Italian self-governing community, with a mandate of four years[33]), in Izola/Isola (nine and three councillors),[34] and in Piran/Pirano (nine and three councillors).[35] Based on the 1994 Law on Self-Governing National Communities, these three municipal self-governing communities established in 1995 the 'umbrella' Coastal Italian self-governing national community.[36] Recently, the municipality of Koper/Capodistria has lost a legal battle to object to the formation of a new municipality of Ankaran/Ancarano; the latter lies in the ethnically mixed area. It was able to hold its first municipal elections in October 2014, which completed the lengthy process of its formation. This will lead to some modifications in the organization of the Italian self-governing community, according to the principal elements and purpose of the autonomy arrangement as provided by law.

5.2.2.2 Language

The self-governing national communities participate in the implementation of linguistic rights, which are widely legislated: ethnically mixed areas are officially bilingual and the right to use the relevant minority language freely and without any restrictions applies to any situation in the private and public spheres in those areas (with a modest exception in the case of Izola/Isola, which allows Italian minority members who live outside the ethnically mixed area the same rights in their contacts with municipal and state bodies[37]). The official use of both languages, according to national[38] and municipal legislation, applies to mandatory bilingual toponomastic signs, signboards, announcements, etc., with the participation of self-governing national communities in the process of bilingual naming. Both official languages can be used in communication with judicial authorities in ethnically mixed areas (where the courts are obliged to guarantee equality of both languages, whereas higher courts elsewhere, when addressing a matter conducted in a minority language at a lower instance, are obliged to provide and pay for translation into the minority language),[39] and in oral and written communication with all public

---

[32] Statute of the Italian Self-Governing National Community in Koper/Capodistria, art 9.
[33] Statute of the Italian Self-Governing National Community in Koper/Capodistria, art 30.
[34] Statute of the Italian Self-Governing National Community—Izola, arts 9 and 29, respectively.
[35] Statute of the Italian Self-Governing National Community—Piran.
[36] Statute of the Italian Coastal Self-Governing National Community 1995, art 1.
[37] Statute of the Municipality of Izola/Isola, art 4(4).
[38] 1991 Constitution, art 11; Law on Slovene in Public Use 2004, art 3.
[39] Law on Courts 2007, 2008, 2010, 2011, 2012, and 2013, art 5.

administrative institutions, which are obliged to reply in the language used by individuals living in the ethnically mixed areas.[40]

Active knowledge of both languages is a condition for higher public officials and those who directly interact with clients, as well as in judicial organs, and it is financially rewarded in the form of a supplement to their salaries. However, in public administration, this requirement has in practice been gradually downgraded from 'active knowledge' to 'knowledge' (much to the disappointment and informal disagreement of national communities).[41] In this respect, the non-binding opinion of self-governing national communities on such high level appointments that were deemed inappropriate due to insufficient language fluency could effectively protect minority interests. The use of minority languages, on an equal footing with Slovene, applies to all official documents issued in ethnically mixed areas. They are compulsory bilingual (in fact, multilingual as all documents are typically also written at least in English) for everyone, regardless of an individual's ethnic identity.[42] However, recent legislative changes have enabled circumvention of this mandatory element of the arrangement.[43]

5.2.2.3 Education

The minority educational system is a public system. Self-governing national communities play an important role in the establishment and functioning of 'minority' schools in ethnically mixed areas:[44] they co-establish Italian schools and Hungarian–Slovenian bilingual schools, they co-manage the schools (e.g. a representative of a self-governing national community is a member of school council), and they play a role in the selection of the school headteacher (they provide an opinion on the candidate, which is legally non-binding). Although self-managing national communities participate in all aspects of the educational system and they nominally have an important role to play, their effectiveness is limited in practice, which is seen as problematic, particularly in the context of the smallness of the minorities on one hand, and the comprehensive nature of the educational system, on the other.[45]

At all levels, education is based on the principles of bilingual fluency of all children from ethnically mixed areas and the promotion and recognition of the multicultural character of those areas.[46] However, for historical reasons (i.e. to prevent the collapse of the Hungarian minority educational system in the 1950s),[47] there are two models of education: the compulsory bilingual education for all children

---

[40] Law on Public Administration 2014, art 4.
[41] Law on Civil Servants 2007, 2008, 2008, and 2012, art 17.
[42] e.g. Law on Identity Card 2011, art 7(2); Law on Passports 2011, art 13.
[43] See section 5.2.2.4.   [44] Law on Self-Governing National Communities 1994, art 4.
[45] Personal interview with a minority representative, Ljubljana, September 2014.
[46] Law on the Special Rights of Italian and Hungarian National Communities in the Field of Education 2001; Law on the Organization and Financing of Education 2007; Law on Kindergartens 2005; Law on Primary Schools 2012; Law on Vocational and Professional Training 2006.
[47] See Constitutional Court U-I-94/96, 1998, para 5.

in the ethnically mixed area of Pomurje (the region with Hungarians), and the monolingual education in the coastal area, where every child has to learn both official languages, his/her mother tongue, and the language of the other national group (Slovenian or Italian). This important element has possibly been relaxed as parents can send their child to any school provided that the school agrees.[48] This could lead to children attending schools outside the ethnically mixed areas, whereby they could avoid the compulsory learning of the minority language.

In Pomurje, there are four bilingual kindergartens, five bilingual primary schools (with units in five settlements), and one bilingual secondary school, whereas for demographic reasons (i.e. the smallness of the community), there is no bilingual tertiary institution; only the possibility of studying Hungarian language and literature at the universities of Maribor and Ljubljana, or in Hungary (based on a bilateral agreement between the two states[49]).[50] Bilingualism applies to most textbooks, administration, and all other activities. In the Italian/Slovenian mixed area, by contrast, a monolingual educational system means that instruction in kindergartens, primary, and secondary schools is conducted in Italian or Slovenian, while the learning of the other official language is compulsory. There are three Italian kindergartens, three Italian primary schools with units in five settlements, and three high schools.[51] Italian is also the language of administration and communication with parents. The teaching staff and other employees in Italian schools are persons whose mother tongue is Italian. At the tertiary level, Italian language and literature can be studied at the universities of Ljubljana and Primorska (in Koper/ Capodistria), or in Italy and Croatia.

The functioning of bilingual education and its results are generally not seen as satisfactory: it 'has led to the absence of vocational/professional [...] minority language, to constant code switching, loss of prestige for the minority mother tongue, marginalisation, and finally language switching'.[52] Some individuals (from the dominant majority) wished to establish the same monolingual education system as in the coastal area, but the Constitutional Court rejected their demand, arguing that 'the Constitution gives the State the responsibility for the establishment of bilingual schools. [...] Historical circumstances have dictated the organization of bilingual education in areas inhabited by the Hungarian ethnic minority, but not in areas inhabited by the Italian ethnic minority'.[53]

---

[48] Law on Primary Schools, art 48.

[49] Agreement on Providing Special Rights of the Ethnic Minority in the Republic of Hungary and the Hungarian Ethnic Community in the Republic of Slovenia 1993.

[50] Government Office for National Minorities, accessed 15 June 2014, <http://www.un.gov.si/si/ manjsine/madzarska_narodna_skupnost/vzgojno_izobrazevalna_kulturna_in_informativna_ dejavnost/>.

[51] Government Office for National Minorities, accessed 15 June 2014, <http://www.un.gov.si/si/ manjsine/italijanska_narodna_skupnost/vzgojno_izobrazevalna_kulturna_in_informativna_ dejavnost/>.

[52] Anna Kolláth, Judit Gasparics, Annamaria Gróf, and Livija Horvat, 'Hungarian in Slovenia: An Overview of a Language in Context', *ELDIA Working Papers in European Language Diversity* no. 2 (2010): p. 10.

[53] Constitutional Court U-I-94/96, 1998, para 26.

5.2.2.4 Media and culture

The autonomy arrangement in the broad area of media and culture seeks to promote and protect culture,[54] by allowing the self-governing communities to decide on and use their national symbols (e.g. their flag or anthem) freely and publicly,[55] and by providing opportunities for minorities to establish cultural institutions, and to create and disseminate information about themselves and the environment in which they live, in their own language; to present minority issues in the mainstream Slovenian media; and to receive information in minority languages, also from their kin-states. Slovenia is legally obliged to support, among others, the development of non-commercial public media intended to inform national communities.[56] The self-governing national communities can register public or private institutions for publishing or other forms of mass communication, thus enabling local production of media content, for which they get also state funding (this is financed separately and does not come from the funds the state pays to the self-governing national communities). The self-governing national communities play a role in managing those institutions and they participate in the selection of the directors. The Hungarian community has been producing its printed newspaper (first as a supplement to the Prekmurje Slovenian newspaper) since 1956, and a radio programme in Hungarian was established in 1958. Hungarian radio and TV programmes, co-financed by the government, are now prepared in the framework of the public RTV Slovenia (radio programme lasting for eighteen hours and fifteen minutes daily, and a TV programme that is broadcast on TV Slovenia nationally, three to four times a week).[57]

A radio station in Italian had already been established in 1949. Italian radio and TV programmes, co-financed by the government, are prepared in the framework of the public RTV Slovenia (radio programme lasting for eighteen hours daily, and a TV programme for nine-and-a-half hours five times weekly). In addition to the broadcasting media, the Italian community also has a publishing house (EDIT, based in Rijeka, Croatia, with an affiliation in Slovenia, which is fully funded by the government), which prints a daily newspaper, and several magazines and other publications.[58]

---

[54] Law on Regulating the Realization of Public Interest in the Field of Culture 2007, 2008, 2010, 2011, and 2013; Law on Protection of Cultural Heritage 2008, 2008, 2011, 2012, and 2013.

[55] 1991 Constitution, art 64; Law on the Coat of Arms, Flag and Anthem of the Republic of Slovenia, and on the Slovenian National Flag 1994, arts 6, 13, 14, and 21.

[56] Law on Mass Media 2006.

[57] Government Office for National Minorities, accessed 15 June 2014, <http://www.un.gov.si/si/manjsine/madzarska_narodna_skupnost/vzgojno_izobrazevalna_kulturna_in_informativna_dejavnost/>.

[58] Government Office for National Minorities, accessed 15 June 2014, <http://www.un.gov.si/si/manjsine/italijanska_narodna_skupnost/vzgojno_izobrazevalna_kulturna_in_informativna_dejavnost/>.

5.2.2.5 *Effective participation in decision-making*

Slovenia's autonomy arrangement enables a broad scope of participatory rights in decision-making processes at the national and municipal levels (there is no regional level of self-government in Slovenia) with: minority representation in political institutions at local and national levels; the veto power; and the (political) self-organization of national minorities in the form of self-governing national communities, established with a view to implementing special minority rights in Slovenia. Self-governing national communities are the only entities that function as political parties. Due to the numerical smallness of both national minorities, there are no minority political parties, but individual minority members can and do participate in party politics, like any other citizen of Slovenia.

The self-governing national minorities are, however, not the only voice of minorities. Minority interests are protected by them, based on their representative and consultative competences, and by directly elected minority representatives to municipal councils and to the national Parliament (where each national minority has one guaranteed seat). And it is these seats that make the minority arrangement for the Italian and Hungarian communities most appealing to other minorities in Slovenia. But because the minority arrangement for the Italians and Hungarians is a comprehensive system that has been in place for decades, it is hard to imagine anything similar being provided for other minorities in the near future. The dual voting right that enables the election of special minority representatives nationally and locally (also the twenty Roma municipal councillors) applies only to minority members that are put on the special minority electoral register that is prepared by the Italian and the Hungarian self-governing national communities (and by the Roma Council for the Roma community).[59] The registers consist of individuals who declare their belonging to their national minority, irrespective of where they live. This right is therefore not territorially confined to the ethnically mixed areas. The competence of the self-governing national communities to prepare and manage the minority electoral registers has, however, proven somewhat controversial (since the first Law on the Voting Rights Register[60] adopted in 1992) as the self-governing national communities have not developed any criteria for the preparation of these registers, which can enable arbitrary decision-making and a legal problem if an individual with a denied application wishes to complain.

Indeed, the formation of such special minority electoral registers was subject to a constitutional enquiry. The Constitutional Court decided that the 1992 Law on the Voting Rights Register[61] was unconstitutional in that the self-governing national communities failed to define the criteria 'according to which [...] the Italian and Hungarian self-governing ethnic communities decide which voters to place on the special electoral register of citizens who are members of the autochthonous national communities'.[62] Interestingly, the Constitutional Court also

---

[59] Law on the Voting Rights Register 2013, art 12.
[60] Law on the Voting Rights Register 1992.   [61] Law on the Voting Rights Register 1992.
[62] Constitutional Court U-I-283/94, 1998.

declared that autochthony was attributed to the Italian and Hungarian national communities and therefore,

> all special rights with which the Constitution protects the ethnic communi-
> ties are applied to the members of the autochthonous Italian and Hungarian eth-
> nic communities—rather than to all persons declaring themselves to be Italians or
> Hungarians. Keeping this in mind, it is insufficient for an individual to exercise the
> special rights (in particular the special voting right) if (s)he only declares him/herself
> to be Italian or Hungarian. [...] The affiliation with the autochthonous Italian or
> Hungarian ethnic communities is not only a matter of the individual's will but also
> a matter of the ethnic community which considers such a person to be its member
> or not.[63]

It is clear that the Constitutional Court's intention was to prevent any abuse by individuals, not any abuse by individuals not deemed as belonging to a minority by the minority itself, but the minorities' 'homework' has yet to be completed. The changed legislation now requires that an individual can be added to the voting register based on his/her declaration as a minority member or on the basis of his/her entry in the register at previous elections, whereby the criteria to be defined should take into consideration: long-lasting ties with a community; an individual's concern for the preservation of a minority identity; or family relations with persons belonging to a community.[64] While no abuse of this right or problematic cases have been reported so far, this is a very significant issue in the context of the decreasing size of both communities, and in the context of aspirations of other communities seeking to be recognized as national minorities (national communities).

The self-governing national communities, established in individual municipalities and for the entire Italian or Hungarian (but not the Roma) national community, are the central political institutions of the communities.[65] Of course, the formation of self-governing national communities does not mean that members of the national communities have no opportunities to establish other (political) organizations to express their political affinities, or to protect and promote their identity. But such organizations cannot replace the self-governing national communities in their roles. These remain the only legal partner in the process of state–minorities dialogue.

5.3 The Effects of the Autonomy Arrangement in Practice

The autonomy arrangement has helped both the national communities to preserve their distinct identity amidst their decreasing numbers and ageing population. It has certainly made it possible for national communities to preserve their cultural and linguistic identity. Furthermore, it has enabled both communities

---

[63] Constitutional Court U-I-283/94, no. 20/98.
[64] Law on the Voting Rights Register 2013, art 12.
[65] 1991 Constitution, art 64(2); Law on Self-Governing National Communities 1994.

to organize politically and to develop into meaningful actors that co-decide on issues of significance to minorities and to their local environments (i.e. ethnically mixed areas). This has been made possible by the collective aspects of the autonomy arrangement whereby both national communities have formed municipal and 'regional'/community-wide self-governing national communities, as publicly financed legal entities. The Hungarian (Pomurje) self-governing national community, which was formed in 1975, has established two important cultural institutions, and co-established another one for culture and promotion as well as a bilingual high school. All these activities are possible as they are financed by the state budget, by Hungary, and through various public tenders.[66] The same is the case for the Italian (Coastal) self-governing national community. Nationally, both communities have been able to acquire the status of actors who participate in national politics through their elective representatives, above all in the legislative processes.

In sum, what the autonomy arrangement has led to is a widely shared understanding that this minority protection is part and parcel of Slovenia's society. However, this also seems to be understood as the final point, and any improvements to the arrangement, or addressing any flaws with regards to its implementation, are hard—if not impossible—to achieve. The autonomy arrangement has therefore not produced autonomous minorities who could decide, on their own, on how to best fulfil their basic interests and address their concerns. Their position is safeguarded to the extent that an outright downgrading of their rights is not possible, but a broad societal support to address the open issues also seems to be missing. Several reasons for this can be identified, but perhaps the most significant one is the reciprocal approach to minority protection that is present in the media, but also occasionally among politicians. The media thus typically report on the difficult situation for Slovenian minorities in neighbouring countries, and compare it with the normative framework of minority protection for the Italians and Hungarians in Slovenia.

The widespread terminology of Slovenia being the 'home-state' for its Slovenian minorities also suggests that Italy and Hungary are 'home-states' for Slovenia's Italian and Hungarian national communities. Slovenia's autonomy arrangement thus appears superior to any other system of rights accorded to the Slovenian minorities across the border, and any improvement becomes an 'unnecessary requirement', possibly by the already well-protected minorities in Slovenia. In such a context, any debate about the changes needed is virtually impossible, and there is also a lot of self-containment among minority members as they seem to be aware of the societal unwillingness to improve what is already deemed good. The recent economic crisis and the smallness of both groups are two additional factors that affect the actual functioning of the autonomy arrangement in practice, and the lack of willingness to address the problems. It is fair to add that the government

[66] For the functioning, organization, and activities of this self-governing national community, see its website, accessed 27 July 2014, <http://muravidek.si/?lang=sl>.

has made it clear, on several occasions, that national minorities should not and will not suffer the severe financial crisis. However, in such a context, they cannot expect any additional funding, either.

Over the years, the autonomy arrangement has suffered indirectly, possibly also unintentionally much to the disappointment and disagreement of both national communities. Two issues warrant special attention: firstly, the process of de-territorialization (whereby several administrative functions are no longer performed solely by a municipality of an individual's permanent residence) has opened up possibilities for persons living in the ethnically mixed areas to have their personal documents, such as identity cards, passports, or driving licences, issued outside those areas and therefore in areas where administrative bodies function in Slovene and where they issue classical documents in Slovene (and other relevant world languages, but not in minority languages). Three individuals (both minority representatives in the Parliament and a member of the majority living in the Slovenian–Italian area) have challenged this change with regards to identity cards,[67] but the Constitutional Court—disappointingly—dismissed their complaint on the basis of inadmissibility (i.e. they could not show a 'direct legal interest').[68]

Secondly, parents now have the right to send their children to any primary school, even outside their area of residence.[69] This means that children from an ethnically mixed area can be sent to schools elsewhere. Although this change was in line with the modern migratory habits of parents,[70] and in some cases also with the mismatch between the number of children and the available school places, it opened up the possibility of parents avoiding bilingual schooling (in Pomurje) if they wished to do so. There are no data on the consequences of this change, but minority representatives (privately) express their fears that this could further diminish the system of minority protection, with one of its principle that some keys elements of the arrangement apply to *all* inhabitants of ethnically mixed areas.[71]

5.4 Minorities as Actors

The autonomy arrangement's core concept and mechanism is the concept of a self-governing national community as a legal entity formed at the level of municipalities, and at the level of a national community (minority), in each of the ethnically mixed areas. No such mechanism exists for the Roma community. The

---

[67] Law on Identity Card, art 7(4).

[68] Constitutional Court U-I-147/11-8, 2012. Correspondence with a minority representative, 5 August 2014.

[69] Law on Primary Schools, art 48.

[70] According to 2002 national census, 16.5 per cent of all Hungarians live outside the ethnically mixed area (Kolláth, 'Hungarian in Slovenia', p. 1).

[71] Informal conversations with minority representatives, 2013 and early 2014; and correspondence with minority representatives in the National Assembly, 5 August 2014.

self-organization of national minorities is an essential part of Slovenia's minority protection. Additionally, national minorities are organized and manage their affairs through associations, whereby the Union of the Italians (which connects the Italian minorities in Slovenia and Croatia) is particularly important. By contrast, the Hungarian minority has no similar umbrella association, which has been described as 'unfortunate'.[72] Municipal self-governing national communities establish their national minority's 'umbrella' organization: the Coastal Self-Governing National Community (Italians) and the Pomurje Self-Governing National Community (Hungarians). The municipal self-governing national communities closely cooperate with the 'umbrella' self-governing national communities and with members of the Parliament. The first type of cooperation is legally based, whereas the other type depends on the practice of individuals holding the functions. The municipal self-governing national communities elect within their community members of the council of the 'umbrella' self-governing national community (the council is therefore elected indirectly), and this self-governing community represents the interests of the entire minority before the government. It is this self-governing community that interacts with the government (or with individual ministries) on behalf of the respective national minority. By contrast, minority members of the Parliament are part of the legislative and they are not legally bound to seek the opinion of the 'umbrella' self-governing community. But in practice, they cooperate closely. Moreover, minority parliamentarians frequently organize meetings with individuals from the executive in Ljubljana, and they often participate at these meetings together with the representatives of the 'umbrella' self-governing national communities.[73]

Whereas the Italian minority governs its own affairs predominantly through the Union of Italians (which is in practice the strongest avenue for cooperation and self-management of the Italians), the Hungarian community governs its affairs in practice in an original manner. The present member of the Parliament, Dr László Göncz, organizes a parliamentary collegium once every month, gathering all presidents of the Hungarian self-governing communities and directors of Hungarian public institutes and institutions, with a view to discussing openly minority issues, resolving them, or taking them to other (parliamentary or governmental) institutions if need be. This approach has been crafted and carried out not only to compensate for the lack of a strong umbrella Hungarian association (like the Union of the Italians), but also and above all to overcome the problems caused by the lack of clearly defined competences of different self-governing communities.[74]

[72] Personal interview with László Göncz, the Hungarian member of the Parliament, Ljubljana, September 2014.
[73] Personal interview with László Göncz, the Hungarian member of the Parliament, Ljubljana, September 2014.
[74] Personal interview with László Göncz, the Hungarian member of the Parliament, Ljubljana, September 2014.

5.5 Minorities' Satisfaction with the Arrangement

Although long established, well developed, comprehensive, and socially widely accepted, the autonomy arrangement does not function to the satisfaction of the national communities. This dissatisfaction is directly related to insufficient implementation of minority protection with obligations that are applicable to all inhabitants of ethnically mixed areas and regardless of the strength of the national communities in question. Because it has been increasingly difficult to implement minority rights and corresponding duties, national communities widely believe that they lack the effective means to prevent this from happening. The limited implementation of minority protection has thus put more pressure on the functioning of the autonomy arrangement. Because both communities are satisfied with the legal framework on minority protection, their performance as actors with decision-making powers to manage their own affairs has been overwhelmingly understood in terms of their ability to guarantee full implementation of minority protection. Accordingly, although they are able to manage their own affairs through the functioning of self-governing communities at different levels of governance, their (dis)satisfaction is defined by how successful they are in securing the functioning of minority protection. Their 'success' in this respect has been mixed: whereas they have managed to secure financial means—despite the very difficult financial situation in Slovenia—for the implementation of minority rights, they have not been able to affect the decision-making on some controversial changes in the application of bilingualism. Moreover, their participation in decision-making on finances tends to be limited and the results can be accorded more to Slovenia's commitment to minority protection, than to the effective participation of minorities in decision-making on this matter.

The implementation of minority protection can be seen as a litmus test for the functioning of the autonomy arrangement. The issue of the problem with the implementation of linguistic rights, which affect functional bilingualism,[75] has been reported by minority members to different institutions. Perhaps the most 'popular' address is the National Assembly's Commission on Nationalities (national minorities) where issues are debated, but not many changes occur afterwards.[76] The extent of the problem has been recently confirmed by an online public opinion poll on the website of the Hungarian minority's daily newspaper *Népújság*, between April and June 2014, according to which 58 per cent of the respondents believe that public use of the language (in offices, at public manifestations, and on signs) lives only in legislation, not in practice, 19 per cent believe that persons belonging to the minority should more consistently use their mother tongue in all situations, whereas only 10 per cent are satisfied with the situation.[77] The

---

[75] Kolláth, 'Hungarian in Slovenia', p. 11.

[76] For further details see, accessed 23 May 2014, <http://www.dzrs.si/wps/portal/Home/deloDZ/seje/sejeDt/poDt/izbranoDt?dt=05>.

[77] Personal correspondence with Jutka Király; *Népújság* newspaper, July 2014, <http://www.nepujsag.net/>.

autonomy arrangement can be seen as having empowered minorities to participate in decision-making processes and use available means to address their concerns,[78] but their participation has not brought about satisfactory results.

Overall, minority decision-making processes, particularly co-decision-making, 'should be arranged more systematically'.[79] Minorities participate in decision-making, but their voice is not necessarily heard, or they are not fully empowered to use the legal means available, such as the veto power to affect the decision-making. As competences of the self-governing communities are not fully defined, there are problems with the functioning in practice of the minority autonomy. The entire system of minority autonomy is critically dependent on personal engagement of minority representatives, be they representatives of the municipal self-governing communities, the respective 'umbrella' self-governing community, or minority members of the Parliament.[80]

To address the arrangement's shortcomings, representatives of both national communities have advocated for a specific solution in the form of a general law on the implementation of the rights of the autochthonous Italian and Hungarian national communities, and in the form of a law on the use of languages of national communities as official languages in ethnically mixed areas.[81] The latter appears a relevant solution given that the 1991 Constitution (art 64) does not mention minority languages as the identity marker in need of special protection. With respect to the former, however, two somewhat more critical remarks seem to be in place: firstly, if some sixty laws have not led to satisfactory results, it is certainly questionable how one general law could overturn this trend, which is the key intention behind this proposal.[82] Secondly and more importantly, a general comprehensive law on minority protection in the form of an autonomy arrangement could possibly question the present approach towards minorities, which is based on the inclusion of minority rights in all general laws that address issues of minorities' concern. This type of minority mainstreaming clearly extends the awareness of the arrangement across different state sectors and among the general public. And the desire of minorities to adopt a general law needs to be understood in the context of supplementing the present approach and making it more efficient. Both minority members of the Parliament have managed to achieve the inclusion of this goal (i.e. the adoption of a general law) in the 2014 governmental coalition treaty.

---

[78] In 2013, Slovenia's Ombudswoman was informed by the Hungarian member of the Parliament about inflammatory writings and messages about the Hungarian national community, and she expected the relevant authorities to investigate the matter (Ombudsman of the Republic of Slovenia, 'Letno poročilo varuha človekovih pravic Republike Slovenije za leto 2013' [Annual Report of the Ombudsman of the Republic of Slovenia for 2013], June 2014, p. 44).

[79] Personal interview with László Göncz, the Hungarian member of the Parliament, Ljubljana, September 2014.

[80] Personal interview with László Göncz, the Hungarian member of the Parliament, Ljubljana, September 2014.

[81] Personal interviews with minority representatives, Ljubljana, May and June 2014.

[82] Kolláth, 'Hungarian in Slovenia', p. 4.

5.6 Conclusions and Recommendations

The Slovenian nation, being typically perceived in ethnic terms, is not welcoming to any ethnic differences being included in the concept (and perception) of the nation on an equal footing, or at least without any negative connotations. These perceptions are closely related to the painful history of neighbouring nationalisms whose goal was also the termination of the Slovenian nation. Ethnic Slovenians have therefore formulated their nation-building policies, including the language policy, in the context of what has been described as 'Slovenian smallness'—that is, a perception that the Slovenian nation is small and endangered by other nations, particularly the bigger ones surrounding the territory of Slovenia.[83] In such a context, minority protection can best be described as a way of controlling the minorities in question, rather than an approach towards empowering minorities and developing minority cultures and languages in the context of the diverse character of the territory. This is reflected in the actual functioning of the autonomy arrangement.

The Slovenian autonomy arrangement involves many positive elements that enable national minorities to participate in decision-making and thus protect, preserve, and promote their identity. Minorities have a say in managing their own affairs, but their participation in public affairs tends to be more declaratory, and not very effective: according to law, not only are minorities responsible for managing their own affairs but they also participate in virtually all aspects of decision-making, locally and nationally, with respect to issues that concern them. However, they do not seem to be content with the effectiveness of their participation. A better implementation of the minority arrangement is therefore a goal frequently heard. The lack of effectiveness in decision-making, which can lead, and indeed has led, to the lowering of minority protection, is somewhat compensated by the characteristics of Slovenia's model of minority protection. At least three such characteristics appear crucial: the application of the model to all inhabitants of the areas in which minorities traditionally live; the application of the model in those areas regardless of the numerical strength of the minorities in question; and the broad scope of rights covered by this arrangement (already in the 1991 Constitution).

However, it is precisely these essential elements of the model of minority protection that appear to present the biggest challenges for its application in practice, and also for the functioning of the autonomy arrangement. It has been obvious for a number of years, as persistently explained by minority representatives at different occasions (including in the context of the first three monitoring cycles under the Council of Europe's Framework Convention for the Protection of National

---

[83] Petra Roter, 'Language Issues in the Context of "Slovenian Smallness"', in *Nation-Building, Ethnicity and Language Politics in Transition Countries*, edited by Farimah Daftary and François Grin (Budapest: LGI/Open Society Institute, 2003), pp. 211–41.

Minorities),[84] that the legal arrangement on minority protection is not fully implemented, whereby the equal use of languages is particularly problematic. Although minorities fully participate in political processes nationally and locally, their representatives tend to express a certain level of dissatisfaction with how effective they can be. For them, the autonomy arrangement seems to be satisfactory based on how well minority rights are implemented, rather than on how much they participate in decision-making processes or how they are listened to in the Parliament or in the government. Some issues, however, have exposed the fragile nature of the autonomy arrangement in Slovenia, particularly in cases where minorities were not able to prevent the changes in legislation that paved the way for the modification of minority protection (such as with regards to bilingual identity cards). Minorities have the right to veto such decisions, but minority representatives have not used it in the Parliament. They have sought solutions through consultation and cooperation, often leading to their further discontent about the adopted legislation.

Minorities appear particularly dissatisfied with their role and ability in securing the implementation of linguistic elements of minority protection to all inhabitants of the ethnically mixed areas. Bilingualism in practice has proven a difficult goal due to several factors, which include the small size of both groups, the changing populations in the Slovenian–Italian mixed areas (whereby many migrants from other parts of the country did not benefit from the mandatory learning of Italian in primary and secondary education) and the economic underdevelopment of the Slovenian–Hungarian mixed area, which has led to out-migration of persons belonging to the Hungarian minority (particularly the educated youth that seeks job opportunities elsewhere in the country or abroad). The autonomy arrangement has been severely tested in this respect as minorities have not been able to effectively prevent further lowering of official bilingualism despite significant attention devoted to this matter by the self-governing national communities.

The application of the model of minority protection in ethnically mixed areas regardless of *the numerical strength* of the minorities in question is of course a positive aspect of any approach to minority protection. However, in the Slovenian case, the two communities in question are so small that this indirectly affects the implementation of some aspects of the autonomy arrangement, particularly their effective participation in decision-making. Additionally, the small size of the communities and mixed marriages have led to a new generation of individuals who may have at least two ethnic identities simultaneously, but the autonomy arrangement in place is based on the assumption that individuals will have a clear dominant identity whose ethnic markers they will seek to promote and protect not only privately, but also in the public sphere.

Thirdly, the *broad scope of minority rights* further presents a problem for the effectiveness of minority participation in decision-making. Namely, the constant comparison between Slovenia's system of minority protection and those of

---

[84] See the Opinions of Advisory Committee on the Framework Convention for the Protection of National Minorities on Slovenia, accessed 4 August 2014, <http://www.coe.int/t/dghl/monitoring/minorities/3_FCNMdocs/Table_en.asp#Slovenia>.

neighbouring states as applicable to the Slovenian minorities living in those states, negatively affects the effectiveness of the Italian and Hungarian autonomy arrangement. Both communities can manage their own affairs, but they find it hard to effectively protect their interests when it comes to addressing their issues of concern (such as the decreasing bilingualism).

Perhaps most importantly, this very comprehensive autonomy arrangement is perceived as Slovenia's claim to the European norms and values in the issue area of human and minority rights. Slovenia and Slovenians typically argue that they have one of the best models of minority protection in Europe (and that ethnic Slovenian minorities in neighbouring countries would be very happy and lucky if they enjoyed the same rights). In this context, and with a view to preserving good relations not just internally but also with those communities' kin-states, it is hard to imagine any changes to the autonomy arrangement to be initiated by the political elites in the near future. But it is precisely this status quo that is negatively affecting Slovenia's approach to diversity management in general.

There are two sides to such negative side effects: one applies to the two national communities, and the other to all other ethnic non-Slovenian citizens of Slovenia. With respect to the former, although the arrangement has its problems in reality, there is hardly any debate about the necessary adjustments to the model that would make minority participation more effective. Any mention of the necessary changes is either taken up by the nationalist voices to call for the abolition of what are described as 'privileges', or is rejected by minority representations out of fear of decreasing the scope of their autonomy arrangement. So far, the only tangible change put forward by minority representatives has remained at the legislative level: they have called for the adoption of a single comprehensive law on minority protection that would complement the mainstreaming of minority protection in relevant legislation. With respect to the latter: this comprehensive arrangement is such that it is not possible to extend it to other communities—both because of its territorial framework and because of its financial and organizational foundations.

This status quo is in the end detrimental for several other minority groups, including 'new' minorities. The latter have been denied the status of constitutionally recognized minorities out of fear that such a status, if granted, would lead to their demands to benefit from a similar arrangement according to the principle of non-discrimination. Consequently, it is very obvious that what is needed is a new approach to diversity management in general, rather than the currently existing autonomy arrangement for some. Such a new approach to diversity management would apply not only to minorities, but it would need to start socializing the dominant nation into understanding that the civic concept of the nation includes several ethno-national communities—not only ethnic Slovenians, Italians, Hungarians, and the Roma, but also all other non-dominant communities, particularly those that share their ethno-national identity with former Yugoslav nations/nationalities.

6

Sámi Parliaments in Finland, Norway, and Sweden

Adam Stępień, Anna Petrétei, and Timo Koivurova

6.1 Introduction

The Nordic solution to Sámi claims—the system of Sámi parliaments—has become one of the most prominent models for addressing indigenous rights questions. With the adoption of the UN Declaration on the Rights of Indigenous Peoples (UNDRIP) and international recognition of the right of indigenous peoples to self-determination, Sámi parliaments in Finland, Norway, and Sweden have also come to be seen as the 'vehicles for Sámi self-determination'.[1] Sámi parliaments are the chief institutions of Sámi autonomy, which due to the dispersion of the Sámi population over the area of Fennoscandia[2] is based on ethnic/identity affiliation rather than territorial boundaries, and thus, constitutes non-territorial cultural autonomy. This chapter presents the Sámi parliaments and examines their role and powers from the perspective of both the legal framework and practical implementation. The analysis focuses on one hand, on the autonomous functions of the parliaments, and on the other, on the possibility of influencing decision-making. Constraints, limitations, difficulties and opportunities are discussed. Such analysis is important not only because Sámi policies are the only European example of indigenous governance apart from Russia and Greenland, but also because the Sámi parliaments are influential institutional models within the indigenous world. Moreover, as the Sámi parliaments enter their third decade of existence, it is a good time to offer an assessment of Sámi parliamentarism.

The chapter opens with an introduction to indigeneity, Sámi identity, and the principle of indigenous self-determination. Then, the historical context of Sámi politics is discussed followed by a presentation of the legal framework and the actual

---

[1] James Anaya, *The Situation of the Sámi People in the Sápmi Region of Norway, Sweden and Finland* (6 June 2011) A/HRC/18/35/Add.2, accessed 21 September 2012, <http://unsr.jamesanaya.org/country-reports/the-situation-of-the-sami-people-in-the-sapmi-region-of-norway-sweden-and-finland-2011>.

[2] Norway, Sweden, and Finland, and in some definitions also Russia's Kola Peninsula or Karelia are considered part of Fennoscandia.

implementation of Sámi self-determination and autonomy as expressed through the Sámi parliaments. The chapter concludes with comments on possible future developments. Throughout the chapter, the term 'Sámi Parliament' is used alongside the North Sámi name *Sámediggi* and the Norwegian, Swedish, and Finnish terms—*Sameting, Sametinget,* and *Saamelaiskäräjät* respectively. As the focus here is on the institution of a Sámi Parliament as a governance/autonomy model, the situation of the Russian Sámi is not discussed, as a popularly elected Sámi representative body does not exist in the Kola Peninsula. However, it should be noted that some Kola Sámi organizations call for the establishment of a Sámi Parliament in Russia, seeing a great value in following the Nordic model.[3] Thus, the attractiveness of the model developed in Nordic countries is evident.[4]

6.2 Indigenous Peoples, the Sámi, and Self-Determination

Indigeneity as a concept, ideology, and movement developed over the twentieth century, and in particular in the 1970s, based on notions of 'unfinished decolonization', a community of suffering as well as opposition to forced assimilation, modernization, and on-going dispossession. International forums and institutions, mainly the United Nations (UN), became the movement's primary locus.[5] The Sámi (also called Lapps—a term presently considered pejorative) are a Finno-Ugric people in Northern Fennoscandia and the Kola Peninsula, which constitute the Sámi homeland or Sápmi. Presently, there are about 65,000–100,000 Sámi (approximately 40,000 in Norway, 15,000 in Sweden, 8,000 in Finland, and 2,000 in the Kola Peninsula). Only in the central and southern Finnmark of Norway, do the Sámi still constitute a majority of inhabitants. In fact, many Sámi presently live in the big cities of Fennoscandia. They are the only indigenous people in the European Union.[6]

Sámi history and the current situation of this ethnic group correspond to the characteristics of indigeneity: minority, non-dominant status in their homeland, close connection between culture, land, and environment, preservation of certain traditional institutions, as well as a history of colonization and dispossession.[7] Therefore, the

---

[3] The Russian Sámi work together with other Russian indigenous groups under the auspices of the Russian Association of Small Indigenous Peoples of the North, Siberia, and Far East (RAIPON), as well as engage in close cooperation with the Nordic Sámi, primarily through the Sámi Council.

[4] Mikkel Berg-Nordlie, 'Striving to Unite. The Russian Sámi and the Nordic Sámi Parliament Model', *Arctic Review on Law and Politics* vol. 2, no. 2 (2011): p. 52.

[5] Ronald Niezen, *Origins of Indigenism: Human Rights and the Politics of Identity* (Ewing: University of California Press, 2002); Irja Seurujärvi-Kari, 'Saamelaisten etnisyyden ja identiteetin rakentaminen saamelais- ja alkuperäiskansaliikkeen kontekstissa' [Sámi Ethnicity—And Identity-Building in the Context of the Sámi and Indigenous Movement] (Doctoral dissertation, University of Helsinki, 2012).

[6] Odd Mathias Haetta, *The Sámi—An Indigenous People of the Arctic* (Karasjok: Davvi Girji, 1993); Hugh Beach, 'The Saami of Lapland', in Minority Rights Group, *Polar Peoples: Self-Determination and Development* (London: Minority Rights Group Publications, 1994), pp. 149–50; Johan Eriksson, *Partition and Redemption. A Machiavellian Analysis of Sámi and Basque Patriotism* (Umeå: Umeå University, 1997).

[7] Patrick Thornberry, 'Who is Indigenous?', in *Economic, Social and Cultural Rights of the Sámi. International and National Aspects,* edited by F. Horn (Rovaniemi: University of Lapland Press,

Sámi are currently clearly identified as an indigenous people. However, even for the Sámi indigenous self-identification was not always self-evident.[8] The embracement of indigeneity was triggered by contacts with other indigenous groups—particularly North American Natives and the Inuit—leading to joining the World Council of Indigenous Peoples (WCIP) in 1975. This shifted Sámi politics towards land rights, livelihood challenges, and culture rather than the typical ethnic minorities' agenda, although issues of discrimination, language, and minority–majority relations certainly continue to be important. Indigenous peoples' claims to autonomy are centred on the indigenous right to self-determination.[9] It is therefore not surprising that the Sámi parliaments (particularly the Norwegian *Sámediggi*) and the Sámi Council (pan-Sámi umbrella non-governmental organization (NGO)) have made self-determination one of their priorities.[10]

The right to self-determination of peoples constitutes one of the bases of the international legal order, as expressed in the UN Charter (art 1) and common article 1 of the International Covenant on Civil and Political Rights (ICCPR 1966) and the International Covenant of Economic, Social and Cultural Rights (ICESCR 1966). As most international legal principles, it is an ambiguous concept. Self-determination, earlier referring primarily to populations of sovereign states and dependent territories (within the process of decolonization), has gradually come to encompass groups seen as distinct populations both within and across state borders. Moreover, it has developed into a collective human right.[11] At the same time, the association of the principle with the notion of secession has become less pronounced, which, as we will see, is particularly relevant in the indigenous context. Self-determination can be conceptualized as a dynamic process of constant negotiation and adjustment to local temporally

1998), pp. 3–8, 22–4; Jose R. Martinez Cobo, 'Study of the Problem of Discrimination Against Indigenous Populations, Sub-Commission on the Promotion and Protection of Human Rights', (1982) E/CN.4/Sub.2/1986/7/Add.4, para 379; International Labour Organization Convention no. 169 concerning Indigenous and Tribal Peoples in Independent Countries (adopted 27 June 1989, entry into force 5 September 1991) C169 (ILO 169), art 1; United Nations Permanent Forum on Indigenous Issues 'Who are Indigenous Peoples?', Factsheet (UNPFII: n.d.); United Nations Declaration on the Rights of Indigenous Peoples (adopted 13 September 2007) General Assembly Resolution 61/295 (UNDRIP), Preamble; James Anaya, 'The Right of Indigenous Peoples to Self-Determination in the Post-Declaration Era', in *Making the Declaration Work*, edited by Claire Charters and Rodolfo Stavenhagen (Copenhagen: Indigenous Work Group for Indigenous Affairs, 2009), pp. 184–98; Elspeth Young, *Third World in the First: Development and Indigenous Peoples* (London: Routledge, 1995).

[8] Regnor Jernsletten, 'The Development of a Saami Elite in Norden', in *Conflict and Cooperation in the North*, edited by Kristina Karppi and Johan Eriksson (Umeå: Norrlands Universitetsforlag i Umeå, 2002), pp. 156–8.

[9] Erica-Irene A. Daes, 'An Overview of the History of Indigenous Peoples: Self-Determination and the United Nations', *Cambridge Review of International Affairs* vol. 21, no. 1 (2008): pp. 7–26.

[10] Anne Julie Semb, 'Sámi Self-Determination in the Making', *Nations and Nationalism* vol. 11, no. 4 (2005): p. 532, 536; Irja Seurujärvi-Kari, '"We Are No Longer Prepared to be Silent": The Making of Sámi Indigenous Identity in an International Context', *Suomen Antropologi: Journal of the Finnish Anthropologial Society* vol. 35, no. 4 (2010): pp. 5–25.

[11] Darlene M. Johnston, 'The Quest of the Six Nations Confederacy for Self-Determination', *University of Toronto Faculty of Law Review* vol. 44 (1986): pp. 31–2; Allen Buchanan, *Justice, Legitimacy and Self-Determination: Moral Foundations for International Law* (Oxford: Oxford

changing conditions.[12] Indigenous peoples see themselves as 'peoples' under international law and their decades-long advocacy finally led in 2007 to the adoption of UNDRIP.[13] Article 3 states clearly:

> Indigenous peoples have the right to self-determination. By virtue of that right they freely determine their political status and freely pursue their economic, social and cultural development.

Indigenous self-determination differs from the understanding of the term associated with notions of decolonization and secession. It is explicitly limited by the states' right to territorial integrity,[14] although some external aspects of self-determination are still in place, such as international representation and cross-border cooperation.[15] Therefore, Sámi leaders perceive states' concerns regarding secession as disfiguring the debate, shifting it away from critical matters of land and self-governance.[16] Indigenous peoples seek control primarily over their lives, lands, and resources[17] and securing the means of subsistence. They wish to achieve cultural autonomy, steer their development as well as to reshape relationships with other peoples inhabiting the same territory under conditions of equality, justice, reconciliation, and acknowledgement of past injustices.[18]

Self-determination broadly refers to two aspects: the right to autonomous governance and own institutions, and, on the other hand, full and effective participation at all levels of decision-making. In internal and local affairs indigenous peoples have the right to autonomy and self-government, including the ways and means of financing self-governing functions.[19] Internal and local affairs are not

University Press, 2004), pp. 331–45; John Howard Clinebell and Jim Thomson, 'Sovereignty and Self-Determination: The Rights of Native Americans under International Law', *Buffalo Law Review* vol. 27 (1978): pp. 669–714; Anaya, 'The Right of Indigenous Peoples', pp. 184–98.

[12] John B. Henriksen, 'The Continuous Process of Recognition and Implementation of the Sámi People's Right to Self-Determination', *Cambridge Review of International Affairs* vol. 21, no. 1 (2008): pp. 27–40; John B. Henriksen, ed., 'Sámi Self-Determination—Scope and Implementation', *Galdu Cala, Journal of Indigenous Peoples Rights*, no. 2 (2008): pp. 1–48; John B. Henriksen, 'Sámi Self-Determination: Autonomy and Self-Government: Education, Research and Culture', *Galdu Cala, Journal of Indigenous Peoples Rights*, no. 2 (2009): pp. 1–48; Ole Henrik Magga, 'The Sámi Parliament: Fulfilment of Self-Determination', in *Conflict and Cooperation in the North*, edited by Kristina Karppi and Johan Eriksson (Umeå: Norrlands Universitetsforlag i Umeå, 2002); Anaya, 'The Right of Indigenous Peoples', pp. 184–98; Semb, 'Sámi Self-Determination in the Making', p. 543.

[13] Daes, 'An Overview of the History of Indigenous Peoples', pp. 7–26.

[14] United Nations Declaration on the Rights of Indigenous Peoples, art 46.

[15] United Nations Declaration on the Rights of Indigenous Peoples, art 36.

[16] Henriksen, 'Sámi Self-Determination—Scope and Implementation'; Barbara Hocking, ed., *Unfinished Constitutional Business?: Rethinking Indigenous Self-Determination* (Canberra: Aboriginal Studies Press, 2005); Shin Imai, 'Indigenous Self-Determination and the State, Indigenous Peoples and the Law: Comparative and Critical Perspectives', *CLPE Research Paper* no. 25 (2008).

[17] As bases for indigenous livelihoods, economies, and cultures, see for instance ILO 169, arts 14, 15.

[18] Sven Jentoft, Henry Minde, and Ragnar Nilsen, eds, *Indigenous Peoples. Resource Management and Global Rights* (Delft: Eburon, 2003); Dave Lewis, *Indigenous Rights Claims in Welfare Capitalist Society: Recognition and Implementation. The Case of the Sámi People in Norway, Sweden and Finland* (Rovaniemi: Arctic Centre, 1998).

[19] United Nations Declaration on the Rights of Indigenous Peoples, art 4.

defined in UNDRIP, but their scope could be better understood by looking at the earlier drafts of the Declaration, where the internal and local affairs included, inter alia: culture, education, religion, information, media, health, housing, employment, social welfare, economic activities, land and resources management, environment, and entry by non-members.[20] In the Sámi context, especially in Finland and Norway, autonomy refers primarily to 'cultural autonomy', which can be understood as 'the right to self-rule, by a culturally defined group, in regard to matters, which affect the maintenance and reproduction of its culture'.[21]

The Nordic states have endorsed Sámi peoplehood and self-determination in various international and domestic contexts, including their support to UNDRIP or reporting under art. 1 of ICESCR (in the case of Sweden).[22] All three Nordic constitutions currently acknowledge the status of the Sámi as a people or an indigenous people.[23] Finnish law officially grants the Sámi 'cultural autonomy'. However, Sámi self-determination has also met with resistance from societies and political systems accustomed to principles of unity and equality.[24] The Nordic-Sámi setting of internal colonization, where currently the Sámi constitute a majority only in a small territory, where livelihoods, land-use, histories, legacies, and cultures have been interlinked for centuries and where the non-Sámi population is concerned with its future position and rights, makes political resolution a difficult task. As a consequence, the role of the Sámi parliaments is still largely limited to partial participation in decision-making rather than actual self-government.[25]

Of importance is also the trans-border setting of the Sámi people as one people with the right to exercise one, collective right to self-determination. International indigenous rights documents, in particular the UNDRIP, provide for strengthened cooperation between divided parts of a group, including for political purposes, and

[20] Timo Koivurova, 'Sovereign States and Self-Determining Peoples: Carving out a Place for Transnational Indigenous Peoples in a World of Sovereign States', *International Community Law Review* vol. 12 (2010): p. 200.

[21] Asbjørn Eide, 'Cultural Autonomy: Concept, Content, History and Role in the World Order', in *Autonomy: Applications and Implications*, edited by Markku Suksi (The Hague: Kluwer Law International, 1998); Alexandra Tomaselli, 'Research Results on Pre-Conditions in the Consultation Procedure of Well-Established Minority Consultative Bodies: Some Examples from the Sámi Parliaments' Experience' (Office of the High Commissioner for Human Rights/EURAC, 2009), accessed 26 April 2015 <http://www2.ohchr.org/english/bodies/hrcouncil/minority/docs/Item%20 IV%20Conditions%20required%20for%20effective%20political%20participation/Participants/ Alexandra%20Tomaselli%20EURAC%20Sami%20political%20participation.pdf>.

[22] Henriksen, 'Sámi Self-Determination—Scope and Implementation'; Eva Josefsen, *The Sámi and the National Parliaments: Channels for Political Influence* (Geneva/New York: IPU and UNDP, 2010); Semb, 'Sámi Self-Determination in the Making'.

[23] Constitution of the Kingdom of Norway, 1985, art 108 (as amended in May 2014); Constitution of Finland, 1995, art 17(3); Constitution of Sweden, 2011, ch 1, art 2.

[24] Seija Tuulentie, 'National Rejection of Saami Claims in Finland', in *Conflict and Cooperation in the North*, edited by Kristina Karppi and Johan Eriksson (Umeå: Norrlands Universitetsforlag i Umeå, 2002), pp. 343–60.

[25] Henriksen, 'Sámi Self-Determination: Autonomy and Self-Government'; Josefsen, *The Sámi and the National Parliaments*; Scott Forrest, 'Indigenous Self-Determination in Finland: A Case Study in Normative Change', *Polar Record* vol. 42 (2006): pp. 229–38.

require states to take measures to facilitate such contacts.[26] In the case of the Sámi, the draft Nordic Sámi Convention (currently under negotiation between Finland, Sweden, and Norway within the Nordic Council of Ministers) would acknowledge the unity of the Sámi people across borders and open the possibility, for instance, of a joint pan-Sámi assembly.[27]

6.3 Historical Context

The contact between the Sámi and Norse traders, settlers, and officials goes back to the Middle Ages, when traders were entitled to collect taxes from the Sámi. As tax collection brought significant income to the southern—Scandinavian and Russian—monarchies and was considered to institute sovereignty over a taxed area, states took over control of taxation, although the Sámi in some regions were forced to pay taxes to two or three monarchs simultaneously.[28] Gradually, christianization, colonization, and agricultural settlement, as well as military and strategic issues, gained importance.[29] In the beginning, the Sámi were considered owners of the land, but this changed over time.[30] Sápmi slowly became divided by state borders. In 1751, Sweden and Norway concluded the Strömstad Border Treaty, which stated that the Sámi would no longer be taxed by both countries even though they made their livelihood in both. However, the treaty also included the so-called 'Lapp Codicil', which for the first time stated the special rights of the 'Sámi nation'. In 1809, Finland became a part of the Russian Empire and Sámi *siidas* (traditional communities) were attached to either Sweden or Finland.[31] Although the border was closed only in 1889, the introduction of borders gradually cut traditional reindeer migration routes, which are critical for the conduct of reindeer husbandry. The Sámi nomadic culture was endangered.[32] Although only around 10 per cent of the Sámi conduct (historically and currently) reindeer herding as their key livelihood, reindeer herding is considered one of the main lifestyles and bases of culture. In Sweden and Norway, reindeer herding currently remains a right reserved exclusively (with only few exceptions) for the Sámi. In 1826, the

---

[26] United Nations Declaration on the Rights of Indigenous Peoples, art 36; Koivurova, 'Sovereign States and Self-Determining Peoples', pp. 203–4, 210–11.

[27] Timo Koivurova, 'The Draft Nordic Sámi Convention: Nations Working Together', *International Community Law Review* vol. 10 (2008): pp. 279–93.

[28] Elina Helander and U. Sand, eds, *The Sami People* (Karasjok: The Sámi Research Institute, 1990); website of the Sámiskt Informationscentrum, 'Sami People', accessed 13 October 2012, <http://www.eng.samer.se/GetDoc?meta_id=1228>.

[29] Helander and Sand, *The Sami People*, pp. 24–5, 28; Hugh Beach, 'The Saami of Lapland', *Minority Rights Group Report*, no. 55 (1998): p. 8.

[30] Veli-Pekka Lehtola, *The Sámi People—Traditions in Transition* (Inari: Kustannus-Puntsi, 2002); Helander and Sand, *The Sami People*, pp. 32–4.

[31] Ulla Maija Kulonen, Irja Seurujärvi-Kari, and Risto Pulkkinen, eds, *The Saami—A Cultural Encyclopaedia* (Vammala: Vammalan Kirjapaino Oy, 2005), p. 389.

[32] Lehtola, *The Sámi People—Traditions*, pp. 36–7.

last area jointly taxed by Russia and Norway became a part of Norway. In 1852, the closing of the border between Norway and Finland resulted in social distress.

In Norway, at the end of the nineteenth century, an assimilative policy of 'norwegianization' was introduced mainly due to the fear of Russian and Finnish (Kven) migration to the Finnmark. This affected the Sámi significantly. It caused language and culture loss, as well as triggering feelings of inferiority.[33] In Sweden, the Sámi were subjected to two different, opposite policies. In line with rationalization policies, the reindeer herders were denied participation in cultural, educational, and technological progress. The rest of the Sámi population was deprived of the right to its own culture and subjected to assimilation.[34] In Russia and Finland, the assimilation was much slower and initially not accompanied by specific policy measures, for example in the 1950s, Utsjoki Municipality Council was still proceeding in the Sámi language.[35] Currently, the Sámi are well integrated into Nordic societies and politics, and thus, marginalization patterns from the past, although still of consequence, are not clearly visible.[36]

Sámi political activism started at the beginning of twentieth century, when the first pan-Sámi meetings took place. However, it was not until the 1960s that a strong pan-Sámi movement emerged. The movement focused on claims to land, natural, and cultural resources. It proved effective in the battle for self-determination and political potency.[37] One manifestation of this new movement was the Sámi Council, established in 1956, as well as active Sámi participation in the global indigenous movement. Sámi activism triggered changes in Nordic policies. In the 1970s, a popularly elected Finnish Sámi Delegation was founded (1973) and the issue of Sámi land rights came to the fore in Norway and Sweden. In Norway, public opinion about the Sámi situation changed fundamentally in the 1980s, mostly due to the conflict over the Kautokeino-Alta river hydroelectric dam project.[38] In the aftermath of the conflict, a commission was established to review Sámi rights and land claims. Its report concluded with a proposal for a Sámi Parliament and constitutional protection of the Sámi culture.[39] In Sweden, the 'Taxed Mountain Case' can be considered a legal case of importance

[33] Helander and Sand, *The Sami People*, pp. 44, 67–70; Lehtola, *The Sámi People—Traditions*; Trond Thuen, *Quest for Equity. Norway and Sámi Challenge* (Canada: Institute of Social and Economic Research, 1995), pp. 146–7; Einar Niemi, 'Saami History and the Frontier Myth', in *Sami Culture in a New Era. The Norwegian Sami Experience*, edited by Harald Gaski (Karasjohka: Davvi Giri, 1997), pp. 72–5.

[34] Lewis, *Indigenous Rights Claims*, pp. 25–8, 42–4; Harald Eidheim, 'Ethno-political Development among Sami After World War II', in *Sami Culture in a New Era. The Norwegian Sami Experience*, edited by Harald Gaski (Karasjohka: Davvi Giri, 1997), pp. 31–2; Beach, 'The Saami of Lapland'; Helander and Sand, *The Sami People*, p. 70.

[35] Helander and Sand, *The Sami People*; Lehtola, *The Sámi People—Traditions*.

[36] See, for instance, Per Selle and Kristin Strømsnes, 'Sámi Citizenship: Marginalisation or Integration?', *Acta Borealia* vol. 27, no. 1 (2010): pp. 66–90.

[37] Christian Jakob Burmeister Hicks, 'Historical Synopsis of the Sámi/United Nations Relationship', accessed 29 September 2012, <http://www.thearctic.is> .

[38] Also known as the 'Alta Dispute'.

[39] Ole Henrik Magga, 'Sámi Past and Present and the Sámi Picture of the World', in *The Changing Circumpolar North: Opportunities for Academic Development*, edited by Lassi Heininen (Rovaniemi: Arctic Centre Publications, 1994).

on a par with the Alta conflict. The court stated that the reindeer herders had a strong claim to usufruct rights on the land where reindeer husbandry had traditionally been practised. Norway, as a result of national developments, ratified the 1989 International Labour Organization Convention No. 169 concerning indigenous and tribal peoples,[40] as well as adopting a broad interpretation of other international standards, such as Article 27 of the ICCPR (1966) referring to minorities' right to culture. According to these standards, state authorities should not only enact legislation that forbids discrimination against minorities but are also obliged to take positive measures promoting the Sámi culture. So far, Finland and Sweden have not ratified the ILO 169. In Finland the issue of land use and ownership is particularly complex, partly due to the fact that the Sámi do not enjoy exclusive rights to reindeer herding.[41]

6.4 The Formal Positioning of Sámi Parliaments

The Sámi parliaments are representative bodies for people of Sámi heritage, democratically elected every four years in Norway (since 1989), Sweden (since 1993), and Finland (since 1996, however, the earlier Sámi Delegation had been elected from 1974). Although perceived as bodies governing Sámi autonomy, particularly in areas such as education, culture, language, and indigenous status, the parliaments still remain primarily advisory bodies without legislative authority, having varied powers in different policy fields in the three Nordic states. In order to establish Sámi parliaments, the creation of an appropriate legal framework was necessary with different solutions adopted across Fennoscandia.

In Norway, the Sámi Act regulates the Sámi Parliament and other Sámi rights.[42] The Sámi Act ensures that the Sámi have their own national elected body, the Sámi Parliament, dealing with all matters relating to the Sámi as a people. Article 108 of the Constitution stipulates that it is the responsibility of the authorities of the State to create conditions enabling the Sámi people to preserve and develop its language, culture, and way of life. In Sweden, Chapter 1, Article 2 of the Constitution (Instrument of Government 1974, amended in 2011) recognizes the Sámi's status as 'a people', granting them the right to preserve and develop a cultural and social life of their own. Although in the past, the legal status of the Swedish Sámi has been dealt with in a number of advisory committees, eventually, it was the Taxed Mountain Case and developments in Norway, which prompted the authorities to acknowledge the need for a Sámi organ. As a result, the Sámi Parliament Act came into force in 1993, during the International Year of the World's Indigenous People.[43] The Finnish Constitution acknowledges the Sámi as an indigenous

---

[40] International Labour Organization Convention no. 169.

[41] Asbjørn Eide, 'Legal and Normative Basis for Saami Claims to Land', *International Journal on Minority and Group Rights* vol. 8, no. 2 (2001): pp. 127–49.

[42] The Sámi Act 1987.

[43] Tom G. Svensson, *The Sámi and their Land* (Oslo: Novus forlag, 1997).

people,[44] and guarantees the Sámi linguistic and cultural self-government in their native region,[45] the Sámi Homeland Area in the northernmost part of Finnish Lapland. Further provisions on Sámi cultural autonomy are set down in the Sámi Parliament Act. According to Section 1 of this Act, the Sámi are an indigenous people, having linguistic and cultural autonomy in the Sámi Homeland. The Act stipulates that for the tasks relating to cultural autonomy the Sámi shall elect a Sámi Parliament.

The tasks and operation of the three Sámi parliaments vary. According to Article 2-1 of the Norwegian Sámi Act, the business of the Sámi Parliament (*Sameting*) is any matter that in the opinion of the Parliament particularly affects the Sámi people. To this end, the Parliament may make proposals and issue statements. The Parliament may on its own initiative raise and state an opinion on any matter coming within its scope, as well as refer matters to public authorities and private institutions. It also has a decision-making power concerning internal appointments. It may establish any boards, councils, or committees that it finds appropriate and delegate authority to them unless it is otherwise provided. The *Sámediggi*, furthermore, has the right to delegate authority to administer the national budget allocations granted for Sámi purposes. Since 1992, the Parliament has had the responsibility for the development of the Sámi language in Norway. The Sámi Parliament has assumed responsibility for the Sámi Culture Fund from the Norwegian Council for Cultural Affairs, and is also responsible for the protection of Sámi cultural heritage sites and for the development of Sámi teaching materials. The Parliament reports to the national Parliament every year on its actions and measures taken in order to support Sámi language, culture, and society.[46]

According to Chapter 2, Section 1 of the Swedish Sámi Parliament Act, the Sámi Parliament (*Sametinget*) in Sweden works for a living Sámi culture, taking initiatives for activities and proposing specific measures. The competences of the Sámi Parliament include the allocation of state subsidies and funds from the Sámi Foundation especially established to protect Sámi culture and Sámi organizations; the appointment of the Board of Directors for Sámi schools; the guidance of work on the Sámi language; the participation in community development and ensuring that Sámi needs are considered, including the interests of reindeer husbandry in the use of land and water; providing information on Sámi conditions; and the performance of additional tasks pursuant to other legislation. The Sámi Parliament may give financial benefits and other assistance to the groups, parties, or similar associations who are or have been represented in the Sámi Parliament (political party funding).[47] The Parliament has also become the central administrative agency for reindeer husbandry.[48]

---

[44] Constitution of Finland, ch 1, s 17(3).   [45] Constitution of Finland, ch 11, s 121(4).
[46] Kulonen, Seurujärvi-Kari, and Pulkkinen, *The Saami—A Cultural Encyclopaedia*, pp. 352–3.
[47] Swedish Sámi Parliament Act 1992.
[48] Website of the Sámi Parliament in Sweden, accessed 21 September 2012, <http://www.sametinget.se>.

The task of the Sámi Parliament (*Saamelaiskäräjät*) in Finland is to promote the Sámi language and culture, as well as to take care of matters related to their status as an indigenous people. The Sámi Parliament may submit initiatives and proposals to authorities, issue statements within its competence, and decide on the distribution of funds allocated for Sámi purposes. The Parliament operates under the auspices of the Ministry of Justice.[49] Importantly, state authorities have an obligation to 'negotiate' with the Sámi Parliament in order to hear its opinion on issues concerning their position. Formally (and formally only), that gives the Finnish *Sámediggi* the strongest legal standing of the three Nordic Sámi parliaments. Such issues include especially community planning, management, use, leasing, and assignment of state lands, conservation areas, and wilderness areas, applications for licences to stake mineral mine claims or file mining patents; legislative or administrative changes to the professions associated with the Sámi culture, the development of Sámi language-teaching in schools, social, and health services; as well as any other matters affecting the Sámi language and culture or the status of the Sámi as an indigenous people.[50] The specific powers of the parliaments, their practical scope and limitations are discussed in section 6.5.

6.4.1 Sámi parliamentary elections

Although state electoral laws generally govern elections, the Sámi parliaments administer their own electoral registers and organs. As an expression of the non-territorial nature of the Sámi autonomous governance, the Sámi elections take place in all three countries throughout the state territory and are open to persons of Sámi origin based on language, family, and historical criteria, with specific definitions varying between the three states. Defining who is eligible to vote or be elected to the Sámi parliaments has become one of the most critical, complex, and contested matters in Sámi legislation. In Norway, all persons who declare that they consider themselves to be Sámi, and who have either Sámi as their domestic language or whose parent, grandparent, or great-grandparent spoke Sámi as his or her domestic language, or who are a child of a person registered in the Sámi electoral register, may demand to be included in the Sámi electoral register in their municipality of residence.[51] In Sweden, a Sámi who registers with the electoral committee needs to be listed on the Sámi electoral roll (again, depending mainly on language criteria, including parents' and grandparents' mother tongue). Importantly, the electoral roll may also include foreigners of Sámi origin, who have been registered in the country for three consecutive years before the day of the election.[52] According to the Finnish Sámi Parliament Act, the right to vote in elections to the Sámi Parliament is granted to every Sámi, provided that he or she is a Finnish citizen, or that he or she

---

[49] Finnish Sámi Parliament Act 1995, ch 2, s 5.
[50] Finnish Sámi Parliament Act, ch 2, s 9.   [51] The Sámi Act, arts 2–6.
[52] Swedish Sámi Parliament Act 1992, ch 3, s 3.

is a foreign citizen domiciled in Finland.[53] A Sámi means a person who considers him or herself a Sámi, provided that s/he or at least one of his/her parents or grandparents have spoken Sámi as his/her mother tongue; that s/he is a descendent of a person who has been entered in a land, taxation, or population register as a mountain, forest, or fishing Lapp;[54] or at least one of his/her parents have or could have been registered as an elector for an election to the Sámi Delegation or the Sámi Parliament. The Sámi definition remains a subject of heated debate in Finland.

In Norway and Sweden, the elections are partisan and based on lists of candidates set up by political parties and other interest groups, similar to national and local elections. The Norwegian Sámi elect thirty-nine members, while thirty-one full members are elected in Sweden.[55] The Swedish Sámi have historically rejected cooperating with national parties and thus parties in the Sámi Parliament are separate from those represented in the Riksdag (Swedish Parliament). In Norway, conversely, Sámi politicians, apart from representing Sámi associations, also compete for support under the name of Norwegian parties, which is a distinctive characteristic of Norwegian Sámi politics. Former president Egil Olli, for instance, represented the Labour Party, which won the 2009 elections.[56] In contrast, in Finland, the elections are non-partisan and individual candidates can be put forward for election. Twenty-one candidates receiving the highest number of votes are elected, provided that among them there are at least three candidates elected from each of the four municipalities of the Sámi Homeland.[57]

6.4.2 International Sámi institutions

Besides the three parliaments, the Sámi have also established international institutions in order to promote pan-Sámi issues and interests. The Sámi Parliamentary Council is a cooperative organization of the Sámi parliaments aiming to harmonize Sámi policies and to promote more democratic participation at both the regional (Fennoscandian, Barents, and Arctic) and international levels. The Council also plays an important role in promoting the rights of indigenous peoples internationally. It contributed, for instance, to the development of the United Nations Permanent Forum for Indigenous Issues.[58] Historically, the Sámi Council (earlier the Nordic Sámi Council), a grouping of Sámi organizations from Norway, Sweden, Finland, and Russia, has been the most prominent pan-Sámi institution. Its task is to enhance the economic, social, and cultural position of the Sámi. The Council aims to protect and develop the social, economic, linguistic, and

---

[53] Finnish Sámi Parliament Act, ch 4, s 21.

[54] Historical registers for Lapps (those practising reindeer herding in the mountains or in the taiga as well as those engaged in fishing), originally connected with tax collection, became commonplace in the eighteenth and nineteenth centuries.

[55] Anna Gremsperger, 'On the Sámi Minority', *JURA* vol. I (2012): pp. 135–47.

[56] Josefsen, *The Sámi and the National Parliaments*.

[57] Website of the Sámi Parliament in Finland, accessed 21 September 2012, <http://www.samediggi.fi>.

[58] Kulonen, Seurujärvi-Kari, and Pulkkinen, *The Saami—A Cultural Encyclopaedia*, p. 354.

cultural rights of the Sámi. Protection of Sámi interests also requires international co-operation, thus the Sámi Council[59] has increasingly worked internationally, especially in the UN and in the venues of Arctic and Barents regional cooperation.[60] Sámi Conferences—which have taken place since 1953 and constitute the highest decision-making organ of the Sámi Council—have acted as forums where crucial policy agendas and political programmes as well as national symbols (the Sámi flag and anthem) were adopted.[61]

6.5 The Practice of Sámi Self-Determination and Autonomy

Direct participation of the Sámi in Nordic national political systems is very limited due to the Sámi's small proportion of the population, and thus, it has been the Sámi parliaments that have become flagships of Sámi politics, self-determination, and autonomous governance.[62] Therefore, there is a need for a critical perspective on the institutional positioning of the Sámi parliaments, their capacity to exercise authority and influence, their financial capacities, and their position within the Sámi society. Formal arrangements, discussed in section 6.4, appear in a different light when confronted with reality. Informal venues of influence and administrative practices significantly affect the actual power of the assemblies.

6.5.1 Influence

The Sámi parliaments are still the primary vehicles for Sámi participation rather than autonomous governance. Therefore attention will firstly be given to the parliaments' participation in and influence on decision-making. Their success and effectiveness depend not only on legal and institutional positioning, but also on actual, as well as informal, influence on decision-making. That influence does not resemble directly legal and constitutional provisions and depends on relationships with authorities, political parties, and the strength of Sámi NGOs. The degree of influence also differs between issue areas. Significant powers are commonplace, for instance, in the area of language and culture while competences in land and resource management are usually significantly restricted.[63] For instance, *Sámediggis* brought about a new type of relationship with state authorities. Sámi activists have become elected representatives and gained direct access to political ministers (rather than Sámi affairs officials). Sámi leaders believe that over time they have developed direct channels to decision-makers and built support bases

---

[59] The Sámi Council is one of the permanent participants in the Arctic Council.

[60] Gremsperger, 'On the Sámi Minority', p. 142.

[61] Kulonen, Seurujärvi-Kari, and Pulkkinen, *The Saami—A Cultural Encyclopaedia*, p. 344.

[62] Josefsen, *The Sámi and the National Parliaments*; Semb, 'Sámi Self-Determination in the Making'; Anaya, *The Situation of the Sámi People*.

[63] John B. Henriksen, ed., 'Sámi Self-Determination: Autonomy and Economy—The Authority and Autonomy of the Sámediggi in the Health and Social Services Sector', *Galdu Cala, Journal of Indigenous Peoples Rights* vol. 2 (2010), pp. 33–4.

both in Lapland and in the Nordic capitals.[64] Thus, the Sámi parliaments play an important role in putting various Sámi issues on the political agenda. Such was the case with Sámi fisheries in Norway, the critical situation of Sámi languages in Finland, or safeguards for Sámi culture in a new Finnish Mining Act and Water Act. In the case of difficult issues (for instance the Finnmark Act, which will be discussed later) lengthy and resource-consuming lobbying was needed.[65] Furthermore, the Sámi parliaments have also played a significant role in Nordic international activities of relevance for indigenous issues, especially regarding the UN Declaration and the establishment and activities of the UN Permanent Forum on Indigenous Issues.[66] Finally, the location of Sámi issues in state ministries affects the Sámi parliaments' influence on decision-making. Some ministries[67] are more resistant to Sámi demands than others.[68] Moreover, awareness of Sámi issues among individual officials appears crucial. Closer, more personal, and on-going cooperation facilitates mutual understanding. However, authorities rarely make an effort to attend *Sámediggis'* sessions, which could enhance such understanding.[69]

All Sámi parliaments act within the frameworks drawn up by their respective governments and therefore to a certain extent implement state policies. However, only the Swedish *Sámediggi* is officially positioned as a governmental agency. The government appoints its chairman on the advice of the Assembly.[70] The situation where an elected representative body is simultaneously an administrative arm of a government—carrying out state policies, which it may want to challenge—is certainly difficult and has been criticized[71] for undermining Sámi self-determination.[72] In Norway, the 2005 Consultation Agreement between

[64] Dave Lewis, 'Ethnic Mobilization: The Case of Indigenous Political Movements', in *Conflict and Cooperation in the North*, edited by Kristina Karppi and Johan Eriksson (Umeå: Norrlands Universitetsforlag i Umeå, 2002), pp. 83–112; Lennard Sillanpää, 'Government Responses to Saami Self-Determination', in *Conflict and Cooperation in the North*, edited by Kristina Karppi and Johan Eriksson (Umeå: Norrlands Universitetsforlag i Umeå, 2002), pp. 83–112; personal communication with Stefan Mikaelsson, 17 September 2012.

[65] Elina Helander-Renvall, 'A Marginalised Minority Remains Marginalized? On the Management of Fjord Resources', in *Conflict and Cooperation in the North*, edited by Kristina Karppi and Johan Eriksson (Umeå: Norrlands Universitetsforlag i Umeå, 2002), pp. 214–15; personal communication with Irja Seurujärvi-Kari (former Vice-President of the Finnish Sámi Parliament), 24 September 2012; Henriksen, 'Sámi Self-Determination: Autonomy and Economy'; Anaya, *The Situation of the Sámi People*, p. 9.

[66] Henriksen, 'Sámi Self-Determination: Autonomy and Economy'.

[67] For instance the Swedish Ministry of Agriculture.

[68] Personal communication with Stefan Mikaelsson, 17 September 2012; Anaya, *The Situation of the Sámi People*.

[69] Personal communications with Irja Seurujärvi-Kari, 24 September 2012, and Stefan Mikaelsson, 17 September 2012; Statement of Finnish Sámi Parliament on the Realization of Sámi People's Right to Self-Determination in Finland, 15 April 2010; Josefsen, *The Sámi and the National Parliaments*, pp. 7, 15–16.

[70] Henriksen, 'Sámi Self-Determination—Scope and Implementation'; Josefsen, *The Sámi and the National Parliaments*, pp. 7, 15–16.

[71] For instance by the Human Rights Council.

[72] Henriksen, 'Sámi Self-Determination—Scope and Implementation'; Anaya, *The Situation of the Sámi People*, p. 12; Rebecca Lawrence and Ulf Mörkenstam, 'Självbestämmande genom myndighetsutövning? Sametingets dubbla roller' [Self-Determining Parliament or Government Agency?

the government and the Sámi Parliament clarified consultation procedures and authorities' responsibilities.[73] Although the UN Special Rapporteur evaluated the agreement as being in line with international standards,[74] so far Sámi politicians appear to be disappointed with the practice. There is a perception that the consultation process is not transparent and that it works well in matters of little significance, while in the case of issues of major economic and political importance (as in the case of recent Mining Law consultations) Sámi input is incorporated to a very limited degree. In the future, greater participation in the work of the *Storting*[75] is advocated, as cooperation experiences with the *Storting*, especially during the adoption of the Finnmark Act, are seen as more satisfactory than with the government.[76] Currently, there are ongoing and so far unsuccessful negotiations on establishing analogous procedures in Sweden.[77] In Finland, a similar consultation agreement would also prove beneficial. Although the Sámi Parliament Act[78] establishes a duty of public authorities to *negotiate* in matters of major importance for the Sámi, in practice that usually means loose consultations, while many proposals are ignored, often in favour of positions presented by municipalities.[79] Although the Constitutional Committee of the *Eduskunta* (the Finnish Parliament) advised that ministries should 'take reasoned Sámi Parliament's initiatives into consideration', often there is no response to Sámi initiatives and no feedback regarding what had been taken into account and with result for the decision-making process.[80]

Institutional access to policymaking is not the only mode of influence. In Norway, as national political parties are present in the Sámi Parliament, the party system has become a significant channel for Sámi postulates.[81] Furthermore, Sámi NGOs play an important role, although that differs from country to country.[82] In

---

The Curious Double Life of the Swedish Sámi Parliament], *Statsvetenskaplig tidskrift* vol. 114, no. 2 (2012): pp. 207–39; website of the Sámi Parliament in Sweden, accessed 21 September 2012, <http://www.sametinget.se>.

[73] Johan Mikkel Sara, 'Indigenous Governance of Self-Determination. The Saami Model and the Saami Parliament in Norway', speech by the Vice-President of the Saami Parliament in Norway during the Symposium on 'The Right to Self-Determination in International Law', organized by Unrepresented Nations and Peoples Organization (UNPO), Khmers Kampuchea-Krom Federation (KKF), Hawai'i Institute for Human Rights (HIHR), 29 September–1 October 2006, The Hague, Netherlands.

[74] Anaya, *The Situation of the Sámi People*.

[75] The Norwegian Parliament, which is not covered by the agreement.

[76] Henriksen, 'Sámi Self-Determination: Autonomy and Economy'; personal communication with John Henriksen, 10 August 2012 (International Representative of the Norwegian Sámi Parliament); Anaya, *The Situation of the Sámi People*.

[77] Anaya, *The Situation of the Sámi People*, pp. 7–8.

[78] Act on the Sámi Parliament (974/1995).

[79] Statement of Finnish Sámi Parliament on the Realization of Sámi People's Right to Self-Determination in Finland, 15 April 2010; personal communication with Irja Seurujärvi-Kari, 24 September 2012.

[80] Personal communication with Irja Seurujärvi-Kari, 24 September 2012; Henriksen, 'Sámi Self-Determination: Autonomy and Economy', p. 38; Anaya, *The Situation of the Sámi People*, pp. 11–12; Statement of Finnish Sámi Parliament on the Realization of Sámi People's Right to Self-Determination in Finland, 15 April 2010.

[81] Josefsen, *The Sámi and the National Parliaments*.

[82] Josefsen, *The Sámi and the National Parliaments*, pp. 17–21.

fact, the establishment of the Sámi parliaments has had certain adverse impacts on NGOs' influence, as the authorities now see the Parliament as the main frame of reference, with NGOs lacking comparable legitimacy. As a result, in Norway and Sweden the position of most NGOs has weakened during the 1990s and 2000s with the exception of the reindeer herders' associations.[83] Moreover, the relative strength of particular Sámi organizations has become dependent on electoral support when they participate in elections. This is particularly visible in Norway.[84] In the same vein, the establishment of the Finnish Sámi Delegation in the 1970s channelled the Sámi movement, hindering the development of strong NGOs in Finland.

Many decisions crucial for the Sámi are taken at the local level, while the role of the Sámi parliaments in municipal governance is often limited. Much depends on individuals and the presence of one Sámi representative on various boards may make a major difference.[85] The relations with municipalities may also become formalized, as in the case of the Norwegian *Sámediggi*'s agreements with the northern counties of Troms and Finnmark, which are considered model examples of such cooperation.[86] Many Sámi leaders still hope for the establishment of one, Nordic Sámi Parliament, and the draft Nordic Sámi Convention provides for such a possibility. While jurisdictional and legal barriers may prove insurmountable, a convention would bring major changes in the legal and institutional positioning of Sámi parliamentarism.[87]

6.5.2 Powers and responsibilities

The notion of incremental expansion of Sámi self-determination and autonomy is reflected in the gradual expansion of the Sámi parliaments' competences, of both the local as well as the non-territorial—referring to the whole territory of the state—character. Nevertheless, the ability to act independently and make autonomous decisions remains limited.[88] Sámi politicians demand greater authority in various sectors for the parliaments, but there is also awareness among Sámi activists of the low capacities of the assemblies and numerous political constraints.[89] However, since the establishment of the Sámi parliaments, there have been a number of positive developments. For instance, recently a number of responsibilities have been transferred from the Swedish Board of Agriculture to the Sámi Parliament. The Norwegian *Sámediggi* has acquired significant autonomous powers over time, including protection of cultural heritage, drawing up of Sámi

---

[83] Josefsen, *The Sámi and the National Parliaments*.

[84] Jernsletten, 'The Development of a Saami Elite in Norden', p. 154.

[85] Magga, 'The Sámi Parliament', p. 308. Personal communication with Stefan Mikaelsson, 17 September 2012 and Irja Seurujärvi-Kari, 24 September 2012.

[86] Henriksen, 'Sámi Self-Determination: Autonomy and Economy', p. 13; Semb, 'Sámi Self-Determination in the Making'; Josefsen, *The Sámi and the National Parliaments*, pp. 4–5.

[87] Personal communications with Irja Seurujärvi-Kari, 24 September 2012, and Stefan Mikaelsson, 17 September 2012; Henriksen, 'Sámi Self-Determination—Scope and Implementation'; Henriksen, 'Sámi Self-Determination: Autonomy and Economy'.

[88] Anaya, *The Situation of the Sámi People*, p. 12.

[89] Personal communication with Irja Seurujärvi-Kari, 24 September 2012; Henriksen, 'Sámi Self-Determination—Scope and Implementation'.

teaching plans, and the right to object to the Planning and Building Act. On the other hand, however, the Norwegian assembly has no effective authority over fisheries, mineral resources, media and, surprisingly, reindeer herding (primarily due to resistance from the herders' association).[90] The Finnish *Sámediggi* assesses itself that its decision-making powers are very limited, even in the sphere of language and culture, where the Parliament is formally a primary vehicle for the Sámi cultural autonomy.[91]

Due to the significance of land and resource issues for Sámi politics and culture, the most important recent development is probably the adoption and implementation of the Finnmark Act (2005) in Norway.[92] Following new legislation, the state transferred its land ownership in the county of Finnmark, constituting 95 per cent of the land and water in the county, to the so-called Finnmark Estate, where the county council and the Sámi Parliament are equally represented. Within the new system, Finnmark residents' usage rights to formerly state-owned lands are reviewed. The *Sámediggi* is entitled to draw up guidelines for non-cultivated land important for reindeer husbandry.[93] In connection with the land rights discussion and the Finnmark Act, some Sámi politicians in Norway have also argued for greater authority for the Parliament as well as influence on specific decisions regarding new mineral exploitation in Sápmi, and there have even been calls for the right to veto.[94] That is, however, a highly unlikely development.

Indigenous peoples have a right to maintain their own education systems[95] and vibrant Sámi languages and high-quality education are seen as prerequisites for Sámi development. Therefore, the area of language, culture, and education is where cultural autonomy of the Sámi finds its expression and where the Sámi parliaments have achieved degrees of autonomy greater than in any other policy field.[96] However, many Sámi leaders see the Sámi parliaments' authority and resources as still overly limited.[97] General national frameworks and parameters restrict the activities of the Sámi parliaments.[98] In Finland, language and culture are at the core of the Sámi Parliament's mandate, but for example language planning is conducted by a governmental research institute rather than the assembly.[99]

---

[90] Henriksen, 'Sámi Self-Determination: Autonomy and Economy', pp. 33–6; Magga, 'The Sámi Parliament', p. 309.

[91] Statement of Finnish Sámi Parliament on the Realization of Sámi People's Right to Self-Determination in Finland, 15 April 2010.

[92] Sara, 'Indigenous Governance of Self-Determination'.

[93] See also Ministry of Justice and Police and the Ministry of Local Government and Regional Development (Norway), *The Finnmark Act—A Guide* [Information brochure distributed in Finnmark], accessed 20 April 2012, <http://www.galdu.org/govat/doc/brochure_finnmark_act.pdf>.

[94] Jonas Karlsbakk, 'Sámi Parliament Wants Veto on Mineral Issues', *Barents Observer*, accessed 20 December 2012, <http://barentsobserver.com>.

[95] United Nations Declaration on the Rights of Indigenous Peoples, art 14.

[96] Michael Tkacik, 'Characteristics of Forms of Autonomy', *International Journal on Minority and Group Rights* vol. 15, no. 2 (2008), p. 375.

[97] For instance regarding the development of autonomous Sámi curricula.

[98] Henriksen, 'Sámi Self-Determination: Autonomy and Self-Government', pp. 21–6.

[99] Anaya, *The Situation of the Sámi People*; Statement of Finnish Sámi Parliament on the Realization of Sámi People's Right to Self-Determination in Finland, 15 April 2010.

A formidable challenge is the demographic shift with more and more Sámi living in southern urban centres.[100] That is particularly visible in Finland, where about 70 per cent of Sámi children live outside the Homeland Area, and are in a disadvantaged position when it comes to access to language education.[101] In Norway and Sweden, the governance of Sámi education is of a non-territorial character, but certain language rights are limited to core Sámi areas.

Sámi politicians see the Sámi parliaments' authority as still insufficient to realize the principle of self-determination and to provide the Sámi with genuine autonomy.[102] Among the demands are a greater role in the protection of cultural heritage and traditional knowledge, the ability to affect health and social services sectors in order to adjust them to the Sámi lifestyle, culture, and language, certain autonomous control over research priorities and funding, as well as, most importantly, authority over traditionally used land and resources. The draft Nordic Sámi Convention proposes a clearer logic for specifying the scope of the Sámi parliaments' competence. The *Sámediggis'* powers would depend on the importance of the issue for Sámi society: from consultation, via negotiation, towards independent decision-making.[103] However, it is nowadays clear for Sámi leaders that new responsibilities need to be followed by appropriate funding and capacity-building, otherwise the Sámi parliaments' powers would remain merely formal ones.

6.5.3 Funding and human resources

In principle, autonomy in internal and local affairs[104] includes the means of financing autonomous functions, indigenous institutions, and initiatives,[105] although this is dependent on the availability of resources. Moreover, the institutions cannot be seen as truly autonomous if each action and project undertaken requires state financial approval. Unsurprisingly, Sámi politicians see the issue of funding as a critical barrier for Sámi parliaments to become truly autonomous institutions for self-determination.[106] Firstly, the available financial resources are seen as inadequate and as not following the transfer of new competences.[107] The Finnish

[100] Henriksen, 'Sámi Self-Determination: Autonomy and Self-Government', pp. 22–3.
[101] Statement of Finnish Sámi Parliament on the Realization of Sámi People's Right to Self-Determination in Finland, 15 April 2010; personal communication with Irja Seurujärvi-Kari, 24 September 2012; Tkacik, 'Characteristics of Forms of Autonomy', p. 375.
[102] Henriksen, 'Sámi Self-Determination—Scope and Implementation'; Henriksen, 'Sámi Self-Determination: Autonomy and Self-Government'; Anaya, *The Situation of the Sámi People*; Tomaselli, 'Research Results'.
[103] Koivurova, 'The Draft Nordic Sámi Convention', pp. 279–93.
[104] United Nations Declaration on the Rights of Indigenous Peoples, art 4.
[105] International Labour Organization Convention no. 169, art 6.
[106] Personal communications with Irja Seurujärvi-Kari, 24 September 2012, Stefan Mikaelsson, 17 September 2012, and John Henriksen, 10 August 2012; Henriksen, 'Sámi Self-Determination—Scope and Implementation'; Henriksen, 'Sámi Self-Determination: Autonomy and Economy'; Anaya, *The Situation of the Sámi People*; Statement of Finnish Sámi Parliament on the Realization of Sámi People's Right to Self-Determination in Finland, 15 April 2010.
[107] Magga, 'The Sámi Parliament', pp. 306–7; Henriksen, 'Sámi Self-Determination: Autonomy and Economy', pp. 10–12.

Sámi Parliament has the lowest budget of the three representative bodies,[108] and financial constraints limit participation in meetings, where the Parliament's input is seen as important, including consultations and the pan-Sámi parliamentary cooperation.[109] In Sweden, it is claimed that the *Sámediggi*'s chairman (responsible for state Sámi policies) does not have sufficient resources to conduct steadily increasing responsibilities.[110] Thus, funding deficiencies undermine the legitimacy of Sámi parliaments. Various institutions[111] fall 'victim to power-play between the *Sámediggi* and the government' and their budgets seem lower than they would have been if they had remained under ministerial supervision.[112] Secondly, the Sámi parliaments are not in charge of all, or even a majority of, governmental spending on Sámi-specific issues. In Norway, only around 40 per cent of Sámi-specific expenditure is channelled via the Sámi Parliament, with the situation in Finland and Sweden being generally similar.[113] Thirdly, large portions of the budget expenditure of the Sámi parliaments are earmarked. Only 7 per cent of the Norwegian *Sámediggi*'s budget is freely disposable,[114] and in Sweden a majority of the funding is dedicated to *Sámediggi* responsibilities as a governmental agency.[115] The dependence on state budgetary decisions, therefore, restricts the independent design of the Sámi's own priorities, long-term plans, and projects.[116]

One reason for the difficulties in all three countries is the budgetary negotiation process.[117] In Norway, the Sámi Parliament remains the only publicly elected institution without its own revenue system, and the 2005 consultation agreement does not cover budget negotiations. Although a governmental assessment conducted in 2006 identified the need for greater involvement of the Parliament in budgetary process, so far little has changed.[118] A lack of good will is not necessarily the chief issue, as major barriers include such issues as poor coordination between ministries, centralized budget decision-making, cost-control focus, and the short institutional history of the *Sámediggis* as well as a lack of awareness among officials.[119] Nordic governments do argue that the situation is improving, including the construction of

---

[108] €1.6 m compared to over €40 m in Norway.

[109] Personal communication with Irja Seurujärvi-Kari, 24 September 2012; Henriksen, 'Sámi Self-Determination: Autonomy and Economy', p. 38; Statement of Finnish Sámi Parliament on the Realization of Sámi People's Right to Self-Determination in Finland, 15 April 2010.

[110] Personal communication with Stefan Mikaelsson, 17 September 2012; Anaya, *The Situation of the Sámi People*, p. 19.

[111] For instance the Sámi national theatre in Norway—*Beaivváš*.

[112] Henriksen, 'Sámi Self-Determination: Autonomy and Economy'.

[113] Henriksen, 'Sámi Self-Determination—Scope and Implementation', pp. 15–16, 31–2.

[114] Henriksen, 'Sámi Self-Determination—Scope and Implementation', pp. 16–17.

[115] Anaya, *The Situation of the Sámi People*, p. 12.

[116] Henriksen, 'Sámi Self-Determination—Scope and Implementation'; Henriksen, 'Sámi Self-Determination: Autonomy and Economy', pp. 11–16, 20–2, 36–7; Anaya, *The Situation of the Sámi People*; personal communications with Irja Seurujärvi-Kari, 24 September 2012, and Stefan Mikaelsson, 17 September 2012.

[117] Anaya, *The Situation of the Sámi People*, p. 12.

[118] Henriksen, 'Sámi Self-Determination: Autonomy and Economy'.

[119] Henriksen, 'Sámi Self-Determination: Autonomy and Economy', pp. 11–13; personal communications with John Henriksen, 10 August 2012, Stefan Mikaelsson, 17 September 2012, and Irja Seurujärvi-Kari, 24 September 2012.

modern parliament buildings in Karasjok and Inari, ongoing analyses of the parliaments' funding schemes, and increasing incorporation of Sámi priorities into state budgets. Indeed, the progress from the early 1990s, when basically all funding was earmarked, is noticeable.[120]

The financial challenges are furthermore mirrored by human resource constraints.[121] Despite improvements over time, the staff and time available for preparing consultation processes and for the analysis of documents are very limited in Finland.[122] In Norway, the Sámi Parliament is the institution with the fifth greatest number of documents to process after four key Norwegian ministries, while its staff number is among the lowest of all state institutions.[123]

6.5.4 Position within Sámi society

In order to exercise influence and become genuine vehicles for Sámi self-determination, Sámi parliaments need to win a strong position within Sámi communities, and that is not always evident. In Norway, reluctance, suspicion, and rejection were apparent before the Parliament's establishment, primarily due to fear of ethnic stigmatization (earlier Sámi identity was seen as a negative label) or because of the aforementioned reindeer herders' interests.[124] These political positions have not disappeared. During the 2013–17 term, two members (three during the 2009–2013 term) of the Norwegian Sámi Parliament came from the Progress Party, which openly calls for the dissolution of the Sámi elected body. Similar voices could be also heard in Sweden.[125] Moreover, the parliaments are troubled by internal conflicts, particularly in the past in Sweden, or by deficiencies in internal decision-making, as is the case with the often questioned, very strong position of the Parliament's President in Finland.[126] Critical challenges are also connected with Sámi demographics. The parliaments' work is focused, and reasonably so, on core Sámi livelihoods,[127] while more and more Sámi live in big cities, increasingly with interests and needs that diverge from the problems debated in the *Sámediggis*.[128] Furthermore, the issue of who is considered a Sámi has remained a problematic one, particularly in Finland. A recent decision of the Finnish Administrative Court to challenge negative decisions of the Sámi Parliament regarding enrolment to the Sámi register is a case in point. Arguments about infringement of indigenous self-determination by the Court and complaints by those denied a place in the

[120] Anaya, *The Situation of the Sámi People*; personal communication with Stefan Mikaelsson, 17 September 2012; Magga, 'The Sámi Parliament', pp. 306–7.
[121] Personal communication with Stefan Mikaelsson, 17 September 2012.
[122] Personal communication with Irja Seurujärvi-Kari, 24 September 2012.
[123] Henriksen, 'Sámi Self-Determination: Autonomy and Economy', p. 19.
[124] Josefsen, *The Sámi and the National Parliaments*; Semb, 'Sámi Self-Determination in the Making'.
[125] Personal communication with Stefan Mikaelsson, 17 September 2012.
[126] Personal communication with Irja Seurujärvi-Kari, 24 September 2012.
[127] Reindeer herding, fishing, hunting, handicrafts, land rights.
[128] Semb, 'Sámi Self-Determination in the Making'; personal communication with Irja Seurujärvi-Kari, 24 September 2012; Sillanpää, 'Government Responses to Saami Self-determination', pp. 98–9.

register are becoming a divisive factor in Finnish Sámi politics.[129] Some Finnish Sámi politicians are concerned that due to very mixed populations and livelihoods in Finnish Lapland, there could potentially be hundreds of thousands of people eligible to register as Sámi voters. Therefore, at the time of writing this chapter, activities are taking place to amend the Sámi Parliament Act in order, inter alia, to specify further the definition of a Sámi. The debate on the issue is, not surprisingly, particularly fervent.

As a result of the aforementioned challenges a certain amount of disappointment is visible. Unsatisfactory enrolment in the Sámi electoral registers, particularly in Norway[130] and Sweden,[131] as well as the electoral participation rate,[132] are signs of the failure of Sámi politicians to develop communication policies and make the Sámi public aware of the position and powers of the *Sámediggis*.[133] Often expectations of the Sámi community do not match the actual powers and financial capacities of the parliaments, which may undermine credibility.[134] There is also some criticism of the fact that the Sámi parliaments are anchored in the institutions of mainstream society and the spirit of the Sámi movement has been replaced by bureaucratic procedures and day-to-day politics.[135] However, the Sámi parliaments cannot be seen as the only incarnation of Sámi self-determination. Sámi professional organizations, especially cultural associations (handicrafts, teachers, artists), reindeer herding organizations as well as autonomous Sámi media still exercise a major influence on Sámi society and on national or local decision-making.[136] Traditional Sámi *siidas* or Swedish *samebys* (Sámi villages—units of local, mainly herding, governance) can also be seen as important elements of Sámi self-determination and autonomy.[137]

---

[129] Permanent Mission of Finland, Verbal Note (adopted 8 July 2012) GEN7062, accessed 28 December 2012, <https://spdb.ohchr.org/hrdb/21st/Finland_09.07.12_%281.2012%29.pdf>; Sámi Council, Observations by the Saami Council with regard to Finland's 20th, 21st, and 22nd Periodic Reports to the Committee for the Elimination of Racial Discrimination. To the Committee for the Elimination of Racial Discrimination, 12 August 2012, accessed 28 December 2012, <http://www2.ohchr.org>.

[130] In the 2009 elections: 13,890 persons registered out of 35,000–70,000 potentially eligible, with turnout among those registered at 68 per cent. For more details see the website of the Sámi Parliament in Norway, accessed 21 September 2012, <http://www.sam ediggi.no>.

[131] In 2011 there were about 8,000 registered voters out of 20,000–35,000 persons potentially eligible to register as voters; see also the website of the Sámi Parliament in Sweden, accessed 21 September 2012, <http://www.sametinget.se>.

[132] In the 2011 election in Finland, turnout was at 55.3 per cent; see also the website of the Sámi Parliament in Finland, accessed 21 September 2012, <http://www.samediggi.fi>.

[133] Henriksen, 'Sámi Self-Determination—Scope and Implementation'; personal communications with John Henriksen, 10 August 2012, and Stefan Mikaelsson, 17 September 2012.

[134] Magga, 'The Sámi Parliament'; Henriksen, 'Sámi Self-Determination: Autonomy and Economy'; personal communications with John Henriksen, 10 August 2012, Irja Seurujärvi-Kari, 24 September 2012, and Stefan Mikaelsson, 17 September 2012.

[135] Henriksen, 'Sámi Self-Determination—Scope and Implementation', pp. 17–18; Henriksen, 'Sámi Self-Determination: Autonomy and Economy', p. 13; personal communication with Irja Seurujärvi-Kari, 24 September 2012.

[136] Henriksen, 'Sámi Self-Determination—Scope and Implementation'; Henriksen, 'Sámi Self-Determination: Autonomy and Self-Government', pp. 33–4; Magga, 'The Sámi Parliament'.

[137] Anaya, *The Situation of the Sámi People*.

6.6 Conclusions

The Sámi have not determined what self-determination and autonomy entails and what the scope of Sámi autonomy should be.[138] This is not necessarily a problem. Ole Henrik Magga,[139] the first President of the Norwegian *Sámediggi*, James Anaya,[140] the UN Special Rapporteur, as well as a number of Sámi scholars[141] are of the opinion that the very existence of Sámi parliaments and their ongoing evolution is a sign of Sámi self-determination, understood as an incremental process of negotiating a new relationship with the modern Nordic nation-states.[142] The Sámi parliaments have been established as advisory bodies with the hope of gradually developing into institutions of some type of self-government and autonomous governance.[143] Lantto and Mörkenstam have stated that the institution of parliaments had provided the Sámi with 'some kind of secure political platform from which they [can] participate in the democratic procedure and legitimately counter-act the power of the nation states in which they live'.[144] The Nordic states are often perceived as a model of indigenous governance,[145] but there is an ongoing need to increase the *Sámediggis'* autonomy and self-governing authority.[146]

The evolution of Sámi parliamentarism has encountered various institutional, jurisdictional, demographic, administrative, and practical constraints.[147] The initial enthusiasm has been replaced, as is often the case, by day-to-day administrative and political realities, and even disappointment. The slow pace of change and opposition (for instance from the Progress Party in Norway) are hardly surprising, as the Sámi parliaments are relatively new institutions, and they challenge to a certain extent the modern concepts of equal citizenship as well as the unitary character of Nordic states.[148] The current legal position of the Sámi parliaments appears fairly strong but is not always mirrored by actual political and decision-making practices. Consultation mechanisms should be developed and strengthened, if Sámi participation is to be full, informed, genuine, and effective. There is a need for more transparency. Feedback mechanisms on how Sámi input is taken into

---

[138] Magga, 'The Sámi Parliament', pp. 303–4; Henriksen, 'Sámi Self-Determination—Scope and Implementation'; Henriksen, 'Sámi Self-Determination: Autonomy and Economy'.

[139] Magga, 'The Sámi Parliament'.   [140] Anaya, *The Situation of the Sámi People*.

[141] See, for instance, Henriksen, 'The Continuous Process of Recognition and Implementation of the Sámi People's Right to Self-Determination', pp. 27–40.

[142] See also website of the Sámi Parliament in Sweden, accessed 21 September 2012, <http://www.samediggi.se>.

[143] Lennard Sillanpää, 'A Comparative Analysis of Indigenous Rights in Fennoscandia', *Scandinavian Political Studies* vol. 20, no. 3 (1997): pp. 197–216.

[144] Patrick Lantto and Ulf Mörkenstam, 'Sámi Rights and Sámi Challenges: The Modernization Process and the Swedish Sámi Movement, 1886–2006', *Scandinavian Journal of History* vol. 33, no. 1 (2008): pp. 26–51.

[145] Anaya, *The Situation of the Sámi People*.

[146] The Human Rights Committee expressed a similar opinion.

[147] Semb, 'Sámi Self-Determination in the Making'.

[148] Tuulentie, 'National Rejection of Saami Claims in Finland', pp. 343–60.

account, as well as what is not and why, are crucial. The success of the Sámi parliaments in influencing decision-making depends largely on the access points in ministries and municipalities and the long-term development of these relations should be seen as one of the priorities.

Practicalities, such as financial schemes and human resources, have a major impact on the functioning of any institution and the Sámi parliaments are no exception. Funding should be sufficient to exercise expanding competences and gradually more financial resources should be freely at the disposal of the *Sámediggis* in order to allow for autonomous prioritization and planning. If the idea of indigenous autonomy is to be taken seriously, decision-making powers need to expand further and the parliaments should be able to take responsibility for more institutions, policies, and decisions.[149] In this way, they can become centres of Sámi political life.[150] However, it does not appear necessary to concentrate all aspects of Sámi autonomous existence within the Sámi parliaments, although the process of such concentration is perhaps inevitable in a long-term perspective.

What has had (and in the future will have) a major influence on the expansion of Sámi autonomy is a certain degree of policy diffusion and convergence between the Nordic states when it comes to Sámi affairs. The current process concerning the draft Nordic Sámi Convention may induce further policy harmonization.[151] The progress in pan-Sámi cooperation and joint decision-making appears a clear future development, although major difficulties both inside Sámi politics and within the Nordic states are to be expected. The draft Nordic Sámi Convention debate is also believed (especially in Finland and Sweden) to put greater emphasis on Sámi issues and further strengthen the pan-Sámi dimension.[152] If adopted, the Convention will open the door to a genuine trans-border pan-Sámi autonomy.

[149] Henriksen, 'Sámi Self-Determination—Scope and Implementation'; Anaya, *The Situation of the Sámi People*; Statement of Finnish Sámi Parliament on the Realization of Sámi People's Right to Self-Determination in Finland, 15 April 2010.

[150] Personal communication with Stefan Mikaelsson, 17 September 2012.

[151] Timo Koivurova and Adam Stepien, 'How International Law Has Influenced the National Policy and Law Related to Indigenous Peoples in the Arctic', *Waikato Law Review* vol. 19 (2011): pp. 135–6; Henriksen, 'Sámi Self-Determination: Autonomy and Economy', p. 33.

[152] Henriksen, 'Sámi Self-Determination: Autonomy and Economy', pp. 38–41; personal communications with Irja Seurujärvi-Kari, 24 September 2012, and Stefan Mikaelsson, 17 September 2012.

PART II

MINORITY SELF-MANAGEMENT

7

Minority Educational Self-Management in Canada

Daniel Bourgeois

7.1 Introduction

Educational self-management through distinct school boards is the most developed minority autonomy arrangement in Canada's official languages communities. School boards are public institutions created by municipalities and counties in the 1800s to build schools, hire teachers, and provide education based on provincial legislation. Education is a provincial purview in Canada, but it was not until the emergence of the provincial welfare states in the 1960s that provinces fully assumed responsibility over schools and the curriculum. Provinces nevertheless maintained locally elected school boards to manage provincial educational programmes while adapting them to local circumstances and decentralized to such boards critical authority and resources to ensure and nurture parents' involvement. Simultaneously, a push for minority educational self-management became an important measure to avoid the national unity crisis spawned by a century of malevolent provincial educational policies against the Francophone minority.

Canada was established in 1867 as an officially bilingual country, but the Anglophone majority in the provinces outside Québec often opposed Francophone parents' wish to educate their children in French. Education became 'the most explosive issue dividing French and English Canadians'[1] because schools are the most important public institution in socializing children and teaching the minority language. Policies against French-language education became critical causes of the national unity crisis fueled by Québec secessionism in the 1960s. To resolve the crisis, the Royal Commission on Bilingualism and Biculturalism recommended, among other things, that minority Francophone parents receive the right to have their children educated in French, that minority-language programmes be developed and managed by minority civil servants, and that the minority manage their particular educational needs. The recommendations would take form in 1982 as

---

[1] Joseph Eliot Magnet, *Official Languages in Canada* (Cowansville, Québec: Éditions Yvon Blais, 1995), p. 139.

Section 23 of the Canadian Charter of Rights. Since then, adapting programmes to local circumstances, decentralizing decision-making, and parent involvement have taken on a whole new meaning in minority Francophone communities. There, local is defined as 'cultural', decision-making is interpreted as 'self-management', and parent involvement is elevated to the status of 'autonomy'.

Francophones outside Québec wield educational self-management.[2] The right to minority-language education and the management of minority schools is enshrined in the Constitution. Twenty-nine minority school boards covering the nine provinces and territories outside Québec manage the French-language schools and their human, material, and financial resources. One of the school boards also manages the curriculum. Another declared itself 'an order of government'.[3] All twenty-nine Francophone school boards go beyond their pedagogical mandate to play a key cultural and community role that majority schools do not. The success achieved towards self-determination by minority Francophones in education has spawned similar minority institutional completeness strategies in health and municipal services.

This chapter will describe and analyse the historical and constitutional basis of minority educational self-management in Canada, minority institutional completeness in education, and the importance of distinct school boards in minority self-determination. It will also explain how the territorial limits imposed to establish schools do not apply to educational self-management exercised through school boards. The twenty-nine minority Francophone school boards may wield functional autonomy differently, but these democratic corporations are protected by constitutional rights and gifted with very significant human, material, and financial resources. They may not be an 'order of government', but minority school boards in Canada are increasingly behaving as such. They are the upper level in the continuum of autonomy arrangements.

7.2 Official Bilingualism in Canada

Canada is a bilingual country. French and English are its official languages because of historic, legal, and demographic reasons. Canada was a former colony of France (1604–1763) and Great Britain (1763–1867). Political vestiges and identities remain from both epochs. Its founding constitution, the 1867 British North America Act (hereafter BNA Act), established a bilingual federal state as well as

---

[2] Michael Behiels, *Canada's Francophone Minority Communities: Constitutional Renewal and the Winning of School Governance* (Montreal and Kingston: McGill-Queen's University Press, 2004).

[3] The Canadian Constitution identifies two *de jure* orders of government: federal and provincial. A popular but erroneous perception considers municipalities as a third order, but provinces can establish, amalgamate, or eliminate municipalities at will and can delegate whatever powers they see fit to their municipalities. Since provinces must establish minority school boards and cannot modify them at will and must award minority school boards specific exclusive powers protected by charter rights and jurisprudence, the argument goes that minority school boards are a de facto 'order of government'.

bilingual provinces in Québec and Manitoba (in 1870). Eight out of ten Canadians have French or English as their mother tongue, and most of the immigrants who represent Canada's remaining 20 per cent speak English or French at home.

However, official bilingualism was limited and mostly symbolic during the first century of Confederation. Section 133 of the BNA Act limited official bilingualism to federal and Québec courts, acts, regulations, minutes, and parliamentary debates. Anglophones blocked most efforts by Francophones to expand bilingualism beyond this minimal framework. Also, official bilingualism established in Manitoba in 1870 by the Francophone majority was illegally eliminated in 1890 by Anglophones once they formed the majority. It would take a century to overturn the decision.[4] Also, even in Québec, where Francophones formed the vast majority of the population, federal services were not always available in French in 1967. Québec's secessionist movement would change the Canadian state in the 1960s.

Ottawa's response was to establish a Royal Commission on Bilingualism and Biculturalism in 1963 and to implement most of its 150 recommendations, including adopting an Official Languages Act.[5] The 1969 Act recognized French and English as Canada's official languages, guaranteed the allocation of public services and communications in both official languages from federal institutions from their headquarters and their peripheral offices where numbers warranted, and established an ombudsman to watch over the actions of federal institutions in respect of the legislation. The Act was revamped in 1988, notably to include the right to work in either official language within federal institutions, and again in 2005 to force federal institutions to take 'positive measures' to contribute to the vitality of the Anglophone minority in Québec and the Francophone minority in the other nine provinces and the three northern territories.[6]

Federal measures stopped the hemorrhaging in minority Francophone communities at the mercy of North American anglicization and helped prevent Québec secession in 1981 and 1995. However, as the Royal Commission duly noted: 'The provision of federal government services in both official languages would be useful, but such measures would be incomplete if the many vital responsibilities of provincial and local governments were disregarded.'[7] The survival and vitality of the official language minority communities (OLMCs) depend mostly on education, health, and other provincial responsibilities.

The federal system thus gave Francophones in Québec control over many key functions—education, health, welfare, justice, municipalities—and the power to adopt the French Charter in 1977[8] and other measures to protect and enhance

---

[4] *Reference re Manitoba Language Rights* [1985] 1 SCR 721.

[5] An Act Respecting the Status of the Official Languages of Canada, 19 Elizabeth II, ch 0–2, Canada, 1969.

[6] An Act Respecting the Status and Use of the Official Languages of Canada, 37 Elizabeth II, ch 38, Canada, 1988.

[7] Royal Commission on Bilingualism and Biculturalism, *Official Languages* (Ottawa: Queen's Printer, 1967), p. 90.

[8] Charter of the French Language, Québec, Assemblée nationale, SQ 1977, ch 5.

French in that province, but it did little for Francophones in a minority setting outside Québec. Canada's first century repeatedly witnessed sociolinguistic conflicts between a vulnerable Francophone minority and intolerant Anglophone majorities in control of provincial functions and institutions. Education, especially when Catholic schools were involved, was the principal battlefield.

Since 1969, all provinces have adopted significant measures that have contributed to the survival and vitality of their respective Francophone minority communities.[9] Most notably, all Anglophone-majority provinces agreed to insert a Charter of Rights and Freedoms in the constitution in 1982.[10] Section 23 provides significant minority rights to distinct schools and the management thereof. Most provinces also agreed to provide health services in French where numbers warrant, notably since 1999. Canada is a far different country than it was fifty years ago when the Royal Commission was appointed.

7.3 Educational Self-Management

Education was 'the most explosive issue dividing French and English Canadians [...] since the origin of racial enmity in Canada; so it remains today'.[11] Francophone minority communities were victims in all conflicts prior to 1969. Section 93 of the BNA Act forced Québec to ensure Protestant (Anglophone) minority education. No major conflicts occurred in that province in the first century of Confederation. Section 93 imposed similar obligations on Ontario concerning its Catholic (Francophone) minority. The province of Ontario disregarded its constitutional obligation, notably by adopting Regulation 17 in 1912 to forbid the use of French as a language of instruction after the first two grades. That decision was legitimate because the constitution protected only religious instruction, but in practice, 'the harshest language law ever enacted in Canada' was 'designed to force the involuntary assimilation of an entire generation of young Franco-Ontarians, and to frighten away any future migrants from Quebec who might hope to raise their families in the ancestral language'.[12] A national uproar ensued.

The situation was no better in the other provinces where Anglophones formed the majority. Only a few years after Confederation, New Brunswick and Prince Edward Island (PEI) adopted public schooling legislation that banned Catholic priests, nuns, and textbooks from Acadian schools. Two men died in riots in New Brunswick. Manitoba was founded by Francophones and Métis in 1870 as a bilingual province, but once Anglophones formed the majority, they illegally repealed

[9] Daniel Bourgeois, Donald Dennie, Wilfrid Denis, and Marc L. Johnson, *Provincial and Territorial Government Contributions to the Development of Francophone Minority Communities* (Moncton: Canadian Institute for Research on Linguistic Minorities, 2007).
[10] Canadian Charter of Rights and Freedoms—Constitution Act, 1982. 31 Elizabeth II, ch 11, Canada, 1982.
[11] Magnet, *Official Languages in Canada*, p. 139.
[12] Scott Reid, *Lament for a Notion* (Vancouver: Arsenal Pulp Press, 1993), p. 53.

French-language rights and privileges. Other nefarious provincial policies in education over the first century of Confederation enticed Francophone minority communities to seek distinct schools and 'educational self-management'.[13]

The mistreatment of Francophones outside Québec throughout the first century of Confederation was one of the key motives behind the Québec secessionist movement. This prompted the Government of Canada to establish a Royal Commission on Bilingualism and Biculturalism in 1963. It was mandated to 'recommend what steps should be taken to develop the Canadian Confederation on the basis of an equal partnership between the two founding races' (read: official sociolinguistic groups), notably in education even if the provinces had 'constitutional jurisdiction over education'.[14]

In its first report, the Commission concluded that 'the unwillingness of the English-speaking majority to recognize the right of French-speaking parents to educate their children in French' was one of the main causes of the national unity crisis and Québec secessionism.[15] Since the school 'is the basic agency for maintaining language and culture, and without this essential resource neither can remain strong', it recommended 'that the right of Canadian parents to have their children educated in the official language of their choice be recognized in the educational system'.[16]

Its second report, titled *Education*, would add key supporting facts, arguments, and recommendations. In summary, it explained how schools were the most significant tool for socialization and the transmission of language and culture outside the home. It also explained how the absence of such schools, as well as bilingual schools, was in great part responsible for the assimilation of Francophones in minority settings. It recommended distinct French-language schools outside Québec, at least where numbers warranted.

The Commission also recommended educational self-management, albeit timidly. Indeed, although it had elsewhere argued in favour of 'self-determination' and 'distinct institutions',[17] the Commission shied away from autonomous minority school boards and complete educational self-management because it feared that this would produce more harm than good. At that time, throughout Canada, the increasingly providential provincial states were centralizing power and taxation from the local school boards to their respective departments of education in order to standardize and improve all educational services. In New Brunswick, for instance, the centralization of education services was part of the Equal Opportunities Program intended to provide the same quantity and quality of services in the poor, rural, and French-speaking areas of the province as were found in

[13] Joseph Eliot Magnet, 'Minority-Language Education Rights', in *The New Constitution and the Charter of Rights*, edited by E. P. Belobaba and E. Gertner (Toronto: Butterworths, 1983), pp. 195–216, 211.

[14] Royal Commission on Bilingualism and Biculturalism, *Official Languages*, p. 174.

[15] Royal Commission on Bilingualism and Biculturalism, *Official Languages*, p. i.

[16] Royal Commission on Bilingualism and Biculturalism, *Official Languages*, pp. 122–3.

[17] Royal Commission on Bilingualism and Biculturalism, *Official Languages*, pp. xlv, xxxiv.

the richer, urban, and English-speaking areas.[18] The Commission feared that small minority-language school boards would miss out on the benefits of state support and centralization, notably task specialization. Indeed, the smaller minority school boards might not be able to 'provide equivalent educational opportunities'.[19]

The homogenizing providential states did raise some concerns, but the Commission did not recommend educational self-management as a counter-measure. Consequently, even if minority students attended distinct schools, they would be governed alongside majority students attending majority schools by the same joint local school board.[20] However, that local school board had to ensure minority representation and, if numbers warranted, had to appoint a minority-language committee to oversee the management of minority schools and the curriculum offered therein. Moreover, the Commission believed minority schools would have to follow the same provincial education programme provided in majority schools.[21] However, the Commission also recommended that the provincial curriculum in the social sciences be adapted to the 'particular situation' of minority students and their communities and that the minority-language programmes be developed and administered by members of the minority community.[22]

This is how the Commission conceived the delicate balance between the integration of the minority system within the providential provincial system to ensure the same level of education and a 'particular administration' that would reflect and respect the minority's values and meet its specific needs.[23] The Commission did not delve into details, leaving the task to experts. Although it shied from full educational self-government, its reports would eventually convince the courts to produce the same result. Its recommendation for distinct schools would be adopted as Section 23 of the 1982 Charter of Rights and Freedoms, and the jurisprudence on Section 23 would produce minority educational self-management.

7.4 Constitutional Rights to Minority Schools and the Management Thereof

Minority education rights in Canada were adopted after many arduous political negotiations between the federal and provincial governments from 1967 to 1981. Bilateral negotiations began soon after the publication of and in reaction to the Royal Commission's first report. The Prime Minister of Canada and the ten provincial Premiers launched a series of high-profile public meetings intent

---

[18] Robert Young, 'The Programme of Equal Opportunity: An Overview', in *The Robichaud Era, 1960–1970*, edited by Roger Ouellette (Moncton: Canadian Institute for Research on Regional Development, 2001), pp. 23–35.

[19] Royal Commission on Bilingualism and Biculturalism, *Official Languages*, p. 10.

[20] Royal Commission on Bilingualism and Biculturalism, *Official Languages*, p. 177.

[21] Royal Commission on Bilingualism and Biculturalism, *Official Languages*, pp. 153–4.

[22] Royal Commission on Bilingualism and Biculturalism, *Official Languages*, pp. 173–6.

[23] Royal Commission on Bilingualism and Biculturalism, *Official Languages*, p. 171.

on repatriating the constitutional text from the British Parliament and inserting therein a charter of rights. They achieved success in 1971, but Québec's Premier withdrew his support soon afterwards. It would take a decade before the goal would be achieved in 1981, although Québec again refused to sign the agreement.

Section 23 is the cornerstone of minority education rights in Canada. Citizens of Canada (a) whose first language learned and still understood is that of the English or French linguistic minority population of the province in which they reside, or (b) who have received their primary school instruction in Canada in English or French and reside in a province where the language in which they received that instruction is the language of the English or French linguistic minority population of the province, or (c) of whom any child has received or is receiving primary or secondary school instruction in English or French in Canada, have the right to have their children receive primary and secondary school instruction in that language in that province. The right applies wherever in the province the number of children of citizens who have such a right is sufficient to warrant the provision to the children out of public funds of minority language instruction and includes, where the number of those children so warrants, the right to have the children receive that instruction in minority language educational facilities provided out of public funds. In short, Canadian parents who meet one of the three qualification criteria have the right to send their children to minority-language schools and these schools must be provided wherever numbers warrant.

Minority education rights to distinct schools and the management thereof have been specified in great part by the courts. The jurisprudence on Section 23 borrowed extensively from the research and the assumptions of the Royal Commission. As noted, the Commission shied away from recommending full minority educational self-management, but it recommended minority control over the linguistic and cultural aspects of the curriculum. The Supreme Court of Canada would eventually interpret Section 23 generously by, among other things, establishing the principles of minority educational self-management.

The most important decision occurred in 1990. In *Mahé v. Alberta*,[24] the Supreme Court rejected local minority parents' request for a distinct French-language school board because the number of students was insufficient. Instead, the Court awarded them seats on the local English-language school board. The Court thereby established the principle of the 'sliding scale'—the higher the number of parents, the more powers they could manage exclusively—to explain why it decided to limit minority autonomy in 1990.

Nevertheless, the Court established five other significant principles that would eventually generate educational self-management. First, it stated the historic purpose of Section 23: it exists to 'repair past torts' and to 'preserve and promote the two official languages of Canada, and their respective cultures' in the future. Consequently, minority education rights must be interpreted and applied generously. Provinces must thus ensure that minority education contributes to minority

---

[24] *Mahé v. Alberta* [1990] 1 SCR 342.

vitality: 'the answers to the questions should ideally be guided by that which will most effectively encourage the flourishing and preservation of the French-language minority in the province'.[25]

Second, after quoting the Royal Commission's argument that language is a 'key to cultural development' and that distinct minority schools 'are essential for the development of both official languages and cultures', the Court concluded that minority schools 'provide community centres where the promotion and preservation of minority language culture can occur; they provide needed locations where the minority community can meet and facilities which they can use to express their culture'.[26] Contrary to majority schools, minority schools have a cultural and community mandate. Thus, education in the OLMCs must not only ensure academic results but also linguistic, cultural, and community vitality.

Third, it established educational self-government by giving precedence to the more precise French-language version of Section 23 over the English-language version the Premiers had agreed to in 1981. The English version refers to 'minority language educational facilities provided out of public funds' while the French version refers to 'des établissements d'enseignement de la minorité linguistique'. The Court ruled that the word *de* (of) meant that the distinct minority schools 'belong to' the minority.[27] It has been argued that translation established minority educational self-management in Canada,[28] but the Supreme Court would not have come to that conclusion without the Royal Commission's arguments. This principle means that once a minority school is established, the minority parents—whether their numbers warrant a distinct school board or merely a seat or two on the local joint school board—must wield 'exclusive control' over the linguistic and cultural aspects of the education system. The Court stated that the parents, through their representatives on the majority-language school board or their own minority-language school board, were to control the educational programmes, the financial resources, and the human resources (teachers and administrators). A decade later, the Court added two more powers to the list of five exclusive powers identified in 1990: the determination of the minority's educational needs and the prerogative to establish minority schools and to determine their location.[29]

Fourth, the Court ruled that minority education is entitled to additional funds if required: 'the funds allocated for the minority language schools must be at least equivalent on a per student basis to the funds allocated to the majority schools. Special circumstances may warrant an allocation for minority language schools that exceeds the per capita allocation for majority schools'.[30] Provinces must therefore

[25] *Reference re Public Schools Act (Manitoba)* [1993] 1 SCR 858.
[26] *Mahé v. Alberta*, 346.   [27] *Mahé v. Alberta*, 370.
[28] Jean-Pierre Proulx, 'Le choc des Chartes: histoire des régimes juridiques québécois et canadien en matière de langue d'enseignement' [Clash of Charters: History of Québec and Canadian Legal Systems in Language Education], *Revue juridique Thémis* vol. 23 (1989): p. 65.
[29] *Arsenault-Cameron v. Prince Edward Island* [2000] 1 SCR 3.
[30] *Mahé v. Alberta*, p. 378.

ensure that the quality of education in minority schools is equal to the one provided in majority schools, and if required, provinces must provide additional funding to minority schools to achieve equality of results.

Lastly, the Supreme Court also outlined the provinces' obligations: they must repair past torts and ensure they do not occur again, provide and promote minority language education, meet the particular educational needs of the minority, ensure that minority language education is of exemplary quality, and restructure their administrative structures to favour minority language education. The last obligation means that Provinces must establish minority school boards to which they grant the 'exclusive' powers.

7.5 School Boards and Minority Institutional Completeness

School boards were established generations ago by provincial legislation to manage educational services in local public schools. In all provinces, an Education Act gives the ultimate authority to the Minister of Education and his/her department, but local school boards are also required because they enable parent involvement, a critical component in effective education, and because civil servants in the provincial headquarters could not manage all the resources and make all the decisions from a central office.

The growth of the provincial welfare states had two opposite impacts on local school boards. On the one hand, the provinces centralized many of their powers to departments of education and most eliminated their taxation authority. On the other, they were regrouped into larger regional entities, thus providing them with scale economies and specialized staff to improve their effectiveness and legitimacy. Their size, powers, and legitimacy have evolved since the 1960s but school boards remain essential institutions.

School boards are local public corporations tasked to implement provincial legislation and policies, albeit with some local adaptations, and to manage the financial, human, and material resources provided by the Province through the annual budgetary process. Boards hire and supervise a superintendent—the Chief Administrative Officer—who implements the legislation and policies, and manages the resources on a daily basis. Board members are elected by universal suffrage every three or four years, depending on the provincial legislation. Elections are usually held on the same day as elections for municipal councils and health boards. Eligible electors must declare for which school board they will vote—the minority or the majority school board in the area—and they will receive one ballot because electors can only vote for one board even if they can send one child to a majority school and another to a minority school. In Ontario, voting is further complicated by the presence of four overlapping school boards in the same area—Francophone Catholic, Francophone Public, Anglophone Catholic, Anglophone Public—but few complications have arisen. Electors and candidates for minority school boards must be Canadian citizens aged 18 or older and qualify for Section 23 rights. Members should be able to read and converse in the minority language in order to participate effectively during Board meetings, but this is not an obligation in many provinces. Many majority boards in the larger urban centres have full-time members, but all the minority school board members are volunteers who receive a small stipend for their time, most of which is spent preparing for and participating in monthly meetings. Boards average nine members.

As noted, although it shied away from minority school boards, the Royal Commission fully appreciated the significance of distinct sub-state institutions to OLMC survival and vitality in Canada. It was aware of the importance of minority institutional completeness outlined by one of its researchers.[31] Raymond Breton's framework posits that relations between ethnic/linguistic/racial groups are embedded in social, economic, and political institutions since many social relations operate within institutions. Institutions have a life of their own that extends beyond the life of their participants. A minority sociolinguistic group often calls upon institutions to give its members the opportunity to live their lives in their language. Such institutions make group membership an asset rather than a liability within the societal structure dominated by another group. They facilitate the minority's social cohesion by shaping the individual members' behaviour. The institutions exist first and foremost to help their members achieve equality with the majority in terms of symbolic and material resources, although Breton conceded that minority-majority conflicts exist even where inequalities in income, for instance, are not a significant issue. Breton also distinguished between institutional segmentation and heterogeneity. Minority groups create segmented (parallel) institutions when they want to segregate from the majoritarian institutions; they establish heterogeneous institutions when they wish to integrate the majoritarian society. The same types of institutions can be used to differentiate or integrate the minority group.

Sub-state institutions are sanctioned by the state and provide legitimacy to the minority policymakers at their helm through regular elections by general suffrage. Sub-state institutions also have access to significant public funds and human resources that can support nationalist projects that the state would not.[32] For instance, a minority school board could offer a course on Acadian nationalism. Budgets are determined by the Department of Education, but school boards have a lot of discretion. Minority-controlled sub-state institutions are better able to ensure services in the minority language and to promote the minority's language,

[31] Raymond Breton, 'Institutional Completeness of Ethnic Communities and the Personal Relations of Immigrants', *American Journal of Sociology* vol. 70 (1964): pp. 193–205. See also Raymond Breton, *Ethnic Relations in Canada—Institutional Dynamics* (Montreal and Kingston: McGill-Queen's University Press, 2005).

[32] The term 'nationalist' means someone who tries to obtain political independence for his or her nation. However, political independence is relative. Acadian nationalists sought an Acadian province detached from the rest of New Brunswick in the 1970s but they no longer do. Instead, they seek independence in the administrative spheres of governance. They could thus be called 'administrative nationalists'. See Daniel Bourgeois, 'Administrative Nationalism', *Administration and Society* vol. 39, no. 5 (2007): pp. 631–55.

culture, and identity. Sub-state institutions, including school boards, can therefore be used by the minority, ironically, to counter state uniformity and homogeneity.[33]

Self-determination and distinct institutions were essential components of official bilingualism and biculturalism, but the Royal Commission did not recommend educational self-management even if education was the most explosive issue and the most important public service in OLMC survival and vitality. Its research and arguments nevertheless enticed the courts to establish minority educational self-management. The Supreme Court refused to grant a distinct minority school board in the *Mahé* case, yet the same ruling granted to the minority a 'political right to manage' its schools.[34] It also ruled that school boards 'constitute, for the minority, institutions which it can consider its own with all this entails in terms of opportunity of working in its own language and of sharing a common culture, interests and understanding and being afforded the fullest measure of representation and control. These are particularly important in setting overall priorities and responding to the special educational needs of the minority'.[35] Thus, provinces must establish minority school boards and they can only modify their number and scope if it benefits the minority. The Court also agreed to force recalcitrant provinces to comply with the affirmative remedies imposed by the courts in a timely manner.[36] For those reasons, among others, some have argued that minority school boards in Canada have become an 'order of government'.[37]

Since 1990, all provinces and territories have established minority school boards that cover the entire nation and serve in principle all minority students. Nine minority English-language school boards cover the entire province of Québec and twenty-nine minority French-language school boards cover the rest of Canada. Minority schools are scattered throughout the country but they are concentrated in a limited number of areas where the minority forms a critical mass. Minority schools are thus established according to the territorial approach defined by the 'where numbers warrant' provision of Section 23. However, minority educational self-management has no geographical limits. Indeed, although school boards have defined service areas, these thirty-eight areas cover the entire country. In addition, regardless of the number of students and schools in each province—260 students attend five minority schools in Newfoundland and Labrador while 110,000 students attend 270 minority schools in Québec—all thirty-eight minority-language school boards should wield the same exclusive powers outlined by the courts since 1990.

Some minority school boards, however, wield more powers than others. For over a decade, the Acadian school board of Nova Scotia has managed the curriculum.

---

[33] Bourgeois, 'Administrative Nationalism', pp. 631–55.   [34] *Mahé v. Alberta*, p. 359.

[35] *Mahé v. Alberta*, p. 373.

[36] *Doucet-Boudreau v. Nova Scotia (Minister of Education)* [2003] 3 SCR 62.

[37] Daniel Bourgeois, 'Bilan de la pleine gestion scolaire assurée par l'application de l'article 23 de la Charte canadienne des droits et libertés' [Assessment of the School Management Guaranteed by Section 23 of the Canadian Charter of Rights and Freedoms], in *Recherche en éducation en milieu minoritaire francophone*, edited by Yves Henry and Catherine Mougeot (Ottawa: Presses de l'Université d'Ottawa, 2007), pp. 212–17.

The Provincial Department of Education gave it relatively free rein to adopt and implement all programmes within provincial guidelines. It also gave the minority school board the human resources to do so; staff were previously employed by the Department. Other minority school boards focus on minority cultural pedagogy: how to adapt the curriculum to the minority's cultural specificities and how to integrate the minority's culture within the curriculum—for instance, teaching the Acadian patois alongside standard French. A school board in south-east New Brunswick declared itself 'an order of government' to protect its decisions and its resources from the provincial government. All minority school boards go beyond their pedagogical mandate to play a key cultural and community role, although some play that role more proactively than others. Most school boards collaborate with local minority volunteer groups and other minority institutions—for instance, municipalities and credit unions—on mutually beneficial projects like minority book fairs and concerts. Minority school boards may not be 'an order of government', but many behave as if they were.

7.6 Parachuting Principles

Success achieved in establishing minority self-management in education through minority (sub-state) institutional completeness, especially since 1990, spawned similar strategies in other public sectors like health and municipal services. There are no constitutional rights to minority hospitals. Section 92 of the BNA Act stipulates that hospitals are provincial institutions while it is silent regarding health care in Canada's official languages. Nevertheless, minority self-management in the health sector has taken root, notably in Ontario and New Brunswick. Similar progress has been achieved with municipal services. The Francophone minority has thus achieved some success in parachuting the principles of educational self-management obtained via court cases onto other sub-state institutions like hospitals and municipalities.

Two Supreme Court decisions on minority language rights—*Reference re Quebec Secession* in 1998[38] and *Beaulac* in 1999[39]—opened the door for critical court victories in the health sector. The first decision ruled that 'the protection of minorities' was one of the four unwritten underlying principles of the Canadian constitution, alongside federalism, democracy, and the rule of law. The second ruled that language rights were not merely individual rights to public services, including court procedures, but also collective rights that nurture an individual's collective identity. Consequently, language rights 'must in all cases be interpreted purposively, in a manner consistent with the preservation and development of official language communities in Canada'.[40] Language rights 'impose on the state the responsibility of ensuring that these rights are respected, which imposes in

---

[38] *Reference re Secession of Quebec* [1998] 2 SCR 217.
[39] *R. v. Beaulac* [1999] 1 SCR 768.   [40] *R. v. Beaulac*, 768, para 25.

turn certain obligations. [...] Language rights are not negative rights, or passive rights; they can only be enjoyed if the means are provided. [...Thus,] the freedom to choose is meaningless in the absence of a duty of the State to take positive steps to implement language guarantees'.[41] Language rights require positive government measures.

The timing of these decisions was opportune for Franco-Ontarians in their struggle against the Ontario government's effort to close the Montfort Hospital.[42] Inspired by *Secession* and *Beaulac*, the Ontario Court of Appeal ruled that the Province's decision was unconstitutional because it did not respect the unwritten principle of minority protection. The Province should protect 'Montfort's broader role as an important linguistic, cultural, and educational institution, vital to the minority francophone population of Ontario'.[43] Montfort's larger-than-health institutional role includes 'maintaining the French language, transmitting the francophone culture, and fostering solidarity in the Franco-Ontarian minority'.[44] As with minority school boards, French-language institutions like hospitals are most effective in ensuring the permanency and quality of services in French, access to services in French, francophone representation in the governance and management of the institution, and accountability.[45] The hospital has since been transformed into the pillar of a province-wide French-language medical services and education network. Franco-Ontarians are elected by their peers to the hospital's board and manage the network with the dual purpose of providing health services and minority institutional governance.

The ruling bolstered other minorities' quest for sub-state institutions and self-management in the health sector. Acadians in Moncton, New Brunswick used similar arguments to protect their Dumont Hospital. They were ambivalent when the Province took over hospitals from municipalities, counties, and religious orders in 1967: some greeted provincial centralization and funding with open arms, but others opposed the loss of decision-making ability in favour of the Department of Health.[46] Opposition grew over the years as the Province multiplied its centralization efforts and came to a boil in 2002 when it refused to designate the Dumont as a 'francophone' institution before finally capitulating.[47] Dumont could thus maintain its distinction from another tertiary hospital nearby—the Moncton Hospital. The south-east region of New Brunswick was able to maintain administrative duality in health: one regional health authority managed the English-language hospitals and clinics and another overlapping regional authority managed the

---

[41] *R. v. Beaulac*, 768, para 20.

[42] Michel Gratton, *Montfort—La lutte d'un peuple* [Montfort—The Struggle of People] (Ottawa: Centre franco-ontarien de ressources pédagogiques, 2003).

[43] *Lalonde v. Ontario (Commission de restructuration des services de santé)* [2001] OJ No. 4768, 56 OR (3d) 505 (CA), para 188.

[44] *Lalonde v. Ontario*, para 171.   [45] *Lalonde v. Ontario*, para 188.

[46] Daniel Bourgeois, 'Acadians', Symposium: 'Autonomy Arrangements in the World', Flensburg, Germany: European Centre for Minority Issues, 14–15 September 2012.

[47] Daniel Bourgeois and Yves Bourgeois, 'Minority Sub-State Institutional Completeness', *International Review of Sociology* vol. 22, no. 2 (2001): pp. 293–304.

French-language hospitals. The six other regions of the Province had a single, common regional health authority. In 2008, the Province replaced the eight health authorities with or by two regional health networks—one for Francophones, another for Anglophones. The overlap in south-east New Brunswick was maintained. Thus, the Dumont Hospital is managed by the Vitalité Regional Health Network while the Moncton Hospital is managed by the Horizon Regional Health Network. The Province also agreed to let Acadians elect the majority of members of the Vitalité Network's Board. Acadians wield less power than in the 1960s but they consider Dumont and Vitalité as 'their' institutions.

Municipalities, like schools and hospitals, are the purview of the Provinces. As with education and health care, municipal services are important to language communities. Over 200 of the 5,000 municipalities in Canada contain a significant number or ratio of language minority members. In fact, the official language minority living in most of these 200 municipalities forms the majority of citizens. Since 1969 but mostly since 1988, municipalities have contributed to their minority's vitality.[48] This is mostly due to minorities taking control of their municipal levers for that purpose, but the Parliament of Canada also contributed to this progress by adding Section 43.1(d) to the Official Languages Act in 1988 to force the Government of Canada to 'encourage and assist provincial governments to support the development of English and French linguistic minority communities generally and, in particular, to offer provincial and *municipal* services in both English and French' (emphasis added). Municipalities have since become nationalist targets.

However, courts have not promoted official languages in municipalities like they have in hospitals. In Québec, Anglophones who formed the majority of citizens in small municipalities in the western half of Montréal Island asked the courts to overturn the Province's 1998 amalgamations with municipalities with a Francophone majority. The claim was rejected on the basis that municipalities are provincial institutions that have no linguistic obligations.[49] Acadians in New Brunswick fared better. As provincial institutions, municipalities have linguistic obligations under the provincial Official Languages Act.[50] Municipalities in New Brunswick wherein the minority forms at least 20 per cent of the population must thus provide bilingual services and communications.[51]

Bilingual services and communications did not suffice. Acadian nationalists also sought municipal institutional completeness. In 1993, after the Government of New Brunswick tried but failed to amalgamate the Acadian-majority city of Dieppe with the English-majority city of Moncton, Acadian nationalists in Dieppe launched efforts to establish that municipality as a 'Francophone' city

---

[48] Daniel Bourgeois and Yves Bourgeois, 'Les municipalités canadiennes et les langues officielles' [Canadian Municipalities and Official Languages], *Canadian Political Science Review* vol. 44, no. 4 (2011): pp. 789–806.

[49] *Baie d'Urfé (Ville) c. Québec (P.G.)* [2001] RJQ 1589 (C.S.); *Westmount (Ville) c. Québec (P.G.)* [2001] RJQ 2520 (C.A.).

[50] *Charlebois v. Mowat* [2001] NBCA 117.

[51] New Brunswick Official Languages Act, 2002, Fredericton: New Brunswick Legislature, ch 0–0.5.

and to erect linguistic identity markers to thwart any future provincial threat of amalgamation.[52]

In Ontario, some municipalities adopted by-laws to impose bilingual commercial signage on new businesses. In *Galganov v. Russell*, the court ruled that the municipality could play a role in 'the protection of its French speaking community'.[53] The minority may thus use municipal institutions on its behalf[54]: 'Russell has established the vulnerability of the French language in its territory and this is the reason for the language policy reflected in the By-law.' The court thus gave credence to Breton's expert testimony to that effect: 'an institutional or governmental recognition of linguistic diversity is based on the desire for social cohesion and the sense of belonging for all groups'.[55]

7.7 Challenges

Minority educational self-government is now a *de jure* reality in Canada,[56] although there are de facto gaps between what the jurisprudence prescribes and what the provinces have conceded.[57] Nevertheless, the pendulum is clearly on the minority's side. In addition to forcing provinces to establish minority school boards and awarding them 'exclusive powers' in education, the Supreme Court also ruled that the 'establishment of programs of instruction' is an exclusive power of the minority school board because 'the majority cannot be expected to understand and appreciate all of the diverse ways in which educational practices may influence the language and culture of the minority'.[58] It would indeed be 'foolhardy to assume that Parliament intended to […] leave the sole control of the program development and delivery with the English majority. If such were the case, a majority language group could soon wreak havoc upon the rights of the minority and could soon render such a right worthless'.[59] However, the Court also ruled that the provinces could establish the 'curriculum'. This begs the question: what takes precedence— 'programs of instruction' determined by the minority school boards or the 'curriculum' determined by Departments of Education? This is a critical issue, yet no administrators working for either minority school boards or for provincial or territorial Departments of Education know the difference between the two judicial concepts, including Nova Scotia where the Government has delegated curriculum

---

[52] Daniel Bourgeois and Yves Bourgeois, 'Territory, Institutions and National Identity: The Case of Acadians in Greater Moncton, Canada', *Urban Studies* vol. 42, no. 7 (2005): pp. 1123–38.

[53] *Galganov v. Russell (Township)* [2010] ONSC 4566, paras 177–8.

[54] *Galganov v. Russell*, para 180.   [55] *Galganov v. Russell*, para 82.

[56] Behiels, *Canada's Francophone Minority Communities*.

[57] Daniel Bourgeois, *Vers la pleine gestion scolaire francophone en milieu minoritaire* [Towards Complete Management of the Francophone School in Minority Communities] (Moncton: Institut Canadien de recherche sur les minorités linguistiques, 2004).

[58] *Mahé v. Alberta*, 344.

[59] *Reference re Minority Language Educational Rights (P.E.I.)* [1988] 69 Nfld. & P.E.I.R. 236, 259.

development to its Acadian school board. Regardless, Nova Scotia's Acadian school board is pleased to control all matters related to the curriculum and programmes.

Another challenge arose when the Supreme Court argued that educational priorities should be those 'of the minority community' since 'the determination of such priorities lies at the core of the management and control conferred on the minority language rights holders and their legitimate representatives by s. 23', and 'it is up to the board, as it represents the minority official language community, to decide what is more appropriate from a cultural and linguistic perspective'.[60] However, the same court also ruled that 'these priorities must be determined and exercised in light of the role of the Minister'.[61] Thus, why let OLMCs determine their educational priorities if the minority school board cannot exercise them without ministerial approval? This needs clarification, although thus far it has not posed a great challenge.

Jurisprudence has also provided little assistance in specifying exactly what minority schools and school boards should do to assume their cultural and community mandate as outlined in *Mahé*. There is little doubt that minority schools 'provide community centres where the promotion and preservation of minority language culture can occur [... and] needed locations where the minority community can meet and facilities which they can use to express their culture'.[62] However, there is no consensus on how education in the OLMCs can contribute to linguistic, cultural, and community vitality. What are the measurable cultural and community objectives to be pursued by minority school boards? And what additional resources should the provinces give to their minority school boards to fully assume their cultural and community mandate? The provinces do not provide additional resources and the minority school boards have seldom insisted they do.

Minority educational autonomy is thus yet to be clearly specified. It is a relative and evolving concept. It is in need of administrative theory to translate the vague and dry legal words into actions. It must move away from the courts and into the realities of educational management. The Supreme Court conceded its limited ability in that regard in *Mahé*: 'It is not possible to give an exact description of what is required in every case in order to ensure that the minority language group has control over those aspects of minority language education which pertain to or have an effect upon minority language and culture'.[63] It assumed that the principles of minority educational self-management would lead to administrative actions.

There has been some progress on the administrative front. In most provinces, administrative discretion has been used to avoid political resistance to minority educational self-management. In most provinces, political and administrative good will has produced interesting results. Most notably, the Government of Nova Scotia was the first (and only) to delegate to its minority school board the curriculum development for French-language schools as well as the six employees

---

[60] *Arsenault-Cameron v. Prince Edward Island* [2000] 1 SCR, paras 51 and 43.
[61] *Arsenault-Cameron v. Prince Edward Island*, para 51.   [62] *Mahé v. Alberta*, 346.
[63] *Mahé v. Alberta*, 376.

responsible for that task formerly assigned to the Department of Education. This was a difficult task to assume for volunteer parents on the school board, but minority board members will not part with that critical function after a decade. The other French-language school boards are somewhat jealous, but none have made serious attempts to emulate their counterparts in Nova Scotia. PEI's minority *Commission scolaire de langue française* provides another interesting exception. Section 23 bestows rights on 'parents', but following a series of court victories by Acadian parents towards educational self-management, PEI's Department of Education discretely allowed the school board to expand the right to grandparents. This led to the construction of a French-language school in the Tignish area, where the Government, in the midst of consolidation efforts, eliminated the six tiny Acadian schools in 1972, which led to massive assimilation.

The progress achieved since 1990 is in great part because of successful court cases initiated by minority parents,[64] but it is also increasingly because of successful initiatives by minority school boards. They are increasingly assuming their role in minority educational self-management. After minority school boards gradually erected the schools required in many minority communities neglected for decades and secured the human, financial, and material resources needed to provide quality education therein, they then started assuming an increasing number of cultural and community responsibilities. For example, New Brunswick's French-language school boards hired cultural officers to organize events and activities both within and beyond school walls in order to increase the students' linguistic and cultural pride and Acadian identity. One of these school boards also developed and offered a course to high school students teaching the ancestral Acadian patois to modern urban Acadian youth.[65] All twenty-nine minority Francophone school boards in Canada integrate their minority culture in their curriculum and participate in joint community projects.[66]

Thus, though the 'sliding scale' is a critical consideration when specifying minority education rights, notably the number, size, and location of schools, the territorial principle is less important beyond the school. School boards cover the entire province or territory. If a child lives too far away from the nearest minority school, even for daily bus transportation, monies are provided for boarding houses and tutors. Cultural officers work beyond the school walls, in some cases outside the community wherein the school is located. Some specialized maths courses are shared through online collaborations between PEI's small French-language school

---

[64] Paul T. Clarke and Pierre Foucher, *École et droits fondamentaux* [School and Fundamental Rights] (Saint-Boniface: Presses universitaires de Saint-Boniface, 2005); Rodrigue Landry and Serge Rousselle, *Éducation et droits collectifs* [Education and Collective Rights] (Moncton: Les Éditions de la Francophonie, 2003).

[65] Jonathan Landry, 'Étude de représentations linguistiques de jeunes Acadiennes et Acadiens en milieu scolaire: Vers un éveil à sa propre langue?' [Study of Linguistic Representations of Young Acadians in Schools: Towards an Awakening to his (their) Own Language?] (Master's thesis, Moncton: Université de Moncton, Faculty of Graduate Studies and Research, September 2012.

[66] Daniel Bourgeois (forthcoming), *Ensuring Cultural and Community Survival: How Canada's Official Language Minority School Boards and Schools Assume their Second Mandate.*

board and the smaller Newfoundland and Labrador French-language school board. The twenty-nine French-language school boards collaborate regularly through formal bodies for both elected school board members (*Fédération canadienne des conseils scolaires de langue française*[67]) and superintendents (*Regroupement national des directions générales de l'éducation*[68]). They also collaborate with Québec's English- and French-language school boards and with the ten provincial Departments of Education and the federal government. Territorial limits inherent in 'where numbers warrant' and the 'sliding scale' caveats have little importance.

The 'sliding scale' is not the only concept that is falling by the wayside as administrators try to make sense of vague court rulings. As minority school boards increasingly assume their role as 'orders of government', they are challenging the court's wisdom in defending the Minister's prerogatives. They argue that the duly elected minority volunteers sitting on the school board and their professional management staff are more competent than the civil servants working in the capital to determine the needs of the minority and the best education policies to meet them. Indeed, the decentralization of the French-language curriculum from Nova Scotia's Department of Education to the provincial Acadian school board demonstrates that the curriculum and the programmes of instruction are best left in the minority's purview. If one pushes the argument to its logical conclusion, it would also be best to let the minority school board determine academic results and tests to that end. Moreover, it would be best to let the minority determine the results sought by the cultural and community mandate awarded by the courts, as well as the best means to that end. It would be difficult to argue that civil servants answering to the Minister of Education responsible for the entire province would more effectively accomplish that objective than minority school board members and district administrators. The 'sliding scale' may survive, but its end point on the minority self-determination side could be pushed further beyond its present limit as minority school boards fully assume their exclusive powers and vital role.

Another challenge is that minority school boards exercise their exclusive powers differently across Canada depending on the administrative arrangements particular to each province. There are legal differences between school boards across Canada—for example, the French-language school board representing the 2,180 Francophones and 260 students in Newfoundland and Labrador can establish a school while in New Brunswick, the three school boards representing the 237,430 Francophones and 29,200 students must defer this decision to the Minister. This example proves that the 'sliding scale' is increasingly irrelevant. There are also differences in resources: the Newfoundland and Labrador school board has a $7.5 m annual operating budget while the one in Nova Scotia has a $46 m annual operating budget for 4,556 students. Most of the budgets incur similar expenses per student for salaries, buildings, bus transportation, equipment, etc., but total costs

[67] Fédération Nationale des Conseils Scolaires Francophones, accessed September 2014, <http://www.fncsf.ca>.
[68] Fédération Nationale des Conseils Scolaires Francophones, accessed September 2014, <http://www.fncsf.ca/rndge>.

and discretionary amounts can vary significantly. This enables the richer school boards to hire more specialized administrative staff (cultural animators and communications officers, for example) that the poorer school boards cannot. There are also differences in functions: the eight French-language school boards in Ontario are responsible for labour negotiations while the provincial government assumes that responsibility elsewhere. Nova Scotia is the only province where the minority school board is responsible for the curriculum. Manitoba's Francophone school board is the only minority school board to collect taxes directly as part of its revenues. Differences in scale also exist: there is a single minority school board in six provinces and three territories, respectively, while there are twelve regional minority school boards (four public, eight Catholic) in Ontario, nine in Québec, five in Alberta, and three in New Brunswick. Finally, there are differences in scope: most minority school boards assume their cultural and community mandate—indeed, most would like to do more but do not have the resources to do so—but a few minority school boards intentionally limit their extracurricular interventions.

If minority-language educational self-management is to eventually look alike in all provinces and territories, it will be because the thirty-eight minority-language school boards and the thirteen provincial and territorial ministers of education make it happen. National standards will not be imposed by Ottawa. Indeed, as noted, education is a guarded provincial purview, so the Government of Canada has no jurisdiction in the field. Nevertheless, it uses its significant spending power to influence provincial policies. Since 1969, it has provided significant funds to provinces and territories to cover the difference in the costs of books and other tools between the minority and majority schools and to encourage the learning of the minority language in majority schools.[69] The Government of Canada also provides scholarships to minority students who attend minority-language universities and colleges. Moreover, it provides funds to minority parents for court action against their province/territory to ensure the minority education rights contained in Section 23 are implemented. But although educational self-management is increasingly uniform, differences will remain. As the Supreme Court of Canada explained in *Mahé*, 'Imposing a specific form of educational system in the multitude of different circumstances which exist across Canada would be unrealistic and self-defeating'.[70]

The most significant differences, however, are not between the minority school boards but between these boards and the majority-language school boards.[71] In many provinces, minority-language school boards are a novelty: half of the twenty-nine French-language school boards outside Québec did not exist before 1990. Minority schools were equally rare. Since 1990, many minority communities have received new schools, but in many cases the community inherited former English-language schools in need of repairs and lacking facilities (e.g. gymnasium,

---

[69] Matthew Hayday, *Bilingual Today, United Tomorrow* (Montreal and Kingston: McGill-Queen's University Press, 2006).

[70] *Mahé v. Alberta*, 376.

[71] Bourgeois, *Vers la pleine gestion scolaire francophone en milieu minoritaire*.

laboratories, library) available in the new English-language schools. In Souris, PEI, for instance, the local Acadian school was located in an abandoned fisheries office with the truck garage acting as the gymnasium. Also, smaller minority school boards do not have the staff—human resources coordinator, communications officer, etc.—to perform basic education management functions.

All of the previous challenges point to a more fundamental challenge: funding. Education is a public service, so minority educational self-management requires public funds. The minority's limited critical mass means higher costs for books and bus transportation, for instance. These are covered by provinces and federal subsidies. A minority community that wishes to force its recalcitrant provincial government to respect its Section 23 rights also has access to federal funds to cover its legal costs. The federal government also funds cultural animators in school settings. However, funds required for the most significant task—determining the minority's educational needs, developing a minority education curriculum, and implementing the school board's cultural and community mandate—have never been addressed by the courts. Administrative arrangements are in place, but most minority school boards argue that funds are inadequate. It may take a court ruling in one particular setting to specify not only how provinces must fund minority school boards so they can ensure the same quality of education as majority school boards, but also how they must fund minority school boards so these can determine their minority community's education needs, develop their minority curriculum and programmes of instruction, and fully assume their cultural and community roles. Courts have been the OLMCs' biggest supporters, and they may be asked to support minority school boards again.

Minority educational self-management remains incomplete, but it has significantly improved since 1990. Assimilation remains rampant in many communities, even where minority schools are located, but there is hope where despair existed a generation ago. Minority school boards are acting increasingly like an order of government by overtly resisting government interventions and assuming their cultural and community mandate in partnership with other minority organizations. They have access to significant financial, human, and material resources and can mobilize these to contribute to the minority's language and culture. They are increasingly assuming their role as the most important public tool for minority survival and vitality. And their success has spawned similar efforts towards institutional completeness in hospitals and municipalities.

The final challenge relates to the validity of minority institutional completeness on which rests much of the Royal Commission's arguments and the jurisprudence on Section 23. Breton's concept was first published in 1964, when he was employed as a researcher by the Royal Commission. It influenced the Commission, although not as much as the Supreme Court when it established educational self-management in *Mahé*. That decision adheres to the Commission's limited support for educational self-management, but it also refers to the concept in establishing the five principles of educational self-management. The concept also influenced lower courts in the *Montfort* and *Russell* cases in which Breton was an expert witness.

The challenge is that the research on minority institutional completeness has been sparse and provides little empirical validation. Academics have developed models using institutional completeness as a variable but they have yet to verify its implications.[72] Researchers who have tackled Breton's assumptions have been supportive but also raised concerns.[73] Thus, although it has influenced the Canadian jurisprudence on minority rights, 'the concept seems ritualistically cited rather than examined'.[74] The lack of empirical validation, however, has not curtailed its value. Indeed, the political use of the concept by nationalists has influenced the courts and governments. It is vague, precarious, and barely understood and mastered by Acadian nationalists,[75] but just like the right to self-management through sub-state institutions like school boards, the perception of what the concept means carries more weight than the literature says.

The right to self-management and the importance of institutional completeness are both vague and precarious concepts yet exist de facto through successful discursive nationalist strategies. Perceptions are critical in politics. Nationalist elites cultivate perceptions. Francophone nationalists have successfully transformed the concepts into an ideology. This does not mean that the concepts are not valid. Indeed, as noted, they exist de facto, albeit on vague and precarious grounds. But the concepts are perceived as more substantive than they are. This does not mean that minority self-determination through sub-state institutions like schools, hospitals, and municipalities cannot become as substantive as envisioned by the nationalists. It simply means that the minority school boards, health authorities, and municipal councils in Francophone communities outside Québec do not fully play their role as 'orders of government', do not wield the exclusive powers required for self-determination, and many do not even attempt to do so. Nevertheless, the trend that began with *Mahé* in 1990 suggests that this may be only a matter of time.

[72] Howard Giles, Richard Bourhis, and Donald Taylor, 'Towards a Theory of Language in Ethnic Group Relations', in *Language, Ethnicity and Intergroup Relations*, edited by Howard Giles (London: Academic Press, 1977), pp. 307–48; Rodrigue Landry, Réal Allard, and Kenneth Deveau, 'Bilingual Schooling of the Canadian Francophone Minority: A Cultural Autonomy Model', *International Journal of the Sociology of Language* vol. 185 (2007): pp. 133–62.

[73] Wilfrid Denis, 'La complétude institutionnelle et la vitalité des communautés fransaskoises en 1992' [The Institutional Completeness and Vitality of Fransaskoises Communities in 1992], *Cahiers Franco-Canadiens de l'Ouest* vol. 5, no. 2 (1993): pp. 253–84; Bourgeois and Bourgeois, 'Territory, Institutions and National Identity', pp. 1123–38; Yves Bourgeois and Daniel Bourgeois, 'La relation entre territoire et identité. Construction de l'identité acadienne et urbaine dans la région du Grand Moncton' [The Relationship between Territory and Identity. Construction of Acadian and Urban Identity in Greater Moncton], in *Balises et références—Acadies, francophonies*, edited by Martin Pâquet and Stéphane Savard (Québec: Presses de l'Université Laval, 2007), pp. 105–26; Edmund Aunger, 'Profil des institutions francophones' [Profile of Francophone Institutions], in *Entre minorité et majorité, un espace francophone sous tension*, edited by Anne Gilbert (Ottawa: Presses de l'Université d'Ottawa, 2009), pp. 56–75; Bourgeois and Bourgeois, 'Minority Sub-State Institutional Completeness', pp. 293–304.

[74] Sheldon Goldenberg and Valerie Haines, 'Social Networks and Institutional Completeness: From Territory to Ties', *Canadian Journal of Sociology* vol. 17, no. 3 (1992): pp. 301–12, 302.

[75] Bourgeois, 'Acadians'.

7.8 Conclusion

Educational self-management is a critical form of non-territorial autonomy for Canada's official language minorities. It goes beyond the right of minority parents to a distinct school within a specific area; it also awards a right to the entire minority community within each province and territory to wield exclusive political powers and important financial, human, and material resources to nurture collective vitality. Thus, minority school boards serving the entire country's minority educational needs expand the powers and resources beyond the spatial judiciary concept of 'where numbers warrant'. Collaboration between the twenty-nine French-language school boards, as well as collaboration between these boards and the nine English-language school boards in Québec, also makes educational self-management spatially neutral. Thus, although minority schools can only be established if a sufficient critical mass of children live within a specific area, the governance and management of the schools spread far beyond the school walls.

Minority education self-management was at the root of the Canadian unity crisis that often exploded during the first century of Confederation, and its implementation since 1990 has provided OLMCs with institutional tools (minority schools and school boards) in the most critical public sector in regards to their vitality. Canada is a different country than in 1963 when the Royal Commission on Bilingualism and Biculturalism was established. Section 23 has significantly enhanced minority survival and vitality and improved relations between the majority and the minority. Nevertheless, education self-management is incomplete and it will remain so until the thirty-eight minority school boards wield all of their exclusive powers—for example, when they determine their curriculum, establish their community's educational needs, and fully assume their cultural and community mandate. Courts have been unable to specify these three critical responsibilities and they probably cannot, so capable ministers and administrators will have to succeed. This will occur if the minority school boards muster the courage to request these critical responsibilities. The biggest challenge seems to be the minority school boards' courage to assume their powers and role. Another challenge is time: assimilation keeps eroding the minority communities. If OLMCs are unable to meet the challenges of educational self-management, autonomy and vitality will become moot points.

8

The Sorbian People in Germany

Detlev Rein

8.1 Introduction

This chapter discusses the issue of whether non-territorial autonomy (NTA) can be granted to the Sorbian people from a mainly juridical—*de lege lata*—point of view, starting off with the debate within the Sorbian people about establishing a corporation under public law (*Körperschaft des öffentlichen Rechts*) for the Sorbs. The contribution starts with a description of the Sorbian people as one of the four national minorities in Germany, its history, its actual private law associations, and public law institutions. Following this is an account of how and why the discussion of NTA being granted to the Sorbian people was initiated. The topic is analysed in the light of German constitutional, state, and public law, including aspects of international law. In concluding, some solutions are proposed for how the Sorbian people's wishes could be accommodated in substance.

8.2 The Sorbs as a National Minority in Germany

The Sorbs, along with the Danes, Frisians, and the German Sinti und Roma, are one of the four recognized national minorities in Germany. In its declarations on the occasions of the signature (1995) and the ratification of the Framework Convention for the Protection of National Minorities (FCNM) in 1998, Germany differentiated between *nationalen Minderheiten* (national minorities) and *Volksgruppen* (ethnic groups).[1] Similar to the FCNM, which uses only the

---

[1] Declaration contained in a letter from the Permanent Representative of Germany, dated 11 May 1995, handed to the Secretary General at the time of signature, on 11 May 1995—Or. Ger./Engl.— and renewed in the instrument of ratification, deposited on 10 September 1997—Or. Ger./Engl.:

> The Framework Convention contains no definition of the notion of national minorities. It is therefore up to the individual Contracting Parties to determine the groups to which it shall apply after ratification. National Minorities in the Federal Republic of Germany are the Danes of German citizenship and the members of the Sorbian people with German citizenship. The Framework Convention will also be applied to members of the ethnic

term 'national minority', modern German usage does not distinguish—neither in terminology[2] nor in the legal consequences—between national minorities, socio-cultural minorities, or ethnic groups, despite the fact that only the Danish minority has a kin-state, Frisians live in both Germany and the Netherlands, and the Sinti and Roma live in (almost) all European countries. In its empirical approach, this chapter uses the term 'national minority' to refer to the totality of groups listed as national minorities in the ratification declarations and/or state reports of the FCNM signatory states.

The Sorbs are a western Slavic people living exclusively in Germany, specifically in the federal states of Brandenburg and Saxony. They speak Upper and Lower Sorbian, which is not spoken anywhere else. Since the settlement, from AD 600 onwards, the Sorbs have been resident in Lusatia. From AD 929, when the Sorbs' settlement area was placed under German rule and increasing numbers of Germans settled there as well, the Sorbs have been living together with the German population for about a millennium. They have no mother country or kin-state. From the various dialects of colloquial Sorbian, two standard languages developed: Upper Sorbian, and Lower Sorbian. Approximately 35,000 Sorbs are still Sorbian speakers; all Sorbs speak (at least) German as well. Today's Sorbian language areas are Upper Lusatia in the north-east of the Free State of Saxony, and Lower Lusatia in the south-east of *Land* Brandenburg. The Sorbs living in Lower Lusatia are still also known as Wends. The number of persons considering themselves Sorbs is not known as in Germany statistics based on ethnic criteria are not gathered. The estimated number is about 60,000 Sorbs, of whom two-thirds live in Saxony, and one-third in Brandenburg. In some local communities in Saxony, they account for up to 90 per cent of the population, and in some villages, the majority of inhabitants are Sorbs, but no municipality is exclusively dominated by Sorbs. They make up about 10 per cent of the population of the overall settlement area, while in the towns they account for less than 2 per cent. The laws of Brandenburg and Saxony clearly define the Sorbs' area of settlement.[3] The constitutions of Brandenburg and Saxony guarantee far-reaching protection for the minority rights of the Sorbs.[4]

With regard to the school system in general the Constitutions and the relevant laws of the two *Länder* guarantee that children's day-care centres and schools may

---

groups traditionally resident in Germany, the Frisians of German citizenship and the Sinti and Roma of German citizenship.

[2] The 'Federal Government Commissioner for Matters Related to Repatriates and National Minorites' is in charge of all the four recognized minorities and the publications of the Federal Ministry of the Interior only use the term 'National Minorities' for all four groups.

[3] Gesetz zur Ausgestaltung der Rechte der Sorben (Wenden) im Land Brandenburg vom 7. Juli 1994 [Act Specifying the Rights of the Sorbs/Wends in the Federal State of Brandenburg of 7 July 1994], para 3, as of 1 June 2014; Gesetz über die Rechte der Sorben im Freistaat Sachsen vom 1. März 1999 [Act on the Rights of the Sorbs in the Free State of Saxony of 1 March 1999], para 3, as of 1 March 2012.

[4] Constitution of the Federal State of Brandenburg of 20 August 1992 (last amended by the Act of 5 December 2013), art 25; Constitution of the Free State of Saxony of 27 May 1992 (last amended by the Act of 11 July 2013), arts 5 and 8.

be established by voluntary bodies, that is, non-governmental institutions. Some of the approximately thirty-five Sorbian and bilingual children's day-care centres are provided by local authorities, others are run by Christian and private law organizations. All other educational institutions of the Sorbian settlement areas are state-provided. In the school systems of Brandenburg and Saxony, schools with teaching in or of Sorbian are offered from the primary school level up to high school, with two Gymnasiums, one in the Lower Sorbian language region and one in the region of Upper Sorbian. Leipzig University offers courses in Sorbian Studies (Sorabistics)—in Lower and Upper Sorbian—for a Master's degree or for the teaching profession.

The Sorbs are organized in a number of civil society associations; most of them registered associations (*eingetragener Verein*). Nearly all of these associations belong to *Domowina*, an umbrella organization which is a registered association. *Domowina* was founded in Hoyerswerda in 1912 to represent the Sorbs (Wends) in their pursuit of national rights. While banned in 1937 and stripped of its assets and forced to operate illegally, the organization reconstituted itself on 10 May 1945. In the German Democratic Republic, *Domowina* had the status of a 'socialist national organization' of the Sorbs. After the end of communism in 1989, it reorganized and changed focus, although its primary goal continued to be the preservation and promotion of the Sorbian language and culture. Since 1991, *Domowina* has functioned as a politically independent and autonomous umbrella organization whose members include five regional associations and a number of sectorial associations (see Table 8.1).

The most important organizations of *Domowina* are the General Assembly (*Hauptversammlung*, every two years), the Managing Committee (according civil law requirements), and the National Executive Board (*Bundesvorstand*).[5] The General Assembly is the highest body, which elects the other organizations, and discusses and decides the principal strategic questions of the national work of *Domowina*. Delegates to the General Assembly are members of the National Executive Board and other members of those private law associations, which are members of the umbrella organization *Domowina*. *Domowina* aims to represent the interests of all 60,000 Sorbs. Its goals are to work on behalf of preserving, developing, promoting, and disseminating the language, culture, and traditions of the Sorbian people, Sorbian identity, the Sorbian community and its rootedness in its traditional homeland; to unite and support the Sorbs and their organizations in their efforts for the good of the Sorbian people; to represent the interests of the Sorbian people in public, to parliaments, institutions, and government agencies; to work for legislation to protect and promote national minorities in Germany; to promote mutual respect between the Sorbian and German populations and their equality; and to promote international friendship with other national minorities and with the Slavic peoples. *Domowina* represents Sorbian civil society in

---

[5] The articles of *Domowina* can be found on the following website, accessed September 2014, <http://www.domowina.de/domowina/satzung-programm-arbeitsrichtlinien-uae/satzung>.

Table 8.1 Member organizations of *Domowina*

Original name	English name
Domowina-Regionalverband 'Handrij Zejler'	*Domowina*—Regional Association
Regionalverband 'Jan Arnošt Smoler' Bautzen	
Regionalverband 'Michał Hórnik' Kamenz	
Regionalverband Niederlausitz e.V.	
Regionalverband Weißwasser/Niesky	
Bund sorbischer Gesangvereine e.V.	Federation of Sorbian Choral Societies
Bund sorbischer Handwerker und Unternehmer e.V.	Federation of Sorbian Craftsmen and Entrepreneurs
Bund sorbischer Studierender	Federation of Sorbian Students
Cyrill-Methodius-Verein e.V., Verein katholischer Sorben	Association of Catholic Sorbs
Förderkreis für sorbische Volkskultur e.V.	Friends' Association for Sorbian Folk Culture
Förderverein sorbischer Kulturtourismus e.V.	Friends' Association for Sorbian Cultural Tourism
Gesellschaft zur Förderung eines Sorbischen Kultur- und Informationszentrums in Berlin (SKI) e.V.	Society for the Promotion of a Sorbian Culture and Information Centre in Berlin
Maćica Serbska e.V.—sorbische wissenschaftliche Gesellschaft	Sorbian Scientific Society
Serbski Sokoł e.V.	Umbrella Organization of Sorbian Sports Clubs
Sorbischer Jugendverein 'Pawk' e.V.	Sorbian Youth Association
Sorbischer Künstlerbund e.V.	Sorbian Artists' Association
Sorbischer Schulverein e.V.	Sorbian School Association

the Consultative Committee on Issues concerning the Sorbian people (*Beratender Ausschuss für Fragen des sorbischen Volkes beim Bundesministerium des Innern*), set up at the Federal Ministry of the Interior in 2002 as a body advising on all domestic policy issues concerning the Sorbian people. *Domowina* is also the only Sorbian member of the Federal Union of European Nationalities (FUEN), and of the Minority Council of the four autochthonous minorities in Germany. This is a body for the associations of the four national minorities in Germany, which is supported by the Secretariat for Minorities in Berlin.

Government grants allocated to the Sorbian institutions are distributed via the Foundation for the Sorbian People (*Stiftung für das sorbische Volk)*, a foundation under public law established in Saxony by an intergovernmental agreement between Brandenburg and Saxony.[6] Based on a co-funding agreement, this Foundation is jointly financed by the federal government and the federal states of Brandenburg and Saxony, and distributes these funds to civil society associations

---

[6] All legal texts in respect of the Foundation for the Sorbian People can be found on the following website, accessed September 2014, <http://stiftung.sorben.com/wobsah_de_42.htm>.

Table 8.2 Funding of the foundation for the Sorbian people in 2013 in euros

Contributor	Amount
Federal Republic of Germany	8,700,000
Free State of Saxony	6,210,700
Land Brandenburg	2,941,700
Total	17,852,400

Table 8.3 Main expenses of the Foundation for the Sorbian People in 2013 in euros

Type of expenses/beneficiary institution	Amount
Repayment to capital	93,000
Administration of property	867,000
Administration of the Foundation	950,000
Structural expenditures	260,000
Sorbian culture information	136,000
Projects of the Foundation's administration	431,000
Sorbian National Ensemble Ltd.	4,407,000
Domowina Publisher Ltd.	2,541,000
Domowina civil law association	2,906,000
Sorbian Institute	1,823,000
German-Sorbian People's Theater	1,220,000
Sorbian Museum Bautzen	371,000
Lower Sorbian Museum Cottbus	137,000
School for Lower Sorbian Language	90,000
Investments	504,000
Project funding	902,000

and Sorbian cultural institutions that are registered corporations under German trade law, such as a music theatre (*Sorbisches Nationalensemble*) and a publisher (*Domowina Verlag*) owned by the Foundation. The funding of the Foundation is shown in Table 8.2, and its main expenses in Table 8.3.

The Foundation has no political mandate. It is not the political voice of the Sorbian people nor does it aim to claim further improvements for the protection of the Sorbian people. The dialogue in such matters between civil society and the political sphere is mainly the subject of *Domowina*. The purpose of the Foundation is purely administrative. The funding by the three donors is pooled in one budget and distributed to the many different undertakings by the Sorbs or in respect of them. In respect of the cultural interests of the Sorbs, the Foundation is important; it decides which portions of the annual budget are spent on the different undertakings in a broad range between, for instance, scientific research, professional theatre, amateur music associations, a daily newspaper, the production of books, and the organization of public events. The distribution of the financial means to the undertakings of and for the Upper Sorbs respectively the Lower Sorbs is a permanent aspect of the decision-making process. The Foundation's Board of Trustees decides the main parameters of the Foundation's activities and its annual budget. Its fifteen members include representatives of the Sorbian people (6), the federal government (2), Saxony (2), and Brandenburg (2), as well as regional/local representatives of the public administration (3). Of the representatives of the Sorbian people, four are elected in respect of Saxony by *Domowina*, and two are elected in respect of Brandenburg by the Council for Sorbian Affairs at the Brandenburg Parliament. In its opinion on Germany's first State Report in 2002, the Advisory Committee to the FCNM (ACFC) came to the conclusion that this Foundation made 'a highly positive contribution as a fine example of good co-operation between the federal authorities and the *Länder* for the benefit of national minorities'. The ACFC noted 'nonetheless that only six of the fifteen members of the Foundation's governing board are representatives of the Sorbian minority—the others belong to the majority. The Sorbian members therefore represent less than half of the board and have no right of veto, even on fundamental issues. The ACFC considered that the authorities should examine ways of strengthening the representation of the Sorbian minority in the functioning of the Foundation and in other fora'.[7]

8.3 The Internal Debate

The debate on awarding the Sorbian self-government institutions the status of a corporation under public law has been ongoing since 2000, especially among the members and within the institutions of *Domowina*. In 2002 the then president was of the opinion that in the case of being a public law body, the Sorbian people would possess an institution with decision-making power in Sorbian matters, binding all Sorbs and so able to overcome controversial trends, which hinder effective work for the Sorbian people.[8] This first phase of discussions about striving for a public law status for the Sorbian people ended in 2007, when opinion spread within *Domowina* that such a change of status—from registered association towards corporation under public law—would not lead to practical improvements for the Sorbs.[9] Instead, focus turned to the efficiency of the Foundation.

[7] Advisory Committee on the Framework Convention for the Protection of National Minorities, Opinion on the First State Report of Germany, (2002) ACFC/INF/OP/I(2002)008, accessed September 2014, <http://www.coe.int/t/dghl/monitoring/minorities/3_FCNMdocs/PDF_1st_OP_Germany_en.pdf>.

[8] Ludwig Elle, *Sorbische Interessenvertretung in Vergangenheit und Gegenwart* [Sorbian Advocacy in the Past and Present] (Bautzen: Sorbisches Institut, 2011), p. 27.

[9] Elle, *Sorbische Interessenvertretung*, p. 31.

By signing the second Agreement on the Co-Funding of the Foundation for the Sorbian People in 2009, the federal government, Saxony, and Brandenburg complied with the request of the German Federal Court of Audit that the bodies and measures funded by the Foundation for the preservation and development of Sorbian language and culture should be reviewed to guarantee their efficiency and future viability. It was not the purpose of the Federal Court of Audit or the three Co-Founders to start a discussion about new public law organizational structures for the Sorbian people. The intention was that the structure of the many undertakings financed by the Foundation should be analysed to find ways of more efficacy, for instance by merging the *Sorbisches* National Ensemble (run by the Foundation) and the *Deutsch-Sorbisches Volkstheater* (run by regional public law bodies) or by avoiding duplication by the Foundation and *Domowina* in respect of publishing books and giving advice to local and regional Sorbian associations. To provide a basis for the review required by the Court of Audit and the Founders, the Foundation commissioned a study. After receiving the study,[10] the Foundation established six working groups tasked with working on proposals for restructuring Sorbian institutions. Five were in charge of performing arts, media, museums/science, language, and administration. As some important members of the Foundation and *Domowina* never had given up the idea of a public law institution, a sixth working group was set up to deal with the question of whether it would be admissible to set up a non-territorial corporation under public law to represent the interests of the Sorbs.[11] The members of the working group felt strongly supported by an expert opinion provided by P. Pernthaler who urged the creation of a public law body consisting of natural persons for the Sorbian people.[12] Thus, the debate was not dead.

The revival in 2010 of the discussion among the Sorbs about the creation of a public law body had different sources. One of the issues discussed was the composition of the Foundation's Governing Board, where representatives of the Sorbian people constitute less than half of the members of the Board. Some feared that decisions of the Board might not conform with the wishes of the Sorbian people. Therefore,

---

[10] Matthias Theodor Vogt and Vladimir Kreck, 'Gesamtkonzept zur Förderung der sorbischen Sprache und Kultur, Teil II, Empfehlungen zur Stärkung der sorbischen Minderheit durch Schaffung eines abgestimmten Selbstverwaltungs-, Kooperations- Projekt- und Institutionenclusters. Im Auftrag der Stiftung für das sorbische Volk erarbeitet am Insitiut für kulturelle Infrastruktur Sachsen' [Overall Concept for the Promotion of the Sorbian Language and Culture, Part II, Recommendations for the Strengthening of the Sorbian Minority by Creating a Coordinated Cluster of Self-Management, Cooperation, Projects and Institutions. Developed at the Institute for Cultural Infrastructure Saxony on Behalf of the Foundation for the Sorbian People], 2009, accessed September 2014, <http://stiftung.sorben.com/usf/IKS_Empfehlungen_Sorben_091205r.pdf>.

[11] In the interest of full disclosure, it should be noted that the author of the chapter acted as chairman of the working group.

[12] Peter Pernthaler, 'Gutachten über die Errichtung einer Körperschaft als öffentlich-rechtliche Vertretung der Sorben (Wenden)' [Opinion on the Establishment of a Corporation as a Public Representative of the Sorbs (Wends)], in *Minderheiten als Mehrwert*, edited by Matthias Theodor Vogt, Jan Sokol, Dieter Bingen, Jurgen Neyer, and Albert Löhr (Frankfurt a. M.: Peter Lang, 2010), p. 543.

they felt that budgetary decisions should be taken by a body of the Sorbian people. Another aspect was the question of who should represent the Sorbian people. Whereas there is no doubt that the Foundation is not entitled to do this, the position of *Domowina* was regarded as controversial. While many members felt that *Domowina* is the representative of the Sorbs in politics and society, others doubted this because *Domowina* is 'only' a private law association. Moreover, there was some dissatisfaction with some of its leading members. However, the idea or perhaps the utopia may be that creating a public law body with an elected parliament will result in other persons having a say. A third argument was connected with the name the 'Sorbian people'. From the term 'people' some Sorbs concluded that they are entitled to derive a right to autonomy from the principle of the right to self-determination of peoples. In the end, *Domowina* decided at its General Assembly in 2013 to follow the proposal of its National Executive Board to retain its actual legal status as a registered association. Nevertheless, the discussion continues among some members of the Sorbian people.[13]

8.4 German Law as the Basis for Legal Structures

Prompted by the above debate within the working group over fundamental aspects of the proposal to erect a public law body for the Sorbian people, and the fact that no decision on that matter was taken by any state institution, it may be instructive to expand on a number of issues that a democratic state based on the rule of law like Germany has to tackle if its national minorities are to be granted NTA. When addressing the issue of appropriate forms of organization, one is soon confronted with the specifics of constitutional, state, administrative, and civil law in European states, although the legal systems in some states may not differentiate between them. Other problems may result from the state structure. Is the state in question a centrally organized state or a federation? Are there any other tiers below the national level able to exercise state authority? Who is authorized to grant partial territorial or non-territorial autonomy? For the purpose of this chapter some terms need to be defined to understand the essence of the Sorbian debates, which were not articulated in legal terms. 'Autonomy' may refer to the legally accepted ability to decide one's own matters. Whether this autonomy is legally accepted or not depends on a higher instance granting or at least tolerating it.[14] Today the definition of the term autonomy is also subject to limitations. It is not possible for a state, let alone a part of its territory or even a clearly defined group within its borders, to be *fully autonomous* in the sense that it is capable of deciding all its matters in full independence without a higher instance also, at least partially, having

---

[13] See the following website, accessed September 2014, <http://www.serbski-sejmik.de/index.php?option=com_content&view=article&id=34&Itemid=23>.

[14] If a remote region splits off from the state it used to belong to and is then recognized as being independent neither by its original state nor by the international community, then this cannot be regarded as autonomy in the sense of this chapter.

a say in matters that regard this state.[15] The following analysis will deal only with autonomy within the territorial boundaries of a state.

For the purpose of the discussion of the issues raised within the two Sorbian debates in the light of German law, it is necessary that a state entity—at the federal or the *Länder* level—allows a group (in this case a minority) or a region to *exercise state authority otherwise exercised by or reserved for the state itself* in order to be regarded as autonomous. Simply exercising a right everyone is entitled to anyway within the given system, whether an individual or a group, does not constitute autonomy. Rather, it amounts to exercising one's human or civil rights.[16] However, if a religious minority organization is allowed to regulate marriage for its members in a state in which all residents fall under the same state law concerning marriage, then it would constitute autonomy. The same holds true for the official language or the language to be used in court. If these languages are recognized by law for the entire national territory, but a specific region is allowed to deviate from this and accept a different language for official and court purposes, it would amount to granting autonomy to this region in this respect. An example would be the language of a minority that has a strong representation in the population of a particular region. However, for obvious reasons the autonomy granted would only be partial autonomy, because if a minority were given full state authority in a specific region, the region would become an independent state. Certain aspects of state action, such as foreign and defence policy, are not usually left to autonomous minority organizations.[17] Furthermore, organizational structures are necessary to exercise autonomy. Such structures may be based on a region or a group of persons. Territorially defined structures in favour of national minorities are probably more

[15] This holds true also for sovereign states that have joined intergovernmental or supranational organizations, military alliances, or customs unions, have entered into bi- or multilateral agreements or for certain matters have subjected themselves to international courts that are not part of their judicial system.

[16] So it is not an act of autonomy if a minority organization builds and runs a museum in a state in which anyone can build and run a museum. This aspect is of particular relevance when it comes to schools where classes are held in a minority language. If the right to run schools is exclusively reserved to a state so that nobody else, i.e. no church, ideological group, or profit-making organization, is allowed to establish a private school, then permitting a minority, by way of exception, to run its own school is tantamount to granting it autonomy, albeit only partial autonomy, at least in the eyes of the minority organization. However, if in principle anyone in a given state has the right to found and run a school under private law, then in the author's view, establishing a school does not amount to exercising autonomy. Consequently, the private schools of the German minority in Denmark and of the Danish minority in Germany, both organized as private law entities (see Bericht der dänisch-schleswig-holsteinischen Arbeitsgruppe zur Behandlung von Gleichstellungsfragen in der Finanzierung der Schulen der dänischen und deutschen Minderheiten Kopenhagen/Kiel im November 2010 [Legal Opinion from the Danish–Schleswig-Holstein Working Group to Consider Equality Issues in the Financing of the Danish and the German Minority Schools 2010], pp. 11–14), are not an expression of a particular degree of autonomy for these minorities, but simply mean that they exercise a right granted to anyone, as can be seen from the fact that in Denmark there are numerous other 'free schools', i.e. independent private schools established either for a profit or with a specific ideological orientation; similarly, many schools in Germany are run by the Christian churches.

[17] John Coakley, 'Approaches to the Resolution of Ethnic Conflict: The Strategy of Non-Territorial Autonomy', *International Political Science Review* vol. 15, no. 3 (1994): p. 311.

common.[18] In contrast, an organizational structure that only consists of members of one specific community and is not primarily defined in terms of a specific territory is NTA.[19]

'Cultural autonomy' and 'functional collective autonomy' (FCA)[20] are not clearly defined legal terms for (public law or private law) organizational structures of minorities. For lawyers they sound more like sociological and/or political descriptions of forms of community self-organization (here: minorities). Legally speaking, in these two forms of 'autonomy', existing individual and/or collective rights are exercised within the framework of private law organizations that are open to anyone. No state authority is transferred and no public law status awarded. This is the difference between autonomy as defined above and collective or functional collective autonomy. The difference lies in the legal frame of the undertakings, not the undertakings themselves. In the case of recognized autonomy, the frame is the public law regime; if important undertakings of the minority are pursued within the civil law regime, this can be called cultural or functional collective autonomy. Malloy, for example, describes how the Danish minority in Germany enjoys cultural and functional collective autonomy and justifies her view with the numerous cultural and charitable undertakings of the minority which 'have a layered FCA embedded mainly in private law, except for official recognition and a right to existence in the Constitution of Schleswig-Holstein'.[21] With regard to the requirements that a democracy and a state based on the rule of law have to meet in order to grant NTA to national minorities, these two forms of autonomy do not really provide an answer, because they do not transfer state powers to national minority communities in a specific and targeted way. These two forms of self-organization

---

[18] For example the Aaland Islands, South Tyrol, or the German-language community in Belgium. The latter, despite its perhaps misleading name, is a territorially defined autonomy, because it is geographically defined and the government of the community has power over all persons resident in this defined region and under certain circumstances over all persons present in that region. According to the former prime minister of the German-language community, this community can be compared to the Länder of the Federal Republic of Germany (Karl Heinz Lambertz, 'Die Verfassung Belgiens und ihre Institutionen' [The Belgian Constitution and its Institutions], *Nordrhein-Westfälische Verwaltungsblätter* vol. 9 (2003): p. 330; Karl Heinz Lambertz, 'Drei Alleinstellungsmerkmale der Deutschsprachigen Gemeinschaft Belgiens' [Three Unique Features of the German-Speaking Community of Belgium], in *La Communauté germanophone de Belgique. Die Deutschsprachige Gemeinschaft Belgiens*, edited by Katrin Stangherlin (Bruxelles: la Charte, 2005), p. 11). In these territorial autonomies, the powers transferred from national or other state authorities to the organizational structures of the autonomy region apply to all residents of this region. The minority regions listed above enjoy partial territorial autonomy.

[19] The best-known example of this kind of autonomy is probably Hungary's system of local, regional, and national minority self-governments. In addition, Hungary's three-tiered structure of minority self-government shows that such an originally purely community-based definition can also be combined with a geographical element in the sense that such minority self-government is reserved only for people who have a specific feature in common (here: ethnicity) and live in the same area and does not cover every inhabitant of that area.

[20] Tove H. Malloy, 'The Lund Recommendations and Non-Territorial Arrangements: Progressive De-Territorialisation of Minority Politics', *International Journal on Minority and Group Rights* vol. 16, no. 4 (2009): p. 667.

[21] Malloy, 'The Lund Recommendations', p. 671.

will only be of interest if it becomes apparent that for legal reasons it is not possible to establish NTA structures.

As noted above, one of the arguments for achieving autonomy was deducted from using the expression 'people' for the Sorbs. In Germany, the legislation and regulations in respect of the four recognized minorities use the terms used by the minorities, *die dänische Minderheit* (the Danish Minority), *die friesische Volksgruppe in Deutschland* (the Frisian People's Group in Germany), *das sorbische Volk* (the Sorbian People), and *die deutschen Sinti und Roma* (the German Sinti and Roma). From the point of view of the state institutions in charge, the different wording does not mean any differentiation between those four groups; it is a matter of courtesy to name the minorities the way they wish to be called. Legally, all four are national minorities in the sense of the FCNM.

It is not the aim of this chapter to discuss the question that was so intensely debated in the 1990s as to whether national minorities can derive a right to autonomy from the principle of the right to self-determination of peoples[22] or whether the right to self-determination and minority rights have to be regarded as two different concepts and therefore must be differentiated with regard to their substance.[23] It is not necessary to provide a final answer to this question because, 'even if we assume a link, international law does not prescribe a specific way in which the right to internal self-determination' has to be implemented; more specifically, it does not create a legal entitlement to found a 'corporation under public law' since international law does not specify how national legal provisions are to be formulated. On the other hand, even if we deny a link, the Sorbian community would still be allowed to establish a 'corporation under public law' since international law would not stand in the way of national law giving a more favourable treatment to certain groups of people than required by international law.[24]

A number of legal forms of organization are relevant under German public law. These include, on the one hand, the law of local and regional government bodies (*Gebietskörperschaften*), and on the other, the law governing corporations under public law such as professional or statutory bodies consisting of natural persons (*Personalkörperschaften*), and public law foundations (*öffentlich-rechtliche Stiftungen*). Furthermore, under private law, registered associations (*eingetragene Vereine*) are of interest. An important feature of the public law entities to be looked at in this chapter

[22] Carmen Thiele, 'Rechtsstellung der Sorben in Deutschland' [Status of Sorbs in Germany], in *Selbstbestimmungsrecht der Völker—Herausforderung der Staatenwelt*, edited by Hans J. Heintze (Bonn: Dietz, 1997), p. 343; Marcus Kotzur, *Die Förderung des sorbischen Volkes: Rechtlicher Status, rechtspolitische Gestaltungsmöglichkeiten, insbesondere die Finanzierungsmöglichkeit des Bundes* [The Promotion of the Sorbian People: Legal Status, Legal Policy Design Options, in Particular the Financing Option of the Federal Government] (Leipzig: Universität Leipzig, Juristenfakultät, 2009), p. 2.

[23] Manfred Mohr, 'Abgrenzung von Selbstbestimmungsrecht und Minderheitenschutz' [Definition of Self-Determination and Minority Protection], in *Selbstbestimmungsrecht der Völker—Herausforderung der Staatenwelt*, edited by Hans J. Heintze (Bonn: Dietz, 1997), p. 139.

[24] Endbericht der Arbeitsgruppe, 'Körperschaft des öffentlichen Rechts' [Public Corporation] (2011), accessed September 2014, <http://stiftung.sorben.com/usf/110713_ENDFASSUNG_Gemeinsames_Papier_AG_KdoeR.pdf>.

is that state bodies[25] are significantly involved in their establishment, either by way of a law, an ordinance, or an administrative act. A corporation obtains its public law status only by an official act of conferment; in this it differs from a registered association (see below).

As a rule, local and regional government bodies exercise state authority over all those who legally reside within their territory (with only a few exceptions, such as diplomats or stationed military personnel). Such local and regional authorities are, for example, the federal states, counties (the *Kreise*), cities, and municipalities.[26] The local and regional government bodies take decisions and carry out administrative acts in accordance with the competences given to them by laws adopted at the higher level. Article 20 of the German Basic Law holds that 'all state authority is derived from the people. It shall be exercised by the people through elections and other votes and through specific legislative, executive and judicial bodies'.[27] Electoral rolls are compiled and elections are carried out in the territory of the local and regional authorities on the basis of the information kept by the registration offices. All residents who meet the general requirements of the electoral law, who have been living for a certain minimum period of time in the territory of the respective local or regional authority and who are German citizens may take part in these elections.[28]

In German law one cannot find an abstract definition of or a law on, '*Personalkörperschaften*'. It may thus be helpful to provide examples to analyse the possibilities and conditions for creating a non-territorial corporation under public law in Germany. For instance, the Federal Code for the Legal Profession (*Bundesrechtsanwaltsordnung*)[29] stipulates that all lawyers who wish to practise their profession in a specific judicial district require permission from the responsible bar association (*Rechtsanwaltskammer,* a public law corporation). With this permission, they become members of the association, take part in its assemblies, may vote in board elections, and be elected to the board.[30] The bar association keeps a list of all its members, who have to pay a fee. Simply put, every practising lawyer is a member of a bar association, and a person who is not authorized to

---

[25] At the federal or the Länder level.

[26] In Germany their residents are registered by the residents' registration office which also must be informed of any change of address and is notified by the civil registrar's office of the birth or death of a resident.

[27] Basic Law for the Federal Republic of Germany of 23 May 1949 (GG) (last amended by the Act of 11 July 2012). Art 28 stipulates that 'the constitutional order in the Länder must conform to the principles of a republican, democratic and social state governed by the rule of law, within the meaning of this Basic Law. In each Land, county and municipality the people shall be represented by a body chosen in general, direct, free, equal and secret elections'.

[28] In addition, 'in county and municipal elections, persons who possess citizenship in any member state of the European Community are also eligible to vote and to be elected in accord with European Community law' (art 28 of the Basic Law).

[29] Federal Code for the Legal Profession (Bundesrechtsanwaltsordnung) of 1 August 1959 (last amended by the Act of 10 October 2013).

[30] On certain grounds, the bar association may refuse to allow lawyers to practise their profession and may institute legal proceedings in order to sanction lawyers by banning them from practice. The decision in such a court proceeding is exclusively taken by members of the bar association.

practise as a lawyer cannot be a member of a bar association.[31] Another example is religious communities. German constitutional law[32] provides that religious communities may take the legal form of a public law corporation, which traditionally has been granted, above all, to the large Christian denominations, but can also be given to new and smaller religious communities 'if their constitution and the number of their members give assurance of their permanency'.[33] The legal form of a public law corporation is not imposed on religious communities by the state; they must decide to adopt it.[34] Although it may seem surprising, it makes sense to say that churches with the status of a corporation under public law fall into the category of NTA, instead of territorial autonomy, as is illustrated by the fact that religious communities which are corporations under public law are entitled to levy taxes collected by the state according to a tax rate established by the respective religious community. A prerequisite for this is the existence of 'civil taxation lists in accordance with *Land* law'.[35] However, these taxation lists comprise only the names of persons who are members of this particular religious community. This, in turn, presupposes that, first of all, it is possible to establish clearly and verifiably who is a member, and, secondly, that there are clear and verifiable rules for the acquisition and termination of membership.[36] German state law applicable to religious organizations also outlines practical procedures for joining or leaving a church. The normal admission procedure for the Christian churches is baptism, usually of children. The church then informs the competent state authority of the

---

[31] Other professions such as medical doctors, dentists, and pharmacists are organized in a similar way. Social insurance funds in Germany with millions of members are also set up as corporations under public law. Both the insured and the contributing employers are members and are jointly responsible for managing the insurance; the members of the self-administration bodies are elected from these two groups.

[32] Art 140 of the Basic Law in connection with art 137 of the Weimar Constitution of 11 August 1919 (WRV) (last amended by the Act of 17 December 1932).

[33] Art 137 V 2 of the Basic Law in connection with art 137 of the Weimar Constitution of 11 August 1919.

[34] Agreements have been concluded between state authorities (the federal and state governments) and religious communities (concordats with the Catholic Church, agreements between the state and the Protestant churches, agreement between the state and non-Christian communities such as the Central Council of Jews in Germany) in which the legal status of a corporation under public law is confirmed or granted. Since the religious communities do not perform state tasks, but order and administer their own matters, they are not on an equal footing with organizations under public law that perform state tasks; instead, they are called 'public law organizations *sui generis*' (Axel Freiherr von Campenhausen and H. de Wall, *Staatskirchenrecht* [State Church Law], 4th edn (München: C. H. Beck, 2006), p. 130).

[35] Art 137 VI of the Basic Law in connection with art 137 of the Weimar Constitution of 11 August 1919.

[36] This shows clearly that a determining factor for the specific legal form of churches in Germany is not territory, but people. While it is true that the organizational structures of the churches relate to a clearly defined geographical area (for example the regional churches or Landeskirchen of the Protestant Church or the dioceses of the Catholic Church), this is a limitation that the churches have in common with all other corporations under public law which otherwise could claim to have global scope. The difference for local and regional authorities, however, is that the latter are responsible for all the people who live in a certain territory, whereas when it comes to corporations under public law consisting of natural persons, the determining factor is specific criteria that the members have to fulfil, rather than a specific geographical territory.

baptism.[37] The church administration and the citizens' registration offices regularly share information on people being baptized, leaving or joining the church, moving from one parish to another, or dying, in order to keep church membership records up to date. This also enables parishes to correctly conduct local church council elections, because, based on this exchange of data between the parishes and the state, it is possible to invite all parish members to take part in the elections and, at the same time, exclude all others who are not entitled to vote. These examples illustrate the advantages a corporation under public law consisting of persons could have for granting autonomy to national minorities. First, people who live scattered across an area in which they do not represent the majority of the population and consequently do not hold a majority in the bodies of territorial autonomy can join forces and look after their own matters together while excluding others who do not belong to that minority. Secondly, services and benefits of the minority organization can be restricted to its members. Thirdly, the organization can exercise authority over its members, and finally, the members can elect the bodies of their organization thus authorizing it to take charge of the matters of the community and to represent it at the political level. The prerequisite for all this is that those who belong to this group can be clearly identified.

The basic idea behind a foundation is that the donated assets are spent to pursue a specific objective and that the most important decisions are taken by the foundation's governing bodies. Ideally, the assets donated are sufficient for the foundation to pursue its objectives with the revenue derived from its assets. In Germany, however, a growing number of public law foundations are endowed with smaller amounts of capital and every year receive additional public funds. A foundation is incorporated under public law if it is established by an act of public authority (a law, an ordinance, or an administrative act). The founding instrument not only sets out the purpose for which the assets are to be used, but also the structure and the composition of the foundation's governing bodies. The members of the bodies may be appointed by the founder or founders from representatives of the government bodies that provide the funds and/or representatives of the beneficiaries or from respected public figures. Or, the representatives of the beneficiaries are appointed or elected by the beneficiaries themselves. In addition, different combinations of these two models are also conceivable. The board of the Foundation for

---

[37] If somebody who is already baptized wishes to switch to another denomination, or if somebody who has left the church now wishes to rejoin it (or a different one), a formalized admission procedure applies; again the state authorities are informed. The procedures for discontinuing church membership are laid down in the laws of the federal states pertaining to leaving a church. The procedure consists of either an oral application stated for the record or a publicly certified written application, both lodged, as a rule, at the local court or the local civil registrar's office.
The Reich Act on the religious education of children applies to children and young people; it assigns responsibility for all religious decisions to a child's parents until the child reaches the age of 12. Between the age of 12 and 14 the child must not be instructed against its will in a faith other than the one he or she was raised in. At 14 the child has reached the age of majority in religious matters and can decide on his or her own whether to join or leave a church; Gesetz über die religiöse Kindererziehung 15 July 1921 [Reich Act on the Religious Education of Children 15 July 1921] (last amended by the Act of 17 December 2008).

the Sorbian People described above is such a combination. An important feature of all foundations under public law is that they are controlled by a public authority to make sure that they comply with the foundation's objectives and that the funds are used efficiently and economically. Such control can be exerted by means of having a decisive vote in the foundation board (e.g. the right of veto granted to the founders' representatives in the foundation's bodies, as in *Domowina*) and/or by obliging the board of the foundation to present its budget for approval and to provide proof of how the funds are used, as well as by means of allocating certain control rights to the Court of Audit.

In a liberal state based on the rule of law, establishing a registered association is an ideal way to cast civic engagement into a legal form. In Germany an association is to be entered in the register of associations if it meets certain conditions: it has to have documents on the appointment of the board, articles of association, and a minimum number of members (seven according to German law[38]). The articles of association must state the foundation's objectives, which may be cast more or less freely, as long as they do not run counter to the free and democratic constitutional order and its expression in criminal and civil law. In its articles, an association is largely free to specify the conditions of membership (as long as it complies with laws prohibiting discrimination), the structure of its governing bodies, and their competences. An important characteristic of registered associations is that, as legal persons under private law, they are entitled to conclude contracts, own property, and take legal action. As a rule, the private law associations of national minorities in Germany (*Domowina, Sydslesvigsk Forening*, Central Council of German Sinti and Roma, *Nordfriesischer Verein, Friisk Forening, Seelter Buund*), their affiliated specialist educational associations (e.g. *Dansk Skoleforening for Sydslesvig, Sorbischer Schulverein*) and their research institutes (*Nordfriisk Instituut, Serbski Institut*) have chosen to establish themselves as registered associations. If the objectives and budgetary behaviour of a registered association prove that it is a non-profit organization it also enjoys certain tax breaks. However, in a less liberal system with a weaker rule of law, a registered association is a much less attractive alternative. For example, it may not be possible to establish a registered association which has political objectives, and establishing an association may be subject to state scrutiny and authorization.

8.5 A Public Law Corporation for the Sorbian People?

The overview of the legal situation in Germany has shown that a legal form under public law that lends itself to granting NTA to national minorities, in particular if these minorities do not make up the majority of the population in their area of settlement or in parts of it, is the public law corporation consisting of natural persons.

---

[38] Bürgerliches Gesetzbuch 18 August 1896 [German Civil Code 18 August 1896] (last amended by the Act of 1 October 2013), para 56.

This legal form allows the creation of bodies that could represent the minority at the political level and govern their internal affairs. In Germany it proved to be the case that an underlying structure and an essential prerequisite of this legal form is that it can be clearly determined in each individual case who is a member of the group in question, in our case a minority. This clarity is needed to be sure that, on the one hand, only persons entitled to join in the decisions of this public law body do so, and, on the other hand, that it is defined who has to obey the decisions of the public law entity. If this public law body were to represent the Sorbian people better than the civil law association *Domowina* and a parliament were to be installed, it is further necessary that all members of that ethnic group are known and invited to the elections of this parliament and non-members of the minority can be rejected.

Regarding the question of being a member of a given national minority, this can be done quite easily in countries where members of a national minority are registered in a public register and/or every ID card indicates the ethnic group the person belongs to. In a state based on the rule of law, this requires that the criteria for establishing ethnicity are defined by law. Two main criteria are conceivable. First, that the individual is a descendant of a member of this minority, and second, that the individual freely decides to declare his or her membership of a minority vis à vis a public authority. Once one of these criteria is met, the following questions have to be asked: is it possible for the individual to leave his or her inherited ethnic group and become a member of another minority or of the majority? What is the legal situation of those whose parents belong to different ethnic groups, either two different minorities or one parent belonging to a minority, and the other to the majority? Do they have the freedom to choose between them and/or belong to two minorities at the same time? What is the procedure for joining, changing, or leaving a minority? And finally, do the representatives or bodies of an organized minority have the right to decide on admitting new members? These questions have to be answered in a logical and practical way if national minorities are to have the possibility of organizing themselves as a corporation under public law consisting of natural persons. To conclude: the decisive prerequisite is the ability to determine whether an individual belongs to a national minority. If the legal form to be granted is a corporation under public law, all documents proving the ethnic affiliation of an individual have to be publicly available for scrutiny.

There may be legal systems in Europe where these conditions are met. In the former Soviet Union, the nationality of individuals was indicated in their passports and thus also recorded in the corresponding administrative files. Elections to the minority self-governments in Hungary are also repeatedly referred to as examples in this context. However, this system has been reformed twice within the past two decades, because it became apparent in practice that its weakness lay in determining those entitled to vote, something which raised doubts as to whether this system was suitable from a rule-of-law point of view. The principal question, at least from the perspective of Germany and some other European states, is whether it is admissible to keep an official register of individuals' minority status. In Germany the following view prevails with the full support of the national minorities' associations.

Since it is every individual's private decision to declare him/herself a member of a minority, such affiliation is neither registered nor recorded officially, and consequently there are no official statistics based on ethnic or linguistic features. Therefore, only estimated figures are available regarding the members of the various national minorities and other ethnic groups traditionally resident in Germany. As a rule, the figures are provided by these groups themselves and have been compiled on the basis of the membership of minority organizations, votes cast for minority party tickets, the number of pupils enrolled in minority schools, and the number of participants in activities or organized events.[39]

Of course, in Germany one could say that declaring one's affiliation with a national minority is comparable to declaring one's religious affiliation, with membership of a religious community not only being recorded but, in the case of employees, also communicated by the competent authorities to employers so that they can deduct church tax on top of income tax.

However, a reservation brought forward is that there are countries that strictly separate church and state and where, for example, the idea of the state recording church membership and collecting church tax on behalf of churches would be inconceivable. This reservation is justified and it relates back to the earlier observation that states differ in terms of their constitutional, state, and administrative law. In many cases it simply has to be accepted that more than one solution is in line with the rule of law and democratic principles. After all, it is also generally accepted that different countries have different election systems. Once a country has decided in favour of a particular solution on the basis of its national law, this solution must be applied consistently. For Germany (in contrast, for instance, to Hungary) this holds true for the principle that one's affiliation to a national minority is a private matter and therefore not registered. Consequently, national minorities in Germany cannot take on the legal form of a corporation under public law consisting of natural persons, because it is not possible to make a list of those persons who are entitled to become members of this corporation and/or vote for its organs.

If one comes to the conclusion that in states where, as a matter of principle, affiliation with a national minority is not registered, a corporation under public law is not a suitable legal form for granting autonomy to a national minority this does not automatically mean that here all efforts to give a national minority the greatest possible degree of self-administration have to stop. In section 8.6, this chapter will therefore take a look at the possibilities offered by a public law foundation and a registered association in order to examine whether these separately or in conjunction could bring about a certain amount of autonomy.

---

[39] Report Submitted by Germany Pursuant to Article 25, Paragraph 1 of the Framework Convention for the Protection of National Minorities, (2002) ACFC/SR(2000)001, accessed September 2014, <http://www.coe.int/t/dghl/monitoring/minorities/3_FCNMdocs/PDF_1st_SR_Germany_en.pdf>.

8.6 Alternative Options

Looking for alternative options, one could follow Oeter's line of argument which suggests not personal but functional autonomy.[40] Since many national minorities are also or above all interested in using funds allocated to them by the state for cultural purposes in the broadest sense of the word, the legal form of a public law foundation is of relevance. Such a foundation is probably the most suitable form of organization for managing and distributing funds, because, after all, this is its main purpose. In addition, it can be equipped with bodies that can also comprise representatives of the beneficiaries of the foundation. There are numerous examples of public law foundations in Germany. They differ with regard to the specifics of their governing bodies, but generally speaking those forces of civil society that work towards achieving the goals for which the foundation was established in the first place are also represented in its bodies. Where several civil society organizations are active in the same sector of society, the founder (i.e. a public institution) tries to mirror the relationship between these forces in society. In order to safeguard public interests, a certain number of seats in the foundation's bodies are, as a rule, reserved for representatives of the state. Where the state is the most important or even the only provider of funds, it can monitor compliance with the principle of efficient and economical use of public money in this way.

If a national minority has just one (umbrella) organization, this organization can be given the task and the right to nominate or even appoint the members that represent the minority in the foundation's bodies. Where there are several major organizations that exist in parallel and do not come under one umbrella organization, it is possible to accommodate interests within the board of the foundation. In a democratic society based on the rule of law, where a parliament decides on the establishment of a public law foundation, the board of the foundation can be expected to achieve an appropriate balance. In order to account for the state's interest in guaranteeing an efficient and economical use of public funds and compliance with the foundation's objective, a second body, for example a management board, could be established to monitor and approve the foundation's budget only with regard to these aspects and not with regard to the content of the foundation's work programme.[41] Thus, in a state that, as a matter of principle, does not register the ethnic origins of its residents, a public law foundation seems to be a suitable legal form to enable minority organizations to decide on the use of funds earmarked for them.

Like corporations under public law consisting of natural persons, a registered association has members. In contrast to corporations under public law, however, it is not necessary for all individuals of a particular group (here: of the national

---

[40] Stefan Oeter, 'Minderheiten im institutionellen Staatsaufbau' [Minorities in the Institutional Structure of the State], in *Das Minderheitenrecht europäischer Staaten, Teil II*, edited by Jochen A. Frowein, Rainer Hofmann, and Stefan Oeter (Berlin: Springer, 1994), p. 498.
[41] Endbericht, 'Körperschaft des öffentlichen Rechts', p. 16

minority) to be a member of this registered association. While the existence of a registered association does not automatically mean that it represents all members of the particular group, the state can nevertheless draw conclusions as to the importance of the registered association depending on the size of its membership and on whether there are other civil society organizations active in the same field. On this basis it can decide whether this particular association could be a suitable recipient of benefits earmarked for a national minority. Examples of this are the afore-mentioned schools and research institutions that have the legal form of a registered association. It would be helpful for minorities if, in addition to having mainly specialized associations, for example for music, dance, drama, youth work, literature, sport, or regional associations, they also created an umbrella organization that could credibly claim to represent all the interests of the minority and at the same time would have enough organizational strength to properly manage public grants. Registered associations are limited in their possibilities where the state is not willing or able to transfer state authority, that is, in the field of legislation or the judiciary.

8.7 Conclusions

It has become apparent that while it is not legally possible to harness the legal form consisting of natural persons of regional or local authorities or of corporations under public law, there are other legal forms of organization, which can be used to achieve partial self-administration of the Sorbian people. In Germany and Denmark one can often find a combination of different legal forms. The German minority in Denmark is organized in many clubs and associations governed by an umbrella organization strong enough to run its own schools successfully. In the political arena this minority is represented by its own political party active at the municipal level. The Danish minority in Schleswig-Holstein is similarly organized, with the exception that its party is, as a rule, represented in the *Landtag*, that is at the regional or *Land* level, and currently even provides a minister to the *Land* government. The Sorbs, on the other hand, have no party activities worth mentioning, but have formed a strong civil society umbrella organization and have their own public law foundation for managing their funds and assets. Unless a minority aspires to be able to pass its own civil laws,[42] to

---

[42] In parts of India no codified family law exists in respect of members of certain smaller religious denominations—which are regarded as minorities— so that the laws and rules of the relevant confessions or Christian beliefs are to be followed in matters regarding marriage and divorce (Alexandra von Oppen, *Eheschließung und Eheauflösung im indischen Familienrecht* [Marriage and Dissolution of Marriage in Indian Family Law] (Frankfurt am Main: Lange, 2004), pp. 42, 50, 52, 60, 68, 207). The Hindu Marriage Act is not applicable to members of 'Scheduled Tribes'. These are indigenous peoples or parts of them, which in the field of matrimonial law are subject to their own rules and customs (Stepahnie Hombach, *Eheschließung und Ehescheidung im modernen Hindu-Recht Indiens im Vergleich zu deutschem Recht* [Marriage and Divorce in the Modern Hindu Law in India in Comparison to German Law] (Göttingen: Cuivillier, 2003), p. 52).

fine members,[43] or levy taxes, it does not seem necessary to establish corporations under public law in order to extend the self-administration competences of minorities. To accommodate the Sorbian wish for as much self-administration as possible and for a representative body for the political discourse, it would be sufficient to make use of other legal forms of organization that exist under public and private law.

Specifically with regard to the Sorbian people, it cannot be denied that certain improvements regarding details seem useful and should be possible. For example, the influence of the state on the Foundation for the Sorbian People should be limited to controlling legal compliance and the budget. This would also relieve the state of 'the delicate task of organising the cultural life of the minority'.[44] This brings us to the crucial point: even if legal forms of organization are chosen that do not come under public law, such as registered associations, it is still possible to speak of granting autonomy. This would not be autonomy in the sense of state law but in the sense of cultural autonomy to national minorities provided that the state does not itself decide on priorities and dimensions. Currently the state decides when establishing and running opera houses, theatres, museums, music schools, or libraries as institutions run by the different levels of the state—federal, *Länder*, or local. Such decisions should be left to the minority institution. By doing so, allocating public funds becomes tantamount to transferring some autonomy, which is not autonomy in the legal sense but that which one could call 'cultural autonomy' or 'functional collective autonomy'.

---

[43] The German bar associations—corporations under public law consisting of natural persons—are entitled by the bar courts to fine members, in the case of severe obligation offences, up to €25,000 or to debar them from advocacy.

[44] Oeter, 'Minderheiten', p. 498.

9

Functional Non-Territorial Autonomy in Denmark and Germany

Tove H. Malloy

9.1 Introduction

The classic definition of non-territorial autonomy (NTA) for cultural minorities[1] seems inadequate in light of the changing nature of minority participation in societal management in the twenty-first century. Classic NTA for cultural minorities may be defined as a policy for accommodating diversity in multicultural societies through delegating powers to distinctly defined and legally embedded institutions[2] of a political, cultural, social, and occasionally economic nature run by minority organizations.[3] However, the frameworks in which NTA is usually adopted no longer provide for neatly defined borders and institutional capacities. Moreover, as societal management is undergoing a change from purely state-managed institutions to new types of multilevel and multidimensional governance structures constructed across the public–private divide, so-called governance networks form as formal/informal thematic movements or processes aimed at solving specific societal issues with greater self-direction.[4] Self-empowerment in terms of minority action[5] within such networks exemplifies the core notion of NTA, the right to

---

[1] This chapter addresses NTA for minorities belonging to ethnic, national, linguistic, or religious minorities, usually determined by history or long-term presence in a homeland region. These types of minorities have enjoyed NTA arrangements in the past. Other minorities, such as women, gays, and lesbians, and disabled people have not, to the author's knowledge, enjoyed NTA arrangements.

[2] In this chapter, the term minority institution refers to the institutional frameworks that minorities have by virtue of minority protection, for instance maintaining schools and cultural associations as well as establishing political parties. Minority organization or association is used when referring to the entities acting on behalf of minority groups. The term actors will also be used as a generic term for organizations and associations.

[3] See for instance, John Coakley, 'Approaches to the Resolution of Ethnic Conflict: The Strategy of Non-Territorial Autonomy', *International Political Science Review* vol. 15, no. 3 (1994): pp. 297–314.

[4] For a good introduction to governance networks, see Eva Sørensen and Jacob Torfing, eds, *Theories of Democratic Network Governance* (Basingstoke: Palgrave Macmillan, 2007, 2008).

[5] Minority action in this chapter refers to civil society–type actions. But unlike mainstream civil society action, which is based on democratic ideals of the universal right to participatory democracy, minority action involves specific rights to participate in democracy based on past experience of

undertake decision-making processes, especially those concerning minority affairs. But the fact that such action is often taken outside neatly defined institutional capacities means that analytical approaches to NTA for cultural minorities require new exploration.

Heretofore NTA institutions and policymaking have been studied from macro-level perspectives in terms of governments devolving power to minority institutions for strategic reasons either based on security threats or imposed norms of protection.[6] This means that not only have top-down policies rather than bottom-up action been in focus, but also scholars have concentrated on NTA as policies for mitigating conflict and tension in culturally diverse societies. NTA has been seen primarily as instrumental (security) but also normative (minority protection), mainly because most NTA policies in culturally diverse societies have been in place on these grounds.[7] However, examinations of minority institutions and organizations in contemporary politics and polity-making will demonstrate that minority actions challenge not only the top-down approach, but also the security and protection strategy views. As minority actors become self-empowered in networks of informal governance, they actually challenge the classic description of NTA as devolved and legally entrenched. In so doing, they force scholars to adjust analytical concepts to the new circumstances. NTA for minority organizations as an analytical tool must, therefore, take into account the changing reality of societal management, including the possibility that NTA as a self-determination tool is assumed bottom-up rather than top-down.

Minority organizations acting in the new reality of governance networks contribute to the development of unstructured responses to circumstances of public administration. For instance, if vacuums emerge due to weakening state powers, minority organizations find opportunities to insert their group power into areas of concern and interest. By assuming collective power through bottom-up action, minority organizations seek to influence or change existing policy or promote new policies. This bottom-up action may be caused by positive as well as negative circumstances: positive, if it springs from an expansion of awareness among minorities about polity-making and societal management; negative, if it emanates from a lack of societal management due to economic, environmental, or social crises. Either way, minority associations are likely to react to issues of their concern, be they social, environmental, economic, or other. Many of these 'reactions' cannot be codified as NTA arrangements; the minorities react to ensure influence or a change in affairs concerning them. Thus, by chance, minority reactions may result in NTA-like functions because the minority actors do not wait for powers to be devolved.

exclusion or persecution. Minority action is thus encouraged in order to protect the identity of minority groups as well as to preserve cultural pluralism.

  [6] See Marc Weller and Stefan Wolff, *Autonomy, Self-Governance and Conflict Resolution: Innovative Approaches to Institutional Design in Divided Societies* (London: Routledge, 2005).
  [7] Codified NTAs exist, among others, in Hungary, Slovenia, and Kosovo.

Functional NTA is one such way to describe the actions of minority actors that provide for minority organizations taking self-empowered decisions about their own affairs. Functional autonomy thus refers to NTA arrangements that do not have specific, neatly drawn frames or correspond to a known model. Functional NTA has not been well defined in the academic literature. However, one description holds that functional NTA represents functional arrangements where opportunity and pragmatics come together to provide local management of relevant functions.[8] Such functions are usually found in the cultural areas protected by minority rights law.[9] Thus, while functional NTA is dependent on individual human and minority rights, it also requires a liberal regulation of the private sector in order to complement the functions that may be established as a result of the respect for human and minority rights. Whereas most classic NTA arrangements are formally enshrined in constitutions or adopted by public law statutes, the basis for functional NTA is more informal and may be as obscure as the footnotes to budgets,[10] that is, programmes which do not need to be adopted as public law instruments. Thus, if minorities see opportunities or need to influence developments in matters concerning them, they may mobilize independently, or in cooperation with mainstream elite actors to access these programmes.[11] And, where these do not exist, they may invent new ones. Such services created by bottom-up action and informal structures take on a similar role as designated institutions of classic NTA as defined above.

This chapter will identify and describe minority institutions and organizations that provide services to members of two cultural minorities in the Danish–German border region, the Danish minority in Schleswig-Holstein, and the German minority in southern Denmark. The focus is on historic minorities with a national identity profile as opposed to immigrants because the historic minorities have certain rights in the border region in their capacity as kin-state minorities of either Germany or Denmark.[12] These rights are not, however, in any way codified as NTA; rather they follow loosely European standards on minority rights. Moreover, while the two national state frameworks are considerably different in that Germany is a federalized state and Denmark a highly centralized state, the two case studies provide a good opportunity for exploring similar approaches to ensuring public services to minorities. Comparison is feasible, as the two countries pledged reciprocity in their approaches to minority protection and minority governance in 1955 when

---

[8] Hans-Joachim Heintze, 'On the Legal Understanding of Autonomy', in *Autonomy, Applications and Implications*, edited by Markku Suksi (The Hague: Kluwer Law International, 1998), pp. 7–32.

[9] For examples, see Markku Suksi, ed., *Autonomy, Applications and Implications* (The Hague: Kluwer Law International, 1998).

[10] See Tove H. Malloy, 'Denmark Adopts Unilateral Legislation in Favour of Kin-Minority', *European Yearbook of Minority Issues* vol. 9 (2010): pp. 669–82.

[11] Tove H. Malloy, 'Creating New Spaces for Politics? The Role of National Minorities in Building Capacity of Cross-Border Regions', *Regional and Federal Studies* vol. 20, no. 3 (2010): pp. 335–52.

[12] For the German framework, see Detlev Rein's chapter in this volume, 'The Sorbian People in Germany'; for the Danish framework, see Martin Klatt, 'Genforening eller mindretal' [Unification or Minority], in *Sydslesvigs danske historie*, edited by Lars N. Henningsen (Studieafdelingen: Dansk Centralbibliotek for Sydslesvig, 2009), pp. 177–236.

the so-called Bonn–Copenhagen Declarations were adopted.[13] Thus, seeking to ensure similar outcomes, the two countries often mirror each other in initiatives, and close cooperation has been established between the two administrations.

First, the chapter will explore the classic concept of NTA from the perspective of governance networks and relate it to minority action and modern-day NTA functions. Next, in the main section of the chapter, a discussion of the case study is provided as well as the structure of minority rights governance in the region and descriptions of minority organizations in five sectors: the political, the cultural, the educational, the social, and the economic. The examples from these sectors aim to show how the minorities have developed a method of bottom-up action to governing their own affairs. The following section discusses the dynamics of minority action and functional NTA, providing an argument for how these minority actions constitute a high degree of self-empowerment even if there are no official frameworks in place. This discussion relies on the assumption that autonomy is empowering. Moreover, it assumes that the informal and fragmented structure of the institutional framework in the region influences the actors and actions within its structure. In the conclusion, I offer a short analysis of functional NTA as policy relevant in culturally diverse societies and what policymakers could take into consideration prior to adopting an NTA scheme for minority governance. The overall argument is that the informal nature of functional NTA may allow for the formation of a more flexible NTA model than the classic and formal, legally defined structures imposed top-down. I hold, therefore, that functional NTA as implemented in the Danish–German border region constitutes more than a functional model; it represents in fact an NTA model almost as strong as a formal NTA model—an NTA model based on self-empowerment as opposed to devolved power.

9.2 Background and Context

The security and protection approaches to studying government strategies and NTA noted in the Introduction do not provide a full picture of the role of minority action in NTA models, because they focus only on the macro-level perspective. One could argue that they look only at the tip of the iceberg because they are both top-down, they both address formal measures, instruments, legal frameworks, and they both see the power relation between dominant and non-dominant groups as hegemonic in a paternalistic and controlling sense, meaning the dominant group

---

[13] The Bonn–Copenhagen Declarations are identical declarations of intent issued simultaneously by the Danish Prime Minister and the German Chancellor in March 1955 providing for a full set of minority rights to be respected in both states. See Jørgen Kühl and Marc Weller, eds, *Minority Policy in Action: The Bonn-Copenhagen Declarations in a European Context 1955–2005* (Aabenraa: Institut for Grænsregionsforskning, Syddansk Universitet, 2005); Knut Ipsen, 'Minderheitenschutz auf reziproker Basis: die deutsch-dänische Lösung in Heintze' [Minority Protection on a Reciprocal Basis: The German–Danish Solution in Heintze], in *Selbstbestimmungsrecht der Völker-Herausforderung der Staatenwelt*, edited by Hans-Joachim Heintze (Bonn: Dietz, 1997), pp. 327–41.

ideology determines what entitlements the non-dominant group may enjoy in terms of devolved power. However, in reality in many societies, bottom-up action by groups, such as minorities, creates political spaces for NTA society management often induced by sector-related issues.[14] One might argue that minorities in such situations act in a new mode of citizenship. They take independent action about society in areas where they see a need for development of services. Civil society action is not new, but whereas civil society activists may provide services, minority action will go a step further and procure decisions based on their right to culture and to be different. Thus, they apply collective agency as well as personal autonomy, and through these actions, they either usurp or diminish the hegemonic monopoly of state authorities in specific sector-related management areas. Such 'acts of citizenship' have been described as a type of action that transforms social institutions and people.[15] On this view, citizens enact themselves as activists, meaning they bond and become activists in various areas of public life, especially in areas which are not yet regulated by law. Hence, the behaviour and actions of minority groups in relation to circumstances of their concern may be seen as self-empowerment in that activists act on rights or lack thereof; they claim their rights in order that justice is exposed against injustice.[16] Self-empowerment, one could argue, takes place when expectations for change begin to materialize, and community empowerment is, therefore, the human activity which is aimed at changing social systems and creating structural alternatives.[17]

This chapter suggests that a third category of NTA analysis that takes into account the structural governance frameworks in which NTA operates is needed in order to expand our theoretical and conceptual knowledge of NTA as well as to make fully informed recommendations about NTA policymaking. This third category may be termed broadly the integration strategy,[18] because it explains the new modes of integration of minority institutions and organizations into societal management.[19] Like the security and protection strategies, the integration strategy presupposes that governments' strategies are both normative and instrumental in aim. Firstly, they are normative as it seeks to ensure the participation of minorities in general as well as to incorporate the contribution of these groups into policymaking and public management. Thus, they are normative in the sense that empowerment promotes integration. This overlaps with the minority protection strategy approach promoted by Article 15 of the European Framework Convention for the Protection of National Minorities (FCNM) which provides for the right to democratic participation in public affairs. Secondly, it is instrumental in the sense that minorities take over a state burden by managing or contributing

---

[14] Malloy, 'Creating New Spaces for Politics'.

[15] Engin F. Isin, 'Theorizing Acts of Citizenship', in *Acts of Citizenship*, edited by Engin F. Isin and Greg M. Nielsen (London: Zed Books, 2008).

[16] Isin, 'Theorizing Acts of Citizenship'.

[17] Sadan Elisheva, *Empowerment and Community Planning: Theory and Practice of People-Focused Social Solutions* (Tel Aviv: Hakibbutz Hameuchad Publishers, 1997, English translation 2004).

[18] Another term would be democratizing strategy.

[19] I would like to thank Alexander Osipov for guiding me in this direction.

to the management of societal affairs. In practice, it may take place through informal mechanisms, such as dialogue mechanisms, specific management agreements, ad hoc and footnote budgeting, specific programming, or public–private partnerships. Thus, the institutional framework of the third approach is rather more complex than well-defined security institutions or legal frameworks of protection. For this reason, a sophisticated study approach is needed.

Governance networks studies are a recent interdisciplinary field that applies several approaches to institutional analysis.[20] Governance networks consist of non-hierarchical forms of governance based on negotiated interaction between a plurality of public, semi-public, and private actors that organize horizontally around interests in the production of public policy. Thus, the processes of policymaking are no longer controlled by governments but subject to a mode of coordination among these various public and private organizations. Unlike the corporatist frameworks, which were controlled by governments, governance networks diminish the degree of government control through higher plurality of stakeholders and joint decision-making, thus rendering governance networks more legitimate as democratic processes. Governance networks may be defined as relatively stable horizontal articulations of interdependent, operationally autonomous actors, interacting through negotiations, taking place within regulative, normative, cognitive, and imaginary frameworks that are self-regulating within limits set by external agencies and which contribute to the production of public policy.[21] As such, governance networks are seen as an alternative to state and markets. Within the governance network research, four academic theories dominate based on observations of interdependency (resource dependencies), governability (calculating gain), integration (improving effectiveness, common goals), and governmentability (reflexive and self-governing), each relying on different conceptions of social action.[22] Whereas the first two allow a degree of government control, the third and fourth are seen as promoting new thinking and greater autonomy for actors. The analysis in this chapter draws on methods used in the latter two, among others the notion that minorities seek to improve effectiveness through creating spaces for politics in regional politics,[23] and the notion that minorities seek to improve services through self-governing through reflexive 'acts of citizenship' in terms of volunteering in public sectors.[24] This type of minority action in terms of functional NTA to be discussed in the next section pushes NTA analysis to take into account the notion of self-empowerment in terms of 'power to' in autonomy. Thus, it invites us to reconceptualize not only the classic notion of NTA, but also the notion of functional NTA.

---

[20] Sørensen and Torfing, 'Governance Network Research'.
[21] Sørensen and Torfing, 'Governance Network Research', p. 9
[22] Sørensen and Torfing, 'Governance Network Research', p. 17.
[23] Malloy, 'Creating New Spaces for Politics'.
[24] See Tove H. Malloy, 'Reflexive Minority Action: Minority Narratives and New European Discourses', in *Globalization and 'Minority' Cultures. The Role of 'Minor' Cultural Groups in Shaping our Global Future*, edited by Sophie Croisy (Brill, 2014).

9.3 Functional NTA in the Danish–German Border Region

The geographic region under examination in this study coincides largely with the old Duchy of Sleswig (1058–1866) which covers the area from the river Eider in today's Schleswig-Holstein to the river Kongeåen in today's Region Syddanmark.[25] Since the tenth century, the Duchy has been under the rule of both Denmark and Germany with predominantly Danish rule until 1866 (fiefdom of the Danish Crown). The permanent division in 1920 after a plebiscite, which offered the people of the Duchy the opportunity to decide to which national state they wished to belong, put an end to the political legacy of the Duchy and began the splintering of a common bi-cultural identity. The events and conflicts of the twentieth century scarred the relationship between Germany and Denmark almost irreconcilably, and the rebuilding after 1945 of a cooperative relationship and a common regional identity has been a slow and difficult process. European Union (EU) integration, Schengen cooperation, and other external factors such as globalization and the new regionalization of the European space have helped speed up the reconciliation process in the border region.

9.3.1 The region

Close to 700,000 people live in the border region, which covers roughly 8,000 km².[26] Approximately 12.5 per cent of the border region population belongs to four historic minorities. In addition to the German and Danish national minorities, a language minority, the North Frisians, live in the north-western corner of Schleswig-Holstein and a small ethnic minority of Sinti (Roma) live in central Schleswig-Holstein. The highest concentration of minorities is found in the town of Flensburg (21 per cent) and in Kreis Nordfriesland (9.7 per cent).[27] In the four Danish communes near the border, the concentration of Germans is between 5 and 8 per cent, whereas the concentration in Kreis Rendsburg-Eckernförde in Schleswig-Holstein where most of the Sinti live is rather low (1.5 per cent). In spite of these numbers, it is little known that the German–Danish border region is culturally one of the most diverse border regions in Europe. In total, including the four minorities, at least eleven different population groups have been identified

[25] The German–Danish border region which is the object of this study constitutes the following districts in Germany and Denmark: Stadt Flensburg (DE), Kreis Schleswig-Flensburg (DE), Kreis Nordfriesland (DE), Kreis Rendsburg-Eckernförde north of the river Eider (DE), Haderslev municipality (DK), Åbenrå municipality (DK), Tønder municipality (DK), Sønderborg municipality (DK).

[26] The region covers roughly 60 km north and 70 km south of the border between Germany and Denmark and coincides with the current Euro-region Sønderjylland-Schleswig; see, accessed 26 March 2014, <http://www.region.de/index.php?id=8&L=1%2Ftrainers.php%3Fid%3D%27__>.

[27] No exact numbers exists as census does not collect data on ethnic origin in Denmark and Germany. The Danish minority usually estimate that they constitute 50,000 and the German minority estimate 15,000 to 18,000.

in the border region.[28] One of these is the category of immigrants, which may be subdivided into numerous nationalities. In addition, the region is home to at least seven different languages or dialects.[29] In spite of this variety of cultures and languages, the region is seldom described as multicultural or multilingual. At most, there is a general recognition that it is a bi-cultural region with two national cultures centred on a national border. But more often the regions on either side of the border are depicted as monolingual. The public discourse in most of the local media is clearly monolingual. The profile of the border region is therefore linked to those aspects of national borders that have dominated Europe in the twentieth century: separation of sovereignties and separation of cultures.

The prevailing religion of the border region is Lutheranism even though the region is also home to many Muslim immigrants. The values fostered through school education are primarily Protestant ethics in both Schleswig-Holstein and Denmark. Although the region may be described as at a stage of historic reconciliation after the large conflicts of the twentieth century, the overall awareness in the general public of this is low. Reconciliation is still the domain of the political elites and more recently the national minorities.[30] Given the history of the border region, it has a long experience of intercultural dialogue, which has intensified considerably in recent years after the opening of the border and the elimination of border control.[31] However, the national sentiments on both sides of the border remain strong, and far from disappearing.[32] Although relations between the two national states have reached a civilized level of neutral politics and a spirit of cooperation, national sentiments still run high on both sides of the border. Members of the national minorities at times experience this when they participate in public debates and local politics.[33] Nevertheless, the region may be classified as one of the most accommodating of national minorities in Europe in that it represents an increasingly sophisticated web of minority protection tools.

Socially, the border region is experiencing demographic patterns similar to many border regions in Europe. The population is ageing, and the young often find a greater variety of opportunities outside the region.[34] The problem of how to retain

---

[28] Martin Klatt, *Fra modspil til medspil? Grænseoverskridende samarbejde i Sønderjylland/Schleswig, 1945–2005* [From Antagonism to Co-operation? Cross-Border Co-operation in the German–Danish Border Region, 1945–2005] (Aabenraa: Institut for Grænseregionsforskning, Syddansk Universitet, 2006). See also Henrik Becker Christensen, 'Fra "mod hinanden" til "med hinanden"' [From 'Against Each Other' to 'with Each Other'], in *Sønderjyllands Historie* vol. 2, edited by H. Schultz Hansen and H. Becker Christensen (Aabenraa: Historisk Samfund for Sønderjylland, 2009), pp. 241–462.

[29] German, Danish, South Schleswig Danish (spoken by members of Danish minority), *Sønderjysk/synnejysk* (spoken by members of the German Volksgruppe and by Danes), Frisian and its dialects, Platt German, Romany.

[30] Frank Lubowitz, 'Oeversee 1864—Entstehung und Wandel eines Gedenktages' [Oeversee 1864—Formation and Transformation of Memorial Day], *Grenzfriedenshefte* vol. 4 (2005): pp. 301ff.

[31] Denmark joined the Schengen agreement in 2001.

[32] Klatt, 'Genforening eller mindretal'.

[33] In 2005, the formation of a coalition government that included the minority party, Sydslesvigske Vælgerforening (SSV) did not receive the confidence vote in the local Schleswig-Holstein parliament, the *Landtag*.

[34] For Schleswig-Holstein 22 per cent are over 65 years of age, see Statistische Ämter des Bundes und der Länder, 'Gebiet und Bevölkerung—Bevölkerung nach Altersgruppen', accessed 26 March

the young is a challenge for both the general population and the minorities. The need to revitalize the region and promote a more progressive and innovative profile to the world is thus a mutual desire of all active members of society. Mobilization of social networks and movements to make the region more competitive and innovative are taking place within the elite groups of society. In order not to end up as a retirement community, the actors and players of the border region are becoming more focused on defining new frameworks for development. The political identity of the border region is a mixture of progressives and conservatives with a growing number of Green citizens who prefer to see the region paying stronger attention to the environment. The region is home to a number of areas in need of environmental protection, such as the Wadding Sea and its bird life on the west coast. Alternative wind energy is also becoming a large part of the local economy thus placing the region in the group of European regions which are more innovative and progressive. At the same time, the border region also represents a number of traditional sectors, such as agriculture, light industry, border trade, shipyards, transport, cruise and cultural tourism, as well as a growing service industry.

Economically, the border region is still experiencing the 'shocks' or aftershocks of German unification in Schleswig-Holstein and the most recent economic crisis in both countries. During the crisis budget negotiations in 2010, in particular the Danish minority saw cuts in funding for their organizations, most notably their educational and social institutions.[35] It is during these times that the self-empowerment of the minorities and their ability to 'take things in their own hands' emerge centre stage both in the formal structures of minority governance and in the informal settings of NTA institutions.

9.3.2 The institutional framework in the region

With regard to minority–majority relations, the post–World War II period saw a slow but steady development of tolerance and respect. Experts attribute this to the joint initiative of the two countries' leaders to issue identical statements of intent on minority protection in 1955.[36] The so-called Bonn–Copenhagen Declarations are not legally binding but have gained strong moral value in the management of minority issues and minority protection.[37] The Declarations were issued on the basis of a political agreement that Denmark, which was a member of NATO, would support Germany's membership. The Declarations stipulate identical civil and political rights for the two national minorities living near the border, the

2014, <http://www.statistik-portal.de/Statistik-Portal/de_jb01_z2.asp>; for Region Syddanmark 19 per cent are over 65, see Danske Regioner, 'Statistik', accessed 26 March 2014, <http://www.regioner. dk/om+regionerne/statistik+ny>.

[35] Jørgen Kühl, *Mindretalsmodel i krise* [Minority Model in Crisis] (Flensburg: Dansk Skoleforening for Sydslesvig, 2012).

[36] Becker Christensen, 'Fra "mod hinanden" til "med hinanden"'.

[37] The Declarations are identical as far as the international standards are concerned, but the Bonn Declaration includes a section on the division of powers between the federal and local level.

Danish minority in Schleswig-Holstein and the German minority in southern Denmark. The Declarations also provide for wide-ranging cultural and educational rights without stipulating any self-government or autonomy. In addition, the Bonn Declaration includes a section on the federal division of powers with regard to minority protection in Germany; specifically, the delegation of powers in the area of education policy. Both the German and the Danish constitutions protect individual civil and political rights. While neither constitution recognizes the minorities, they both provision special rules for minority parties.[38] Both countries have signed and ratified the most important European and international legal instruments, such as the European Convention on Human Rights (1950), the European Charter on Regional or Minority Languages (1992), the European Framework Convention for the Protection of National Minorities (1995), and the United Nations' Covenants (1966) on human rights. Both countries have recognized the minorities in connection with the signing of the European Framework Convention. After the Bonn–Copenhagen Declarations were in place, work to create feasible corporate structures began on both sides of the border; in Germany at the sub-federal level of Schleswig-Holstein and in Denmark at the national level.

Schleswig-Holstein had already recognized the cultural rights of the Danish minority in 1949 in the so-called Kiel Declaration, which reiterated the rights and responsibilities of the minority according to the federal German constitution as well as the right to freedom of belonging to the minority and to send their children to Danish minority schools.[39] The first decree on minority schools was issued in 1950. This political recognition was made legally binding through the revision of the Schleswig-Holstein Constitution in 1990, which expanded the scope of rights. Following this, Schleswig-Holstein has adopted legislative acts on education,[40] elections,[41] and day care[42] as well as media.[43] These acts provide for the formalization of minority institutions in the respective areas. Thus, minority schools in Schleswig-Holstein are regulated as private schools, or substitute schools (*Ersatzschulen*), but hold recognition as fulfilling public school requirements. Minority political representation and participation in regional and local elections is guaranteed on the basis of an exemption from the general requirements

---

[38] The German Constitution provisions exemption from the 5 per cent threshold to enter national and local parliaments. The Danish Constitution exempts the German minority from collecting the required signatures to run for the national parliament.

[39] Klatt, 'Genforening eller mindretal', p. 216.

[40] The first legislation addressing minority schools was adopted in 1978 but currently the schools are regulated by the Education Act of 1990, arts 4, 58, 60, 63, accessed 27 February 2014, <http://www.schulrecht-sh.de/archiv/schulgesetz/index.htm>.

[41] Elections Act of 1991, art 3(1), accessed 27 February 2014, <http://www.gesetze-rechtsprechung.sh.juris.de/jportal/?quelle=jlink&query=WahlG+SH+%C2%A7+3&psml=bsshoprod.psml&max=true>.

[42] Day Care Act of 1991, arts 5, 7, 12, accessed 27 February 2014, <http://www.gesetze-rechtsprechung.sh.juris.de/jportal/?quelle=jlink&query=KTagStG+SH&psml=bsshoprod.psml&max=true&aiz=true#jlr-KTagStGSHV4P5 jlr-KTagStGSHV1P5 jlr-KTagStGSHV2P5 jlr-KTagStGSHV3P5>.

[43] Media Act of 1995, arts 17, 24, 26, 34, 45, 54, accessed 27 February 2014, <http://www.rafraenkel.de/cgi-bin/gesetze/data/67.pdf>.

on representativeness.[44] Minority cultural education in kindergartens is guaranteed through a requirement to accommodate the wishes of parents, whereas a multicultural representation is required in the public media. The Danish minority organizations in Schleswig-Holstein are, therefore, incorporated mainly as private associations under German law.[45]

Denmark follows somewhat the same line albeit in practice rather than formal standard-setting. Firstly, there is no formal recognition of the German minority in the Constitution, and no specific law addresses the rights of the minority. Prior to World War II, the public schools in those areas where Germans lived were obliged also to teach in German. This right was eliminated after the War but in 1946 it was reinstated. In 1949, the Danish government issued a protocol, the so-called Copenhagen Protocol, enumerating the rights of the German minority, including the right to maintain German identity and speak German as well as the right to established German kindergartens. The German minority schools are regulated as private schools (*Friskoler*) and are recognized as providers of public education.[46] All other organizations operated by the German minority are incorporated as sub-committees of the minority's main organization, Bund Deutscher Nordschleswiger, which is established as a private association.[47] The Danish law on elections recognizes the exemption from the requirement to submit voters' declarations for the German minority party when registering the party for general elections.[48] Since the German minority party has not been participating in national elections since 1964, there are special rules for local elections.[49]

9.3.3 Five sectors of functional NTA

Functional NTA minority organizations are found in five major sectors in the border region. These are the political and cultural sectors, education and social services, as well as the economic sector, with the latter representing sub-domains, such as agriculture, finances, the environment, energy, and cultural heritage

---

[44] The Danish minority is exempt from the requirement to elect one representative in every local district.

[45] See also Detlev Rein's chapter in this volume, 'The Sorbian People in Germany'.

[46] Act on Free Schools of 1991 with amendments, accessed 27 February 2014, <https://www.retsinformation.dk/Forms/r0710.aspx?id=145519>.

[47] Bund Deutscher Nordschleswiger, accessed 26 March 2014, <http://www.bdn.dk/>.

[48] Elections (consolidated) Act of 2013 (in English), accessed 27 February 2014, <http://valg.oim.dk/media/502465/FT-electionsUK-2013.pdf>.

[49] New rules for local and municipal elections in 2007 guaranteed the German minority party a non-voting mandate in the event that it did not reach the minimum requirement of 25 per cent of the votes for a mandate. See report, 'Responsum fra den dansk-slesvig-holstenske arbejdsgruppe til behandling af ligestillingsspørgsmål ved finansieringen af det danske og det tyske mindretalsskoler' [Legal Opinion from the Danish-Schleswig-Holstein Working Group to Consider Equality Issues in the Financing of the Danish and the German Minority Schools], accessed 27 February 2014, <http://www.uvm.dk/Aktuelt/~/UVM-DK/Content/News/Int/2010/Nov/~/media/UVM/Filer/Om%20os/Int/PDF10/101112_Bericht_Minderheitenschulen_DK.ashxhttp://www.uvm.dk/Aktuelt/~/UVM-DK/Content/News/Int/2010/Nov/~/media/UVM/Filer/Om%20os/Int/PDF10/101112_Bericht_Minderheitenschulen_DK.ashx>.

tourism.[50] At the political level, the two minority parties as well as a number of representative and consultative bodies have been established over the years. With regard to the political parties, favourable conditions for the Danish minority party in Schleswig-Holstein, the Sydslevisk Vælgerforening (SSV), have enabled it to remain active in the *Landtag* since 1958 due to an exemption from the 5 per cent threshold. In general, the SSV is considered an important contributor to the political debate and decision-making process in Schleswig-Holstein, and most recently, since 2012, the party has been in the ruling coalition holding the cabinet posts of Justice, Culture, and European Affairs. At the municipal level, the SSV holds 195 seats in municipal councils, and in the town of Flensburg, where it also constitutes one of the largest parties in the council; it also holds the post of lord mayor.[51] The German minority party in Denmark, the Slesvigske Parti (SP) has not been represented directly in the Danish Parliament since 1964 but it has been successful at the local level, particularly in connection with the elections to the four most southern municipalities after the restructuring of Danish districts in 2007.[52] This success was due in large part to an innovation of ideas implemented in the election campaign and the fact that the individual members of the party attracted majority votes. The SP also negotiated with the Danish authorities to implement a special right to representation. The so-called Hungarian model allows the SP party list to be entitled to a delegate if it does not win at least one seat, but obtains at least 25 per cent of votes corresponding to the lowest electoral quota carrying a seat at the election.[53] The SP holds a total of nine posts in all the four municipal councils in southern Denmark, and in one municipality it also holds a committee chair.[54] Therefore, without specific devolution of powers but ad hoc special rights, both minority parties are able to participate actively in the decision-making processes at the municipal level, and in Schleswig-Holstein also at the sub-federal state level.

In a less formal manner, the sheer number of organizations established between 1949 and today keep the political dialogue between the minorities and the majority

---

[50] The discussion of minority institutions is based to a large extent on findings published in *Competence Analysis*, 2007 where the reader can find detailed empirical data for each of the sectors discussed. See 'Competence Analysis: National Minorities as a Standortfaktor in the German–Danish Border Region', accessed 26 March 2014, <http://www.landtag.ltsh.de/export/sites/landtagsh/parlament/minderheitenpolitik/download/kompetenzanalyse_en.pdf>. See also, Adrian Schaeffer-Rolffs, 'Paternalistic versus Participation Oriented Minority Institutions in the Danish–German Border Region', *ECMI Working Paper* no. 67 (2013).

[51] See Sydslesvigsk Forening, 'Dansk virke i Grænselandet—Sydslesvigsk Årbog 2013' [Danish Action in the Border Region—South Schleswig Yearbook 2013] (Flensburg: Sydslesvigsk Forening, 2013).

[52] The German minority did cooperate with the centre-right party, Central Democrats from 1973 to 1979 and held indirectly a mandate through one of its member's membership of this party. See Bund Deutscher Nordschleswiger, 'Vorgeschichte des Kopenhagener Sekretariats', accessed 16 March 2014, <http://www.bdn.dk/vorgeschichte.8635.aspx>.

[53] See Third Report submitted by Denmark Pursuant to Article 25, Paragraph 2 of the Framework Convention for the Protection of National Minorities of 30 March 2010 (ACFC/SR/III(2010)004), accessed 26 March 2014, <http://www.coe.int/t/dghl/monitoring/minorities/3_FCNMdocs/PDF_3rd_SR_Denmark_en.pdf>.

[54] See Bund Deutscher Nordschleswiger, accessed 26 March 2014, <http://www.bdn.dk/>.

open. These organizations are usually considered consultative bodies in that they provide for a platform where minorities can be heard.[55] However, they also aim to bring all parties together on an equal footing to discuss matters of concern. In the border region there is an abundance of these types of institutions.[56] While none of these organizations have legal standing, they function as intercultural dialogue and consultation fora based on good will and trust. Through these organizations the minorities voice their concerns and at times also claim their rights in those areas that are not included in the overall frameworks established over the years, such as tourism or economic development fora as well as the example of the special right of the SP in municipal elections. The minorities also use these fora to voice their concerns in regard to Denmark and Germany's compliance with international law standards adopted by the two countries. For instance, the cyclic monitoring of the Council of Europe's Framework Convention for the Protection of National Minorities and the European Charter for Minority or Regional Languages is often the focus of debates in these organizations.

The field of culture, together with education, is the area where the minorities exert the highest level of autonomy in terms of self-management over their own institutions. In the cultural sector alone, both minorities maintain organizations, such as theatre, museums, youth clubs, and sports clubs, and organize concerts, annual festivals, and religious activities. In terms of membership, the largest minority organizations are the youth and sports clubs. Most activities are open to the general public with or without membership, and many events are offered on a commercial basis. While many events and activities can be shared with members of the majority, there are of course activities that would require attendees to be bilingual. On an annual basis, the Danish minority alone organizes a dozen symphony concerts as well as ballets; more than seventy theatre performances of which more than half are for children. The minorities also maintain libraries and archives. The Danish minority's library, Dansk Centralbibliotek for Sydslevsig, and the German minority's library, Verbandes Deutscher Büchereien Nordschleswig, function as the intellectual depositories of the border region's history of minority cultures. They also have research staff that undertakes research. The minorities also safeguard the preservation of local history and culture through the maintenance of their museums. Both minorities operate museums which catalogue minority as well as regional history. While some of these museums are partially funded by

---

[55] Marc Weller and Katherine Nobbs, eds, *Political Participation of Minorities. A Commentary on International Standards and Practice* (Oxford: Oxford University Press, 2010).

[56] The Liaison Committee for the German Minority to the Danish State (1964); the Advisory Committee for Danish Minority Issues (1965); the Committee for Issues Concerning the German Minority in North Schleswig (1975); the Representation Office of the Germany Minority in Copenhagen (1983); the European Bureau for Lesser-Used Languages (EBLUL) in Germany (1986); the Commissioner of the Minister-President for Minority Affairs and Culture, Schleswig-Holstein (1988); the Representation Office of the Danish Minority to the Danish Parliament (1992); the Commissioner for German Minority Issues and German Embassy Contacts in the Border Region (2000); the German Federal Government Commissioner for Emigrant Issues and National Minorities (2002); the Trans-Factional Initiative for Regional and Minority Languages (2003); DialogForumNorden (2004) and the Secretariat for Minorities to the *Bundestag* (2005).

national funds and kin-state funding, others are entirely funded by the minorities themselves or through private donations. Common to all the museums is that they are operated by members of the minorities, either as salaried personnel or as volunteers.

The minorities participate in the public debate through the two daily minority newspapers, *Der Nordschleswiger* in Denmark and the *Flensborg Avis* in Schleswig-Holstein. These newspapers are considered among the most important minority dailies in Europe. *Flensborg Avis,* a bilingual newspaper, was founded in 1868 and became a limited company in 1930. Today it has 1,400 stockholders and is estimated to have around 20,000 readers. *Der Nordschleswiger,* which is only published in German, was established in 1946. Together, the two newspapers represent many years of minority news reporting and intercultural dialogue experience. In total, they print almost 10,000 copies per day and employ forty-four journalists. Both newspapers have also established publishing houses, and *Der Nordschleswiger* produces five minutes of radio news per day. Journalists from both newspapers have received prizes for good journalism. Although the two newspapers were initially established as the voice of the minorities, they now also take part in the shaping of public opinion on specific regional issues. The newspapers are also read outside the border region and in Copenhagen and Berlin.

With regard to education, the minority schools in the border region date back to 1920 in Schleswig-Holstein and to 1949 in Denmark. The schools are seen as an instrument in the maintenance and furthering of minority culture and identity while also preparing the pupils for life in the majority culture. This means that the curriculum is taught in both the minority and the majority languages in parallel and as mother tongues. All minority educational establishments in the border region are self-administered by the minorities, meaning that they do not require input from the majority administration. The Danish minority operates fifty kindergartens, forty-six schools, and two high schools,[57] and the German minority operates twenty-one kindergartens, fourteen schools, and one high school.[58] Given the rural location of some minority schools, classes are often smaller in size and have fewer pupils per class than the average public schools. This is particularly pronounced in the schools on the west coast of Schleswig-Holstein and poses challenges in terms of expense. A complex funding scheme has emerged over the years rendering the minority schools dependent on funds from both Germany and Denmark. Both countries provide basic subsidies according to number of pupils and on a par with majority schools. In addition, the minority schools receive funding specifically aimed at securing bilingual education. Significant with regard to the external funding received from kin-states is that it is lobbied for and negotiated directly between the minorities and their respective kin-state authorities. This means that the minorities are not only carrying out a public administration service

---

[57] See Dansk Skoleforening for Sydslesvig e.V., Vores Institutioner, accessed 26 March 2014, <http://www.skoleforeningen.org/institutioner>.
[58] See Deutschen Schul- und Sprachverein fur Nordschleswig, accessed 26 March 2014, <http://www.dssv.dk/>.

that would otherwise have to be conducted by the local and national administrations but they are also actively entering into power relations with the authorities of both national and kin-state.

The need to provide social services to members of minorities was first identified in 1945, when living conditions after the War were difficult on both sides of the border but especially in Schleswig-Holstein. This was also a period when many border region non-governmental organizations (NGOs) were established by kin-states to distribute humanitarian help. Today, the Danish and the German minorities operate sophisticated social service centres offering services mainly to elderly members of the minorities but also offering counselling, medical care, and maternity advice. The two minority organizations, Dansk Sundhedstjeneste for Sydslesvig in Schleswig-Holstein and Sozialdienst Nordschleswig in Denmark, offer services on a par with the national services. Both services operate homes for the elderly as well as assistance in the homes of the elderly. Thus, there is no longer a need for the kin-state NGOs to fill that space. Other social services provided by the minorities include the long-standing tradition among the Danish minority of organizing working class members in the Sønderjysk Arbejderforening, which, among other activities, has been instrumental in supporting victims of the Nazi regime in getting compensation. This organization dates back to the early post-war years when the sociological composition of the Danish minority consisted of primarily labour and wage earners. The Danish minority also administers humanitarian help through the I.C. Møller Foundation, which donates small grants to the needy and the sick. Similarly, the German minority supports needy members through the Deutsche Selbsthilfe Nordschleswig which offers small loans as well as co-financing to young families with children wishing to buy or build a home. Finally, voluntary work is also performed in the area of care for the elderly with both cultural and physical activities. Humanitarian help is thus a large part of the social services rendered by the minorities to their members.

The fifth sector, the economic, is rather broad in terms of identifying minority organizations, which provide self-administered services to members of the minorities. Arguably, the aforementioned cultural organizations and their activities may also be seen as part of the economic sector. The minority cultural heritage museums are also relevant here. The museums are operated by the minorities often on a voluntary basis. This is the case with many of the small cultural heritage and archaeological sites on the west coast and on the coastal islands. Moreover, the Danish minority has taken the lead in getting the entire Dannevirke area (fortifications dating back to around AD 500) in Schleswig-Holstein declared a UNESCO protected site. The economic sector further includes a number of minority organizations that may be seen as culture neutral but nonetheless are established and organized by minorities. These are organizations where minorities create economic activity, not only as members of minorities but also as members of mainstream society.[59] These include agricultural organizations and financial establishments,

---

[59] For the value of regional networks, see Susanne Gretzinger and Susanne Royer, 'Social kapital i regionale netværk skaber værdi—den sønderjyske mektronikklynge' [Social Capital in

environmental action, organizations focusing on energy, the print media, and minority heritage tourism.

With regard to agriculture, for instance, a high percentage of members of the German minority in Denmark are farmers, and agriculture is both an economic and a political issue to the German minority. The agricultural sector has traditionally been one of Denmark's strongest sectors for centuries. With modernization of the agricultural sector in the second half of the twentieth century, monopolization took over. In this process, the German minority positioned itself in a pioneering position as organic farmers.[60] The German minority runs its own farmers' association, the Landwirtschaftlicher Hauptverein für Nordschleswig (LHN). The LHN is one of the smallest agricultural associations in Denmark, but nonetheless one of the pioneering ones. It offers advice to farmers and is an important participant in ensuring and developing a well-functioning agricultural sector in southern Denmark. Its strategy aims at securing the cultural identity of farmers and the farming sector as well as the maintenance of memberships and the dynamic and modern structure of the association. In Schleswig-Holstein, the Danish minority has a long tradition in farming. The history of Danish minority agricultural cooperation goes back 150 years in Schleswig and is thus a product of both Prussian politics in the region and the simultaneously emerging movement of cooperative farming in Denmark. It became natural to cooperate on issues of farming, financing, and information. Fælleslandboforeningen for Sydslesvig is a fully functioning support organization for Danish minority farmers in Schleswig-Holstein. It provides advisory services on animal husbandry, cultivation, machinery, and buildings, and it provides a cultural guide function to visiting interest groups. In spite of its fairly small size, Fælleslandboforeningen for Sydslesvig's members have received prizes for their star productions. In addition, the Danish minority has established a trade association, the Dansk Erhvervsforening i Sydslesvig, which represents Danish commercial interests by being the link to the majority society through the activities of its members. It also participates actively in the local debate about the economic development of the border region. Finally, with regard to regional development, the German minority in Denmark holds observer status in a Regional Growth Forum established by the Region Syddanmark, and both minorities have had seats in the cross-border INTERREG Commission.

Just as the need of the minorities for obtaining credit was important in the social sector, so it is in the agricultural sector. Both the Danish minority in Schleswig-Holstein and the German minority in Denmark have long-standing traditions of providing credit loans to their own farmers. Both credit unions offer favourable conditions and low interest rates for loans. The Danish minority first established a credit facility during the years immediately following the annexation

Regional Networks Create Added Value—the Southern Denmark Mekatronik Cluster], *Pluk* (May 2012): pp. 15–19.

[60] See Landwirtschaftlicher Hauptverein für Nordschleswig, accessed 26 March 2014, <http://www.lhn.dk/Forside.htm>.

of the Duchy of Sleswig by Prussia. The need to support farmers financially was paramount. Today, the Danish minority has its own bank, the Union Bank and Slevigs Kreditforening eG. In Europe, few minorities have their own banks. The fact that the minorities in the border region have credit unions shows how serious the establishment of permanent and viable economic life was to the minorities. The farming traditions in the minority communities were a factor both in creating permanency in the region and stability in local society. To obtain loans, one has to prove membership of the minorities. However, today the Union Bank is open to normal business with the majority. Loans can only be had for purposes of farming in South Schleswig. In Denmark, the Kredit-Garantie-Ausschuss des BDN services the farmers from the German minority with loans for various purposes.

The minorities also see the environment and alternative energy as important aspects of their responsibility as citizens in the border region. In fact, the minorities' environmental activities show the interest of the minorities not only in developing the region but also in preserving the region as part of preserving their cultural homeland. The environment is of interest to many people living in the border region due to the large coastlines of both the western coast and the eastern coast. Both coastlines are of concern in terms of environmental protection. The protection of the coastlines, particularly the Wadden Sea on the west coast, has been a concern of the Danish minority, which supported an application by the Schleswig-Holstein government to UNESCO for protection of a 'Schleswig-Holstein Wadding See' national park. In addition, a member of the political party SSV (as well as of the North Frisian minority) emerged as a tireless speaker and defender in the *Landtag* of the environment in Schleswig-Holstein. Likewise alternative energy is also of great concern. The German minority's farmers have taken the lead in the quest for developing bioenergy in the border region. While the border region is also one of the leading wind energy regions in Europe, the German minority is actively promoting bioenergy, and the head of the LHN is now a principal figure in a new bioenergy park established close to the border. Finally, young members of the Danish minority have initiated a 'think globally, act locally' initiative within the minority which seeks to mobilize individual members to become more environmentally conscientious. The so-called Glokale Sydslevigere have established an association called Handle/forvandle (act and change) and are seeking to involve members directly through meetings and events. It has furthermore challenged the corporate body of the Danish minority, the Sydslesvigske Forening (SSF), to adopt green budgeting in the administrations of its organizations.

9.4 The Dynamics

Underlying the self-empowerment argument of this chapter are two assumptions upon which the functional NTA analysis must rely. First, in so far that the focus is on action and activist-type citizenship, the notion of autonomy applied assumes 'power to' and 'freedom to' in contradistinction to 'freedom from'. This means that there are at least three specific dimensions of autonomy characterizing the processes that emerge as functional NTA in the border region. These are the independent variables *choice, capability*, and *will*. I will discuss these separately below. The second assumption defines the dependent variable of the system or the structure within which the minority organizations are able to act autonomously when opportunities arise. This framework is based on the assumption of 'freedom from' in so far that it is a framework that seeks to prevent cultural assimilation as set out in the minority protection standards. It is guided by the international and national norms that the two countries have decided to follow, such as the Bonn–Copenhagen Declarations and the Council of Europe's FCNM. However, in both case studies, that is, the Danish and the German accommodation models, the structures are fragmented, combining loosely statutes and programmes at multiple levels but without any central legal framework established. Because the fragmented framework is spread over several levels and is informal in character, it allows for outcomes to emerge that would not normally emerge from traditional NTA. This, therefore, renders the functional NTA model self-empowering in praxis, if not in legal terms.

With regard to the first specific dimension of the notion of autonomy, the aspect of *choice*, this is exemplified in terms of the desire to seek change through activism and acts of citizenship. This is seen in the minorities' visions about their communities, and the fact that they participate actively in politics not only as members of a minority but also as members of a majority that seeks a well-functioning society. Particularly important for the issue of choice is the fact that the minorities seek leading posts, such as mayorships in the case of the Danish minority and chairs of municipal committees as in the case of the German minority. Any politician who takes on a leading role in public administration must be able to exercise choice and discern good from bad. The choice dimension is also exemplified in the work of the German minority in the agricultural sector taking a lead in the transformation to organic farming and to alternative energy production. To the minorities these are matters of homeland preservation acted upon on the basis of conscious choices regarding that homeland. The survival of the homeland region is vital to most historic minorities in Europe, as homeland regions provide the nurture for identity formation and self-identification with regional and national traditions. There is, therefore, a strong inner motivation and direction in the choice to protect both the food chain in terms of organic farming and the environment in terms of alternative energy.

The second dimension is the aspect of *capability*, which is exemplified in terms of the power to seek change by creating new or alternative functions of service provision through bottom-up activism and to sustain these through self-administration and self-governance. This is seen in some of the sectors discussed, most notably the cultural sector, education, and social services as well as the credit unions. Procuring cultural education and options for acquiring cultural sustenance as well as producing cultural products, as opposed to relying passively on cultural dissemination from the kin-state, is exemplified in both the minorities' heavy emphasis on cultural activities, in particular for children, youth, and the elderly. Procuring a high number of cultural events and activities requires the capability to organize institutions that will procure the desired cultural products. Theatres, museums, youth clubs, sports clubs, concerts, and festivals are established, organized, and managed by both minorities independently. Similar capacity is required for the management of minority education. While policy frames may be dictated by the respective governments in terms of regulations about schools, both minorities must be able to adopt their desired educational goals as well as to operationalize and manage these goals. Materializing one's goals as a cultural human being is dependent on the nature of the education that one receives in the formative years, and education in one's own language and about one's own culture is a vital aspect of protecting and promoting minority cultural identity for historic minorities in most countries. For both minorities in the border region, a comprehensive educational process is considered vital. Thus, both minorities insist on educating their children from the first day of kindergarten through to the last year of obligatory education, usually high school. Minority education is arguably the most resource-demanding sector for the minorities to operate but at the same time it is the most important resource-providing institution in so far that it educates new members of the minorities. The capability to manage their own educational institutions is the survival tool of the minorities, and therefore the tool that can ensure autonomy is guaranteed for the future.

With regard to the provision of specific social services to minority members it is difficult to argue that it is a survival tool given that the care is given usually in the last years of a member's life. Nevertheless, minorities see the capacity to take care of the elderly in particular as part of the overall survival of the minority culture because social care is a birthright in Denmark and Germany. Both minorities in the border region live in states with well-functioning social models based on a view that the state takes care of you 'from the cradle to the grave'. The problem is that traditional elder care services are not equipped to be culture sensitive. So in those cases where there might be a communication and understanding issue, the minorities see a need to step in to assist in communication. In other words, they fill a gap in that cultural communication at the end of a person's life becomes very important and at times life saving. This is thus an example of bottom-up action that creates services based on capability, including language capacities. In short, the capability to provide specific services to members is not only a question of self-management but it actually becomes a type of self-governance and may, therefore, be seen as self-empowering NTA.

The third dimension is the aspect of *will* which is exemplified in the ability to seek change through self-direction and self-rule. While choice and capability denote desire and survival, will denotes direction and perseverance. This is exemplified in the minorities' actions in the informal political sector described in section 9.3.3. The participation as minority representatives in the consultative bodies designated to intercultural dialogue and minority issues requires not only determination and resolution about one's demands but also about the outcome even if it means less desirable compromises. Through these institutions the minorities have to achieve and materialize those aspects of minority rights that in a formalized, legalized setting of NTA would be established in law and adopted through a formal democratic process. Since such formal settings do not exist under conditions of functional NTA, the minority representatives have to show the will of their communities in order to claim their rights. Both the Danish and the German minority in the border region have a long history of successes in this respect. These range from matters of permission to fly the kin-state's flag in public spaces to securing funding and additional funding for activities in the established areas of protection, such as education and culture, as well as in new areas of cooperation, such as tourism. Most recently, the Danish minority also had to use these channels to secure access to kin-state media after digitalization. In other words, the dialogue institutions fill a function of minority governance that allows for self-determination if minorities possess the will to exercise their rights. Choice, capability, and will are, therefore, drivers for action that not only render the accommodation model in the border region functional but also autonomous.

The second assumption of the analysis of minority bottom-up action, the dependent variable of a *fragmented*, multilevel structure, allows for self-empowering NTA to emerge through the opportunities that procure pragmatic solutions. Firstly, the fact that the central and federal administration level is little involved in the functioning of the accommodation models means that there is room for bottom-up action at the micro-level. This is exploited by the minorities in their actions, and it promotes in fact the aim of traditional NTA, namely self-direction and self-government. Secondly, the fact that the fragmented structure allows for a public–private model in so far that some of the framework regulations are public and at the same time many if not most of the minority institutions are established under private law, means that there is considerable flexibility in devising new modes of service provision as well as in resolving normative issues. This is exemplified in the combination of establishing minority schools under private law while endowing them with public functions and powers. Thirdly, the fragmented structure opens up spaces for public administration that classic NTA would not because the latter delineates often strictly the boundaries and limits of areas of self-governance. Functional NTA being flexible allows for minorities to engage with public administration functions that would normally be closed areas for minorities, such as the social sector and some of the areas of the economic sector described in section 9.3.3. Whereas classic NTA is often restricted to cultural and educational areas, functional NTA need not be because there is no clear definition of the boundaries of the cultural and educational functions. Thus, the lack of clearly defined models in the Danish–German border region allows for a pragmatic approach to NTA that does not impose strict boundaries. In other words, the degree of fragmentation and the informal, bottom-up approaches to management at the micro-level allow for pragmatic solutions when opportunities arise. Pragmatic solutions, therefore, penetrate boundaries that classic NTA must respect.

9.5 Conclusions and Policy Analyses

The aim of this chapter was to demonstrate that the informal nature of functional NTA examined in the Danish–German border region may allow for the formation of a more flexible scope of NTA management than normally assigned to functional NTA. Functional NTA has traditionally been placed at the bottom of the normative scale of autonomy for minorities, implying that it is the weakest form of autonomy due to its lack of establishment in law and political structures. This chapter suggests otherwise. The examination of the functional model of NTA in the border region demonstrates that the minorities have been able to enter into networks of governance in public administration areas that are normally not included in classic NTA, such as the social and economic sectors. By grasping opportunities to act bottom-up in situations of vacuum or neglect, they have exercised choice, capacity, and will to establish pragmatic solutions in areas of societal management that concerned them and their members. In exercising strong abilities to act and seek change through a variety of instruments available to them via the fragmented and multilevel minority governance system, they have created self-management structures and exercised self-empowerment without established rights to self-government. I argued that not only have the minorities forged a self-empowerment NTA model, they have in certain sectors also been able to go beyond what classic NTA agreements would allow. In doing so, they have expanded their rights beyond traditional NTA rights as they have empowered themselves through the drive for policy change. It would seem, therefore, that functional NTA creates a paradox in minority governance that defies authoritative studies of NTA.

To put NTA in perspective, I argued that government strategies to control and pacify minorities through paternalistic security and protection programmes provide an inadequate picture of minority governance in the twenty-first century. Modern multilevel and multicultural society management requires provisioning of diversified public services especially in highly diverse settings, and states no matter how efficient may not have the resources and capacities to meet cultural demands in all service sectors. Whereas classic NTA models fill this gap in a number of service areas, usually the culture and education sectors, they are often restricted by tight definitions of public administration impact areas, thus excluding NTA in other areas. To begin broadening our perspective of NTA to include a governance networks perspective, I argued that two assumptions underpin the approach in the Danish–German border region, the specific notion of autonomy as 'freedom to' and 'power to', on the one hand, and the fragmented, multilevel accommodation models, on the other. While the first assumption may be characterized as an independent variable in that the capabilities of the minorities to exercise their 'power to' must rely on and is determined by the level of their human and social capital, the second assumption may be characterized as a dependent variable in that the two accommodating states, Denmark and Germany, have decided to follow similar approaches to minority rights governance, that is, low-level, fragmented, and informal institutionalization of societal management delivery to minorities framed by the international norms that the states have signed up to as a matter of international policy. Therefore, in the setting of diverse modern societies, there is a need to study NTA from new perspectives, in particular from the point of view of governance networks.

From the point of view of policymaking in culturally diverse societies, functional NTA as integration strategy provides policymakers with options of degrees of control. To some it could be considered a low-risk model in that it does not require codification at high levels of law; sovereignty is not threatened and power-sharing is not in question. On this basis, one might argue it is a low cost model for policymakers in that it does not demand any binding guarantees; with regard to the Danish–German border region the Bonn–Copenhagen Declarations were not legally binding and the international norms adopted by Denmark and Germany are binding but do not require constitutional codification nor do they provision any collective autonomy rights. On the other hand, to some policymakers the unpredictability of the functional approach as to areas of impact potentially becoming expanded through bottom-up action induced by informal structures may provide avenues for power-grabs by the minorities that could impact on the level of government control. Since public administration in democratic societies requires that public services are disbursed in a consistent manner, one might argue that the risk of power-grabs could render it a very expensive model in that it addresses public administration functions where state revenue should be applied as a matter of state responsibility. Thus, in the event of having to withdraw services in cases of emergency or severe economic constraints, situations could occur where opportunistic and pragmatic solutions emerge and consequently increased revenue disbursement is needed. The predictability of functional NTA as a control mechanism is, therefore, questionable.

For policymakers who are not concerned with control, but rather with celebrating diversity, functional NTA provides an option in terms of integration of minorities and majorities in culturally diverse societies. The assumption of the notion of autonomy as 'freedom to' and 'power to' allows for higher degrees of participation in mainstream society than 'freedom from' because the former two engender minority action. Described as 'acts of citizenship' that spring from bottom-up action, the behaviour of minorities who act upon societal issues contributes to enhancing their ability to participate in public affairs, such as societal management. The ensuing opportunities for self-management can furthermore result in self-empowerment and the ability of minorities to participate on an equal footing with the majority. In liberal democratic societies where individual autonomy and empowerment are seen as democratic ideals, equal access to empowerment is more likely to result in integration than control mechanisms. The question policymakers have to ask themselves is, therefore, whether they seek policy for control purposes or policy for democratic changes.

PART III

SYMBOLIC PARTICIPATION

10

Non-Territorial Autonomy in the Post-Soviet Space

Alexander Osipov

10.1 Introduction

Non-territorial autonomy (NTA) occupies a specific place in the current scholarly and political debates around ethnic relations. The notion has been extensively referred to as a policy tool or a normative idea and even implanted in some international soft law instruments[1] and domestic legislations, but its meaning and content remain unclear. One can talk rather about a multiplicity of interpretations loosely connected to each other than a single normative principle or coherent model. In numerous scholarly publications and political statements NTA is considered as either a general principle according to which people can jointly pursue their interests related to preservation and expression of their ethnic identity in a variety of organizational forms;[2] or as a special shape of organization on ethnic grounds—as a rule as a vertically integrated corporation based on fixed membership of persons belonging to a certain ethnic group;[3] or/ and as a performance of public functions or competences by the said organizations.[4]

---

[1] Such as the Lund Recommendations on the Participation of National Minorities in Public Life (adopted 1 September 1999) of the OSCE High Commissioner on National Minorities.

[2] Brendan O'Leary, 'The Logics of Power-Sharing, Consociation and Pluralist Federations', in *Settling Self-Determination Disputes: Complex Power-Sharing in Theory and Practice*, edited by Barbara Metzger, Marc Weller, and Niall Johnson (Leiden: Martinus Nijhoff Publishers, 2008), pp. 47, 54–5; Hans-Joachim Heintze, 'On the Legal Understanding of Autonomy', in *Autonomy: Applications and Implications*, edited by Markku Suksi (The Hague; Boston: Kluwer Law International, 1998), pp. 15–16.

[3] Christofer D. Decker, 'Contemporary Forms of Cultural Autonomy in Eastern Europe: Recurrent Problems and Prospects for Improving the Functioning of Elected Bodies of Cultural Autonomy', in *The Participation of Minorities in Public Life* (Strasbourg: Council of Europe Publishing, 2008), pp. 89–90; Yash Ghai, 'Ethnicity and Autonomy: A Framework for Analysis', in *Autonomy and Ethnicity: Negotiating Competing Claims in Multi-Ethnic States*, edited by Yash Ghai (Cambridge, New York: Cambridge University Press, 2000), p. 8; Thomas Benedikter, *The World's Modern Autonomy Systems. Concepts and Experiences of Regional Territorial Autonomy* (Bozen/Bolzano: European Academy of Bozen/Bolzano, 2009), pp. 39–40.

[4] Tove Malloy, 'The Lund Recommendations and Non-Territorial Arrangements: Progressive De-Territorialization of Minority Politics', *International Journal on Minority and Group Rights* vol. 16, no. 4 (2009), pp. 665–79; Markku Suksi, 'Personal Autonomy as Institutional Form—Focus on

At first glance, NTA rests on the assumption that ethnicities can and should be regarded as internally cohesive social entities possessing will, interests, and ability to make decisions collectively, and thus behaving as social actors. If one discards this 'groupist'[5] assumption, the construction collapses and the idea loses any sense in most of its interpretations. Moreover, the ideas labelled as NTA have very few unquestionable substantive referents in the current or past ethno-political designs and thus basically remain a sample of wishful thinking. Therefore, one may also ask the question whether NTA can go beyond the domain of political rhetoric and serve as an analytical tool with a definite conventional meaning.

My suggestion is to address NTA in terms of 'frame' and regard it as a framing mode in ethno-politics employed both by experts and practitioners. I assume that from this perspective, the notion of NTA can serve for mapping certain rhetoric, decisions, and institutional settings within broader politics. For the purposes of this chapter, I confine my analysis to official ethno-cultural policies pursued 'from above'. Therefore, 'policies of non-territorial autonomy' can be analysed as interactions between certain ways of framing multi-ethnicity, the adoption of respective normative models, and ultimately their implementation. Briefly, these policies can be defined as top-down arrangements which are designed for the accommodation and facilitation of collective activities pursued on behalf of identity-based groups and which imply special treatment of certain activities and organizations.

10.2 Theoretical Considerations

I assume that NTA is non-existent as a single coherent theoretical or practical model, but that the term can depict a certain way of framing attitudes and action with regard to ethnic and cultural heterogeneity. One can pinpoint similar discursive patterns, descriptive models and popular approaches to contextualize and problematize ethnicity-related issues that share some features with the major interpretations of NTA; sometimes these patterns lead to political decisions and institution-building. Such terms as 'frame' or 'framing' lack a clear and uniform meaning and still generate controversies,[6] although they have been employed in social sciences for about forty years starting from the seminal work of Erving Goffman who defined frames as 'schemata of interpretation' which enable people to 'locate, perceive, identify and label' 'infinite number of concrete occurrences'[7].

Europe against the Background of Article 27 of the ICCPR', *International Journal on Minority and Group Rights* vol. 15, nos 2–3 (2008): pp. 157–78.

[5] Rogers Brubaker, 'Ethnicity without Groups', *Archives Européennes de Sociologie* vol. XLIII, no. 2 (2002): pp. 163–4.

[6] Robert Entman, 'Framing: Toward Clarification of a Fractured Paradigm', *Journal of Communication* vol. 43, no. 4 (1993): pp. 51–8; Kim Fisher, 'Locating Frames in the Discursive Universe', *Sociological Research Online* vol. 2, no. 3 (1997), accessed 19 March 2014, <http://www.socresonline.org.uk/2/3/4.html>.

[7] Erving Goffman, *Frame Analysis: An Essay on the Organization of Experience* (London: Harper and Row, 1974), p. 21.

Basically, 'frame' is understood as a 'scattered conceptualization'[8] way to contextualize certain social phenomenon and to define its primary characteristics in public communication.[9] Sometimes 'frame' is defined as a 'second level agenda setting'[10] or 'strategic communication'—the imposition of a way to perceive, assess, and prioritize certain issues.[11] Most often the notion of framing serves for the purposes of analysing mass media and activities of public movements.[12] Nothing precludes us from regarding policymakers and experts as an environment, a 'discursive community,'[13] that provides for the problematization and contextualization of ethnic policies and this makes the notion of 'framing' relevant in the given context.

Some authors argue that frame comprises four major elements which are (1) setting up the context; (2) formulating the problem; (3) pointing out the problem's source; and (4) putting forward a solution.[14] Respectively, NTA as framing (1) sets up the context as a multi-communal society where ethnicities as such appear as its founding blocks; (2) describes the problem as a need for mutual accommodation and reconciliation of ethnicities taken as social entities; (3) defines the source as a conflict between territorial/political domination of a certain ethnicity and the needs of other ethnicities to pursue their own interests and to develop themselves socially and culturally; and (4) offers a solution in self-organization of ethnic groups and redistribution of resources among them notwithstanding their territorial belonging. This general mode of framing prompts acknowledgement (at least rhetorically) of the need for certain decisions, such as self-organization of ethnic groups, their organizational consolidation and transfer of competences and resources. A complex interrelation between declarations, normative frameworks, decisions, actions, and institutional settings can hardly be addressed as a linear one-way connection; rather one should expect a mosaic of loosely linked 'talks', 'decisions', 'actions', and organizational set-ups. Official statements do not necessarily entail the respective action, but nevertheless in some way set up or change public agendas; similarly, an established practice or rule may lack legal underpinning or explicit clear-cut justification, but nevertheless channel public activities and deliberations.

---

[8] Entman, 'Framing: Toward Clarification', p. 51.

[9] Zhongdang Pan and G. M. Kosicki, 'Framing as a Strategic Action in Public Deliberation', in *Framing Public Life: Perspectives on Media and our Understanding of the Social World*, edited by Stephen D. Reese, Oscar H. Gandy, and August E. Grant (Mahwah, NJ: Lawrence Erlbaum Associates, 2001), pp. 37–40.

[10] Maxwell McCombs and Salma Ghanem, 'The Convergence of Agenda Setting and Framing', in *Framing Public Life: Perspectives on Media and our Understanding of the Social World*, edited by Stephen D. Reese, Oscar H. Gandy, and August E. Grant (Mahwah, NJ: Lawrence Erlbaum Associates, 2001), pp. 67–81.

[11] Marie-Eve Desrosiers, 'Reframing Frame Analysis: Key Contributions to Conflict Studies', *Ethnopolitics* vol. 11, no. 1 (2012): pp. 1–23.

[12] Robert D. Benford and David A. Snow, 'Framing Processes and Social Movements: An Overview and Assessment', *Annual Review of Sociology* vol. 26 (2000): pp. 11–39; Dietram A. Scheufele, 'Framing as a Theory of Media Effects', *Journal of Communication* vol. 49, no. 4 (1999): pp. 103–22.

[13] Pan and Kosicki, 'Framing as a Strategic Action', p. 43.

[14] Entman, 'Framing: Toward Clarification', p. 55.

As mentioned before, I regard 'policies of non-territorial autonomy' (or 'NTA policies') as activities (including rhetorical exercises) of public authorities purporting the need to create conditions for self-organization and activity of ethnic groups as such. In my view, this approach must be instrumental particularly in the analysis of ethnic policies in post-Soviet countries, most of which are still far from the ideals of liberal democracy and which demonstrate the 'unrule of law',[15] a symbiosis of formal and informal institutions[16] and 'systemic hypocrisy'[17] in the form of a gulf between official representations and actions. Respectively, my task here is to trace where and under what circumstances the above-mentioned way of framing multi-ethnicity leads to conceptualization of NTA in legislation and political decisions and subsequently to setting up institutions. We can also expect movements in the opposite direction when certain organizations and practices generate certain discourses and justifications. For the purpose of this study, I single out three potential directions for framing and for the respective practical decision-making: (1) general approval of ethnicity-based public activities as self-organization and self-determination of ethnic groups per se; (2) facilitation of ethnic groups' self-organization; and (3) vesting of the groups and their representative structures with competences and resources.

10.3 Between Frames and Normative Models

Public authorities in all post-Soviet countries as a rule recognize explicitly the multi-ethnicity of their populace. Sometimes the official wording goes far beyond merely general formulations on equal rights and minority protection and includes recognition of different communities as social entities possessing distinct identities as well as the right to 'development' and participation in public life. In a few cases such symbolic recognition is stipulated in constitutional provisions. The 1993 Russian Constitution refers to the country's people as 'multinational' (the Preamble) and also includes such tropes as 'national development' (in the meaning of ethno-cultural development, art 72 (f)) and 'peoples' rights' with regard to the preservation of languages (art 68, part 3) and to small indigenous peoples (art 69). Similar provisions are present in constitutions and charters of most constituent entities of the Russian Federation. For example, the Republic of Buryatia (eastern Siberia) in Article 4(2) of its Constitution declares 'free development of all nations and nationalities groups resident on its territory' and in this regard

---

[15] Vladimir Gel'man, 'The Unrule of Law in the Making: The Politics of Informal Institutional Building in Russia', *Europe-Asia Studies* vol. 56, no. 7 (2004): pp. 1021–58.

[16] Gero Erdmann and Ulf Engel, 'Neopatrimonialism Reconsidered: Critical Review and Elaboration of an Elusive Concept', *Commonwealth & Comparative Politics* vol. 45, no. 1 (2007): pp. 95–119; Vladimir Gel'man, 'Subversive Institutions, Informal Governance, and Contemporary Russian Politics', *Communist and Post-Communist Studies* vol. 45, nos 3–4 (2012): pp. 295–303.

[17] Nils Brunsson, *The Organization of Hypocrisy. Talk, Decisions and Actions in Organizations* (Chichester, N.Y.: John Wiley & Sons, 1989).

encourages activities of 'national-cultural centres and associations'. The Belarusian Constitution of 1994 (art 14) refers to 'relations' between national [ethnic] communities' which are to be regulated by the state on the basis of their 'equality' and 'respect towards their rights and interests'. The 1996 Constitution of the separatist and internationally unrecognized Transnistrian Moldovan Republic (art 8) contains the same formulation. The 1992 Constitution of Turkmenistan mentions 'equality between social and national [ethnic] communities' (art 11). More often references to communal 'right' or group development are scattered over pieces of sectoral legislation, in by-laws or official conceptual outlines of ethnic policies. For example, the Concept of Nationalities Policy of Moldova adopted by the Law No. 546-XV from 19 December 2003 contains such notions as 'interests' and 'development' of 'ethnic and linguistic communities'. The Ukrainian Declaration of Nationalities' Rights of 1 November 1991 (which amounts to a constitutional law) stipulates that the 'state guarantees' of 'equal political, economic, social and cultural rights' are granted to all 'peoples, ethnic groups and citizens resident on its territory' (art 1). The Russian State Concept of Nationalities Policy (in force from 1996 until 2012) defined 'national-cultural autonomy' as 'national-cultural self-determination' of 'peoples', and this was on a par with numerous references to 'interests', 'co-operation', and 'development' of ethnicities.

Most post-Soviet countries allow ethnicity-based non-governmental organizations (NGOs) and consultative or advisory bodies for minorities; official ethno-cultural policies mostly revolve around these two types of institutional settings. For example, Russia has, according to different estimates, between 2,500 and 3,500 NGOs which represent minorities and indigenous populations; Belarus officially reports about 180 minority NGOs on its territory.[18] Moldova has a national Coordinative Council of National Minorities—a consultative body on minority issues composed of around 100 ethnic NGOs under the governmental Bureau for Inter-Ethnic Relations.[19] The Council of National Minorities functions under the auspices of the Georgian Public Defender (Ombudsman);[20] the Council is closely linked to the voluntary coalition of minority NGOs—the Association 'Multinational Georgia'.[21] Several territories of Ukraine (such as the Odesa or Chernivtsy provinces) and constituent regions of the Russian Federation have established minority consultative councils under their governments or executive bodies in charge of ethno-cultural affairs. I would consider these kinds of settings as belonging to 'policies of non-territorial autonomy' only under the condition that public authorities consistently frame and justify these arrangements as self-organization and representation of ethnic groups per se. This condition will be

---

[18] The official lists are on the Plenipotentiary's website, accessed 13 October 2014, <http://www.belarus21.by/ru/main_menu/nat/nat_cult_ob/obyed/new_url_1579289175>.

[19] Website of governmental Bureau for Inter-ethnic Relations, accessed 13 October 2014, <http://www.bri.gov.md/index.php?pag=sec&id=91&l=ru>.

[20] For details, see the website of the European Centre for Minority Issues Caucasus, accessed 13 October 2014, <http://www.ecmicaucasus.org/menu/fora_cnm.html>.

[21] Website of the Association 'Multinational Georgia', accessed 13 October 2014, <http://pmmg.org.ge/index.php?m=7&lang=Eng>.

met when ethnicity-based NGOs function within a special ideological and normative framework, and consultative or representative bodies are officially supposed to
speak on behalf of ethnic 'communities' as such rather than individual NGOs or
experts. In this regard, the space for NTA policies remains rather limited although
the domain's boundary is blurry and flexible. If we reserve the notion of NTA
policies for the translation of general vague wording into clearly defined workable
models resting on the 'groupist' ideas, then only three major frameworks would
match this requirement. These are cultural (or 'national-cultural') autonomy; bodies supposed to represent the entire ethnicities (so-called congresses of peoples);
and structures supposed to be representative of several ethnicities as such before
the authorities and to provide dialogue and reconciliation between themselves (in
most cases referred to as 'Assemblies of Peoples').

Four post-Soviet countries (Estonia, Latvia, Russia, and Ukraine) have laws on
cultural or 'national-cultural' autonomy. In Estonia, the idea of cultural autonomy
for minorities is also stipulated in the 1992 Constitution (art 50). In Latvia and
Ukraine, the minority laws which contain provisions on cultural autonomy do
not create new types of organization, and autonomy is understood to as a general
permission for self-organization on ethnic grounds in various forms. In Russia
and Estonia cultural autonomy is interpreted both as a general principle and a
particular form of organization on an ethnic basis.[22] The term 'people's congresses'
carries two meanings: a one-off event for discussing issues pertinent to the given
ethnic group, and a mass movement (usually formed by a congress in the first
sense) supposed to consolidate this group and respectively, to have an organizational structure, governing bodies, and a network of regional branches. Hundreds
of 'congresses' as single events were summoned within the former Soviet Union
from the late 1980s onwards, and most took place in Russia. Congresses in the second meaning are also present basically in Russia (the major ones number thirteen),
and most represent so-called titular ethnicities of Russia's constituent republics
(among those groups are Tatars, Bashkirs, Komi, Mordovians, Buryats, Udmurt,
etc.)[23] and receive financial and administrative support of the respective regional
authorities.[24] A specific but similar case is the Association of the Nenets People,
Yasavey, which has functioned since 1989 in the Nenets Autonomous District (the

[22] David J. Smith, 'Non-Territorial Autonomy and Political Community in Contemporary
Central and Eastern Europe', *Journal on Ethnopolitics and Minority Issues in Europe* vol. 12, no. 1
(2013): pp. 27–55.

[23] A rationalization of these endeavours rests on the fact that most people belonging to these ethnicities reside outside the respective 'kin' regions; for example, approximately three-quarters of Tatars
live outside Tatarstan.

[24] Alexander Osipov, 'The "Peoples' Congresses" in Russia: Failure or Success? Authenticity
and Efficiency of Minority Representation', *ECMI Working Paper* no. 48 (2011), accessed 15
March 2014, <http://www.ecmi.de/uploads/tx_lfpubdb/Working_Paper_48_Final.pdf>; Yuriy P.
Shabaev and Anna M. Charina, *Regional'nye etnoelity v politicheskom processe: (finno-ugorskoe dvizhenie: stanovlenie, evolyuciya, ideologiya, lidery)* [Regional Ethnic Elites in the Political Process
(Finno-Ugric Movement: Establishment, Evolution, Ideology, Leaders)] (Syktyvkar: KRAGSiU,
2008), pp. 107–8.

north of European Russia).[25] Outside Russia, one can mention first and foremost the Congress (*Qurultay*) and the Parliament (*Mejlis*) of Crimean Tatars, nominally formed through public vote of all Crimean Tatars.[26]

The Assembly of People of Kazakhstan (APK—before 2007, the Assembly of Peoples of Kazakhstan) is a special body created by the president of the Republic of Kazakhstan, who is *ex officio* the APK chair.[27] The status of the APK is protected by the Constitution of Kazakhstan (art 44) and it operates under a special law. The APK is composed of 350 members who represent ethnic and civil society associations, and various state official and public figures all acting in a personal capacity.[28] Each province of Kazakhstan also has its Small Assembly of People which also operates under the heads of regional administrations. Candidates for the main APK are nominated by those provincial 'small assemblies' upon recommendations of ethnicity-based NGOs as well as other civil society organizations and are then appointed by the president of Kazakhstan. Officially, the major objectives of APK are to elaborate proposals for public policies that take into account the interests of all ethnic groups and also to facilitate and promote social dialogue to preserve the unity of the people of Kazakhstan. The agenda and working plans for APK are officially defined by its chair. The Assembly of Peoples of Russia (APR) is a nationwide NGO established in 1998.[29] The very idea of the APR as a kind of inter-ethnic parliament and even an annex to the supreme legislative body has been discussed since the early 1990s[30] and was even mentioned in the 1996 Concept of State Nationalities Policy of the Russian Federation. Despite its pretentious name, APR is simply a voluntary association with no public law powers or functions although it works in close cooperation with the government. APR receives public support including funding and is often commented on by high-ranking public officials as an important tool in the management of ethnic relations in Russia. The main proponent of APR has been Ramazan Abdulatipov,[31] who started his political career

---

[25] For a description of Yasavey, see its official website, accessed 15 March 2014, <http://www.yasavey.org/>.

[26] OSCE High Commissioner on National Minorities, *The Integration of Formerly Deported People in Crimea, Ukraine: Needs Assessment* (The Hague: OSCE HCNM, 2013), pp. 16–17.

[27] L. Shaimerdenova, 'Assambleya narodov Kazakhstana—novyi institut obshestvenno-politicheskoi konsolidatsii' [Peoples' Assembly of Kazakhstan—New Institute of Sociopolitical Consolidation], *Russkaya kul'tura vne granits* no. 6 (1997): p. 16; Bhavna Dave, 'Management of Ethnic Relations in Kazakhstan: Stability without Success', in *The Legacy of the Soviet Union*, edited by Wendy Slater and Andrew Wilson (Basingstoke: Palgrave Macmillan, 2004): p. 93; G. Baybasheva, '"Rol" Assamblei narodov Kazakhstana v sovershenstvovanii mezhetnicheskih otnoshenii v Respublike Kazakhstan' [The Role of Peoples' Assembly of Kazakhstan in Current Inter-Ethnic Relations in the Republic of Kazakstan], *Ekonomika i Pravo v Respublike Kazakhstane* no. 22 (2008): p. 33.

[28] For a description of the APK and of the regional assemblies, see the APK's official website, accessed 15 March 2014, <http://www.assembly.kz/pravovaya-baza-ank.html>.

[29] See the APR Charter and Programme, as well as a description of the regional Assemblies history on its official website, accessed 15 March 2014, <http://anrussia.ru/> and Mikhail N. Guboglo, 'Assambleya narodov Rossii. Teoriya i praktika' [Peoples' Assembly of Russia: Theory and Practice], in *Etnicheskaya mobilizatsiya i mezhetnicheskaya integratsiya* (Moscow: TsIMO, 1999), pp. 105, 117–18.

[30] Leokadiya M. Drobizheva, *Social'nye problemy mezhnacional'nyh otnoshenii v postsovetskoi Rossii* [Social Problems in Inter-Ethnic Relations of Post-Soviet Russia] (Moscow: Tsentr obshechelovecheskih tsennostei, 2003), p. 29; Guboglo, 'Assambleya narodov Rossii', pp. 105, 117–18.

[31] See Ramazan Abdulatipov's website, accessed 15 March 2014, <http://www.abdulatipov.ru>.

in the federal institutions in 1990 as a Member of Parliament and the Chairman of the Council of Nationalities—one of the two chambers of Russia's Supreme Soviet (the parliament). To date, Abdulatipov remains APR's permanent and irreplaceable leader. The governing bodies of APR are also composed of retired nomenclature figures and parliamentarians of the 1990s and 2000s with a background in ethnicity-based public movements.

There are dozens of 'peoples' assemblies' in a number of Russian regions. Many of them were established before the federal APR (for instance, in Yakutia in 1994, and in Saratov province—in 1997),[32] and for the most part the creation of those organizations was initiated by the regional governments.[33] At present, all regional 'assemblies' are considered regional branches of APR, but not all regional offices of APR are named 'assemblies'. According to the APR website, the organization includes seventy-two regional offices; all regional assemblies are also NGOs and include representatives of ethnic ('national-cultural' in Russian terminology) societies.[34] The Assembly of People of Kyrgyzstan has been established in 1994 under the country's president's auspices as an NGO; to date it is composed of twenty-eight nationwide minority associations under the principle 'one minority—one member' and four multi-ethnic social organizations. The organization defines its major goal as the consolidation of Kyrgyzstan's people through inter-ethnic dialogue, the facilitation of cultural activities, and the coordination of minority communities' public initiatives. Although the Assembly is a non-governmental association, several ministers (ministers of culture, education, youth affairs; Director of the Public Management Academy under the president; Director of the State Cadre Service and Chair of the Language Board) are considered members of its Council *ex officio*.[35] The Belarusian Consultative Inter-Ethnic Council (CIEC) functions under the Plenipotentiary on Religious and Nationalities Affairs.[36] In Belarus, CIEC includes only heads of national minority associations. It is stipulated that one ethnic group has only one representative council and the Plenipotentiary's Office makes the appointment only when all NGOs speaking on behalf of a certain group have agreed on their common nominee. In addition, organizations represented in CIEC commit themselves to regard all decisions of the Council as binding.

---

[32] Information about the regional assemblies up until June 2014 was available at the APR's old website: Deyatelnost regionalnukh otdelenii ANR, accessed 12 May 2014, <http://www.anrorg.ru/Regions/Reg_Index.htm>. See also <http://www.анпр.рф/Regions/Reg_Index.htm> for a brief description of several individual organizations.

[33] e.g. see Decree of the President of the Republic Sakha (Yakutia) No. 39 of 3 February 1997 on Holding the Second Assembly of Peoples of Sakha (Yakutia); Resolution of the Administration Head of Cheliabunsk Oblast No. 711 of 3 December 1996 on the Assembly of Peoples of Cheliabinsk Oblast; Decree of the President of the Republic of Bashkortostan No. UP-493 of 18 August 2000 on Holding the Assembly of Peoples of Bashkortostan. The texts are stored on the legal database 'Consultant+'.

[34] Deyatelnost regionalnukh otdelenii ANR, accessed 12 May 2014, <http://www.anrorg.ru/Regions/Reg_Index.htm>.

[35] Information about the Assembly's structure and activities is available on its official website, accessed 15 March 2014, <http://www.assembly.kg/>.

[36] See the official website of the Belarusian Plenipotentiary on Religious and Nationalities Affairs, accessed 15 March 2014, <http://www.belarus21.by/ru/main_menu/nat/consultation_centre>.

10.4 Legal Frameworks

Virtually all post-Soviet countries have constitutional provisions which recognize ethno-cultural heterogeneity and the need to create conditions for the preservation and expression of individual and group ethnic identity. All post-Soviet countries are parties to multilateral human rights treaties as well as bilateral agreements which contain provisions on the protection of national minorities. Some countries of the region have special laws on national minorities or on broadly understood ethno-cultural policies, or at least provisions of sectoral laws related to the protection of minorities. These laws are generally declarative and stipulate only general principles; the mechanisms of implementation are set up in by-laws, political decisions, or informal practices. Russia's federal structure makes the situation in this country even more complex: the constituent regions have their own laws on ethnic relations (which are basically in line with the federal ones), and much of the resources and authority in the sphere of ethno-cultural policy has been transferred to the regional level.

In general, the principle of a 'narrowing funnel' applies: states' obligations are being gradually reduced on the way from general declarations and constitutional provisions to implementation through a series of laws, executive programmes, and individual decisions of the executive. The only real guarantee of implementation is the good will of the executive; no action can be taken in courts on the grounds of declarations, concepts, and programmes on ethnic relations, and the executive branch has a broad discretion in interpreting laws as well as in broader decision-making.[37] This description is fully relevant to the legislation on cultural autonomy. As mentioned in section 10.3, the related legislative provisions are present in the national laws of four countries; while in Latvia and Ukraine they mean general approval of civil activities aimed at the protection and promotion of minority languages and cultures, in Estonia and Russia the respective pieces of legislation also envisage specific types of ethnicity-based organizations. Entities referred to as 'cultural autonomies' in Estonia and 'national-cultural autonomies' in Russia have a special legal framework. In Russia, the latter comprises the 1996 Federal Law 'On National-Cultural Autonomy', respective provisions in other pieces of federal legislation, eleven regional laws on the public support of 'autonomies', provisions of other regional laws and numerous by-laws, as well as executive orders and target programmes. Estonia has a special law 'On Cultural Autonomy' of 1993. In both cases, national legislation offers fewer opportunities and instead creates more difficulties for community initiatives and public support than the laws on 'ordinary' non-profit organizations do.[38]

---

[37] Advisory Committee on the Framework Convention for the Protection of National Minorities, Third Opinion on the Russian Federation (adopted on 24 November 2011), ACFC/OP/III(2011)010, para 20, pp. 66–70.
[38] Ilya Nikiforov, 'National'no-kul'turnaya avtonomiya v Estonii: povtorenie proidennogo' [Ethnocultural Autonomy in Estonia: Repetition of the Past], in *Natsional'no-kul'turnaya avtonomiya. Ideya i realizatsiya. Estonskii opyt*, edited by Alexander Osipov and Ilya Nikiforov (Tallinn: Tsentr

'National-cultural autonomies'[39] (NCAs) in Russia are a type of civil society organization ('social organizations' in terms of Russian law); NCAs are obliged to be incorporated as legal persons.[40] They are established on behalf of an ethnic group or a national minority within a defined territory (until 2003 all ethnicities were allowed to establish NCAs); since 2003 only mono-ethnic NCAs are allowed. NCAs may have three levels of territorial organization: local (within a municipality), regional (within a federation unit), and all-Russian 'autonomies'. The procedures for the establishment of an NCA are more complex than for other types of NGOs. NCAs can be established only on a bottom-up basis: a group of persons belonging to a certain ethnicity (until 2003, only ethnicity-based NGOs) can establish a local NCA; several local NCAs can form a regional one; in turn several regional NCAs can found the federal 'autonomy'. Parallel federal autonomies of the same ethnicity are not allowed under any version of the 1996 NCA law. The existence of more than one NCA of the same ethnicity within a region is not allowed in accordance with the Constitutional Court decision of 5 March 2004;[41] and parallel local autonomies are precluded and denied official registration by the authorities. Local autonomies are not obliged to become members of the respective regional NCA, and regional NCAs can exist independently of their co-ethnic federal 'autonomies'. The rights of NCAs are restricted in comparison with 'ordinary' NGOs which can also be ethnicity-based; only one organizational form based on fixed individual membership is possible, and NCAs until December 2014 were allowed to carry out activities related exclusively to the issues of language, culture, and education. Like 'ordinary' social organizations, NCAs can establish mass-media outlets, cultural and educational institutions, own property, and conclude contracts. NCAs, like other ethnic NGOs in Russia, receive small-scale support from public authorities and only a few can rely on regular private sponsorship.

Minority self-governments (also referred to as 'cultural autonomies') in Estonia are established by minority cultural NGOs. With permission of the authorities, the founders can set up a register (a list) of persons wishing to be members of the self-government and they may then arrange for the board's elections. Four 'traditional' minorities and other groups that number more than 3,000 persons can set

informatsii po pravam cheloveka, 2008), pp. 43–55; Alexander Osipov, 'National Cultural Autonomy in Russia: A Case of Symbolic Law', *Review of Central and East European* Law vol. 35, no. 1 (2010): pp. 27–57.

[39] The word 'autonomy' is used in Russian and Estonian to mean organization or body; to avoid further remarks and explanations I follow this approach here.

[40] Most of post-Soviet legislative frameworks do not draw a clear distinction between entities of public and private law; most types of social organizations can function without obtaining legal personality.

[41] Postanovlenie Konstitutsionnogo Suda RF ot 3 marta 2004 goda No. 5 'Po delu o proverke konstitutsionnosti chasti tret'ei stati 5 Federal'nogo zakona "O natsional'no-kul'turnoi avtonomii" v sviazi s zhaloboi grazhdan A.H.Dits i O.A.Shumacher', Sobraniye Zakonodatel'stva Rossiiskoy Federatsii (2004) No. 11, item 1033 [Decision No. 5 of the Constitutional Court of the Russian Federation from 3 March 2004 on the Constitutionality of the Federal Law (part 3, art 5) 'On National-Cultural Autonomy' made in response to A. H. Dits's and O. A. Shumacher's appeal', Compendium of Legislation of the Russian Federation (2004) No. 11, item 1033].

up self-governing bodies. Minority self-governments are not legal entities, and at best, a self-government established under the law may function as a coordinating council for 'its own' minority.[42]

People's congresses in Russia are social movements, and as such almost all of them have not been underpinned by any specific legal framework. Only two constituent units of the Russian Federation—the Komi Republic in the Russian European north and the Khakass Republic in south Siberia—had laws between 1992 and 2003, respectively on the Komi People Congress and on the *Chon-Chobi*—the Khakass Congress.[43] In addition, the Association of the Nenets People, *Yasavey*, which is not established as a 'congress', claims to be the only one spokesperson of this 'titular' indigenous ethnicity in the Nenets Autonomous District in Russia's North. It enjoys a special representative status enshrined in the regional Charter (arts 16 and 29). In the other cases, an ethnic congress is convened by the governing body of the movement and the official authorities of the respective republic, where the movement is based. For example, the *Kurultay* (Congress) of the Bashkir people was convened and incorporated on the basis of and in pursuit of the decrees of Bashkortostan's president.[44] In a formal sense, the 'congresses' exist as NGOs in legal forms, such as 'social movement' (organization with no fixed individual membership) or as unions or associations of social organizations.

The position of coalition-type representative organizations looks more complex. The Assembly of Peoples of Kazakhstan was established in 1995 by a presidential decree as a consultative body under the president; currently it is working on the basis of the national law, On the Assembly of People of Kazakhstan, as a special body formed by the president (art 44 of the Constitution of Kazakhstan).[45] In contrast, the Assembly of People of Kyrgyzstan has no specific legislative provisions as functions as a social association. The very idea of the APR is present in the Concept of Nationalities Policy of the Russian Federation adopted by a president's decree in 1996. Some APR documents as well as statements of its leaders argue that the Assembly was created in response to the Concept,[46] which is not quite true—the government did not partake in the federal Assembly's establishment, and still the organization has no public competences and enjoys quite limited support.

---

[42] Vadim Poleshchuk, 'Changes in the Concept of National Cultural Autonomy in Estonia', in *The Challenge of Non-Territorial Autonomy: Theory and Practice*, edited by Ephraim Nimni, Alexander Osipov, and David J. Smith (Bern: Peter Lang, 2013), pp. 149–62.

[43] Law of the Republic of Komi on the Status of the Congress of Komi People 1992; Law of the Republic of Khakassia on the Status of the Congress of Khakass People (*Chyylyf*) 21 April 1994. Copies of the originals are at the author's disposal.

[44] Decree of the President of the Republic of Bashkortostan No. UP-493 from 18 August 2000 on Holding the Assembly of Peoples of Bashkortostan; Decree of the President of the Republic of Bashkortostan No. UP-229 from 30 May 2007 on Holding the Assembly of Peoples of Bashkortostan.

[45] The texts are available at, accessed 15 March 2014, <http://www.assembly.kz/pravovaya-baza-ank.html>.

[46] Ramazan G. Abdulatipov, 'Doklad Predsedatel'a Soveta ANR R. G. Abdulatipova' [Report of the Council Chairman Ramazan G. Abdulatipov], *Istoricheskoya dukhovnoya naslediye druzhby narodov Rossii: Traditsii i sobremennost. Materialy Kongressa Narodov Rossii* (2007): p. 31.

A number of Russian regional assemblies like the ones in the Republic of Sakha (Yakutia), the Republic of Tatarstan, the Saratov province, and others were created earlier than the federal APR with the direct interference of the regional governments. Accordingly, in some regions these local assemblies, being NGOs, are referenced in the regional official conceptual outlines and programmes of nationalities policy.[47] As a rule, they also gain the direct support of the authorities; for instance, their conventions are held at the initiative of the regional executive authorities and are in part publicly funded. However, there are no local laws and regulations dealing specifically with regional assemblies. The Consultative Inter-Ethnic Council (CIEC) in Belarus was established in 2004 in accordance with the Statute on the Plenipotentiary on Religious and Nationalities Affairs enacted by the Council of Ministers. The CIEC predecessors were the Coordinating Council for National Minorities under the Council of Ministers (established in 1995) and the latter's successor, the Coordinating Council for National Minorities under the State Committee for Religious and Ethnic Affairs (founded in 1998). The CIEC rules of procedure are set up by acts of the Plenipotentiary.[48]

10.5 Between Normative Frameworks and Praxis

Little can be said about 'cultural autonomies' in Russia and Estonia. In Russia, NCAs occupy the same niche as all other ethnicity-based NGOs; they engage basically in activities pertinent to the expression and preservation of their groups' cultural traits. It is worth noting that the number of NCAs is growing although lagging far behind 'ordinary' ethnicity-based NGOs; by March 2014 the total number of registered NCAs reached 1,014 throughout the country.[49] It should be noted that since 1993 only two self-governments of small minorities, namely the Ingrian Finns and the Swedes, have been established in Estonia, and both are inactive.[50] Basically, minority activists work through the already established NGOs which are legal entities or benefit from educational and cultural institutions run by the state and municipal authorities.

The 'congresses' and 'assemblies' in Russia have no special legal framework, but in fact they occupy a special privileged niche. They represent so-called governmental

---

[47] For examples see: Law of the Republic Sakha (Yakutia) No. 259-Z from 13 July 2005 on the Collaboration of the Governmental and Municipal Organs of the Republic Sakha (Yakutia) with Social Associations; Law of Saratov Oblast No. 166-ZSO from 11 September 2007 on the Regional Target Programme National-Cultural Development of the Peoples of Saratov Oblast for 2008–10.

[48] Rules of the Consultative Inter-Ethnic Council under the Plenipotentiary on Religious and Nationalities Affairs, adopted by the Order the Plenipotentiary on Religious and Nationalities Affairs No. 7 from 23 January 2010, accessed 15 March 2014, <http://www.belarus21.by/ru/main_menu/nat/consultation_centre/new_url_1285022831>.

[49] According to the data on the Ministry of Justice official website, accessed 15 March 2014, <http://unro.minjust.ru/NKAs.aspx>.

[50] Vadim Poleshchuk, ed., *Chance to Survive: Minority Rights in Estonia and Latvia* (Moscow, Paris, Tallinn: Foundation for Historical Outlook, 2009), p. 63.

NGOs (GONGOs), which are directly or indirectly set up and guided by the government. Within this context, their relations with public authorities, funding, and formation of the governing bodies are subject to informal practices which are closed to the public, non-transparent, and quite often in conflict with the law. The latter means, first of all, that state interventions in the convention of 'congresses' and 'assemblies' (particularly, in setting up their organizing committees) directly contravenes the legislation on social and non-profit organizations; selective budgetary funding is arbitrary and thus must be deemed discriminatory. In fact, financial support to congresses and 'assemblies'—like many other organizations and initiatives under the auspices of the public authorities—is provided by enterprises and businesspeople dependent on the government. Thus, the relationships in this triangle (government–donor–recipient) remain closed to the public. Also opaque is the selection of delegates to the conventions of 'congresses' and 'assemblies'. Most 'congresses', in the meaning of representative fora, are formed through a two-step scheme. The organizing committee sets up numerical quotas based on the estimated number of people belonging to the respective ethnicity within certain territories; then a meeting of all stakeholders at the local level nominates and elects electors to the regional meeting; afterwards the electors at their regional conferences nominate and cast votes for the delegates to the congress.[51] The way in which these meetings and conferences are convened remains non-transparent and still insufficiently studied, especially with regard to the provision of access to those who wish to take part in the electoral procedures, the setting of agendas and rules, and particularly personal nominations and voting, Preparatory processes to all the conventions are also blurred: it is unclear who formulates the agenda and how, and what are the scenarios and internal regulations. In any case, a congress as a meeting of several hundred delegates and guests who work altogether within a short time at plenary sessions and thematic sections can, in principle, be easily manipulated by the organizers.

Similar procedures employed by APR and regional 'assemblies' in Russia turn out to be even more confusing. Nominally, 'assemblies' claim to represent ethnic groups, but until recently the long-lasting debates about the ways to achieve 'genuine' and 'legitimate' representation have generated no satisfactory output. As a rule, governing bodies of the assemblies are formed during congresses, and delegates are selected under mixed and complicated principles. The situation is aggravated, first, by the fact that most assemblies also envisage personal membership (and individual members are usually retired high-ranking officials, politicians, and secret service officers) and, second, by an unwritten tradition that the governing bodies of most assemblies are formed during the congresses by a general vote of the delegates and not by the constituent organizations or the ethnicities. These procedures are also vulnerable to manipulations given that 'assemblies' are dependent and that all decision-making is closed to the constituencies. A clear and accurate judgment on whether all these opportunities were really employed looks

---

[51] Osipov, 'The "Peoples' Congresses" in Russia', pp. 6–9.

impossible, because no reliable and comprehensive study of the assemblies has been done so far.

In other countries, the situation looks simpler. In Kazakhstan, the president directly appoints representatives of ethnic associations as well as prominent public figures like authoritative persons active in public administration, academia, higher education, fine arts, business, and veterans' organizations. The process of nomination of prospective members of the Assembly is done through regional 'small assemblies', which are supervised by regional heads of state administrations.[52] In Belarus, CIEC includes only governmental appointees. In addition to making recommendations to the government of Belarus on ethnic issues, CIEC plans and coordinates joint activities of the national-cultural societies and makes decisions on the distribution of public grants and subsidies for ethno-cultural projects of the non-governmental sector. In Kyrgyzstan, the governing bodies of the Assembly of People of Kyrgyzstan are elected during its congresses (except for the ministers who are the Council's members *ex officio*); however the selection of candidates and their nomination is strongly (but informally) dependent on the government.

10.6 From Symbolic Policies to Resource Distribution and Institution-Setting

Such initiatives as NCA, 'peoples congresses' and multi-ethnic assemblies first and foremost provide for the symbolic presence of ethnic groups in the public space. Almost none of these structures play any independent role in politics; they are orchestrated by governments even if they have not been created by the state directly. The role of each in resource distribution, services delivery, and decision-making is highly dependent on the local context, the motivation of the activists, the position of the local authorities, and the availability of sponsors. Theoretically, all structures described here provide multiple opportunities, but are rarely realized in full. Nevertheless, the structures in question claim to partake in cultural and educational projects. For the cultural autonomies this is the main form of activity, while it is an auxiliary one for the 'congresses' and 'assemblies'. All three forms of organization basically have not contributed to the formation of other institutional structures, as well as to setting up standards and sustainable practices related to the protection of minorities. Rather, they engage in holding events like folk festivals, conferences, or round tables on ethnic issues. Only a few NCAs in Russia establish and maintain private educational institutions, basically training courses

---

[52] Nikolay N. Turetskii, 'Assambleya naroda Kazahstana—knou-how kazahstanskoi mezhetnicheskoi politiki' [Peoples' Assembly of Kazakhstan—Know-How of Kazakh Ethnopolitics], *Yevraziiskaya integratsiya: ekonomika, pravo, politika* no. 5 (2009): pp. 118–21; Gulbakhsha N. Musabaeva, 'Aktual'nye voprosy mezhetnicheskih otnoshenii v Kazahstane i mezhdunarodnoe sotrudnichestvo' [Topical Issues of Interethnic Relations in Kazakhstan and International Cooperation], *Vestnik Tverskogo gosudarstvennogo universiteta. Seriya: Pravo* no. 28 (2011): pp. 31–40.

and Sunday schools. The 'congresses' and 'assemblies' do even less. The APR in the early 2000s contributed to the setting up of a non-governmental House of Peoples' Friendship in Moscow which comprised a museum, a theatre, and a library.[53] This endeavour was funded by private donors, and by 2009 had faded. The APR and the regional assemblies try to create subsidiaries, such as 'Youth Assemblies'; however, effective social activities of these derivatives remain highly questionable. The Assembly of Peoples of Tatarstan in Russia functions on the basis of the state institution, House of Peoples of Tatarstan, and gets public funding through this channel. The Assembly of Peoples of Tatarstan runs language courses;[54] the republican government considers the Assembly as an intermediary between the authorities and migrants,[55] and the Assembly is authorized to provide legal aid to newcomers belonging to ethnic minorities.

With regard to resource allocation and distribution, all three types of organizations depend on private donors and on governmental subsidies. In Estonia, no public authority is obliged to provide pecuniary support to minority self-governments or any other minority organizations (however, public subsidies to minority NGOs do take place). Russian authorities also bear no financial obligations to NCAs or other minority associations. In these cases, public donations are selective and not guaranteed. In Russia, direct contributions by public authorities are mainly confined to the provision of free of charge or low rent premises for minority organizations (usually at the regional level there are special public institutions called House of Peoples Friendship or House of Nationalities) or involve minority organizations as junior partners in the preparation of cultural events (such as festivals, exhibitions, and conferences). Private financial sponsorship is irregular and often takes place on the initiative of or under pressure from public authorities. In Kazakhstan, Kyrgyzstan, and Belarus, ethnic organizations' financial dependence on the state is higher than in Russia, as all activities are carried out under the control of the state and quite often with budgetary funding. In other countries, minority organizations have more independence, but also more problems with financing. Noteworthy is the role of the Belarusian CIEC. Among other things, it makes decisions about the distribution of public subsidies for the projects of national-cultural societies, and also makes recommendations on granting tax-exempt status to ethnic NGOs. Although, formally the final decisions on both issues are made by the Plenipotentiary on Religions and Nationalities Affairs, CIEC recommendations are usually always accepted.

Another issue is the acquisition and fulfilment of public competences and authorities. The largest amount of power has been formally granted to the

---

[53] *Dom narodov Rossii. 2000–2005* (Moscow: Vserossiiskii Vystavochnyi tsentr, 2006).

[54] A. V. Nabiullina, 'Osobennosti natsional'noi politiki kak faktora mezhetnicheskogo vzaimodeistviya v Respublike Tatarstan' [Characteristics of National Policy as a Factor of Interethnic Cooperation in the Republic of Tatarstan], *Kazanskaya nauka* no. 1 (2012): p. 287; Liliya V. Sagitova, 'Dom druzhby narodov kak ob'ekt i sub'ekt sotsial'nogo reformirovaniya: ot sovetskoi modeli k globalizatsionnoi?' [Home of the Commonwealth of Peoples as an Object and Subject of Social Reform: From the Soviet Model to Globalization], *Zhurnal issledovanii social'noi politiki* vol. 9, no. 4 (2011): p. 504.

[55] Sagitova, pp. 501–6.

APK. The APK selects nine MPs (out of 154) to the national parliament and takes part in drafting laws and executive regulations which concern minorities or ethnic relations.[56] Neither Russian nor Estonian legislation entitles cultural autonomies to participate in government decision-making, in the development of any professional standards and codes, or in the management of public cultural and educational institutions.[57] It should be noted that the 1925 Law on Cultural Autonomy in Estonia provided for the transfer of authority to manage minority schools with corresponding budgetary resources to minority self-governments.[58] Nothing like this is present in the current law. In practice, authorities in several Russian republics have recognized 'peoples' congresses' as lobbying organizations and authoritative conventions. As a rule, heads of those regions where 'congresses' of the respective 'titular' nations convene (Komi, Mordovia, Bashkortostan, Tatarstan) report before those meetings, and in turn the 'congresses' address their wishes and demands to the republican governments. In the Komi Republic, there has been an established practice of regular reporting of the republican ministries before the Komi Congress and of the local authorities before the local branches of the Congress. On several occasions the Komi Congress has successfully initiated amendments to regional legislation, and such a right was provided for in previous laws on the status of the Komi Congress.[59] Similarly, governmental consultations with the Association of the Nenets People, *Yasavey*, in the Nenets Autonomous District are mandatory under the district's Charter (art 16), and the Association has the right to take legislative initiatives in the regional parliament (art 29). Federal and regional 'assemblies of peoples' in Russia have been conceived as bodies entitled to participate in government decision-making, particularly in the assessment of draft laws and executive acts affecting minorities. In reality, the assemblies remain merely civil society organizations enjoying some ritual piety from regional authorities. There is no evidence that 'assemblies' have affected the decision-making processes or that their initiatives materialized in new laws or policy changes. This mode of existence fits in the general framework in which almost all other coalition-type and consultative bodies function in all post-Soviet countries: their real influence on decision-making looks negligible. Something of an exception is the Belarusian CIEC which decides on the allocation of budget funds and on granting tax benefits to national-cultural societies.

---

[56] Musabaeva, 'Aktual'nye voprosy mezhetnicheskih otnoshenii', pp. 31–40; L. S. Zhakaeva, 'O proportsional'noi sisteme formirovaniya Mazhilisa parlamenta Kazahstana' [On Proportional Structuring of Mazhilis—Kazakh Parliament], *Konstitucionnoe i munitsipal'noe pravo* no. 7 (2009): pp. 27–32.
[57] Nikiforov, 'National'no-kul'turnaya avtonomiya'; Osipov, 'National Cultural Autonomy in Russia'.
[58] David J. Smith, 'Non-Territorial Cultural Autonomy as a Baltic Contribution to Europe between the Wars', in *The Baltic States and their Region: New Europe or Old?*, edited by David J. Smith (Amsterdam: Rodopi, 2005), pp. 209–24.
[59] Osipov, 'The "Peoples' Congresses" in Russia', pp. 14–15.

10.7 Social Context and Perceptions

The former Soviet Union basically followed the ethno-nationalist doctrine of state-building, or, more precisely, the ruling elites regarded their country as a form of organization of the 'titular' ethnicities. These perceptions were present in national legislations and political declarations in varying degrees of transparency and consistency; in practical terms they served as a basis for preferential treatment of persons belonging to the 'titular' groups and of their languages.[60] Today, Russia and Belarus can be regarded as partial exceptions. Russia is a federation, and part of its regions are considered 'ethnic' entities and follow ethno-nationalist doctrines in legislation and domestic policies, while at the federal level the patronization of ethnic Russians has not manifested itself as a clear-cut trend so far. In Belarus, the ethno-national character of the state is not articulated; Russian remains an official language on a par with Belarusian, and government officials exploit the rhetoric of 'civil' nation widely.[61]

All post-Soviet countries seek to prevent or mitigate social cleavages along ethnic lines, and thus they strive to establish counterweights to ethno-nationalist ideology and to avoid radical manifestations that could provoke civil unrest. For this purpose, official authorities resort to limited and rather symbolic recognition of multi-ethnicity or multi-nationality and support cultural and educational activities on behalf of and for 'non-titular' populations. The governments have at their disposal numerous institutions that allow for the promotion and organization of cultural activities on behalf of minorities, as well as for the public recognition of their positive role in society. The post-Soviet official rhetoric derives in large part from the Soviet understanding of the 'nationalities question'. Throughout the Soviet period, official declarations (including the main programmes of the Communist Party and the founding documents of the Soviet state) as well as semi-official academic publications regarded ethnic groups as social entities with their own integral social and economic life, able to 'develop', to pursue interests of their own and therefore to hold group rights, primarily the right to self-determination.[62] 'Self-determination' was regarded primarily in territorial forms, through the creation of 'own' statehood or territorial autonomy.[63] The main objective of the Soviet

---

[60] Zoltan Barany and Robert G. Moser, eds., *Ethnic Politics after Communism* (Ithaca: Cornell University Press, 2005).

[61] Nelly Bekus, *Struggle over Identity: The Official and the Alternative 'Belarusianness'* (Budapest, New York: Central European University Press, 2010).

[62] Terry Martin, *The Affirmative Action Empire: Nations and Nationalism in the Soviet Union, 1923–1939* (Ithaca, NY: Cornell University Press, 2001); Ronald Suny, *The Revenge of the Past: Nationalism, Revolution, and the Collapse of the Soviet Union* (Stanford: Stanford University Press, 1993).

[63] Ian Bremmer, 'Post-Soviet Nationalities Theory: Past, Present and Future', in *New States, New Politics: Building the Post-Soviet Nations*, edited by Ian Bremmer and Roy Taras (Cambridge: Cambridge University Press, 1997); Teresa Rakowska-Harmstone, 'The Dialectics of Nationalism in the USSR', *Problems of Communism* vol. 23, no. 3 (1974): pp. 1–22; Philip Roeder, 'Soviet Federalism and Ethnic Mobilization', *World Politics* vol. 43, no. 2 (1991): pp. 197–9.

'nationalities policy' was modernization and alignment of social and economic conditions for all ethnic communities; therefore, this policy was primarily aiming at economic, social, and cultural investments in ethnic and geographic peripheries of the country and at radical social engineering extensively labelled with the notion of 'development'.[64] Ethnicity-based administrative-territorial units were viewed as an institutional framework for the 'development' of the respective 'nationalities'.[65] Even more important is the fact that the underlying assumptions of NTA were compatible with the communists' understanding of ethnicity's role in the society. In particular, the idea of non-territorial self-organization on the basis of ethnicity can be easily derived from a theoretical construct of 'national sovereignty' (in the sense of ethnic) put forward by some Soviet legal theorists in 1940s and 1950s.[66] According to these ideas, sovereignty was in principle threefold: it included popular, state, and 'national' (ethnic) institutions; each type was not restricted to one or the other; and 'national' sovereignty was enjoyed by all ethnic groups, but could be implemented in different ways and forms of 'self-determination'.[67]

Numerous ethnic conflicts of the late 1980s and early 1990s, which were accompanying the Soviet Union's breakdown, triggered wide political and academic debates about the ways of mitigating tensions on ethnic grounds. A common wisdom of policymakers in Russia and beyond was that driving ethnicity out of the political domain and preventing territorial claims by satisfying minorities' cultural needs and facilitating inter-ethnic dialogue would be the right strategies. Various forms of cultural and non-territorial autonomy and consultative mechanisms for minorities were extensively referred to as adequate organizational settings.

Having been created in the late 1980s or the first half of the 1990s, all three types of 'autonomous' non-territorial organizations continue to exist to date, and two achievements can be noted. First, these structures involve almost all activists and experts (especially at the local and regional levels), who can formulate positions and demands on behalf of minorities, and therefore secure governmental control and domination. Second, they provide for the agendas, scenarios, and communication protocols which are comfortable for the government and which allow avoiding all disputes and controversies on substantive issues related to social justice and resource allocation. Last, but not least, these undertakings allow governments

---

[64] Walker Connor, *The National Question in Marxist–Leninist Theory and Strategy* (Princeton, NJ: Princeton University Press, 1984); Victor Zaslavsky, 'Ethnic Group Divided: Social Stratification and Nationality Policy in the Soviet Union', in *The Soviet Union. Party and Society*, edited by Peter J. Potichnyj (Cambridge: Cambridge University Press, 1988), pp. 218–28.

[65] Dmitri Gorenburg, *Minority Ethnic Mobilization in the Russian Federation* (Cambridge: Cambridge University Press, 2003).

[66] Yuriy G. Sudnitsin, *Natsional'nyi suverenitet v SSSR* [National Sovereignty in the USSR] (Moscow: Gosyurizdat, 1958); Kiti D. Korkmasova, *Natsionalno-gosudarstvennoye ustroistvo SSSR* [Ethno-State Structure of the Soviet Union] (Rostov-on-Don: Rostov State University Publishing House, 1984).

[67] Liudvig M. Karapet'an, *Federativnoe ustroistvo Rossiiskogo gosudarstva* [Federative Structure of the Russian State] (Moscow: Norma, 2001), pp. 229–41; Milena V. Zolotareva, *Federatsiya v Rossii: problemy i perspektivy* [Federation of Russia: Problems and Perspectives] (Moscow: Probel, 1999), pp. 59–109.

to refer to minority self-organization and inter-ethnic dialogues as evidence of how successful ethnic policies are. One can hardly speak about the failures of the organizations described here, because their rationales were vaguely formulated and not always in line with actual official policies. Thus, cultural autonomy in Russia and Estonia were widely acknowledged as a device for the consolidation of ethnic groups, but they could not perform this function because of legislative flaws, and no one made any real attempt to stimulate self-organization of minorities in the framework of 'autonomies'. The APR has not acquired any public competence (as assumed before its establishment), but it really benefits from its privileged position and close ties with the government. Likewise, it is also hard to talk about the efficiency of 'peoples' congresses' because of the uncertainty in their goals and objectives.

The main beneficiaries in the cases described above are the governments, because they have established instruments for control over ethnic activists, public agendas, and large support groups. Leaders and activists of ethnic organizations also benefit from those policies since they get a channel of regular communication with public authorities, acquire a high symbolic status, and receive additional material resources and political weight. Ordinary members of ethnic movements and organizations are also favoured with symbolic recognition of their ethnic communities and with the opportunity to participate in politics at least symbolically. The general public also gets a comfortable narrative about the state of ethnic relations. It should perhaps be admitted that in some cases the respective organizations can solve particular problems, for example in Tatarstan, they secure control over immigrants through ethnic 'communities' and help governmental agencies to carry out cultural activities. Over the last twenty years, there have been no public critics of those institutions' fundamentals in Kazakhstan, Russia, and Belarus, and no one has used them as a means to oppose or criticize policies pursued by the authorities. Moreover, there have been no attempts to work out alternative scenarios or frameworks in these countries, even in the early 1990s when the political regimes were much more liberal. Official authorities evaluate all policies of NTA positively, as a remarkable achievement of their own. 'Cultural' or 'national-cultural' autonomy receive mostly positive assessments by the governments, ethnic activists, and scholars, despite the fact that 'autonomies' offer fewer opportunities than 'ordinary' non-profit organizations both in Russia and Estonia. Critics touch upon minor details like insufficient public finding, but never the basic issues.

This phenomenon can be explained by the high symbolic status of NCA in public opinion. However, attitudes to cultural autonomy inside Estonia are generally more sceptical than in Russia because of this institution's complete impracticality.[68] 'Peoples' congresses' are evaluated in the local academic literature in two opposite ways: there are either apologetic or highly critical judgements, speculative in both instances. The admirers argue that the 'congresses' are legitimate and efficient

---

[68] Nikiforov, 'National'no-kul'turnaya avtonomiya'; Andrei Shiryaev, 'Eshe k voprosu ob avtonomizatsii' [More on Autonomy Issues], *Vesti Dnya* (19 March 2009).

mechanisms for the formulation and representation of ethnic interests through democratic procedures.[69] The critics state that they are formed through backroom machinations and fake ballots while the conventions themselves are directly manipulated by the governments and a handful of activists.[70] It's almost impossible to confirm or refute these statements because there have been no reliable empirical studies of those organizations. It may be noted that a large social survey conducted in 2007–8 by the society Finland–Russia showed that only a small part of the 'titular' population in Russia's regions had ever heard of the 'congresses' they had supposedly voted for.[71] For more than twenty years there has been no evidence of bottom-up oppositional criticism toward 'congresses' or attempts to hijack those institutions or change their mode of operation. Finally, people's assemblies are also judged from opposite directions. Apologetic statements dominate, mainly in Kazakhstan.[72] In Russia most positive assessments have been gained by the Assembly of Peoples of Tatarstan which performs a specific job in language training and legal aid for immigrants.[73] Mostly critically assessed was the very idea of multiple ethnic groups' 'representation' within a common forum. Nonetheless, critics and apologists draw very little interest from the wider public.

10.8 Conclusions and Recommendations

NTA as a mode of framing ethnic issues as relations between ethnic groups which exist as social entities regardless of territorial definition and which perform as social actors, as one can see, persists and has concrete embodiments. Sometimes these frames shape public agendas to a certain degree and are also translated into practice, having contributed to institutional set-up. From this perspective, NTA deserves theorists' and practitioners' attention as a process affecting ethnic policies at large and leading to concrete substantive consequences. A condition for an

---

[69] Vladimir K. Abramov, *Mordovskii narod ot s'ezda k s'ezdu* [Mordovian People from Congress to Congress] (Saransk: no publisher, 2004); Vladimir K. Abramov, *Mordovskoe natsional'noe dvizhenie* [Mordovian National Movemement] (Saransk: no publisher, 2007); V. Markov, *Vozrozhdeniye v epokhu peremen. S'ezdy Komi naroda: dokumenty i kommentarii* [Renaissance in the Era of Change: The Congress of the Komi People: Documents and Commentaries] (Syktyvkar: no publisher, 2011).

[70] Shabaev and Charina, *Regional 'nye etnoelity v politicheskom processe'*, pp. 107–8; Valeriy Aleksandrovich Tishkov, 'Kazanskie strasti' [Kazan Passions], *Nezavisimaya gazeta* (4 October 2002).

[71] Alexei K. Konyuhov, ed., *Finno-ugorskie narody Rossii: vchera, segodnya, zavtra* [Finno-Ugra People of Russia: Yesterday, Today, Tomorrow] (Syktyvkar: no publisher, 2008), p. 104.

[72] R. S. Aryn, 'Vzaimodeistvie gosudarstvennyh institutov i etnicheskih soobshestv—vazhneishii faktor stanovleniya gosudarstvennosti Respubliki Kazahstan' [Cooperation of State Authority Institutes with Ethnic Communities—Key Factor of Statehood's Establishment in the Republic of Kazakhstan], *Vestnik Tomskogo Gosudarstvennogo Universiteta* vol. 300, no. I (2007): pp. 79–81; Turetskii, 'Assambleya naroda Kazahstana'.

[73] Sagitova, 'Dom druzhby narodov kak ob'ekt i sub'ekt sotsial'nogo reformirovaniya', pp. 495–512.

effective application of this approach would be avoidance of the 'groupist' attitudes and taking NTA not at face value, as a way of group self-organization, but rather as a mode of framing, often introduced on a top-town basis.

Processes entailed by or related to framing also deserve a thorough examination. One may argue that all three organizational forms described here are not authentic models of representation and self-organization of ethnic groups, since they are guided and controlled by authoritarian governments (as in Russia, Belarus, and Kazakhstan) and/or governments pursuing 'ethnic control'[74] (as in the cases of Estonia and Kyrgyzstan). This objection becomes irrelevant if one questions the very notion of 'authentic' self-organization or representation. The role of state coercion must also be questioned in the light of the fact that in most countries of the former Soviet Union most ethnic activists within the last two decades strive to be loyal to their governments and to accept all their offers no matter how authoritarian these are. Given the lack of opposition and alternatives to such mode of behaviour, one may assume that this model of interaction with authorities is legitimate and is as a rule endorsed by those who wish to take part in social activities on behalf of minorities.

It would be a mistake to assess the legitimacy of NTA from the point of whether they were initiated 'from above' or 'from below'. This perception reflects in some way a 'republican' vision of ethnicities as aggregates of individuals thinking in a similar way because of their 'identity' and respective 'genuine' interests and thus being able to adopt and implement collective decisions through democratic procedures. If these assumptions about 'genuine' collective interests and 'true' substantive representation are discarded, one can talk about a broader range of perspectives and realistically suggest that ethnic politics like other politics in the post-Soviet space develops in a similar neo-patrimonial framework where public activities are subject to patron–client networks and informal institutions, and resources are allocated in exchange for personal and institutional loyalties.[75] Ultimately, ethnic activists as a rule do not pursue strategies other than being a loyal junior partner and an agent of the state and its representatives. In turn, governments easily find performers for such initiatives as NCAs, 'assemblies', and 'congresses'.

One may also assume that the experience of the former Soviet republics can be relevant in other contexts in the following respects. First, such initiatives are important as a symbolic policy, or as a way to publicly recognize the role ethnic groups play in society. Symbolic status or a specific label for an organization (such as 'autonomy') turns out to overweigh utilitarian considerations; ethnic activists often demonstrate that they feel comfortable with agendas which have little if

---

[74] Ian Lustick, 'Stability in Deeply Divided Societies: Consociationalism versus Control', *World Politics* vol. 31, no. 3 (1979): pp. 325–44.

[75] Shmuel Noah Eisenstadt, *Traditional Patrimonialism and Modern Neopatrimonialism* (Beverly Hills, CA: Sage, 1973); Daniel Bach, 'Patrimonialism and Neopatrimonialism: Comparative Trajectories and Readings', *Commonwealth & Comparative Politics* vol. 49, no. 3 (2011): pp. 275–94; Erdmann and Engel, 'Neopatrimonialism Reconsidered'; Robin Theobald, 'Patrimonialism', *World Politics* vol. 34, no. 4 (1982): pp. 548–59.

any relevance to people's daily life. The high level of legitimacy of NTA policies and the institutions set up in this framework (in that they encounter no public criticism) leads to the conclusion that many potential controversies or conflicts can be mitigated or avoided by imitative forms of social participation and social activism. It is also important that such forms of activity and participation really bind people of different political views and really allow removing from public agendas the issues which may cause social unrest. Second, the forms of organization and the related activities described here can be regarded as good examples of neo-patrimonialism[76] in ethnic policies resting on patronage relationships, resource distribution in exchange for loyalties, and prevalence of informal institutions partly independent of legal frameworks. An important question in this regard is whether the neo-patrimonialist framework applies only in illiberal environments and whether its components can be observed in countries with a market economy, rational bureaucracies, and the rule of law as well.[77] Third, one may assume that the organizational forms in question apply not only in the field of symbolic politics. Organizations of these types can in fact implement ethno-cultural and educational projects, and their affiliation with state institutions can in theory raise capacities. These types of organizations offer flexible and thus potentially efficient schemes of public participation. Particularly interesting are the electoral procedures employed by 'peoples' congresses'—a public vote at local and regional 'primaries' in theory gives the opportunity to participate in the public movement for everyone who appears in person at the local meeting without establishing any ethnic or other qualifications. Fourth, all models of interaction between civil society and the state must be of potential interest in various social and political contexts because they further joint participation in decision-making as well as the distribution and utilization of public resources for ethnic and cultural policy. Fifth, multi-ethnic coalition-type organizations like an 'assembly' seem promising organizational forms. In theory, they can help to overcome ethnic barriers and encourage leaders and activists of different ethnicities to coordinate and reconcile their interests and stances. In addition, multi-ethnic organizations can provide minority organizations with additional recourses such as legal aid, support staff, and premises, and such cooperation may in certain instances be more efficient than separate investments of each individual organization.

[76] Neo-patrimonialism is a term that means (1) a type of social systems and political regimes based on a combination of patronage and clienteles, established and utilized by office holders, and legal-rational bureaucratic rule; and (2) a theoretic framework designed for the analysis of these phenomena; this approach is applied to the 'Third World' as well as most post-communist societies.

[77] Bach, 'Patrimonialism and Neopatrimonialism', pp. 283–90; Theobald, 'Patrimonialism'.

11

Russian National Cultural Autonomy in Estonia

Vadim Poleshchuk[1]

11.1 Introduction

Estonia is routinely referred to as a country that successfully implemented the principles of national cultural autonomy in the interwar period. Cultural autonomies were also established in Estonia after 1991, that is, when its independence was regained. The national administration treats the very idea of autonomy rather seriously. Will Kymlicka argued in 2000 that in Estonia 'Russian settlers did not see themselves as immigrants, nor were they admitted by the host society as future citizens. But as both sides rethink their initial attitudes, the immigrant model (supplemented with some forms of cultural autonomy) might form the basis for a stable arrangement'.[2] However, the failure of the local Russian minority to establish autonomy raises the question of whether this concept might meet the requirements of the largest minority group, which makes up at least a quarter of the population. In the national context autonomy is understood in practice as a specific organization of a national minority group. Nevertheless, the concept of autonomy was also repeatedly used to demonstrate the liberal character of Estonian ethnic policies.

11.2 The Interwar Period

A hundred years ago the percentage of minority groups in Estonia was modest. According to the 1897 census there were about 945,000 inhabitants in Estonia. Of them, 90.6 per cent were Estonians, 4.0 per cent Russians, and 3.7 per cent Germans.[3] After Estonia became an independent country, the first census was

[1] The author is grateful to Stuart Sweeney (UK) for his kind assistance.
[2] Will Kymlicka, 'Estonia's Integration Policies in a Comparative Perspective', in *Estonia's Integration Landscape: From Apathy to Harmony: Interviews with Estonian Leaders of Public Opinion, Materials of International Conference, Estonia's Integration Projects, Monitorings*, edited by Jaan Tõnissoni Instituut (Tallinn: Jaan Tõnissoni Instituut, 2000), p. 49.
[3] Ene-Margit Tiit, *Eesti rahvastik. Viis põlvkonda ja kümme loendust* [Estonian Population. Five Generations and Ten Censuses] (Tallinn: Statistikaamet, 2011), p. 23.

organized in 1922. The population had increased and reached 970,000. On the basis of the Tartu Peace Treaty with Bolshevik Russia, Estonia incorporated territories which were inhabited predominantly by Russians. As a result the percentage of Russians soared and reached 8.2 per cent, while the percentage of Germans dropped to 1.7 per cent; Jews and Swedes were below 1 per cent. Eighteen thousand persons were stateless, mainly refugees from Soviet Russia.[4] There were very significant changes in the structure of the local Russian population after the 1917 Russian Revolutions. According to some estimates in 1897 every fifth Russian and every fourth German were professionals. In interwar Estonia, the Russian share among professionals dropped and was only a few per cent.[5] Russian intellectuals, professionals, and skilled workers left Estonia en masse in early 1918 just before the German military occupation. Thus, in Revel (Tallinn) in 1917 there were 158,000 inhabitants and only 103,000 in the following year.[6]

The Estonia of the time can be described as a typical Eastern European country of the interwar period starting as a democracy in the early 1920s and ending up as an authoritarian regime in the late 1930s. The country consisted of the 'main' ethnic nation(ality) (*rahvus*) and minority nationalities. However, the 1920 Constitution referred to the people (*rahvas*) as the supreme executor of state power (art 27). It guaranteed to national minorities the right to found autonomous institutions for the promotion of the interests of their national culture and welfare insofar as these did not run contrary to the interests of the State (art 21). The Law on Cultural Autonomy of National Minorities was passed at the beginning of 1925.[7] It was the result of a compromise between the leading political forces and it was classified as a temporary legal act. It dealt only with culture, not welfare. The law (art 8) recognized as national minorities Germans, Russians, and Swedes as well as other groups numbering 3,000 or more (in practice, the only additional group were the Jews). A Greek proverb says that nothing is more permanent than the temporary: the 1925 law was in use until the collapse of Estonian independence in 1940.

Much attention has been paid to the 1925 autonomy law by international academia. Estonia was the first country to apply in practice the old idea of Austro-Marxists, and it was praised in international fora as early as the 1920s and the early 1930s. Many writings describe in detail the circumstances of the adoption of this Act; regretfully, much less ink was expended on explaining how autonomy bodies worked and what their efficiency was. Reintroduction of the national minority autonomy law in once again independent Estonia in 1993 has also drawn much attention. Regretfully, there were almost no attempts to provide a thorough comparative analysis of the 1925 and 1993 Acts. Kari Alenius provided

---

[4] Tiit, *Eesti rahvastik*, p. 35.

[5] Sergei Issakov, *Путь длинною в тысячу лет. Русские в Эстонии. История культуры. Часть I* [The Thousand-Year Road. Russians in Estonia. The History of Culture. Part I] (Tallinn: INGRI, 2008), pp. 162–206.

[6] Raimo Pullat, *История Таллина с начала 60-х годов XIX столетия до 1970 года* [The History of Tallinn from the 1860's up to 1970] (Tallinn: Eesti Raamat, 1972), p. 171.

[7] Riigi Teataja 1925 [National Gazette 1925], no. 31/32.

a comprehensive overview of all major factors that might influence the adoption of the autonomy law in 1925. He concluded that 'there are many factors explaining why Estonia became the only country in the world to pass a law on cultural autonomy during the period between the world wars. These factors, which were different, yet interconnected and similar in their impact, together provided sufficient impetus to make it possible to approve autonomy'.[8] He believed that highly significant factors were the readiness and ability of the newly established national majority to address the needs of minorities, as well as the removal of political and economic power from autonomy in the text of a draft law. Among moderately significant factors were the demographic make-up of Estonia (relatively small percentage of minorities); lobbying by German minority activists; demonstration of loyalty by local Germans and Russians to the new regime so that Estonians might feel that they achieved 'sufficient historic revenge on their former ruling powers'. Contrary to widespread opinion, Alenius did not find evidence of great significance of the influence of the League of Nations with its pro-minority requirements ('political conditionality' of the early 1920s) or evidence of the pressure from the kin-states of minorities. The influence of the failed communist coup of 1924 should not be overestimated; it gave some impetus to the process of the adoption of the Act.[9]

In accordance with the 1925 law, two national minorities, the Germans (1925) and the Jews (1926), soon established national cultural autonomies. They both elected cultural councils with electorates based on 'nationality lists'. The Russians, the largest minority, did not follow them. The Germans were the main proponents of the 1925 law. As worded by Housden,

> Germany's defeat in the war, upheaval in Russia and the establishment of the Estonian state (bringing with it the expropriation of the massive baronial estates) left the once ruling German elites of Estonia and Latvia facing marginalization. It speaks volumes for the depth of their sense of pride that, from such an unpromising position, they looked to construct a system suited to the reservation of autonomy in some form. Inevitably such a system had to play to their traditional identity and fit with existing political possibilities. Cultural autonomy fitted the bill.[10]

And Nikiforov has added, that 'a higher social status of the entire national group stimulated them to secure their position by separation in legal terms from a common social body'.[11] Similar to the Germans, the Jews were a small and relatively

[8] Kari Alenius, 'The Birth of Cultural Autonomy in Estonia: How, Why, and for Whom?', *Journal of Baltic Studies* vol. 38, no. 4 (2007): p. 458.
[9] Alenius, 'The Birth of Cultural Autonomy'.
[10] Martyn Housden, 'Cultural Autonomy in Estonia: One of History's "Curiosities"?', in *The Baltic States and their Region: New Europe or Old?*, edited by David J. Smith (Amsterdam: Rodopi, 2005), p. 235.
[11] Ilja Nikiforov, 'Национально-культурная автономия в Эстонии: повторение пройденного' [National Cultural Autonomy in Estonia: Repetition of the Past], in *Национально-культурная автономия. Идея и реализация. Эстонский опыт* [National Cultural Autonomy. Idea and Realisation. Estonian Experience], compiled by Vadim Poleshchuk (Tallinn: Legal Information Centre for Human Rights, 2008), p. 45.

prosperous group, dispersed through the cities.[12] Germans and Jews were very different from the largest minority, the Russians, who resided in the countryside; many of them faced problems of poverty and lack of land.[13]

On the basis of the 1925 Act, the autonomy bodies enjoyed two basic rights. Firstly, they enjoyed the right to organize, manage, and supervise both public and private educational institutions working in their mother tongue, and second, they were allowed to take care of cultural needs and to establish appropriate bodies and associations of relevance (art 2). Without doubt, the right to control publicly funded schools was of utmost importance. Furthermore, on the basis of the 1925 law, state and local governments were to provide autonomy bodies with financial resources in accordance with the valid legislation (art 6). Thus, by the early 1930s the German bodies took over one-quarter of all German-language schools in Estonia; most of their funds were spent on education.[14] The Jewish autonomy also controlled several educational institutions and most of the Jewish youth attended these institutions in 1938 and 1939.[15] The Estonian system of minority school with (partial) autonomy was not unique, however. For instance, in neighbouring Latvia the head of the German school authority Wolfgang Wachtsmuth argued that the Germans there should enjoy more independence from the authorities as compared with Estonian Germans.[16]

The Estonian Constitution of 1920 guaranteed national minorities the right to mother tongue education (art 12). While the text provides no definition of minorities, three groups (Germans, Russians, and Swedes) were explicitly mentioned in Article 23 of the Constitution. Constitutional provisions were observed in practice. Thus, in 1925, there were 204 Russian-language publicly funded basic schools (the level of obligatory education); two-thirds of all pupils attended rural schools.[17] In 1923, there were twelve Russian upper secondary schools and four of them were funded by the state.[18] Contrary to the Germans and Jews, the Russians could not control the mother tongue educational system through autonomy bodies. However, they still could influence them. According to the Constitution of 1920 (art 22), local government institutions might function (internally) in the

---

[12] However, they had a significantly lower level of prosperity than Baltic Germans or Latvian Jews. Anton Weiss-Wendt, 'Thanks to the Germans! Jewish Cultural Autonomy in Interwar Estonia', *East European Jewish Affairs* vol. 38, no. 1 (2008), pp. 90–1.

[13] Isaakov, *The Thousand-Year Road*, pp. 205–6.

[14] Housden, 'Cultural Autonomy in Estonia', p. 234.

[15] Tõnu Parming, 'The Jewish Community and Inter-Ethnic Relations in Estonia, 1918–1940', *Journal of Baltic Studies* vol. 10, no. 3 (1979): p. 247.

[16] John Hiden and David J. Smith, 'Looking beyond the Nation State: A Baltic Vision for National Minorities between the Wars', *Journal of Contemporary History* vol. 41, no. 3 (2006): p. 394.

[17] Tatjana Shor, 'Проблемы культурной автономии на страницах русской периодики в Эстонии 1925–1930 гг' [The Issue of Cultural Autonomy in the 1925–1930 Russian Periodicals of Estonia], in На перекрестке культур: русские в Балтийском регионе. Часть 2 [At the Crossroad of Cultures: Russians in the Baltic Region. Part 2] (Kaliningrad: Kaliningrad State University, 2004), p. 124.

[18] Sergei Issakov, *Русское национальное меньшинство в Эстонской Республике (1918–1940)* [The Russian National Minority in the Republic of Estonia (1918–1940)] (Tartu: The Crypt, 2000), p. 197.

language of 'minority nationals' if the latter constituted a majority. Ethnic Russians dominated in four districts east of the River Narva, two districts near Lake Peipus, and six districts in Petseri (Pechory) region. Russians dominated in the cities of Mustvee, Kallaste, and Petseri (Pechory).[19] The demographic strength of ethnic Russians in particular in local government bodies permitted them to resolve relevant issues without establishing cultural autonomy bodies. Dispersed Germans and Jews were deprived of this opportunity (as well as those Russians who lived in large numbers in the cities of Tallinn, Narva, and Tartu).

The second major task of cultural autonomy bodies related to culture and cultural associations. Actually, the establishment of a cultural autonomy was not necessary in order to make use of the right to deal with cultural activities in an organized manner. In interwar Estonia, the Ministry for the Interior registered more than 6,600 associations and one-tenth of them were 'Russian' (as compared with 3 per cent which were 'German').[20] By default many (if not most) local Russians were engaged in social and cultural activities of the Russian community. Last but not least, it would be useful to examine the reasons why Russian cultural autonomy was not created according to the explanations of the Russian community leaders themselves. Tatjana Shor carefully studied interwar Russian-language printed media to find answers to the question why Russians did not establish national autonomy in the late 1920s or early 1930s. Initially, the establishment of Russian cultural autonomy was seen as a difficult task considering the demographic and geographic factors. Additionally, Russian activists were unsure if their group representatives were able to cover the expenses necessary to maintain the work of the educational facilities. Shor also showed that in the late 1920s, another important reason was the contradictions between the various political groups of local Russians involved in an 'information war'.[21]

According to the 1934 census Estonians made up 88.1 per cent of the population. The percentage of Russians remained the same (8.2 per cent) while their community increased in absolute numbers. The German community had decreased to 1.5 per cent of the population. There was also a noticeable decrease of stateless people from 1.6 per cent in 1922 to 0.7 per cent in 1934.[22] In 1934 Estonia's second Constitution was adopted preserving the right to national minority cultural autonomy (art 21). However, after the 1934 coup the authoritarian regime of Konstantin Päts pursued a policy of Estonianization, which raised well-founded concerns among local minorities. Representatives of the Russian minority managed to submit their application for creation of the autonomy in 1937. There are good reasons to believe that this attempt was (at least partially) a reaction to the new political reality when previous compensatory mechanisms did not function well enough and greed for cultural autonomy was based on deep concerns and

[19] Issakov, *The Thousand-Year Road*, p. 205.
[20] Galina Ponomarjeva and Tatjana Shor, *Русская печать и культура в Эстонии в годы Второй мировой войны (1939–1945)* [Russian Printed Media and Culture in Estonia during the Second World War (1939–1945)] (Tallinn: Tallinn University Publisher, 2009), pp. 7–8.
[21] Shor, 'Проблемы культурной автономии'. [22] Tiit, *Eesti rahvastik*, p. 40.

fears of the minority leaders. However, the Russian application was unsuccessful: the authorities refused, referring to the planned changes in the Constitution.[23]

While the authoritarian regime of Päts can hardly be qualified minority-friendly, the German and Jewish autonomy bodies survived the 1934 coup. Anton Weiss-Wendt made a good point referring to the good relations between the Estonian and the German government, which might essentially be explained by economic reasons. Under these circumstances it was impossible to put limits on the functioning of German cultural autonomy and this situation was also beneficial for Jews and their cultural autonomy.[24] The links between the proponents of German cultural autonomy (such as Werner Hasselblatt and Ewald Ammende) and the Nazi regime are well known. These links might also shed some light on suspicions that their contemporaries might feel regarding the activity of the Baltic Germans in propagating the idea of cultural autonomies internationally.[25] 'Repatriation' of Germans to the Third Reich in the late 1930s was quick and well organized and it physically removed most German minority members from Estonia.[26] Interestingly, the Estonian authorities used the very first opportunity to abolish German cultural autonomy for formal reasons. Article 15 of the 1925 law permitted the abolition of autonomy if the number of 'minority nationals' dropped below half of the number recorded in the previous population census. With reference to this provision, the government by its decree of 21 December 1939 abolished the German autonomy and took over its property.[27]

The new Constitution of 1938 reintroduced the right to establish autonomy (art 20). However, the leaders of Russian cultural organizations complained in a 1939 memorandum addressed to President Päts: 'While the institution of cultural self-government is provided for in the Constitution of the Republic, for some reasons any interest paid to this topic is considered to be a sign of disloyalty.'[28] The same Russian leaders complained about de facto Estonianization of Russian elementary schools in the border regions as well as other policies of Estonianization. Securitization of the Russian minority issue could only partially explain these

---

[23] Natalja Lesnaja, 'О сохранении преемственности в развитии русской культуры в Эстонии в XX веке' [On the Preservation of Continuity of the Russian Culture in Estonia in the Twentieth Century], in *Русские в Эстонии. Сборник статей* [Russians in Estonia. The Compendium of Articles], edited by Viktor Boikov and Naftoli Bassel (Tallinn: Russian Research Center in Estonia, 2000), p. 92.

[24] Weiss-Wendt, 'Thanks to the Germans'.

[25] Housden, 'Cultural Autonomy in Estonia', pp. 239–40.

[26] Kalev Katus, Allan Puur, and Luule Sakkeus, 'The Demographic Characteristic of National Minorities in Estonia', in *The Demographic Characteristics of National Minorities in Certain European States*, edited by Werner Haug, Youssef Courbage, and Paul Compton (Strasbourg: Council of Europe Publishing, 2000), p. 50.

[27] Riigi Teataja 1939 [National Gazette 1939], no. 117.

[28] 'Обращение председателей правлений Союза русских просветительных и благотворительных обществ в Эстонии и Русского национального союза к президенту Эстонской Республики, февраль 1939 года' [Appeal to the President of the Republic of Estonia of the Chairmen of the Boards of the Union of Russian Educational and Charitable Societies in Estonia and the Russian National Union, February 1939], available from: Эстония (Estonia Daily), 3 July 1993.

negative trends. In general, the authoritarian regime was playing games with ethnic nationalism, and the concept of cultural autonomy did not always accord with the new state ideology, which did not provide support to minorities. In contrast to the German community, the Russians enjoyed no support from their kin-state (Soviet Russia). The only remnant of the democratic period to survive was the Jewish autonomy. However, it was dissolved by the Soviet authorities in 1940 together with all other 'bourgeois associations'.[29]

The Swedes were another big ethnic group that did not utilize the right to establish cultural autonomy. They emigrated from Estonia in 1944 during the Nazi occupation just before the return of the Red Army. Paradoxically, the lists of 'repatriates' were drafted on the basis of the same rules as the 'nationality lists' envisaged in the cultural autonomy law. While this was practically the only legal way granted by the German authorities to leave the country, many ethnic Estonians managed to be included on the lists.[30]

The German cultural autonomy bodies assisted the Germans in preserving their community in interwar Estonia based on a specific identity and to organize the swift and smooth resettlement of the former rulers of the country. The chroniclers of the local Jewish community argued that while autonomy played an important role in organizing and directing the educational and cultural life of Estonian Jews, 'it led to certain isolation. Jews communicated mainly among themselves with the exception of work relations, and contacts with Estonians were quite limited'.[31] The Germans and Jews had chosen self-segregation in the Estonian nation state, which slowly but steadily slipped into the trendy fashion of the epoch, that of ethnic nationalism. As for the Russians, no one could undermine the 'natural' isolation of peasants living in the border regions. However, Russian urban intellectuals had also managed to preserve their specific social and cultural life under the conditions of the authoritarian regime. Whether they could save the Russian-language schools remained an open question.

11.3 The Cultural Autonomy Law of 1993

There were considerable changes in the ethnic composition of Estonia during the Soviet period. In addition to mass emigration before and during World War II (Estonians, Germans, Swedes), there were demographic losses due to the war (all ethnic groups), to the atrocities of Nazi occupation (especially Jews and Roma), to Stalinist repression (all groups), and to changes to the state border (border districts inhabited mostly by Russians became a part of core Russian regions (Russian Soviet Federative Socialist Republic) in 1944). After the war, the national population

---

[29] Eugenia Gurin-Loov and Gennadi Gramberg, *The Jewish Community of Estonia* (Tallinn: Jewish Community of Estonia, 2001), p. 11.
[30] Katus et al., 'The Demographic Characteristic', p. 52.
[31] Gurin-Loov and Gramberg, *The Jewish Community*, p. 11.

started to grow. However, there was also considerable migration from other territories of the Soviet Union, which began to alter significantly the ratio between different ethnic and linguistic groups. According to the last Soviet census of 1989, the total population numbered 1.565 million people. The percentage of ethnic Estonians was 61.5 per cent. Russians reached 30.3 per cent but only a small part of them were descendants of the pre-war Russian community. Other large minority groups consisted of Ukrainians (3.1 per cent), Belarusians (1.8 per cent), and Finns (1.1 per cent). Most of them spoke Russian as their mother tongue or as the preferable language of public communication; in fact, one-third of the Estonian population became Russian-speaking. However, almost all ethnic Estonians preserved Estonian as their mother tongue.[32]

Trends of minorization of Estonians in their traditional territory were accompanied by widening use of Russian. This should not be ignored when analysing the factors promoting pro-independence mobilization of ethnic Estonians in the late 1980s and early 1990s. Neil Melvin explained that

> [w]ithout the developed political institutions of civil society, it was the bonds of culture, language and family that provided the foundations of political organization against Soviet rule. The cultural-linguistic basis for mobilization was further reinforced by perceptions of Russian expansion in the region and gradual assimilation of Baltic and Finno-Ugric peoples by Russian society. In this context, Baltic national identities became even more closely wedded to language and culture than in other Soviet republics. Protecting Estonian and Latvian language and culture therefore became the central justification for political activity in the Baltic states during *perestroika*.[33]

The Estonian historian Toomas Hiio rightfully pointed out that some policies of Estonianization of the late 1930s helped to preserve Estonian identity under the conditions of the Soviet regime.[34] Ironically, ethnic identities were reinforced by Soviet 'nationality policies' which combined promotion of civic identity (the Soviet people) and use of the Russian language ('language of interethnic communication') with affirmative action measures to support 'titular' ethnic groups in their homelands. Under Soviet rule ethnic Estonians enjoyed a certain degree of ethno-territorial autonomy. Paul Kolstoe has stressed that while in the Soviet Republic, Russians enjoyed certain cultural facilities in the 1970s and 1980s, they

---

[32] Vadim Poleshchuk, 'Вопросы об этничности, языке и религии в переписи населения Эстонии' [Issues of Ethnicity, Language and Religion in the Census in Estonia], in *Этнологический мониторинг переписи населения* [Ethnological Monitoring of Population Census], edited by Valery Stepanov (Moscow: Russian Academy of Sciences, Institute of Ethnology and Anthropology, 2011), pp. 449–51.

[33] Neil Melvin, *Russians Beyond Russia. The Politics of National Identity* (London: Chatham House Papers, 1995), p. 25.

[34] Toomas Hiio, 'Служба государственной пропаганды Эстонской Республики 1934–1940 гг' [The State Propaganda Service of the Republic of Estonia in 1934–1940], in *Образ Другого. Страны Балтии и Советский Союз перед Второй мировой войной* [Images of the Other: Baltic States and the Soviet Union before World War II], edited by Reinhard Krumm, Nikita Lomagin, and Denis Hanov (Moscow: Rosspen, 2012), p. 50.

were still handicapped in most places over access to political power.[35] Tamara Dragadze has explained that

> ethnically defined provinces, or administrative units, in the Soviet experience engendered a two-way experience: the ethnicisation of political, cultural and economic discourse in the local context and the territorialisation of ethnicity. Thus the Soviet system reinforced the local view that a given territory has emblematic significance for a people's understanding of self and their ethnicity.[36]

Local traditions and Soviet policies embedded a set of views that characterize Estonians as a 'culture nation', which has very special (if not mystical) ties with the Estonian soil. In the early 1990s many Russian-speakers were condemned by members of the majority for being 'people without roots' and they were teased by the words of a popular Soviet song ('my address is neither a house nor a street, but the Soviet Union'). Estonian intellectuals failed to recognize that many (if not most) of the settlers basically switched to the civic Soviet identity and that they were obsessed with romantic ethnic nationalism, which is quite 'natural' for the initiation of the pro-independence struggle. Vojin Dimitrijević observed in 1994 that in Eastern and Central Europe 'socialist' states were replaced with those heavily loaded in favour of the dominant ethnic groups. Furthermore, most of these states are based on strict adherence to the ethno-nationalist concept of the 'nation states' primarily belonging to the dominant group.[37] The Estonian majority supported the text of the new Constitution adopted by a 1992 referendum. The preamble of the Constitution explains that the people of Estonia founded the Estonian state with the aim of preserving ethnic Estonians and Estonian culture through the ages. In 2007 the preamble was amended to include reference to the Estonian language.[38] After twenty years of independence there is much discussion about 'Estonian-ness' (*eestlus* or *eesti meel*) and its importance for local minorities. 'Estonian-ness' is in fact a slightly modernized 'culture', which is hard to combine with specific world views of minority communities.

In a number of legal acts Estonia has also proclaimed its adherence to the principle of state continuity and policies of restitution. From this point of view, the Soviet regime and its policies, including migration policies, lacked any legitimacy. In practical terms, restitution mostly concerns international treaties, (immovable) property rights, and citizenship. The Estonian Supreme Soviet reintroduced the Law on Citizenship of 1938 and defined the citizens of Estonia as those who were in possession of citizenship prior to 1940 and their descendants.[39] While this decision does not contradict restitution logic, it adversely affected the local

---

[35] Paul Kolstoe, *Russians in the Former Soviet Republics* (London: Hurst, 1995), p. 102.

[36] Tamara Dragadze, 'Ethnic Conflict as Political Smokescreen', in *Ethnicity and Intra-State Conflict: Types, Causes and Peace Strategies*, edited by Hakan Wiberg and Christian Scherrer (Aldershot: Ashgate, 1999), p. 267.

[37] Vojin Dimitrijević, 'Democracy versus Nation. The Post-Communist Hypernational State and the Position of its "Ethnically Different" Citizens', *Helsinki Monitor* vol. 5 (1994): p. 23.

[38] Riigi Teataja I [National Gazette I], 2007, no. 33, art 210.

[39] Riigi Teataja [National Gazette], 1992, no. 7, art 109.

Russian-speaking community and this outcome was quite predictable. According to official estimates, about one-third of the total Estonian population did not have Estonian or any other citizenship in early 1992.[40] Estonia did not follow the example of Lithuania that restored its citizenry but permitted easy access to citizenship for Soviet-era settlers. In short, most Russian-speakers were not recognized as either citizens or as members of a national minority. The majority of Russian-speakers were expected to 'repatriate'. Pre-war Russian community members were recognized as citizens on an equal footing with members of the majority. However, as Kees Groenendijk has argued, '[b]oth the fact that the new nationality legislation does not explicitly exclude non-Baltic residents and the fact that some descendants of citizens of 1940 were of non-Baltic origin do not alter the discriminatory effect of the legislation'.[41]

The 'ethnic neutrality' of Estonian citizenship legislation is problematic. Chapter II of the Estonian Constitution titled 'Fundamental Rights, Freedoms and Duties' starts with Article 8. Section 1 of this article reads as follows: 'Every child of whose parents one is an Estonian citizen has the right to Estonian citizenship by birth.' Ironically, this appears to be the most important fundamental right for the drafters of the Estonian Constitution. In the late 1990s *ius sanguinis* stipulated by Article 8 of the Constitution was interpreted by Estonian political scientist Rein Ruutsoo as conferring ethnic privileges on Estonians.[42] Klara Hallik studied several characteristic elements in the ethnic policy stances of all mainstream parties represented in Parliament in the period 1995–9. According to her findings, there was

> a strong ethnic self-defense reflex among the various Estonian parties, where Estonia's Russians [were] still seen as the main existential threat to the Estonian people … All Estonian-based parties [were] unanimous in the need to encourage non-Estonian out-migration … With only a few, though minor differences, all of the Estonian-based parties view[ed] the nation state as an ethnicity-based state and therefore none of their platforms [had] any plans to organize a political dialogue with the non-Estonians.[43]

These statements are fully applicable to the Parliament of 1992–5, which adopted the new Law on Cultural Autonomy of National Minorities in 1993.[44]

There is no contradiction between the very tough minority policies of the early 1990s and the reintroduction of the concept of national cultural autonomy. First,

---

[40] Citizenship and Migration Board, *Yearbook 2003* (Tallinn: Citizenship and Migration Board, 2003), p. 8.

[41] Kees Groenendijk, 'Nationality, Minorities and Statelessness: The Case of the Baltic States', *Helsinki Monitor* vol. 4, no. 3 (1993): p. 20.

[42] Rein Ruutsoo, 'Eesti kodakondsuspoliitika ja rahvusriigi kujunemise piirjooned' [Estonian Citizenship Policies and a Sketch of an Emerging Nation State], in *Vene küsimus ja Eesti valikud* [The Russian Issues and Challenges for Estonia], edited by Mati Heidmets (Tallinn: Tallinna Pedagoogikaülikool, 1998), p. 176.

[43] Klara Hallik, 'Rahvuspoliitilised seisukohad parteiprogrammides ja valimisplatvormides' [Parties' Programs and Electoral Platforms on Ethnic Issues], in *Vene küsimus ja Eesti valikud* [The Russian Issues and Challenges for Estonia], edited by Mati Heidmets (Tallinn: Tallinna Pedagoogikaülikool, 1998), p. 95.

[44] Riigi Teataja I [National Gazette I], 1993, no. 71, art 1001.

the concept initially took the form of symbolic policies. In their appeal to the Congress of People's Deputies of Russia of 14 May 1990, the Estonian Parliament stated that in Estonia 'the Russian national minority is guaranteed all civil rights and cultural autonomy'. For Estonian policymakers it was important to highlight the link between interwar policies and the policies of Estonia, which was about to regain independence. It was of utmost importance to prove the liberal character of policies in a (reborn) Estonian nation state. Second, the right to national auton-omy was included in the 1992 Constitution (art 50) similar to all pre-war con-stitutions. This law was also specifically referred to in Article 104 which included the list of the most important 'constitutional' laws (these acts may be passed and amended only by a majority of the membership of Parliament). Actually some public discussions about a cultural autonomy act started in the late 1980s and were actively supported by the minorities themselves, for example through the umbrella organization Association of Estonian Nationalities (*Eestimaa Rahvuste Ühendus*). There were some discussions in the committee of national policies of the Supreme Soviet and a special expert group convened to deal with the issue. The draft sub-mitted by a group of experts[45] in April 1991 drew significant attention at least in expert circles. This draft never became law.

The new bill was submitted to the Estonian Parliament elected in 1992. The aim of the bill was inter alia to replace the Law on the National Rights of the Citizens of the Estonian Soviet Socialist Republic of 1989.[46] Therefore, the draft included the list of basic rights of national minorities (e.g. the new list did not include the right to receive education in Estonian, Russian, and other languages which could be found in the 1989 law). The draft cultural autonomy Act was discussed in plenary sessions three times: on 28 June 1993 (first reading), on 30 September 1993 (second reading), and 26 October 1993 (continuation of the second reading and adoption).[47] Not a single Russian-mother-tongue speaker was elected to the 1992–5 Parliament; however, there were a number of radicals of the ethnic major-ity who attacked the bill in plenary meetings as an act that might please 'the civil garrison' of the former occupying power. The views of Russian-speakers were only sporadically presented by some MPs. They were labelled as 'imperialistic' and their views were not discussed in detail, at least in the plenary meetings. Ants-Enno Lõhmus, who presented the Act in the 28 June meeting, stated clearly that the new law would *not* give anything to those national minorities whose educational and cultural problems 'have already been solved'. At the same session he explained that the autonomy would provide 'additional rights to preserve one's cultural traditions and to found educational institutions to preserve one's education and language'. On 30 September Lõhmus explained that the draft law did not provide for 'special rights' of autonomies in the field of schooling: these issues would be regulated by

---

[45] A. Kirch, O. Samorodni, M. Kirch, T. Tuisk, and H. Koitel. The text is on file with the author.
[46] ENSV Teataja [Estonian Soviet Socialist Republic Gazette], 1989, no. 40, art 618.
[47] The minutes of the plenary meeting as well as all draft laws are publicly available on the official website of the parliament, accessed September 2014, <http://www.riigikogu.ee>.

general laws. Mart Nutt, another MP presenting the bill, explained to the audience that Russians did not need autonomy because they were a very large community. Some MPs were worried that the law would recognize Estonia as a 'multinational state'. In a meeting held on 26 October Lõhmus stressed that in Estonia there is only one ethnic nation(ality) (*rahvus*) and several national minorities.

Karl Kössler and Karina Zabielska have argued the widespread belief that

> Estonia's current Law on Cultural Autonomy for National Minorities follows the outline for the law of 1925 quite closely. From a comparative perspective, the law of 1993 is more detailed, while the less comprehensive regulations of its predecessor were given more substance by means of extensive interpretation.[48]

Estonian MPs who voted for this law in 1993 would be surprised: for most of them it was clear that these two laws were essentially different. Asbjørn Eide explained that the 1925 law explicitly dealt with responsibilities for cultural autonomies with organization, administration, and supervision of public and private schools in the mother tongue, whereas the 1993 Act did not cover these issues in any detail.[49] Importantly, cultural autonomies were not supposed to take over existing publicly funded schools.

Cultural autonomies in 1925 and in 1993 were similar in form, that is, a cultural council elected on the basis of 'nationality lists', the same privileged groups (Germans, Russians, Swedes, and Jews), plus the right to establish autonomy for groups that have more than 3,000 Estonian citizens (citizenship was required by the 1925 law as well, see art 10). However, the two were very different in essence. According to Article 4 of the 1993 law, the main objective of a cultural autonomy body was (1) to organize study in the mother tongue and supervise the use of the assets prescribed for such a purpose; (2) to establish cultural institutions of national minorities and organize their activities, and to organize national cultural events; as well as (3) to establish foundations, and to grant stipends and awards for promoting the culture and education of national minorities. Furthermore, national minorities had the right to establish their own institutions of cultural self-administration, which, in dealing with matters within their competence, should adhere to Estonian legislation and abide by the interests of the national culture. In other words, cultural autonomies received no special rights; the above-mentioned rights are not autonomy-specific and may be realized by other natural and legal persons. The status of cultural autonomies was anything but clear, and most importantly, it was not a legal person.[50] The 1993 law laconically stated that 'the cultural autonomy of a national minority shall mean the right of persons belonging to a national minority to establish cultural autonomy bodies

---

[48] Karina Zabielska and Karl Kössler, 'Cultural Autonomy in Estonia—Before and after the Soviet Interregnum', in *Solving Ethnic Conflict through Self-Government. A Short Guide to Autonomy in South Asia and Europe*, edited by Thomas Benedikter (Bozen/Bolzano: EURAC, 2009), pp. 58–9.

[49] Asbjørn Eide, 'Cultural Autonomy and Territorial Democracy: A Recipe for Harmonious Group Accommodation?', *Working Group on Minorities* (E/CN.4/Sub.2/AC.5/2001/WP.4), 2001.

[50] Vallo Olle, 'Mõned vähemusrahvuse kultuuriomavalitsuse õiguslikud probleemid' [Some Legal Issues Regarding Cultural Autonomies for National Minorities], *Juridica* vol. 2 (2009), pp. 86–97.

in order to perform culture-related rights granted to them by the Constitution' (art 2(1)). Aleksei Semjonov argued that

> the law by no means affords an opportunity for self-governance, since the cultural councils have only the right to 'request' financial help from official and public foundations and organizations. Yet all existing non-governmental organizations (NGOs) enjoy the same right and can do this. To create an additional body through a rather complex and expensive bureaucratic procedure only to be able to do more or less the same things seems useless for most minority societies.[51]

Semjonov also asked an open question: who is the subject of the cultural autonomy law? Actually the same question posed by MP Kalev Kukk was not properly answered during the Parliament debate. Kukk was especially puzzled by the group rights approach of the bill's drafters (in the 26 October plenary meeting). In 2012 the Ministry of Culture finally provided an answer to this question: cultural autonomy is a form of self-government that may be realized by a legal person and the latter may be a non-profit association or a foundation.[52] In other words, cultural autonomy is an additional form of organization of people who have already self-organized voluntarily.

For a decade the 1993 law could not be applied, as the necessary legal acts for implementation did not exist before 2003. The proponents of autonomy became representatives of a small Ingrian Finnish minority, establishing autonomy in 2004. The Swedish minority followed in 2007. The Swedish cultural council has since been elected three times—in 2007, 2010, and 2013; the election was organized in Tallinn and Haapsalu (Estonia), and in Stockholm (Sweden).[53] The state supports cultural autonomies by providing assistance to 'contractual partners' of the Ministry of Culture.[54] That means that autonomies, which are not legal persons and therefore have no bank accounts, are supported by grants paid to umbrella organizations of the Ingrian Finns and the Swedes. There are good reasons to believe that neither the Finns nor the Swedes received many benefits after finalizing the clumsy and time-consuming procedures necessary to found a cultural autonomy.[55]

---

[51] Aleksei Semjonov, 'Estonia: Nation-Building and Integration—Political and Legal Aspects', in *National Integration and Violent Conflict in Post-Soviet Societies: The Cases of Estonia and Moldova*, edited by Pål Kolstø (Lanham, Boulder, New York, Oxford: Rowman and Littlefield Publishers, 2002), p. 132.

[52] Ministry of Culture, written communication of 5 July 2012, no. 7.15/907 (on file with the author), 2012.

[53] This information is provided on the official site of the Cultural Council of Swedish Minority, accessed 5 May 2014, <http://www.eestirootslane.ee/index.php/et/valimised>.

[54] Ministry of Culture, written communication.

[55] During the last decade the FCNM Advisory Committee has also changed its approach to Estonian national cultural autonomy. Initially it criticized the cultural autonomy law for a restrictive definition of a national minority (only citizens of Estonia). In 2001 the Advisory Committee raised concerns that in the cultural autonomy law 'some elements are not suited for the present situation of minorities in Estonia and need to be revised or replaced in order for them to be effective. This pertains in particular to their personal scope of application' (Advisory Committee of the Framework Convention for the Protection of National Minorities, Opinion on Estonia (ACFC/INF/OP/I (2002)005), s 68, adopted on 14 September 2001. Ten years later the factor of citizenship criteria became less important. At least half of all minority members became Estonian citizens: according to

Symptomatically, in 2011 the Advisory Committee on the Framework Convention for the Protection of National Minorities (FCNM) started to criticize the very concept of cultural autonomy. It encouraged the Estonian authorities 'to consider reviewing their minority policy and legislation in broader terms, rather than focussing their attention on amending the [Law on Cultural Autonomy of National Minorities] that is generally considered ineffective and impractical'.[56]

The rigid ethnic policies of the 1990s were somewhat liberalized with the adoption of the first comprehensive integration programme in 2000. These developments were often interpreted as a sign of a new, more inclusive approach towards minorities. The document paid significant attention to the cultural autonomy law and its failures:

> Although the act was passed in as early as 1993, the possibilities provided for in the act have not been implemented. This primarily concerns the question of the formation of cultural self-governments, as the main objectives of the formation of the cultural self-governments to be formed were, among other things, the organization of the teaching of the mother tongue and supervision of the use of funds anticipated for that purpose, as well as the formation of cultural institutions and the organization of their activities, etc. As a result, an analysis of the act must be performed in co-operation with the President's Round Table and other parties.[57]

Symptomatically, the next integration programme for 2008–13 mentioned cultural autonomy only once in the context of supporting 'Estonian indigenous minorities and cultural autonomies'.[58]

In 2006 the leader of the Ingrian Finnish autonomy, Toivo Kabanen, pointed out some grey areas in the relevant legislation, for example the undefined legal status of a cultural autonomy; the lack of specific regulation of relations between autonomy, state, and local governments; the issue of financial support, etc.[59] The government tried to amend the law twice to make cultural autonomy a legal person—in 1997 (bill no. 636) and in 1999 (bill no. 23). Thus, in the 1999 draft law the government proposed to provide cultural autonomies the status of non-profit organizations with some specificities. Some minor changes in the law were made in 2002.[60]

---

the data of the 2011 census the percentage of non-citizens in all populations dropped to 15 and the percentage of ethnic non-Estonians to 31 (Statistics Estonia, 'Statistical Yearbook of Estonia', 2014, accessed August 2014, <http://www.stat.ee/72571>). The threshold of 3,000 citizens of Estonia is an obstacle for very small groups like Armenians. It should be noted that according to the 1993 law (art 6) non-citizens may take part in the activities of cultural and educational institutions and religious communities of national minorities even if they are not able to participate in the elections of the directing bodies of institutions of cultural self-administration.

[56] Advisory Committee on the Framework Convention for the Protection of National Minorities, Third Opinion on Estonia, adopted on 1 April 2011, ACFC/OP/III(2011)004, s 65.

[57] State Programme 'Integration in Estonian Society 2000–2007', 2000, s 6.2.1.

[58] Estonian Integration Strategy 2008, s 3.2, accessed August 2014, <http://ec.europa.eu/ewsi/UDRW/images/items/docl_3700_459328622.pdf> (unofficial translation).

[59] Toivo Kabanen, 'Soome vähemusrahvuse kultuuriautonoomiast' [About Cultural Autonomy of Finnish National Minority], presentation at the Follow-up Seminar on Implementation of the FCNM, 9 October 2006, Tallinn. On file with the author.

[60] Amendments published: Riigi Teataja I [National Gazette I], 2002, no. 53, art 336; Riigi Teataja I [National Gazette I], 2002, no. 62, art 376.

The cultural autonomy law was, however, never substantially amended. The Minister of Culture convened a special working group to draft the necessary amendments in 2010.[61] Nevertheless, no relevant bills had been presented by mid-2014.

11.4 Russian Minority and Cultural Autonomy after 1991

After independence, authorities were able to draft on the basis of census data a long list of 'nationalities' residing in Estonia. In practice, however, Estonian society is divided into two basic ethno-linguistic groups: Estonian and 'Russian'. In the early 1990s many expected the start of a process of re-ethnification of certain groups within the local Russian community, among Russified non-Russian minorities. It seems, however, that non-Estonian/non-Russian minorities are now consolidated around Estonian or Russian cores of society. According to the preliminary data of the 2011 census, the Estonian population has diminished to 1.294 million. The percentage of Russians in the total population has declined to 25 per cent (as compared with 30 per cent in the 1989 census). However, both in 1989 and in 2011, Russians made up about 80 per cent of all ethnic non-Estonians; the percentage of native Russian-speakers has been and still exceeds the percentage of ethnic Russians.[62]

Considering their demographic strength and existing parallel cultural and educational institutions working in Estonian and Russian, Russians and Russian-speaking minorities expected to become one of two constituent groups in a reborn Republic of Estonia. However, they failed to secure these common objectives in the early 1990s. The August 1991 coup in Moscow resulted unexpectedly in the rapid restoration of independence and the majority politicians chose not to address the concerns of the minority community. On 20 August 1991 the Supreme Soviet voted on the declaration proclaiming restoration of Estonian independence. Before the final vote, MP Claudia Sergiy explained why the representatives of four pro-minority groups decided to abstain: 'We cannot take part in voting on the issue of state independence of Estonia while we were provided with no guarantees and we cannot guarantee to our electorate peace and prosperity in independent Estonia'.[63] Even if the decision to abstain from voting was wrong, the forthcoming events proved that the concerns of the minority MPs were not without reason. Decisions regarding the restoration of Estonian citizenship (February 1992), began with the 'legalization of Soviet settlers' who were issued temporary residence permits (July 1993). This, together with new linguistic policies (February 1995), put

---

[61] Ministry of Culture, written communication.

[62] Statistics Estonia, 'Statistical Yearbook of Estonia'.

[63] The minutes of the plenary session of the Supreme Soviet (20 August 1991) are on file with the author.

non-dominant ethnic groups at risk of social marginalization. The socio-economic situation of minorities had also deteriorated:

> The 1990s were clearly years of decline, not only of political status, but also of the social-economic status of ethnic non-Estonians. 'Nationalising policies' had been found to result in an unequal division of cultural, economic, and political resources between majority and minority populations. Ethnic non-Estonians experienced collective downward mobility and shrinking labour market opportunities.[64]

Against this background many pro-minority leaders (especially of Russian origin) began to fight for minority and human rights and for the status of a national minority. There were some debates regarding the establishment of cultural autonomy, and concerns were voiced that Russians were not able to financially maintain their own cultural and educational institutions. Some experts argued that Russians regarded cultural autonomy as a useless mechanism when public funds were still provided to Russian-language schools. Moreover, cultural activities were supported to some extent by national and local authorities. Scholars Aidarov and Drechsler referred to sociological studies arguing that 'Estonian Russians have identities that rather sustain and develop social and political passiveness and individualism than activ[ism] and solidarity'.[65]

During the Soviet period, education in Estonia was provided in two languages—Estonian and Russian (from kindergarten through elementary and secondary schooling to university level). However, the number of students in Russian-language schools gradually decreased from the early 1990s. This might be explained both by the overall decrease in the number of Russian-speaking children in Estonia (due to migration and lower birth rates) and to the reorientation of some non-Estonians towards education in Estonian. In autumn 1990, first-year students of Russian-language general education schools made up 40.6 per cent (and 36.8 per cent in all grades); in 1999 the respective figures were 20 per cent and 28 per cent.[66] In the 2011–12 academic year, Russian was the language of instruction of 19.1 per cent of all schoolchildren, and 3.4 per cent of all students (those of minority origin) studied in Estonian language immersion classes, that is, mostly in Estonian.[67] In 2007–11, Russian upper secondary schools switched to a minimum of 60 per cent instruction in Estonian. The transition was initiated in spite of lack of support by the minority: in 2007 the transition was completely or partially supported by as few as 31 per cent of Russian-speakers surveyed.[68]

---

[64] Vadim Poleshchuk and Jelena Helemäe, 'Estonia—In Quest of Minority Protection', in *International Obligations and National Debates: Minorities around the Baltic Sea*, edited by Athanasia Spiliopoulou Åkermark et al., (Mariehamn: The Åland Islands Peace Institute, 2006), p. 154.

[65] Aleksandr Aidarov and Wolfgang Drechsler, 'The Law and Economics of the Estonian Law on Cultural Autonomy for National Minorities and of Russian National Cultural Autonomy in Estonia', *Halduskultuur/Administrative Culture* vol. 12, no. 2 (2011): p. 55.

[66] Integration Programme 2000, s 6.1.1.1.

[67] Estonian Educational Database, 2011, available from the Ministry of Education and Research, data provided on request on 24 January 2012, data on file with the author.

[68] However, more minority support was observed the following year, thanks to the smooth start of the transition. Ivi Proos and Iris Pettai, *Russian-Speaking Youths: The Position and Expectations of a New Generation. Brief Summary of Materials of Sociological Study* (Tallinn: Estonian Open Society Institute, 2008), p. 28.

11.4.1 Failed attempts to establish Russian cultural autonomy

The proactive approach of the Ingrian Finns and the Swedes, as well as gradual but consistent Estonianization of minority school education, promoted discussions regarding Russian cultural autonomy. In recent years at least three applications were submitted to the authorities to establish Russian cultural autonomy. The first application was filed by a group close to the ethnic Russian Party in Estonia (now non-existent). It was rejected and all court appeals were in vain.[69] If successful, the new body would have faced the problem of legitimacy within the Russian minority due to the image of those involved in the procedures. Two other applications were also submitted by organizations that are questionable as cultural (umbrella) associations of the local Russians. These application procedures are still pending.[70] It will be difficult to report on active measures of the Estonian state to support the foundation of Russian cultural autonomy. According to David Smith,

> in these recent debates one discerns a fear on the part of ethnic majority repre-
> sentatives that institutions of Russian NTA[71] would become a 'state within a
> state' and a vehicle for external influence by Russia, especially given the numeri-
> cal size of the Russian-speaking minority and its territorial concentration, espe-
> cially in north-eastern Estonia. Perhaps more importantly, the presence of the large
> Russian-speaking minority has been framed within the dominant political discourse
> as a threat not just to state security, but also to the societal security of the majority
> ethno-national group.[72]

The failure to organize cultural autonomy occurred along with several attempts to consolidate ethnic Russians and other Russian-speakers residing in Estonia. As regards political participation, all these attempts failed. At the moment no eth-nic Russian parties exist in Estonia. However, Russians were able to consolidate around the mainstream Party of the Centre, especially in the context of 'a World War II monument controversy' in April–May 2007.[73] The party has been routinely criticized by other political actors for their allegedly pro-minority and pro-Russian policies. Russian-speakers have maintained their support for the Party of the Centre up to the present.[74] Lack of interest towards a Russian cultural autonomy might be partially explained by the opportunity to solve certain pending issues at the level of local governments. Residents who are non-citizens in Estonia can vote in local elections. Therefore, local authorities are quite receptive towards minority

---

[69] Information from the Baltic News Service of 5 November 2010.

[70] Ministry of Culture, written communication.

[71] NTA stands for non-territorial autonomy.

[72] David J. Smith, 'Non-Territorial Autonomy and Political Community in Contemporary Central and Eastern Europe', paper presented at the panel 'Non-Territorial Autonomy and New Modalities for National Self-Determination', Political Studies Association Conference, Belfast, 3–5 April 2012, p. 5.

[73] Vadim Poleshchuk, 'The War of the Monuments in Estonia: The Challenges of History and the Minority Population', report from the Åland Islands Peace Institute, no. 1 (2009), pp. 20–2.

[74] Thus, before the most recent national election in March 2011, 81 per cent of Estonian citizens of minority origin claimed to support the Party of the Centre (vs 11 per cent of majority members). See Delfi.ee (News portal), 25 February 2011, accessed September 2014, <http://www.delfi.ee/>.

requests, especially in Tallinn and in the big municipalities of the north-east where the minority communities are present in significant numbers or are the dominant group, and the Party of the Centre has taken power.

Article 21(3) of the Law on Basic Schools and Upper Secondary Schools of 2010[75] permits that the language of instruction may be a language other than Estonian in municipal upper secondary schools. However, permission to pursue studies in another language or bilingual studies is granted by the government on the basis of an application from a rural municipality or a city. The board of trustees of the school is entitled to make such a proposal to the municipality. The municipalities of Tallinn and Narva, controlled by the Party of the Centre, decided to support requests by fifteen general education schools and applied to the central government, however, with a negative result.[76] To prevent 'municipalities' tricks' the Parliament introduced amendments to the Law on Private Schools, which prevented municipalities from establishing private upper secondary schools working in Russian without the government's permission.[77] Formerly, it was carried following the proposal of the Chancellor of Justice (constitutionality control body and ombudsman). These developments highlight the weakness of minorities vis-à-vis majority-supported polices, even if minorities enjoyed the support of local governments.

Economic and political stabilization in the Russian Federation in the 2000s resulted in more comprehensive policies to promote Russian culture and Russian-language education in neighbouring countries. One example of these changes is the so-called compatriots' policies, which are regarded by the Estonian security service as a risk factor in terms of protection of the constitutional order. Thus, the Estonian Security Police alleged in its 2011 annual review that the 'real' purpose of Russia is not culture but manipulation of the local Russian minority for political reasons. Furthermore, some activities of pro-minority politicians in support of Russian-language education are criticized in the Security Police review, not because of violations of the law but because of the suspected influence or involvement of Russian diplomacy in these activities.[78] There are good reasons to believe that active support of Russian minority interests might be interpreted as a security threat in its own right. As argued by Aidarov and Drechsler, Russian cultural autonomy may be and is perceived

> as a vehicle for Russians in Estonia to organize, to form a more cohesive group [...], and, seeing that they are not infrequently perceived to be the 'national enemy', thus to turn more easily against the integrity of Estonia. In other words, Russians may mobilise themselves politically via culture—and that would be too high a price to pay for the advantages of Russian [cultural autonomy].[79]

[75] Riigi Teataja I [National Gazette I], 2010, no. 41, art 240.
[76] Riigi Teataja III [National Gazette III], 2012.
[77] Riigi Teataja I [National Gazette I], 2013, art 3.
[78] Security Police of the Republic of Estonia, *Annual Review 2011* (Tallinn: 2012), pp. 9–11.
[79] Aidarov and Drechsler, 'The Law and Economics', p. 52.

The failure to organize a cultural autonomy does not mean that all other attempts of self-organization were unsuccessful. In the early 1990s there were also several attempts to create representative bodies for the 'community', for example the Russian Democratic Movement, the Representative Assembly, the Russian Community.[80] As for very recent civil society initiatives, it is worth mentioning the Russian District Council, a body elected in 2011 by free elections conducted by a group of volunteers.[81] The pro-Russia spectrum is represented, for example, by the Union of Organizations of Russian Compatriots[82] whose activities are directly supported by the Russian authorities. However, none of these bodies did or does enjoy the support of a decisive majority of local Russians. As for cultural associations, there are many examples, including large and important umbrella organizations uniting both Russians and non-Russian minorities. One external observer noted that

> for many of the non-titular, non-Russian NGOs the working language remains largely Russian. Hence the general policy of the Estonian state to sponsor the fragmentation of the minority communities into speakers of different languages was particularly aimed at formerly russified non-Estonians.[83]

11.5 Conclusions

In the case of Estonia, national cultural autonomy, the specific organization of a national minority group, proved a useful solution in the interwar period for small, consolidated, and wealthy minority groups who sought differentiation (if not isolation) from main society. However, cultural autonomies in pre-war Estonia were hardly beacons of hope. They led to or preserved the self-segregation of local Germans and Jews. It is evident that nowadays the Estonian authorities have repeatedly used the autonomy concept to establish the liberal character of ethnic policies. In the national context, cultural autonomy seems to belong to the domain of symbolic rather than instrumental policies. After 1993, small, motivated ethnic groups, the Ingrian Finns and the Swedes, were the first to establish autonomies and to realize their limited practical importance.

As for Estonian Russians, the creation of a single representative body for a large heterogeneous group seems not to be feasible. In a heterogeneous community, elections may lead to the creation of governing or representative bodies that lack legitimacy among many community members. The 1993 cultural autonomy law was not envisaged for local Russians who were demographically very strong and who enjoyed publicly funded educational and cultural arrangements. Furthermore,

[80] Semjonov, 'Estonia: Nation-Building and Integration', p. 146.

[81] See details on ruszemsovet.eu, accessed 5 May 2014, <http://www.ruszemsovet.eu/home>.

[82] See details on rusest.ee, accessed 5 May 2014, <http://rusest.ee>.

[83] Timofey Agarin, *A Cat's Lick. Democratisation and Minority Communities in the Post-Soviet Baltic* (Amsterdam and New York: Rodopi, 2010), pp. 297–8.

there are fears that autonomy might be a form of (potential) mobilization of a (politically 'dangerous') minority group. The reduction of Russian-language classes in minority schools gave rise to controversies and thus stirred up public interest towards Russian cultural autonomy. However, only some community leaders demonstrated interest in this, and it failed to arouse great enthusiasm among the minorities.

There are good reasons to doubt that the concept of cultural autonomy as a specific self-organization of minorities is 'suitable' in the context of modern approaches to democracy and minority protection. However, the concept fits well in the idea of a nation state based on genuine ethnic nationalism, which is typical of Estonian policymakers. Such a nation state consists of an ethnic majority, which 'tolerates' national minorities by permitting them a certain amount of autonomy, while the state does not essentially belong to them and is not perceived to address minorities' needs and aspirations. John Packer has argued that 'the nationalist project of the 'nation state' is incompatible with respect for human rights since it favours one cultural association (core nation) over all others: a regime of human rights virtually presumes one pluralist state'.[84]

Cultural autonomy is interpreted in Estonia as a special right of association of particular ethnic minority groups. The interwar and modern history of Estonia provides us with evidence that the very existence of autonomies will always be dependent on political will and voluntarism of the authorities. Therefore, cultural autonomies cannot serve as a substitute for comprehensive minority protection mechanisms, which are essentially based on the protection of individual rights deducible from and inspired by respect for human dignity. The idea of isolation and (self-)segregation, which is enshrined in the very concept of institutionalized cultural autonomy, is hardly in line with the modern approach to fully-fledged participation of minorities in political, social, and economic life.

---

[84] John Packer, 'Problems in Defining Minorities', in *Minority and Group Rights towards the New Millennium*, edited by Deirdre Fottrell and Bill Bowring (The Hague: Martinus Nijhoff Publishers, 1999), p. 271.

Conclusion

Levente Salat

The aim of this book has been to assess non-territorial autonomy (NTA) as a statecraft tool and/or policy instrument deployed in countries faced with the challenge of ethno-cultural diversity. The chapters of the volume were supposed to provide detailed and comparably structured information on cases of NTA arrangement in various regions of the world, from Canada to the post-Soviet space, through Western Europe, Central and South-East Europe, and the North of Scandinavia. The sharp focus on the institutional approach was meant to facilitate a better understanding of the rich, though largely under-researched political phenomena which come under the heading of NTA arrangements, often conflated with minority rights, or even human rights sometimes, and clearly shadowed by more systematic research on territorial autonomy (TA). One of the ambitious targets of the editors has been to shed light on the boundaries of the so far poorly defined NTA concept, by mapping the institutions, functions, and outcomes of the arrangements which are allegedly considered to be instances of NTA, paying attention, however, to various contextual determinants, too. Beyond terminological clarity, the aim of contributing to knowledge production helpful in policy analysis and policy advice has been another common denominator of the editors' motivation.

The final chapter of the book will attempt to evaluate the outcomes of this bold undertaking, by focusing on two core issues. First, the chapter will try to assess the overall contribution of the cases included in the book to the study of NTA, in general, and to highlight, in particular, the tentative elements of the 'new methodological platform for NTA research', suggested by Tove H. Malloy in the Introduction. Second, the issue of the optimistic expectation regarding the advantages of NTA over TA, put forward by Sherrill Stroschein in Chapter 1, will be addressed, in a methodologically less underpinned discussion, informed though by the cases included in the volume, and building on additional literature, too. The chapter will conclude by a brief set of advice for policymakers.

1. Contributions to NTA Research

In terms of definition, the baseline which guides the volume is Ruth Lapidoth's emphasis on self-regulating institutions, without which personal (cultural) autonomy cannot exist, as specified in the Introduction. In order to assess the extent to which the cases included in the book provide evidence for this demarcation, or, to the contrary, sustain the need for alternative approaches, the NTA arrangements discussed in the previous chapters will be analysed from the perspective of (1) the terminology they use, (2) the ideological background and the main element of justification of the arrangement, (3) the context of adoption and specific objectives followed by the implementing authorities, (4) types of entrenchment, (5) institutional particularities and competences, (6) legitimacy and popular support, and (7) outcomes and level of satisfaction of the members of the target groups—following the conceptual framework put forward by the Introduction. Based on the findings of the comparative analysis, conclusions will be drawn regarding the intensity of self-rule characteristic to each of the NTA arrangements.

1.1 Terminology

The general idea of self-rule has several types of legal–institutional embodiments in the analysed cases. A more or less common assumption is that NTA can be seen, in the end, as the outcome of collective rights which include entitlements to elect—with a wide range of significance of the term, however—a body that will serve as a representative forum, on the one hand, and, on the other, an administrative tool of the specific arrangement. The elected body is called 'minority/nationality self-government' (Hungary), 'self-governing ethnic communities' (Slovenia), 'national councils' (Serbia and Croatia), 'Sámi Parliaments' (Norway, Sweden, and Finland), 'cultural autonomy' (Estonia and Russia[1]), or peoples' congresses and the 'assembly of peoples' (Russia[2]). When the institutional framework of the arrangement is less clear or it is more complex, the idea of the self-rule is reflected in descriptions like 'self-management in sub-state institutions' or 'institutional completeness' (Canada), 'self-administration competences exercised through public law corporations' (Germany, with reference to the Sorbian people) or 'self-management within a fragmented and multilevel minority governance system' (the Danish–German border region).

Regardless of the terminology, all the cases are based on the personal/personality principle (as defined by Renner), although the importance of territoriality pops up

---

[1] Elections are not a critical part of establishing national cultural autonomies in Russia, as will be explained later.

[2] The electoral processes characteristic of these types of representative bodies on ethnic grounds lack a clear legal basis and are not transparent to the general public.

in a number of instances (Croatia, Slovenia, Hungary, Norway). The associated competences are limited in general to the fields of education, language, culture, religion, and mass media, with the notable exception of the Sámi Parliaments, in the case of which the right to autonomous governance includes competences in economic activities, land-resource management, environment, and control of entry of non-members. The arrangements characteristic for the Danish–German border region are atypical, too, since the five sectors in which self-administered services are offered include—in addition to culture and education—political representation, social services, and services in the economic sector. An interesting further exception in this regard is the case of Canada, where the concept of 'institutional completeness' includes minority self-management in the health sector. The cases also include instances of functional autonomy, both in the sense of the concept proposed by Heintze (Germany and the Danish–German border region), and Tkacik (Canada).

1.2 Ideological background, justification

Justification for NTA arrangements is usually rooted in the commitment for collective rights or other forms of special rights stipulated in constitutions. Beyond that, the ideological background referred to in the analysed cases unravels interesting regional patterns. In Serbia, Croatia, and Slovenia the Yugoslav legacy seems to have influenced the dominant patterns of diversity management, in both a positive (Serbia) and a negative sense (Slovenia). International minority rights standards, especially the Council of Europe's Framework Convention for the Protection of National Minorities have also been regularly invoked in the Western Balkans. With regard to the post-Soviet space, it is suggested that the interest for non-territorial self-organization of ethnic groups can be derived from the theoretical construct of 'national sovereignty', understood in ethnic terms, put forward by Soviet legal theorists in the 1940s and 1950s. The Sámi Parliaments in the three Scandinavian countries are rooted in the Sámi identity and the principle of indigenous self-determination, as stipulated in the UN Declaration on the Rights of Indigenous Peoples adopted in 2007. In Canada, the emerging institutional completeness of the Francophone minority is the result of the activity of the Royal Commission on Bilingualism and Biculturalism and subsequent court ruling which has gradually created a legal environment favourable for the survival and vitality of the French linguistic minority, in line with the provisions stipulated in Section 23 of the Canadian Charter of Rights adopted in 1982. In the case of Hungary, the underlying philosophy of the implemented NTA arrangement has to do with the country's assumed obligation for the large communities of Hungarians lost in Trianon, who live in neighbouring countries as national minorities. In Germany and the Danish–German border region the discussed examples of NTA are based on the principle of public–private partnership: informal structures resulting from bottom-up community activism provide public services to the minorities in a relatively wide area of activities.

1.3 Context of adoption, objectives of the implementing authorities

The most eloquent information with regard to the multiple objectives followed by the implementing authorities is provided by the Serbian case study. We learn that the authorities of post-Milošević Serbia were primarily interested in strengthening their position in the Kosovo debate, and in improving, in the longer run, the country's human rights record in order to facilitate accession to membership of the Council of Europe and later the EU. But it is not less important that they were equally preoccupied with providing a political environment in which minorities accept Serbia as their own state, that the democratically elected national councils cooperate with the institutions of the state, that authorities are more open and sensitive to the minorities and, last but not least, that more radical claims, like TA, by territorially concentrated minorities can be downplayed.

In other instances the commitment to NTA has been included in the new constitutions adopted after regime change (Hungary: 1989), or independence (Slovenia: 1991, Croatia: 1992, Estonia: 1992). The reasons for doing so were often motivated by more or less hidden political agendas. In the Hungarian case study we are informed that in the domestic debate arguments referring to the standard-setting ambitions of the Hungarian legislator occasionally resurfaced: some authors argue that in the early 1990s, when the Hungarian Parliament was not exposed to any political pressure, neither domestic, nor international, the granting of group rights to minorities and the legislation on minority self-governments adopted for domestic minorities was intended, in fact, to serve as a model for neighbouring countries hosting sizable Hungarian minorities. Hidden agendas might be suspected in the Slovenian case, too, where the 1991 Constitution grants special rights to the 'autochthonous Italian and Hungarian national communities', modest in numbers and steadily shrinking, while similar rights are denied to the third 'autochthonous' community recognized by the Constitution, the Roma, as well as to the constitutionally non-recognized national minorities like the Croatian, Serb, Bosniak, Muslim, or Albanian communities that are ten or even twenty times larger.

The Sámi Parliaments are a result of Sámi political activism started in the beginning of the twentieth century, succeeding in changing gradually the trends of internal colonization which threatened their traditional homelands, and managing to break the resistance of the dominant majorities against their claims. The endeavours of the Sámi have been strongly supported by developments in international public law like the 1989 International Labour Organization Convention (No. 169) on indigenous and tribal peoples, or the UN Declaration on the Rights of Indigenous Peoples adopted in 2007. Their status as indigenous people is recognized by the three Nordic constitutions (Norway: 1985, Finland: 1995, Sweden: 2011), and their right to self-determination is endorsed both in domestic and international contexts.

In Canada, the gradual change which eventually led to the emergence of the specific NTA arrangement was triggered by the activity of the Royal Commission on Bilingualism and Biculturalism which resolved, at least temporarily, the Québec secessionist crisis of the 1960s. Among other causes, the crisis emerged due to the refusal of the authorities of Anglophone provinces to let Francophone parents educate their children in French. Self-management of the French linguistic minority first in education, later in health care, and more recently in municipal services is the result of the sustained dialogue between minority activists and state authorities for improved relations between the majority and the minority.

The NTA arrangements in the Danish–German border region have deeper roots in history in both countries: in 1949 the Kiel Declaration recognized the cultural rights of the Danish minority in Germany, while in the Copenhagen Protocol, issued in the same year, the Danish Government recognized the rights of members of the German minority in Denmark to maintain their identity. These commitments were elevated to the level of bilateral statements, the Bonn–Copenhagen Declarations issued in 1955, as part of the political bargaining meant to secure Denmark's support for the German candidacy to NATO membership.

1.4 Types of entrenchment

In addition to official recognition and commitment to collective rights enshrined in the Constitutions, the NTA arrangements discussed in the analysed cases are regularly entrenched in public law. Special laws stipulating the particularities of the respective arrangements were adopted in Hungary (1993, 2005, 2011), Croatia (2002), Serbia (2002, 2009), Slovenia (1994), Norway (1987), Sweden (1993), Finland (1995), and some of the cases included in the analysis of the post-Soviet space: Estonia (1993), Russia (1996), Latvia (1991), and Ukraine (1992). Two interesting exceptions are provided by the Canadian case and the Danish–German border region. In Canada, the steps towards institutional completeness for the Francophone minority emerged through rulings of the Supreme Court, based sometimes, as we are informed, on generous interpretation of Section 23 of the Canadian Charter of Rights. Since no favourable court decision exists yet with regard to bilingualism in municipal services, by-laws adopted by some Ontario municipalities seem to pave the way in this direction.

The legal–institutional particularities of NTA in the Danish–German border region are remarkable since those arrangements are neither enshrined in constitutions, nor regulated by public law statutes. The bases of the arrangements are to be found in the Bonn–Copenhagen Declarations which are not legally binding, and it is mainly their strong moral value, rooted among others in the reciprocity principle, that provides for the spectacular impact they produce on minority protection and minority governance. The activity of the various corporate structures which provide the relevant services is regulated at the sub-federal level in Schleswig-Holstein, and at the national level in Denmark. In essence, those institutions are private institutions (schools) or associations which hold recognition as fulfilling public functions.

1.5 Institutional particularities of the arrangements

Though the picture provided by the cases included in the volume is rather complex, the institutional particularities of the analysed NTA arrangements can be framed with the help of four complementary aspects: (i) issues related to the election of the representative body of the NTA; (ii) legal standing of the arrangements' main institutions; (iii) competences associated with the elected bodies or other relevant institutions of the arrangement; (iv) budgeting.

1.5.1 Elections

The issue of elections is relevant in the post-Yugoslav area, Hungary, Estonia, and the Nordic countries.[3] In most of these cases the underlying philosophy of the arrangements holds that persons belonging to national or ethnic minorities have the right to elect special bodies—called 'national councils', 'minority self-governments', 'councils of self-governing ethnic communities', 'parliaments' or 'national cultural autonomies'—in order to be able to exercise self-governance in certain fields, limited regularly to activities considered crucial for identity reproduction. While fair and transparent elections are essential for the legitimacy and democratic character of the arrangement, this aspect generates most of the problems for both minorities and majorities. Though the data provided by the case studies are not fully comparable, it is apparent that two aspects are especially critical for attempts which are meant to achieve the objectives mentioned above: the territorial bases of the elections, on the one hand, and the issue of electoral registers, on the other.

With regard to territory, the cases included in the volume offer two alternative answers: (a) elections for minority councils, national cultural autonomies or parliaments are organized in one single electoral district covering the state territory in Serbia, Estonia, and the three Nordic countries; and (b) the electoral process is tied to the administrative sub-units and/or layers of the country in Hungary, Croatia, and Slovenia. In the latter cases two further issues need to be handled: special thresholds are utilized in order to single out territorial administrative sub-units where elections for minority councils can be organized, and regulations are in place for specifying the way in which minority councils or 'umbrella organizations' with competences at state level can be established. In Hungary, until 2011, elections have been organized at local and national levels. The new law adopted in 2011 introduced a third level: minority self-governments can be elected now at the county level and for Budapest, too. At the local level elections for nationality self-governments of a certain minority ('nationality' according to the official terminology in use since 2011) can be organized in those territorial administrative units (localities) where at least thirty members of the respective nationality live, according to the last census. In addition, in localities where Slovaks, Slovenes, or

---

[3] Certain electoral procedures are in place in the Russian Federation, too, where 'peoples' congresses' and the Assembly of Peoples in Russia are 'elected' in a rather non-transparent way. These cases will be addressed briefly later.

Roma live traditionally, but their presence is not reflected in the census or is lower than the mentioned threshold, the respective nationality self-governments with state-level competences can propose the organization of elections for local minority self-governments. Elections for minority self-governments in Budapest or at the county level can be organized if the criteria for electing at least ten minority self-governments in the respective county or in the capital city have been met. Elections for the national (state) level nationality self-governments—indirect before 2011 and direct since—are organized without any threshold requirements. According to the provisions of the law, elections for minority self-governments can be held if at least fifteen persons register as electors.

In Croatia, national minority councils are elected at two levels: towns and municipalities, on the one hand, and at the level of counties and Zagreb, the capital, on the other. The election of the council meant to serve the interests of a particular national minority can be organized in administrative units where the respective minority represents at least 15 per cent of the population, and the number of persons belonging to the same minority is above 200 in towns and municipalities, or 500 in counties and the capital city. The functions of representing a particular national minority in relations with the Croatian state can be fulfilled by umbrella organizations called 'coordinations', established—in principle—by at least half of the national minority councils existing at regional level. Coordinations can be created by the national minority councils which exist at the local and regional level by the means of association, and can be both mono- or multi-ethnic.

In Slovenia, the Italian and Hungarian ethnic communities can 'found', as the law stipulates, 'municipal self-governing ethnic communities' in the so-called ethnically mixed territories (recognized as such by the Law on the Establishment of Municipalities and Municipal Boundaries). All municipal self-governing communities (five in the case of Hungarians and four in the case of Italians) form the 'umbrella' self-governing national community which represents the respective national minority in relations with local authorities and institutions of the state. Direct elections are organized in order to elect the councils of the self-governing communities at the municipal level, while the councils of the umbrella organizations are indirectly elected by members of the councils at the municipal level.

Territory bears additional significance in the way in which elections for NTA are organized in two cases. In Hungary, minority self-governments elected in localities where a certain nationality forms a local majority can be transformed into a territorial minority self-government if more than half of the citizens with voting rights in the respective locality have been recorded in the voting register of the nationality concerned, and if at least half of the elected members ran as the candidates of the given nationality. Though it is less clear what it means in practice, we are informed by the relevant chapter that the autonomy arrangement in Slovenia has a mixed character, including elements of territorial, personal, and functional autonomy.

Electoral registers exist in all countries where representative bodies of national minorities are directly elected. In Serbia there are two systems in place. The members of the national councils are directly elected if at least 40 per cent of all persons belonging to a national minority according to the latest census voluntarily register on a separate voting list. If this requirement is not fulfilled within twenty-four hours of the elections starting, members of the national councils for the respective minorities will be elected by electors. Electors are persons formally supported by at least twenty to one hundred people enrolled in the electoral register of the respective minority. No objective criteria are used and no formal control is exercised over applications for registration on minority electoral rolls.

In Hungary a registry of voters was introduced in 2005 as an attempt to curb the 'ethno-business'-like consequences of the previous arrangement, which allowed all Hungarian citizens to vote and to stand for candidacy (based on five recommendations only) in the elections for minority self-governments. The application for registration remains, however, optional; it is based on self-declaration and no further objective criteria are used. From 2014, refugees and residents without citizenship may also ask for registration in elections for minority self-governments. Voting rights for the nationality self-governments will be cancelled if a person registered on the electoral role asks to be deleted from the register.

In the three Nordic countries registering on the Sámi electoral roll is conditioned by various objective criteria (mother tongue of parents and grandparents, registration of parents in electoral rolls, ancestors listed in registers relevant to traditional Sámi preoccupations). In Sweden and Finland the right to register on special electoral rolls is extended to foreigners (non-citizens) of Sámi origin, too. Defining Sámi origin objectively remains, however, the most complex and controversial aspect of Sámi legislation in the Nordic countries.

In Slovenia a special kind of difficulty emerged from the mixed—territorial and personal—character of the autonomy arrangement. Special electoral registers are compiled by the self-governing national communities, with a clear territorial basis. The registers may include, however, any individuals who declare their belonging to the respective national minority, regardless of where they live. Registering on the special electoral roll of the minority is tempting since it allows for directly electing minority representatives in the municipal councils, as well as for the two seats reserved for the Italian and Hungarian minorities in the Parliament. Based on a ruling of the Constitutional Court which tried to resolve the apparent conflict between the constitutional protection provided to communities, on the one hand, and individuals belonging to those communities, on the other, the new Law on Voting Rights Registers introduced more or less 'objective' criteria of identification: long-lasting ties with the community, concern for the preservation of the relevant minority identity, family relations with a person belonging to the community. Electoral registers, called 'nationality lists', are also used in Estonia, for a similar purpose: in addition to the four privileged groups (Germans, Russians, Swedes, and Jews), any group that has more than 3,000 Estonian citizens as members can establish a cultural autonomy body and elect its council based on the nationality list.

In terms of presenting candidates, the adopted solutions are varied as well. In Sweden and Norway lists of candidates put forward by political parties or other interest groups compete. In Finland elections are non-partisan, and individual candidates can run if they are nominated by at least three other persons.

In Serbia, lists of candidates can be proposed by political parties and NGOs of the respective minority, as well as groups of citizens from the same minority provided that they hold the support of at least 1 per cent of the voters registered in the relevant minority electoral roll. In Hungary, candidates can be nominated by registered organizations—but not political parties—provided that in their by-laws it is clearly stipulated that the purpose of the organization is to serve the respective minority, this provision being enshrined for at least the previous three years. It is interesting to add that in terms of candidacy the law adopted in 2011 requires that candidates declare that they are willing to represent the respective nationality, know its traditions and culture, and speak the relevant language (in the case of Roma and Armenian candidates, Hungarian is accepted as the nationality language). In Croatia, candidates for the national minority councils can be nominated by minority organizations or groups of minority members from the territory of the municipality, city, or the county. Political parties cannot nominate candidates, but candidates are not forbidden from being members of political or ethnic parties. Elections for the various NTA arrangements are organized simultaneously with local elections in Hungary and in Slovenia, special elections are organized for the representative bodies of minorities in Serbia, Croatia, and the three Nordic countries.

With regard to the issue of elections of representative bodies in what is called the post-Soviet space in the volume, it is important to add that while in the case of more genuine forms of NTA, like 'national cultural autonomies' (defined in the 1996 Federal Law) elections do not seem to play any significant role in the process of establishment, whereas in what concerns the so-called congresses and assemblies of peoples in Russia, set up and controlled mainly by the government, two-tier electoral schemes are in place. Organizing committees establish numerical quotas based on the ethnic composition of the relevant territories, which are used in nominating and electing electors by all 'stakeholders' participating in a regional meeting. Electors meet then in regional congresses, where they nominate and cast their votes for the delegates to the congress. The governing bodies of the congresses are elected and governed by unwritten tradition, and remain controversial both in terms of membership (retired high-ranking officials) and non-transparent procedures, closed to the constituencies. In Kazakhstan, the members of the Assembly of People are directly appointed by the president, whereas in Belarus, members of the Consultative Inter-Ethnic Council are governmental appointees.

1.5.2 Legal status of relevant institutions

Elected national councils and nationality self-governments are legal entities recognized under public law in the three Nordic countries as well as in Serbia, Hungary, Croatia, and Slovenia. In Slovenia, both the self-governing communities at the municipal level and the corresponding 'umbrella' organizations are legal persons, the directly elected councils being the highest representative organs of the respective legal entities. In Croatia only the directly elected councils are non-profit legal entities, while the 'coordinations' do not have legal personality. In the Acadian case, two of the three levels of the targeted institutional completeness, which gives substance to minority self-management, education, and health services, are regulated by public law at the provincial level, while the achievements at the third, municipal level, exist so far in the form of by-laws adopted by three Ontario municipalities. In the Danish–German border region, the institutions relevant to minority self-administration are incorporated mainly as private associations under German and Danish law. However, those organizations perform various public functions in education, political representation, social services, and media, based on specific legislation. The chapter on the Sorbian people in Germany addresses the dilemma whether the current legal status of the minority—based on a strong umbrella organization incorporated under private law and a public law foundation for managing funds and assets—is sufficient to exercise minority self-administration, or whether incorporation under public law is necessary in order to extend the boundaries and deepen the substance of NTA.

In the post-Soviet space, the situation is rather complex and often controversial. In Estonia, 'cultural autonomies' established under the 1993 law are not legal entities, as we are informed by the two relevant chapters of the book, though this aspect is still debated by the authorities of the Estonian state. In Russia the term 'autonomy' refers to organizations or bodies of a certain kind: 'national-cultural autonomies' (NCAs), as defined by the 1996 Federal Law are 'social organizations' with legal personality, established in a bottom-up manner. NCAs at the local level can be established by groups of citizens belonging to a certain ethnicity, several local NCAs can establish regional NCAs, more regional NCAs can found the federal 'autonomy'. On regional level one ethnicity may have just one NCA; parallel autonomies are denied registration. Compared to other ethnically based NGOs, which exist as well, NCAs are disadvantaged both in terms of establishment and attracting public support. Peoples' congresses are social movements (organizations without registered individual membership), or 'unions of associations of social organizations', as specified in the respective chapter of this volume, but in some cases they may provide examples of more genuine forms of representation like the Komi People Congress, the Khakas Congress, or the Congress of the Bashkir People. Assemblies of peoples have various legal forms: in Russia, they are non-governmental organizations (NGOs), established and run, however, in close cooperation with the governments, both at the federal and regional level (practically GONGOs); in Kazakhstan the Assembly of People was established by a Presidential Decree and is working on the basis of a special law, while in Kyrgyzstan it exists as a 'social association', without any specific legal underpinning.

1.5.3 Competences

Since the information offered by the chapters of the volume regarding the competences associated with the various NTA arrangements are extremely detailed and complex, the big picture carved out by the comparative analysis cannot escape being reductionist and oversimplifying. In broad terms, the cases addressed in the chapters can be divided in four categories: (α) effective competences with rather strong legal and institutional bases; (β) effective competences without strong institutional or legal bases; (γ) symbolic competences with strong legal bases; (δ) vague competences with no clear legal bases.

(α) In terms of effective competences, the most salient example of the reviewed cases is offered by the Sámi Parliaments in the three Nordic countries, where the tasks and operation of the three Parliaments are defined in the so-called Sámi Parliament Acts. Though the Parliaments are primarily frameworks of Sámi participation rather than autonomous governance, and their ability to make autonomous decisions and act independently remains limited, the arrangements in place in the three Nordic countries provide significant power to the Sámi in the area of language, culture, and education, and fair competences in traditionally used land and resource management (with considerable differences, however, if the three countries are compared). The Parliaments are in charge of any issue concerning the Sámi: making proposals, issuing statements and opinions on any matter affecting the situation of Sámi, both as far as public authorities or private institutions are concerned. Parliaments decide on internal appointments in Sámi educational and cultural institutions, and decide—in various formats—on the distribution of funds allocated for Sámi activities.

Incremental expansion of Sámi self-determination in the past decades has gradually widened the Parliaments' competences, of both local and non-territorial character. The situation is especially impressive in Norway, where the 2005 Consultation Agreement signed between the government and the Sámi Parliament clarified the procedures and responsibilities. In Sweden, the Sámi Parliament has the official status of government agency implementing state policies, which provides it with considerable leverage, but is often the basis of criticism, too, for undermining, in fact, Sámi self-determination. Formally, the Sámi Parliament in Finland has the strongest legal standing compared to the other two Nordic Sámi Parliaments (including important competences in resource management and community planning); however, its effective leverage is often weaker than would be expected. All in all, the three Sámi Parliaments in Norway, Sweden, and Finland are eloquent examples of NTA arrangements (with important territorial components, however) which can be classified under the category of effective competences with strong legal underpinning.

(β) Two cases, the Danish–German border region and the Acadians in Canada can be classified under the category of effective competences without strong institutional or legal bases. In the Danish–German border region five major areas of NTA competences are identified in the relevant chapter: political participation, on the one hand, and services in educational, cultural, social, and economic sectors, on the other. Political participation is carried out essentially by minority parties which have representatives at the local and regional level (in Schleswig-Holstein), who participate in decision-making and, occasionally, in the executive power, too. A considerable number of consultative bodies—with no legal standing—provide frameworks for the political dialogue between the majority and minorities, based on good will and mutual trust. Culture and education are the two areas where both minorities, Danish in Germany and German in Denmark, enjoy the highest level of autonomy. All minority educational institutions in the border region are self-administered by the minorities, and due to complex funding schemes provided by Germany and Denmark, minorities entertain direct relations with the authorities of both national and kin-state. In terms of culture, minorities maintain theatres, museums, youth and sport clubs, libraries and archives, and they publish two influential daily minority newspapers. Social services are provided by sophisticated centres assisting mainly elderly members of the two minorities, but counselling, medical care, and maternity advice is also included in the list of services offered by the centres. Activities in the economic sector are carried out by agricultural organizations (motivated, beyond the well-functioning of the agricultural sector, by the preservation of the cultural identity of farmers), financial institutions (providing credit loans), as well as organizations focusing on the environment and energy (interested in forms of regional development compatible with the preservation of the cultural homelands), and print media and minority heritage tourism.

In the case of the Acadians, minority self-management through distinct institutions in education and health care is not clearly regulated in spite of the spectacular progress made towards institutional completeness by the Francophone minority: some of the minority school boards are more powerful than others, especially in terms of managing the curriculum, and a lot depends on the people in charge. A number of minority school boards in New Brunswick declare themselves 'an order of the government', seemingly without any clear legal bases, in order to protect their autonomous decision-making and resources from the provincial government. Though the concept of institutional completeness has undeniable legal underpinning (s 23 of the Canadian Charter of Rights and subsequent court rulings), the success of the Canadian NTA arrangement is rooted essentially in various forms of activism of the members of the minority, which makes it comparable with the case of the Danish–German border region.

(γ) The third category, symbolic competences with strong legal bases, includes the cases in which national councils or minority self-governments are elected (Croatia, Estonia, Hungary, Serbia, and Slovenia). In those cases, the legal acts which define the elected representative body and regulate the process of election provide detailed descriptions of remits and competences, too. The lists are regularly long and comprehensive (especially in the case of Hungary and Serbia), though, in essence, the elected bodies have mainly consultative functions (especially in Croatia and Slovenia). Decision-making competences are usually attached to the management of those public institutions, cultural and educational mainly, which have been taken over from the state or are created and maintained by the empowered minority (Hungary, Serbia, and Slovenia). On rare occasions effective (Serbia) or formal (Hungary and Slovenia) veto rights are also included in the list of competences, however state authorities are not obliged to accept the opinions expressed by minorities. In general, the effectiveness of the national councils and elected minority self-governments depend to a large extent on the relationships they manage to establish with local and/or central authorities (Serbia provides an interesting example in this concern: while provincial authorities are regularly cooperative and local authorities sporadically cooperative, central state authorities are reluctant to comply with the law which transfers important competences to elected national councils). In addition, generous provisions of the relevant legal documents often remain a dead letter since no institutional leverage is attached to the declared competences (especially in Estonia), and funding regularly falls short of what would be necessary.

(δ) In the post-Soviet space, the main function of NCAs, peoples' congresses and assemblies of peoples is, as we are informed by the relevant chapter, to provide for the symbolic presence of ethnic groups in the public space. Though all the organizations included in one of the three types of structures claim to have competences in the fields of culture and education, they have no clear activity measurable in setting up institutions or providing standards and good practices in minority protection. The examples, however, fluctuate on a large scale. A number of NCAs in Russia established and maintain private educational institutions, and in isolated cases museums, theatres, and libraries have also been created. The largest degree of power has been formally granted to the Assembly of People in Kazakhstan, which takes part in the process of drafting laws and executive regulations of concern for minorities and ethnic relations. In some cases, peoples' congresses (Komi) and organizations with similar functions (Nenets People Association) are successful as lobby organizations, initiating amendments to the regional legislation. All in all, the competences of the various NTA arrangements in the post-Soviet space are vague, lacking any clear legal and institutional basis.

1.5.4 Financial aspects

Though NTA arrangements seem to be generally underfinanced, the case studies included in the volume offer interesting counter-examples. One notable exception is the Danish–German border region, where a significant part of the funding is provided by the authorities of the two states within the framework of reciprocity. The institutions of the Sorbian people in Germany are quite generously financed as well from three sources: the federal government, on the one hand, and the federal states of Brandenburg and Saxony, on the other. The chapter on Serbia includes no reference either to any shortage of the rather complicated funding scheme in place. This could be due to the fact that the analysis has been written from the perspective of the Hungarian National Council in Serbia, which receives significant subsidies from the Hungarian kin-state. This aspect makes the arrangement somewhat similar to the Danish–German case, at least as far as Serbian–Hungarian relations are concerned. The Slovenian case study informs us, too, that the two autochthonous minority communities which are beneficiaries of the NTA arrangement have managed, in general, to secure the necessary financial means. In these cases, the role played by the two kin-states, Italy and Hungary, is probably important as well.

Though Sámi Parliaments receive considerable subsidies from the three Nordic states, funding in their case is seen as a critical barrier of self-determination. An interesting aspect of this shortage is that Sámi Parliaments in all three countries are in charge of approximately only 40 per cent of governmental spending on

Sámi-specific issues. The right to self-determination is curbed too by the fact that funding deficiencies undermine the legitimacy of Sámi Parliaments: certain institutions prefer to remain under governmental supervision, rather than accepting being transferred under Sámi jurisdiction which secures them less funding. Among several other reasons, a similar logic hinders the establishment of the Russian cultural autonomy in Estonia, where cultural autonomy institutions lacking appropriate public funding are regarded as potentially useless while central and local authorities provide public funds to Russian language education and cultural activities of the sizeable Russian minority.

In Hungary and Croatia, where the elected representative bodies depend on local authorities in terms of funding, the effectiveness of the arrangement is seriously hindered. In Croatia, the persistent problem of inadequate funding obstructs the activity of national minority councils, while in Hungary one of the strongest elements of cultural autonomy—the right to take over from the state or the local government minority serving public institutions—is undermined by the serious financial risks incurred. The shortage of appropriate funding seems to undermine the effectiveness of educational self-management in the Canadian case, too, at least in some cases. In the post-Soviet space NCAs, peoples' congresses, and assemblies of peoples depend on governmental subsidies and private donors. In Russia, where state authorities bear no formal financial obligations for these organizations, public funding is selective and occasional. In Kazakhstan, Kyrgyzstan, and Belarus financial dependence of ethnic organizations on the state is higher.

1.6 Legitimacy

The level of acceptance and legitimacy of the arrangements in place can be appreciated based on the popular support in cases where elections are held. However, only three case studies offer useful information in this regard; in two further cases indirect answers are available. The chapter on Serbia informs us that the number of individuals who have voluntarily enrolled on the separate minority voting registers indicates that national minorities see the advantages of national councils as forms of self-governments. Moreover, the elections organized so far show an increasing tendency to register. In this case, the legitimacy and representativeness of the arrangement can be considered as fair. In Croatia, although the number of national minorities which nominate candidates for national council elections is relatively high (fourteen), the percentage of effectively elected national councils is between 58 and 37 per cent, with a strongly decreasing tendency. The voter turnout at around 10 per cent, is more or less constant. Based on these data, the legitimacy of the institutions which are meant to provide the frameworks of effective minority participation in Croatia can be seriously questioned. In the case of the Sámi, the voter turnout is higher (around 60 per cent), but the enrolment to the Sámi electoral registers is unsatisfactory: around 20 per cent of the potentially eligible in all three countries. Though generally viewed as institutions of salient importance for Sámi self-determination, the legitimacy of the Sámi Parliaments in the three Nordic countries can be questioned as well.

The chapter on Estonia also provides an implicit answer to the question of legitimacy: the lack of interest of members of the Russian minority towards the provisions of the 1993 law on cultural autonomy can be explained, beyond evident imperfections of the regulations, by several alternative institutions through which Russians see their interests more effectively represented. However, the Estonian state's general policy of aiming to provide incentives for the fragmentation of minority communities also contributes to the minority demobilization, as the relevant chapter suggests. In the post-Soviet space the legitimacy of NTA policies is apparently high, especially if it is measured against the low level of public criticism. This is seriously misleading, though, since in most of the cases the whole arrangement is based, as we are informed by the chapter, on patron–client relations which generate networks of clientelistic resource distribution and exchange of loyalties. In fact, the three institutional frameworks of apparent NTA analysed in the relevant case studies are not genuine forms of political activism on behalf of minorities, but institutional arrangements through which ethnic control is exercised by the government (in Estonia and Kyrgyzstan) or through which authoritarian governments guide and control inter-ethnic relations (Russia, Belarus, and Kazakhstan).

1.7 Outcomes

The level of satisfaction within the arrangements' target groups and the contribution of NTA to the vitality and survival of the minorities are two indicators with the help of which the overall outcomes of the reviewed cases can be assessed more broadly. Although the degree of acceptance within the majority communities would be of interest as well, the chapters provide only sporadic information in this regard. In Slovenia, the results of the arrangement are deemed unsatisfactory by the two targeted autochthonous communities, Italians and Hungarians, since the competences of self-governing communities are not effectively defined, their empowerment and participation in decision-making are rather symbolic, and the voice of the minorities is often not heard. In spite of considerable efforts and permanent attention dedicated to language protection, the indicators of bilingualism continue to diminish to the disadvantage of the two minorities, which is an important vitality test of the arrangement. In general, the arrangement is viewed with considerable reserve both by the majority and by other minorities, in some cases significantly larger as far as the number of members is concerned.

In Croatia, NTA arrangements do not contribute significantly to the living conditions of minorities, as we are informed by the relevant chapter. Since the interest of the constituencies in taking advantage of the activity of minority councils is generally low, the high costs incurred by direct and separate elections seem to be unjustified. The arrangement apparently generates ethno-business-like phenomena, too: in bigger cities and wealthier regions the more generous financial support offered to some of the national minority councils seems to contribute to the 'politicization of ethnicity' in an inappropriate sense, candidates in elections being motivated by financial incentives, rather than dedication to minority interest representation. Ethno-business is quite a salient unintended consequence of the nationality self-governments in Hungary, too, as the relevant case study suggests, and it has been only partially curbed by the subsequent changes in the legislation. Since few examples are known in which the strongest element of cultural autonomy—taking over minority-serving public institutions from the state or local government—has produced effects, the overall impact of the arrangement cannot be assessed in very positive terms. The revitalization of largely assimilated minority communities remains a difficult task, and the complex and rather expensive system of nationality self-governments cannot address effectively the most serious challenge: the problems of the country's Roma community.

In spite of evident shortcomings, Sámi self-determination seems to be institutionally well underpinned in the three Nordic countries, and the authorities in the three states increasingly endorse, through complex and promisingly developing institutional solutions, Sámi peoplehood. The level of involvement and participation within the Sámi community, however, remains low, and Sámi self-determination is met occasionally with resistance on behalf of host societies, due to political systems based on the prevailing wisdom of the nation-state. Two further limitations emerge from the arrangements in place. First: though Sámi Parliaments are, in essence, institutional forms of NTA, the importance of territoriality in enhancing success is highlighted by the significant autonomous powers gained by the Norwegian Sámi in the county of Finnmark where they are territorially concentrated, on the one hand, and by the relative ineffectiveness of the Sámi Parliament in Finland in educational matters, on the other hand. This is due to the fact that 70 per cent of the Sámi children of the country live outside the Homeland Area. Second: the Sámi is essentially a trans-border community which would require institutional arrangements beyond the ones which reflect fragmentation by nation-state borders.

In the Danish–German border region, in Canada (Acadians), in Germany (with reference to the Sorbian people), and in Serbia (with reference to the Hungarian minority), the active involvement of various actors on behalf of the target groups is an important explanatory variable of the arrangements in place. This seems to result in a higher level of satisfaction. Due to the strong bottom-up character of the developments in these four cases, self-empowerment is apparently the most eloquent indicator of the minorities' vitality and desire for survival. It is interesting to note that in those cases further improvements are seen as being dependent on the minorities themselves, in the first instance, and only secondarily on further institutional developments (especially in Canada and Serbia). The case of the Sorbian people in Germany seems to be problematic in this regard, since the relevant chapter discusses the ongoing debate of the advantages and disadvantages of claiming public law status for the main actor speaking in the name of the minority (which is incorporated, for the time being, under private law and performs quite well, as we are informed).

With regard to Estonia, the fact that Russians, the very minority which could benefit most from the provisions of the 1993 Law on NCAs are not interested in setting up their own cultural autonomy is an indirect, though strong indicator of the level of (dis)satisfaction of the main target group. In the post-Soviet space the real beneficiaries of the NCAs, peoples' congresses, and assemblies of peoples seem to be the governments, on the one hand, and ethnic activists and entrepreneurs, on the other. Since symbolic policies and neo-patrimonialism trigger imitative forms of participation and activism, the level of satisfaction—or dissatisfaction—of the target groups themselves cannot be appreciated objectively on the basis of the information provided in the relevant chapter. It can be inferred, however, that in most of the cases there are no real causes for satisfaction. The impact on people's daily life of the arrangements is practically almost non-existent (with perhaps the exceptions mentioned above regarding the Komi, Nenets, Khakas, and Bashkir peoples).

1.8 The intensity of self-rule

Table C.1 summarizes the main findings of the chapters, according to the structure recommended by the methodology set forth in the Introduction. Regarding the core research question—the intensity of the self-rule exercised by empowered minorities through self-regulating institutions (the Lapidoth thesis)—it is interesting to observe that there are at least three complementary dimensions of the assessment: (a) the message sent by the terminology used by the various arrangements; (b) the formal/legal status of the self-regulating bodies, and (c) the effectiveness of the whole institutional arrangement.

In terms of terminology, there is an increasing scale which ranges from self-administration to self-determination, through the intermediary categories of self-management, national-cultural autonomy, and self-government. As far as self-ruling bodies are concerned, the intensity scale seems to range from symbolic structures to parliaments, through private law organizations, on the one hand, and various types of bodies with (more or less clear) public (law) status, on the other. With regard to effectiveness, the cases can be divided into three categories: low, fair, and strong. Table C.2 classifies the analysed cases according to these three sets of categories.

A few interesting conclusions follow from this. First, terminology can be misleading in at least two ways: (a) preference for terminology with a strong message may be justified by hidden agendas and may not be backed in all instances with effective institutional arrangements, as in the cases of Hungary and Slovenia; (b) effectiveness is not always supported by bold ambitions suggested by the prevailing terminology: the Sámi Parliament in Sweden, being a governmental agency, and outstanding, for that reason, in terms of effectiveness, finds itself in a rather uncomfortable position with regard to the ideology of self-determination. Secondly, the existence of self-regulating institutions is not a guarantee in itself of effective NTA arrangements, as the experience of national councils in Croatia and Slovenia or that of the nationality self-governments in Hungary proves. If the self-regulating bodies are fragmented at the local and regional level, their chance of becoming an effective actor with a sufficiently strong voice on behalf of the minorities diminishes significantly. Self-regulation does not produce the desired consequences either if

Table C.1 Comparative overview

	Canada (Acadians)	Danish–German border region	Germany (Sorbs)	Slovenia	Croatia	Serbia	Hungary	Sámi (Norway, Sweden, Finland)	Estonia	Post-Soviet space
Terminology, ideological background, context of establishment										
Terminology	Institutional completeness	Self-management (multilevel minority governance)	Self-administration (through private law organizations)	Self-governing ethnic communities	National councils	National councils	Minority/nationality self-governments	Parliaments	Cultural autonomy	Cultural autonomy; peoples' congresses; Assembly of People
Ideological background, justification	Bilingualism in Canada	Bilateralism, public–private partnerships	Support for the Sorbian (Wend) national movement	Yugoslav legacy, autochthonous communities	Yugoslav legacy	Yugoslav legacy, state-building	Commitment for kins abroad, standard-setting for neighbours	Self-determination of indigenous peoples	Legacy of the 1925 Law on cultural autonomy	Soviet legal theorists: national (ethnic) sovereignty; Austro-Marxism; authorities' desire to prevent territorial claims and disputes
Context	Secessionist crisis in Québec	The acceptance of West Germany in NATO	German reunification (*Domowina*, first founded in 1912, re-registered in 1991)	New constitution after independence	New constitution after independence	Kosovo debate, CoE membership, perspectives of EU accession	New constitution after regime change	Success of the indigenous peoples' international movement	New constitution after independence	New constitutions after independence
Entrenchment	Canadian Charter of Rights, s 23 (1982), subsequent court rulings, municipality by-laws	Bonn-Copenhagen Declarations (1955)—not legally binding, relevant state or federal legislation	Private law corporation (umbrella organization), public law foundation (for finances)	Constitution (1991), Special Law (1994)	Constitution (1992), Special Law (2002)	Special Law (2002, 2009)	Constitution (1989, 2011) Special Law (1993, 2005, 2011)	Constitutions: (Norway: 1985; Sweden: 2011; Finland: 1995) Sámi Acts: (Norway: 1987; Sweden: 1993; Finland: 1995)	Constitution (1992), Special Law (1993)	Russia: Constitution (1993), Special Law (1996), etc.

Institutional particularities

Elections	What is elected	School boards	Minority party candidates in local and general elections	Managing committee, executive board	Councils of self-governing communities and state level 'umbrella' organizations	National councils at local and regional levels ('coordinations' are established)	National councils at state level	Minority/ nationality self-governments at local, county, and state levels	Parliaments	National-cultural autonomies	Russia: peoples' congresses at federal and federal state levels
	Type of elections	N/a	General and/or local	Indirect, by members of the General Assembly (delegates of member organizations)	Direct (councils); indirect (umbrella)	Direct	Direct (if registration on the electoral roll is over the threshold); indirect otherwise	Direct at local and county levels, and at state level too (since 2011)	Direct	Direct	Indirect, two-tier, with no clear criteria on who can participate
	Electoral lists	N/a	N/a	N/a	Yes (some objective criteria)	Yes (without objective criteria)	Yes (without objective criteria)	Yes (since 2005, without objective criteria)	Yes (some objective criteria)	Yes (without objective criteria?)	N/a
	Thresholds	N/a	Exemptions for minority parties	N/a	?	1.5% of the unit's population, and 200 in towns, 500 in counties	40% of minority as reflected in census register on electoral rolls; electors: proposed by 20–100 persons from the minority's electoral roll	Administrative units where at least 30 persons declared to belong to a minority; 15 persons register on the separate lists		3,000 members	N/a
	Timing	N/a	N/a	N/a	Simultaneous with local elections	Separate from local or general elections	Separate from local or general elections	Simultaneous with local elections	Separate from local or general elections	Separate from local or general elections	Nd

(Continued)

Table C.1 (*Continued*)

	Canada (Acadians)	Danish–German border region	Germany (Sorbs)	Slovenia	Croatia	Serbia	Hungary	Sámi (Norway, Sweden, Finland)	Estonia	Post-Soviet space
Legal status of relevant institutions	Public law (education and health), by-laws (municipalities)	Private law	Private law corporation and public law foundation	Public law	Non-profit legal entities (coordinations are not legal entities)	Public law	Public law	Public law	No clear legal status	NCAs: social organizations; peoples' congresses: social movements
Competences	(β): Education, health, municipality	(β): Political representation, education, culture, social care, economic sectors	(?): Interest representation in public and government institutions, language, culture, and homeland preservation	(γ): Consultative, formal veto, managing educational, cultural, and media institutions	(γ): Largely consultative	(γ): Consultative, veto, decision-making in educational, cultural, and media institutions	(γ): Consultative, formal veto, decision-making in institutions taken over from the state	(α): Education, language, culture, land and resource management	(γ): Education in mother tongue, establishment of cultural institutions, grants to promote minority cultures	(δ): Symbolic presence of ethnic groups in public life
Financial aspects	Somewhat problematic	Satisfactorily financed (German and Danish states)	Generously financed (federal government, two federal states)	Nd	Critically underfinanced (local authorities)	Satisfactorily financed (central and regional state budgets)	Critically underfinanced (local, regional, and central authorities)	Underfinanced, several critical aspects of control over funding	Nd	Selective and occasional public funding
Legitimacy	N/a	N/a	N/a	Nd	Low (10% voter turnout)	Fair	Nd	Low (20% register on electoral rolls)	Nd	Fake, in fact ethnic control
Outcomes	Bottom-up activism, self-empowerment is the sign of vitality and will of survival	Bottom-up activism, self-empowerment is the sign of vitality and will of survival	Bottom-up activism, self-empowerment is the sign of vitality and will of survival	Symbolic participation in decision-making, diminishing vitality	Ineffective and costly arrangement, with little impact on target groups' life	Relatively stable arrangement with fair signs of vitality and will of survival	Ineffective, the most important competences remain under-utilized due to lack of funding	Stable arrangement with promising dynamics, strong signs of vitality and will of survival	Ineffective, the main target group remains uninterested	Imitative forms of participation, in ethnic activists' and governments' interests

N/a: not applicable

Nd: no data

(α): effective competences with rather strong legal and institutional bases

(β): effective competences without strong institutional or legal basis

(γ): symbolic competences with strong legal basis

(δ): vague competences with no clear legal basis

Table C.2 Dimensions of assessment

Terminology	Self-administration	Self-management	National-cultural autonomy	Self-government	Self-determination
	Germany (Sorbs)	Danish–German border region, Acadians in Canada	Croatia, Serbia, Estonia, Russia, other post-Soviet	Hungary, Slovenia	Sámi (Norway, Sweden, Finland)
Self-regulating institutions	*Symbolic bodies*	*Private law organizations*	*Public law bodies*		*Parliaments*
	Russia, Estonia, other post-Soviet	Danish–German border region, Germany (Sorbs)	National councils (Serbia, Croatia, Slovenia), self-governments (Hungary), school boards and health districts (Canada)		Sámi (Norway, Sweden, Finland)
Effectiveness	*Low*	*Fair*		*Strong*	
	Slovenia, Croatia, Hungary, Estonia, Russia, other post-Soviet	Sámi (Finland), Serbia, Danish–German border region, Germany (Sorbs), Acadians (Canada)		Sámi (Norway, Sweden)	

the decisions of the empowered bodies are not binding for the majorities. An eloquent example is offered in this sense by the Sámi Parliaments which have the most far-reaching competences in self-regulation among the analysed cases, the effects of which are seriously cut back, however, by the fact that they control less than half of the budgets allocated by the respective governments to Sámi purposes. Thirdly, effectiveness is not necessarily tied to the public status or type of entrenchment of the self-regulating institutions. The strong public standing of self-regulating bodies in Slovenia, Hungary, or Croatia produces very modest effects, while the remarkable results produced by the arrangements in place in the Danish–German border region or by the *Domowina* in the case of the Sorbs in Germany prove that entrenchment under public law is not a key to success in itself. An interesting example is provided in this sense by the Nordic countries, too. Although the Sámi Parliament in Finland has the strongest legal standing, its effectiveness is lower in several concerns than that of the other two similar institutions in Norway and Sweden.

Comparing the analysed cases from this point of view, it seems that NTA effectiveness requires the providential combination of three circumstances: appropriate legal standing, bottom-up activism of the members of the target groups and adequate funding. In a somewhat surprising way, the most balanced example in these three regards seems to be the given by the case study on Serbia, closely followed by the Danish–German border region (where the lack of a more spectacular legal standing before public law appears to be effectively compensated by the cooperation between the two states). The case of the Acadians in Canada seems to suggest the generative order of the three elements, too. Bottom-up mobilization can trigger appropriate legal response and, with perseverance, satisfactory funding schemes, too. The Croatian, Slovenian, Hungarian, and Estonian cases prove, on the other hand, that top-down arrangements which are not based on the will of the sufficiently mobilized minority communities have little chance of success, especially if appropriate funding mechanisms are not in place. What, therefore, have we learned about NTA from the cases discussed in the chapters of this book? What, in fact, is NTA? I will try to summarize a few concluding remarks in the next section.

2. The Concept of NTA, Revisited (Once More)

NTA is commonly assumed to be a particular form of autonomy. But is it, indeed, justified to use the concept of 'autonomy' if we analyse more carefully the cases which are regularly referred to as autonomies with non-territorial bases? In order to answer this question, we need to recapitulate first, based on the vast literature invoked in the previous chapters, what we have to think of when we operate with the autonomy concept with reference to political–institutional arrangements meant to regularize majority–minority relationships in diverse societies. For any type of autonomy arrangement in this particular sense of the term we need to have (1) a state, the authorities of which are willing to share the power they have with (2) some kind of sub-state entity or entities, (3) within a framework of an institutional set-up, legally underpinned, which stipulates the rights and duties of the two main actors, describing in detail the manner in which power is shared. The rationale (4) of the arrangement is to provide guarantees to the sub-state entity that its right to continued existence as such is recognized, politically warranted, and institutionally safeguarded. The (5) outcome of the whole arrangement should be a redefined political community within which democracy and diversity are reconciled, and the principle of self-determination is not monopolized. Several important questions follow from the above. First: where does the autonomous power of the state, which has to be shared in certain circumstances, come from and is the claim to share it reasonable? Secondly: what are the specific sub-state entities which claim share of the power and are their objectives feasible? Thirdly: which are the most suitable procedures and institutional arrangements for complying with the rationale and providing for the expected outcomes simultaneously?

There are many ways in which we can think of the sources of the autonomous power states possess in relation to various actors in societies; it can result from the desire of peoples for self-determination, from the emergence of political communities as a result of various kinds of 'social contracts', or from empowerment by international circumstances. As one of the possible answers, Michael Mann has pointed out that state autonomy is the result of the usefulness of enhanced territorial centralization of social life.[4] According to the way in which states exercise autonomous state power, they can be divided into despotic and infrastructural states, Mann suggests. Despotic states are regularly unstable, among other reasons exactly because they lack appropriate logistical infrastructure to penetrate and coordinate social life. They become infrastructural by creating diffused power structures, according to the complexities of the social life they are meant to coordinate. As a result states are sometimes obliged to devolve part of the autonomous power they possess exactly for the sake of their main purpose, recognizing that social life is territorial in many complex ways. Or, they can refuse to do so, risking becoming despotic. Sub-state entities, which claim part of the autonomous political power of a state, are regularly components of society distinguished by various markers (language, culture, religion, etc.) that are interested in self-reproduction. In some cases they may have strong territorial bases, and their interest lies in proceeding in a similar way as states do: by providing for territorial centralization of power within a limited jurisdiction. In other cases, the territorial basis is lacking and sub-state entities might be interested in protecting less evident identity boundaries.

In terms of procedures, the first critical thing is recognition. A state can decide which sub-state entities claiming part of the autonomous state power are in its interest to recognize. Recognizing a sub-state entity means implicitly that its claim to self-reproduction is acknowledged, and the next task is to reach agreement regarding the institutional details of the shared power which can provide for the desired outcome. With regard to these two aspects one can grasp the core differences between TA and NTA. Recognizing a sub-state entity with territorial basis is politically more costly, but in practical terms significantly simpler. In order to know

---

[4] Michael Mann, 'The Autonomous Power of the State: Its Origins, Mechanisms, and Results', in *States in History*, edited by John A. Hall (Oxford: Blackwell, 1986), p. 135.

who is the agency of the recognized sub-state entity with no territorial basis, special lists are necessary. This could violate, as we have seen, several constitutional provisions. However, it is difficult to think of arrangements which can guarantee the stability of identity boundaries, if the jurisdiction of the arrangement is not clear.[5] Institutional arrangements which can provide for the desired outcome of the recognized entities' self-reproduction are more easily available in the case of sub-state entities of territorial character, while similar solutions in the non-territorial version are far more complicated. For instance, with regard to language, which is often one of the core concerns of NTA arrangements, this aspect is particularly salient: the chances of the long-term survival of a language, which is not dominant in a certain territory, are low if not doomed to failure. Similarly, the appropriate institutional frameworks within which effective self-rule without territorial jurisdiction can be imagined are, as we have seen in most of the discussed cases, very difficult to design and even more difficult to administer properly.

Based on the above, one might ask if it is justified at all to talk about *autonomy* in the case of non-territorial arrangements. Indeed, Renner's[6] confidence that nations are not necessarily territorial in nature is probably right, but autonomy is a matter of state construction, rather that nation-building; power is not shared by nations, but by states which have a territorial character by definition. The question is, therefore, can state power, which is territorial in nature, be shared in non-territorial arrangements? The chapters of this book provide plenty of arguments regarding the merits of NTA arrangements, while also shedding light on conditions and institutional particularities which may contribute to the success and the desired outcomes of the various set-ups. The analysis of the bottom-up processes which give substance to self-empowerment and generate interesting frameworks of private–public partnership is, without doubt, one of the valuable contributions of this book to the literature on NTA. The concept of institutional completeness, though it is rooted in a very particular legal and historical context, might inspire further discussions exactly on the critical edge: what is autonomy in an NTA arrangement? The limits of internal self-determination, as highlighted in the chapter on the Sámi Parliaments, might also be stimulating for further research.

3. Policy Recommendations

Practitioners and experts interested in statecraft may find solutions in this book. They might discover the value of the experiences shared in the case studies, and

---

[5] It is an interesting and strange consequence of this dilemma that two chapters of the book—the chapter on Estonia and the case study on the post-Soviet space—question in essence the whole rationale of the NTA arrangements, labelling them as 'groupist', in the sense given to the term by Brubaker (Rogers Brubaker, *Ethnicity without Groups* (Cambridge, MA: Harvard University Press, 2006)), and suggesting that they reinforce ethnic boundaries, instead of overcoming them. Though the empirical bases of the stance taken by the two authors is most probably unquestionable, this is a self-defeating argument since it eliminates the very scope of the recognition: acknowledging the right to self-reproduction. A similar argument often pops up in the literature on consociationalism, too.

[6] Karl Renner, 'State and Nation', in *National Cultural Autonomy and its Contemporary Critics*, edited by Ephraim Nimni (London, New York: Routledge, 2005), pp. 15–41.

realize that a state which is rejecting autonomy claims runs the risks of turning despotic (in Michael Mann's sense). Considering autonomy arrangements as specific instruments of state-building, like in the Serbian case, certain components of society can be more effectively connected to the state and the reach of the state to those components can become more operative. Once openness for considering autonomy is given, NTA arrangements could be good trial procedures, which are relatively easy to test: if arrangements provisionally set up based on the claims of minority elites do not trigger mass support in a reasonable time, they can be closed down for reasons which are difficult to contest.

In the event that there is political will for setting up NTA arrangements, in order to make them effective and capable of exercising devolved power, the agency of the arrangement needs to be as wide as possible (not fragmented at local and regional levels), and it needs to be directly elected. Direct elections require separate electoral rolls, based on voluntary registration and minimal objective criteria (like mother tongue), which in a democratic open society should not trigger special problems. Elections should be held simultaneously with general elections: this could reduce costs and guarantee higher turnout. Furthermore, the more democratic and transparent the elections are, the more power can be devolved to the limited jurisdiction of the agency: the more empowered the members of the target group feel, the higher the level of satisfaction will be. Since the chances of securing the desired outcome—long-term survival and vitality of the target group—are relatively low, being too restrictive in terms of devolved competences might, on the other hand, prove counterproductive. Institutional completeness in the sense carved out by the case of the Acadians in Canada might be an objective measure of success, both for majorities and minorities. In addition to solutions entrenched in public law, the cases analysed in this volume provide compelling arguments regarding the potential of private law alternatives. Encouraging self-empowerment and fostering service delivery within public–private partnerships could unleash constructive energies in the context of divided societies, too.

In terms of funding, the burden is difficult to avoid. It can be shared, and bilateral agreements with kin-states can provide the arrangement with additional stability. If the level of satisfaction with the outcomes is high, collecting taxes from registered members could also contribute to sustainability. Besides appropriate funding, the sustainability of any NTA arrangement critically depends on the level of acceptance on behalf of the majority. To this end, the public opinion of the majority should be assisted by appropriate policy measures in accepting the arrangement as legitimate. Moreover, state authorities should be prepared to carry out their responsibilities in dealing with the agency of the NTA and the institutions managed by it. The measure of success of a balanced, well-functioning NTA is that its benefits are felt not only by the protected minority, but the political community as a whole.

Bibliography

BOOKS

Abramov, Vladimir Kuzmich. *Mordovskii narod ot s'ezda k s'ezdu* [Mordovian People from Congress to Congress] (Saransk: no publisher, 2004).

Abramov, Vladimir Kuzmich. *Mordovskoe natsional'noe dvizhenie* [Mordovian National Movemement] (Saransk: no publisher, 2007).

Agarin, Timofey. *A Cat's Lick. Democratisation and Minority Communities in the Post-Soviet Baltic* (Amsterdam/New York: Rodopi, 2010).

Barany, Zoltan and Robert G. Moser. eds. *Ethnic Politics after Communism* (Ithaca: Cornell University Press, 2005).

Bárdi, Nándor, Csilla Fedinec, and László Szarka. eds. *Minority Hungarian Communities in the Twentieth Century* (Boulder, CO: Atlantic Research and Publication Inc., 2011).

Barry, Brian. *Culture and Equality* (Cambridge, MA: Harvard University Press, 2001).

Barsenkov, Aleksandr Sergeevich et al. *O kontsepcii natsional'noi politiki v Rossiiskoi Federatsii* [On the Concept of National Politics of the Russian Federation] (Moscow: KIT, 1992).

Behiels, Michael. *Canada's Francophone Minority Communities: Constitutional Renewal and the Winning of School Governance* (Montreal/Kingston: McGill-Queen's University Press, 2004).

Bekus, Nelly. *Struggle over Identity: The Official and the Alternative 'Belarusianness'* (Budapest/New York: Central European University Press, 2010).

Benedikter, Thomas. *The World's Modern Autonomy Systems. Concepts and Experiences of Regional Territorial Autonomy* (Bozen/Bolzano: European Academy of Bozen/Bolzano, 2009).

Bertrand, Jacques and Oded Haklai. eds. *Democratization and Ethnic Minorities* (London/New York, Routledge, 2014).

Birnir, Jóhanna Kristín. *Ethnicity and Electoral Politics* (New York: Cambridge University Press, 2007).

Bíró, Gáspár. *Az identitásválasztás szabadsága* [Free Choice of Identity] (Budapest: Századvég, 1995).

Bourgeois, Daniel. *Vers la pleine gestion scolaire francophone en milieu minoritaire* [Towards Complete Francophone School Management in Minority Communities] (Moncton: Institut Canadien de recherche sur les minorités linguistiques, 2004).

Bourgeois, Daniel, Donald Dennie, Wilfrid Denis, and Marc L. Johnson. *Provincial and Territorial Government Contributions to the Development of Francophone Minority Communities* (Moncton: Canadian Institute for Research on Linguistic Minorities, 2007).

Breton, Raymond. *Ethnic Relations in Canada—Institutional Dynamics* (Montreal/Kingston: McGill-Queen's University Press, 2005).

Breuning, Marijke and John T. Ishiyama. *Ethnopolitics in the 'New Europe'* (Boulder, CO: Lynne Rienner, 1998).

Brubaker, Rogers. *Ethnicity without Groups* (Cambridge, MA: Harvard University Press, 2006).

Brunsson, Nils. *The Organization of Hypocrisy. Talk, Decisions and Actions in Organizations* (Chichester, NY: John Wiley & Sons, 1989).

Buchanan, Allen. *Justice, Legitimacy and Self-Determination: Moral Foundations for International Law* (Oxford: Oxford University Press, 2004).

Bugajski, Janusz. *Ethnic Politics in Eastern Europe: A Guide to Nationality Policies, Organizations, and Parties* (New York: Sharpe Armonk, 1993).

Bugajski, Janusz *Political Parties of Eastern Europe. A Guide to Politics in the Post-Communist Era* (Armonk, NY/London: M. E. Sharpe, 2002).

Citizenship and Migration Board. *Yearbook 2003* (Citizenship and Migration Board: Tallinn, 2003).

Clarke, Paul T. and Pierre Foucher. *École et droits fondamentaux* [School and Fundamental Rights] (Saint-Boniface: Presses universitaires de Saint-Boniface, 2005).

Connor, Walker. *The National Question in Marxist-Leninist Theory and Strategy* (Princeton, NJ: Princeton University Press, 1984).

Cordell, Karl. ed. *Ethnicity and Democratisation in the New Europe* (New York: Routledge, 1999).

Dahl, Robert. *Polyarchy: Participation and Opposition* (New Haven: Yale University Press, 1971).

De Winter, Lieven and Huri Türsan. eds. *Regionalist Parties in Western Europe* (London: Routledge, 1998).

Drobizheva, Leokadiya Mikhailovna. *Social'nye problemy mezhnacional'nyh otnoshenii v postsovetskoi Rossii* [Social Problems in Inter-Ethnic Relations of Post-Soviet Russia] (Moscow: Tsentr obshechelovecheskih tsennostei, 2003).

Eisenstadt, Shmuel Noah. *Traditional Patrimonialism and Modern Neopatrimonialism* (Beverly Hills, CA: Sage, 1973).

Elle, Ludwig. *Sorbische Interessenvertretung in Vergangenheit und Gegenwart* [Sorbian Advocacy in the Past and Present] (Bautzen: Sorbisches Institut, 2011).

Eötvös, József. *The Dominant Ideas of the Nineteenth Century and their Impact on the State. Vol. I-II*, translated, edited, and annotated by D. Mervyn Jones. (New York: Columbia University Press, 1996).

Eriksson, Johan. *Partition and Redemption. A Machiavellian Analysis of Sámi and Basque Patriotism* (Umeå: Umeå University, 1997).

Ernő, Kállai. *Helyi cigány kisebbségi önkormányzatok Magyarországon* [Local Roma Minority Self-Governments in Hungary] (Budapest: MTA Etnikai-nemzetiségi Kisebbségkutató Intézet—Gondolat Kiadói Kör, 2005).

Federal Ministry of the Interior. *National Minorities in Germany* (Berlin: Federal Ministry of the Interior, 2010).

Freiherr von Campenhausen, Axel and H. de Wall. *Staatskirchenrecht* [State Church Law], 4th edn (München: C. H. Beck, 2006).

Gal, Kinga. ed. *Minority Governance in Europe* (Budapest: Local Government and Public Service Reform Initiative, 2002).

Gaski, Harald. *Sámi Culture in a New Era. The Norwegian Sámi Experience* (Karasjohka: Davvi Girji, 1998).

Ghai, Yash. ed. *Autonomy and Ethnicity: Negotiating Competing Claims* (Cambridge: Cambridge University Press, 2000).

Goffman, Erving. *Frame Analysis: An Essay on the Organization of Experience* (London: Harper and Row, 1974).

Gorenburg, Dimitry. *Minority Ethnic Mobilization in the Russian Federation* (New York: Cambridge University Press, 2003).

Gratton, Michel. *Montfort—La lutte d'un peuple* [Montfort—The Struggle of People] (Ottawa: Centre franco-ontarien de ressources pédagogiques, 2003).

Gurin-Loov, Eugenia and Gennadi Gramberg. *The Jewish Community of Estonia* (Tallinn: Jewish Community of Estonia, 2001).

Haetta, Odd Mathias. *The Sámi—An Indigenous People of the Arctic* (Karasjok: Davvi Girji, 1993).

Hannum, Hurst. *Autonomy, Sovereignty, and Self-Determination. The Accommodation of Conflicting Rights* (Philadelphia: University of Pennsylvania Press, 1990).

Hayday, Matthew. *Bilingual Today, United Tomorrow* (Montreal/Kingston: McGill-Queen's University Press, 2006).

Helander, Elina and U. Sand. eds. *The Sami People* (Karasjok: Sami Institutta [The Sami Research Institute], 1990).

Henriksen, John B. *Sámi Parliamentary Co-Operation. An Analysis* (Kautokeino/Copenhagen: Nordic Sámi Institute, 1999).

Hocking, Barbara. ed. *Unfinished Constitutional Business?: Rethinking Indigenous Self-Determination* (Canberra: Aboriginal Studies Press, 2005).

Hombach, Stepahnie. *Eheschließung und Ehescheidung im modernen Hindu-Recht Indiens im Vergleich zu deutschem Recht* [Marriage and Divorce in the Modern Hindu Law in India in Comparison to German Law] (Göttingen: Cuivillier, 2003).

Imre, Mikó. *Nemzetiségi jog és nemzetiségi politika* [Nationality Law and Nationality Policies] (Kolozsvár: Minerva, 1944).

Issakov, Sergei. *Путь длинною в тысячу лет. Русские в Эстонии. История культуры. Часть I* [The Thousand-Year Road. Russians in Estonia. The History of Culture. Part I] (Tallinn: INGRI, 2008).

Issakov, Sergei. *Русское национальное меньшинство в Эстонской Республике (1918-1940)* [The Russian National Minority in the Republic of Estonia (1918-1940)] (Tartu: The Crypt, 2000).

Jackson Preece, Jennifer. *National Minorities and the European Nation-States System* (Oxford: Oxford University Press, 1998).

Jászi, Oszkár. *Magyar kálvária, magyar feltámadás* [Hungarian Calvary, Hungarian Resurrection] (Budapest: Magyar Hírlap Kiadó, 1989).

Jentoft, Sven, Henry Minde, and Ragnar Nilsen. eds. *Indigenous Peoples. Resource Management and Global Rights* (Delft: Eburon, 2003).

Josefsen, Eva. *The Sámi and the National Parliaments: Channels for Political Influence* (Geneva/New York: IPU and UNDP, 2010).

Kantor, Zoltan. ed. *Autonomies in Europe: Solutions and Challenges* (Budapest: L'Harmattan, 2014).

Karapet'an, Liudvig. *Federativnoe ustroistvo Rossiiskogo gosudarstva* [Federative Structure of the Russian State] (Moscow: Norma, 2001).

Karppi, Kristina and Eriksson, Jonas. eds. *Conflict and Cooperation in the North* (Umeå: Norrlands Universitetsforlag, 2002).

Kaufmann, Eric. ed. *Rethinking Ethnicity: Majority Groups and Dominant Minorities* (London: Routledge, 2004).

Klatt, Martin. *Fra modspil til medspil? Grænseoverskridende samarbejde i Sønderjylland/Schleswig, 1945-2005* [From Antagonism to Co-operation? Cross-Border Co-operation in the German-Danish Border Region, 1945-2005] (Aabenraa: Institut for Grænseregionsforskning, Syddansk Universitet, 2006).

Kolstoe, Paul. *Russians in the Former Soviet Republics* (London: Hurst, 1995).

Komac, Miran. ed. *Priseljenci. Študije o priseljevanju in vključevanju v slovensko družbo* [Immigrants. Studies on Immigration and Integration into Slovenian Society] (Ljubljana, INV: 2007).

Konyuhov, Alexei Kimovich. ed. *Finno-ugorskie narody Rossii: vchera, segodnya, zavtra* [Finno-Ugra People of Russia: Yesterday, Today, Tomorrow] (Syktyvkar: no publisher, 2008).

Korkmasova, Kiti Dzelalovna. *Natsionalno-gosudarstvennoye ustroistvo SSSR* [Ethno-State Structure of the Soviet Union] (Rostov-on-Don: Rostov State University Publishing House, 1984).

Kotzur, Marcus. *Die Förderung des sorbischen Volkes: Rechtlicher Status, rechtspolitische Gestaltungsmöglichkeiten, insbesondere die Finanzierungsmöglichkeit des Bundes* [The Promotion of the Sorbian People: Legal Status, Legal Policy Design Options, in Particular the Financing Option of the Federal Government] (Leipzig: Universität Leipzig, Juristenfakultät, 2009).

Krivokapić, Boris. *Zaštita manjina u međunarodnom i uporednom pravu—Knjiga III—Zaštita manjina u nacionalnim porecima država* [The Protection of Minorities in International and Comparative Law—Volume III—Protection of Minorities in National Orders of State] (Beograd: Ministarstvo za ljudska i manjinska prava Srbije i Crne Gore, 2004).

Kulichenko, M. *Natsiya i sotsialny progress* [Nation and Social Progress] (Moscow: Nauka, 1983).

Kulonen, Ulla Maija, Irja Seurujärvi-Kari, and Risto Pulkkinen. eds. *The Saami—A Cultural Encyclopaedia* (Vammala: Vammalan Kirjapaino Oy, 2005).

Kühl, Jørgen. *Mindretalsmodel i krise* [Minority Model in Crisis] (Flensburg: Dansk Skoleforening for Sydslesvig, 2012).

Kühl, Jørgen and Marc Weller. eds. *Minority Policy in Action: The Bonn-Copenhagen Declarations in a European Context 1955-2005* (Aabenraa: Institut for Grænsregionsforskning, Syddansk Universitet, 2005).

Kymlicka, Will. *Multicultural Citizenship* (Oxford: Oxford University Press, 1995).

Landry, Rodrigue and Serge Rousselle. *Éducation et droits collectifs* [Education and Collective Rights] (Moncton: Les Éditions de la Francophonie, 2003).

Lapidoth, Ruth. *Autonomy. Flexible Solutions to Ethnic Conflicts* (Washington, D.C.: United States Institute of Peace, 1996).

Lehtola, Veli Pekka. *The Sámi People—Traditions in Transition* (Inari: Kustannus-Puntsi, 2002).

Levy, Jacob. 'Classifying Cultural Rights'. In *Ethnicity and Group Rights*, edited by Ian Shapiro and Will Kymlicka (New York: New York University Press, 2000).

Lewis, Dave. *Indigenous Rights Claims in Welfare Capitalist Society: Recognition and Implementation. The Case of the Sámi People in Norway, Sweden and Finland* (Rovaniemi: Arctic Centre, 1998).

Lijphart, Arend. *Democracy in Plural Societies: A Comparative Exploration* (New Haven: Yale University Press, 1977).

Magnet, Joseph Eliot. *Official Languages in Canada* (Cowansville, Québec: Éditions Yvon Blais, 1995).

Markov, V. *Vozrozhdeniye v epokhu peremen. S'ezdy Komi naroda: dokumenty i kommentarii* [Renaissance in the Era of Change: The Congress of the Komi People: Documents and Commentaries] (Syktyvkar: no publisher, 2011).

Martin, Terry. *The Affirmative Action Empire: Nations and Nationalism in the Soviet Union, 1923-1939* (Ithaca, NY: Cornell University Press, 2001).

Melvin, Neil. *Russians Beyond Russia. The Politics of National Identity* (London: Chatham House Papers, 1995).

Niezen, Ronald. *Origins of Indigenism: Human Rights and the Politics of Identity* (Ewing: University of California Press, 2002).

Nimni, Ephraim J. ed. *Otto Bauer: The Question of Nationalities and Social Democracy* (Minneapolis: University of Minnesota Press, 2000).

Nimni, Ephraim, Alexander Osipov, and David J. Smith. eds. *The Challenge of Non-Territorial Autonomy. Theory and Practice* (Oxford: Peter Lang, 2013).

OSCE High Commissioner on National Minorities. *The Integration of Formerly Deported People in Crimea, Ukraine: Needs Assessment* (The Hague: OSCE HCNM, 2013).

Pettit, Philip. *Republicanism. A Theory of Freedom and Government* (Oxford: Clarendon Press, 1997).

Poleshchuk, Vadim. ed. *Chance to Survive: Minority Rights in Estonia and Latvia* (Moscow/ Paris/Tallinn: Foundation for Historical Outlook, 2009).

Ponomaryeva, Galina and T. Shor, *Русская печать и культура в Эстонии в годы Второй мировой войны (1939-1945)* [Russian Printed Media and Culture in Estonia during the Second World War (1939-1945)] (Tallinn: Tallinn University Publisher, 2009).

Proos, I. and I. Pettai. *Russian-Speaking Youths: The Position and Expectations of a New Generation. Brief Summary of Materials of Sociological Study* (Tallinn: Estonian Open Society Institute, 2008).

Pullat, Raimo. *История Таллина с начала 60-х годов XIX столетия до 1970 года* [The History of Tallinn from the 1860's up to 1970] (Tallinn: Eesti Raamat, 1972).

Reid, Scott. *Lament for a Notion* (Vancouver: Arsenal Pulp Press, 1993).

Reilly, Benjamin. *Democracy in Divided Societies* (New York: Cambridge University Press, 2001).

Renner, Karl. *Das Selbstbestimmungsrecht der Nationen in besonderer Anwendung aug Österreich* (Leipzig/Vienna: Franz Deuticke, 1918).

Roach, Steven C. *Cultural Autonomy, Minority Rights and Globalization* (Aldershot: Ashgate, 2005).

Roeder, Philip. *Where Nation-States Come From: Institutional Change in the Age of Nationalism* (Princeton: Princeton University Press, 2007).

Sadan, Elisheva. *Empowerment and Community Planning: Theory and Practice of People-Focused Social Solutions* (Tel Aviv: Hakibbutz Hameuchad Publishers, 1997, English translation 2004).

Salat, Levente and Monica Robotin. eds. *A New Balance: Democracy and Minorities in Post-Communist Europe* (Budapest: Local Government and Public Reform Initiative, 2003).

Sartori, Giovanni. *Parties and Party Systems: A Framework for Analysis* (Cambridge: Cambridge University Press, 1976).

Schöpflin, George. *Nations, Identity, Power: The New Politics of Europe* (London: Hurst, 2000).

Shabaev, Petrovich Yuriy and Anna Mikhailovna Charina. *Regional'nye etnoelity v polit-icheskom processe: (finno-ugorskoe dvizhenie: stanovlenie, evolyuciya, ideologiya, lidery)* [Regional Ethnic Elites in the Political Process (Finno-Ugric Movement: Establishment, Evolution, Ideology, Leaders)] (Syktyvkar: KRAGSiU, 2008).

Sillanpää, Lennard. *Political and Administrative Responses to Sámi Self-Determination* (Helsinki: Societas Scientarum Fennica, 1994).

Skurbaty, Zelim A. ed. *Beyond a One-Dimensional State: An Emerging Right to Autonomy?* (Leiden/Boston: Martinus Nijhoff Publishers, 2005).

Smith, David J. and Karl Kordell. eds. *Cultural Autonomy in Contemporary Europe* (London: Routledge, 2008).

Solbakk, John Trygve. ed. *The Sámi People—A Handbook* (Tromsø: Davvi Girji OS, 2006).

Sørensen, Eva and Jacob Torfing. eds. *Theories of Democratic Network Governance* (Basingstoke: Palgrave Macmillan, 2007, 2008).

Sudnitsin, Yuriy G. *Natsional'nyi suverenitet v SSSR* [National Sovereignty in the USSR] (Moscow: Gosyurizdat, 1958).

Suksi, Markku. ed. *Autonomy, Applications and Implications* (The Hague: Kluwer Law International, 1998).

Suny, Ronald. *The Revenge of the Past: Nationalism, Revolution, and the Collapse of the Soviet Union* (Stanford: Stanford University Press, 1993).

Svensson, Tom G. *The Sámi and their Land* (Oslo: Novus forlag, 1997).

Sydslesvigsk Forening, 'Dansk virke i Grænselandet—Sydslesvigsk Årbog 2013' [Danish Action in the Border Region—South Schleswig Yearbook 2013] (Flensburg: Sydslesvigsk Forening, 2013).

Szabó, Róbert Győri. *Kisebbségpolitikai rendszerváltás Magyarországon* [Transformation of Regime in Minority Policy in Hungary] (Budapest: Osiris, 1998).

Tamir, Yael. *Liberal Nationalism* (Princeton: Princeton University Press, 1995).

Tatalović, Siniša. *Nacionalne manjine u Hrvatskoj* [National Minorities in Croatia] (Split: Stina, 2005).

Taylor, Charles. *Multiculturalism and the Politics of Recognition* (Princeton: Princeton University Press, 1992).

Thuen, Trond. *Quest for Equity. Norway and Sámi Challenge* (Canada: Institute of Social and Economic Research, 1995).

Tiit, Ene-Margit. *Eesti rahvastik. Viis põlvkonda ja kümme loendust* [Estonian Population. Five Generations and Ten Censuses] (Tallinn: Statistikaamet, 2011).

Tilly, Charles. *Democracy* (New York: Cambridge University Press, 2007).

Von Oppen, Alexandra. *Eheschließung und Eheauflösung im indischen Familienrecht* [Marriage and Dissolution of Marriage in Indian Family Law] (Frankfurt am Main: Lange, 2004).

Weller, Marc and Katherine Nobbs. eds. *Political Participation of Minorities. A Commentary on International Standards and Practice* (Oxford: Oxford University Press, 2010).

Weller, Marc and Stefan Wolff. eds. *Autonomy, Self-Governance and Conflict Resolution: Innovative Approaches to Institutional Design in Divided Societies* (London: Routledge, 2005).

Woelk, Jens, Francesco Palermo, and Joseph Marko. eds. *Tolerance through Law: Self-Governance and Group Rights in South Tyrol* (Leiden: Martinus Nijhoff Publishers, 2008).

Young, Elspeth. *Third World in the First: Development and Indigenous Peoples* (London: Routledge, 1995).

Zolotareva, Milena Valerievna. *Federatsiya v Rossii: problemy i perspektivy* [Federation of Russia: Problems and Perspectives] (Moscow: Probel, 1999).

CHAPTERS AND ARTICLES

Abdulatipov, Ramazan Gadzhimuradovich. 'Doklad Predsedatel'a Soveta ANR R. G. Abdulatipova' [Report of the Council Chairman Ramazan Gadzhimuradovich Abdulatipov]. *Istoricheskoya dukhovnoya naslediye druzhby narodov Rossii: Traditsii I sobremennost. Materialy Kongressa Narodov Rossii* (2007): pp. 26–39.

Aidarov, Aleksandr and Wolfgang Drechsler. 'The Law and Economics of the Estonian Law on Cultural Autonomy for National Minorities and of Russian National Cultural Autonomy in Estonia'. *Halduskultuur/Administrative Culture* vol. 12, no. 2 (2011): pp. 52–5.

Alenius, Kari. 'The Birth of Cultural Autonomy in Estonia: How, Why, and for Whom?'. *Journal of Baltic Studies* vol. 38, no. 4 (2007): p. 458.

Anaya, James. 'The Right of Indigenous Peoples to Self-Determination in the Post-Declaration Era'. In *Making the Declaration Work*, edited by Claire Charters and Rodolfo Stavenhagen (Copenhagen: Indigenous Work Group for Indigenous Affairs, 2009), pp. 184–98.

Aryn, R. S. 'Assambleya narodov Rossii' [Peoples 'Assembly of Russia]. *Zhizn' natsional'nostei* (1999): pp. 2–3.

Aryn, R. S. 'Vzaimodeistvie gosudarstvennyh institutov i etnicheskih soobshestv—vazhneishii faktor stanovleniya gosudarstvennosti Respubliki Kazakhstan' [Cooperation of State Authority Institutes with Ethnic Communities—Key Factor of Statehood's Establishment in the Republic of Kazakhstan]. *Vestnik Tomskogo Gosudarstvennogo Universiteta* vol. 300, no. 1 (2007): pp. 79–81.

Aunger, Edmund. 'Profil des institutions francophones' [Profile of Francophone Institutions]. In *Entre minorité et majorité, un espace francophone sous tension*, edited by Anne Gilbert (Ottawa: Presses de l'Université d'Ottawa, 2009), pp. 56–75.

Bach, Daniel. 'Patrimonialism and Neopatrimonialism: Comparative Trajectories and Readings'. *Commonwealth & Comparative Politics* vol. 49, no. 3 (2011): pp. 275–94.

Bašić, Goran. 'Društveni identitet i etnokulturalna politika' [Social Identity and Ethno-Cultural Policy]. In *Položaj nacionalnih manjina u Srbiji*, edited by Vojislav Stanovčić (Beograd: Srpska akademija nauka i umetnosti, 2007), pp. 97–116.

Batt, Judy. 'Eötvös "Fuzzy Statehood" versus Hard Borders: The Impact of EU Enlargement on Romania and Yugoslavia. "One Europe or Several?"'. *Working Paper* no. 46 (2002): pp. 4–10.

Baybasheva, G. '"Rol" Assamblei narodov Kazakhstana v sovershenstvovanii mezhetnicheskih otnoshenii v Respublike Kazakhstan' [The Role of Peoples' Assembly of Kazakhstan in Current Inter-Ethnic Relations in the Republic of Kazakstan]. *Ekonomika i Pravo v Respublike Kazakhstan* no. 22 (2008): pp. 33–5.

Beach, Hugh. 'The Saami of Lapland'. In *Minority Rights Group, Polar Peoples: Self-Determination and Development* (London: Minority Rights Group Publications, 1994), pp. 149–50.

Benford, Robert D. and David A. Snow. 'Framing Processes and Social Movements: An Overview and Assessment'. *Annual Review of Sociology* vol. 26 (2000): pp. 11–39.

Beretka, Katinaka. 'National Councils of National Minorities in Serbia: Pros and Contras of an Ethnic Self-Governance'. In *Challenge of Non-Territorial Autonomy: Theory and Practice*, edited by Ephraim Nimni, Alexander Osipov, and David J. Smith (Oxford: Peter Lang, 2013), pp.181–96.

Berg-Nordlie, Mikkel. 'Striving to Unite. The Russian Sámi and the Nordic Sámi Parliament Model'. *Arctic Review on Law and Politics* vol. 2, no. 2 (2011): pp. 52–76.

Bieber, Florian. 'Power-Sharing at the Governmental Level'. In *Political Participation of Minorities: A Commentary on International Standards and Practice*, edited by Marc Weller and Katherine Nobbs (Oxford: Oxford University Press, 2010), pp. 414–33.

Bíró, Gáspár. 'Az 1993. évi törvény létrejöttének körülményei' [The Circumstances of the Creation of the 1993 Act]. *Barátság* vol. 21, no. 1 (2014): pp. 7765–87.

Bourgeois, Daniel. 'Administrative Nationalism'. *Administration and Society* vol. 39, no. 5 (2007): pp. 631–55.

Bourgeois, Daniel. 'Bilan de la pleine gestion scolaire assurée par l'application de l'article 23 de la Charte canadienne des droits et libertés' [Assessment of the School Management Guaranteed by the Application of Section 23 of the Canadian Charter of Rights and Freedoms]. In *Recherche en éducation en milieu minoritaire francophone*, edited by Yves Henry and Catherine Mougeot (Ottawa: Presses de l'Université d'Ottawa, 2007), pp. 212–17.

Bourgeois, Daniel. 'Acadians'. Symposium: 'Autonomy Arrangements in the World', Flensburg, Germany: European Centre for Minority Issues, 14–15 September 2012.

Bourgeois, Daniel and Yves Bourgeois. 'Minority Sub-State Institutional Completeness'. *International Review of Sociology* vol. 22, no. 2 (2001): pp. 293–304.

Bourgeois, Daniel and Yves Bourgeois. 'Territory, Institutions and National Identity: The Case of Acadians in Greater Moncton, Canada'. *Urban Studies* vol. 42, no. 7 (2005): pp. 1123–38.

Bourgeois, Daniel and Yves Bourgeois. 'Les municipalités canadiennes et les langues officielles' [Canadian Municipalities and Official Languages]. *Canadian Political Science Review* vol. 44, no. 4 (2011): pp. 789–806.

Bourgeois, Yves and Daniel Bourgeois. 'La relation entre territoire et identité. Construction de l'identité acadienne et urbaine dans la région du Grand Moncton' [The Relationship between Territory and Identity. Construction of Acadian and Urban Identity in Greater Moncton]. In *Balises et références—Acadies, francophonies*, edited by Martin Pâquet and Stéphane Savard (Québec: Presses de l'Université Laval, 2007), pp. 105–26.

Bowring, Bill. 'Austro-Marxism's Last Laugh? The Struggle for Recognition of National-Cultural Autonomy for Rossians and Russians'. *Europe-Asia Studies* vol. 54, no. 2 (2002): pp. 229–50.

Bowring, Bill. 'The Tatars of the Russian Federation and National-Cultural Autonomy: A Contradiction in Terms?'. *Ethnopolitics* vol. 6, no. 3 (2007): pp. 417–36.

Bremmer, Ian. 'Post-Soviet Nationalities Theory: Past, Present and Future'. In *New States, New Politics: Building the Post-Soviet Nations*, edited by Ian Bremmer and Roy Taras (Cambridge: Cambridge University Press, 1997).

Breton, Raymond. 'Institutional Completeness of Ethnic Communities and the Personal Relations of Immigrants'. *American Journal of Sociology* vol. 70 (1964): pp. 193–205.

Broderstad, Else Grete. 'Political Autonomy and Integration of Authority: The Understanding of Sámi Self-Determination'. *International Journal on Minority & Group Rights* vol. 8, no. 2 (2001): p. 151.

Brubaker, Roger. 'Ethnicity without Groups'. *Archives Européennes de Sociologie* vol. XLIII, no. 2 (2002): pp. 163–89.

Brunner, Georg and Herbert Küpper. 'European Options of Autonomy—A Typology of Autonomy Models of Minority Self-Governance'. In *Minority Governance in Europe*, edited by Kinga Gál (Budapest: Local Government and Public Service Reform Initiative, 2002), pp. 11–36.

Cârstocea, Andreea and Mindaugas Kuklys. 'Contemporary Accommodation of Minority Groups: A Continuum of Institutional Approaches'. *ECMI Handbook* (2015 forthcoming).

Christensen, Henrik Becker. 'Fra "mod hinanden" til "med hinanden"'[From 'Against Each Other' to 'with Each Other']. In *Sønderjyllands Historie* vol. 2, edited by H. Schultz

Hansen and H. Becker Christensen (Aabenraa: Historisk Samfund for Sønderjylland, 2009), pp. 241–462.

Clinebell, John Howard, and Jim Thomson. 'Sovereignty and Self-Determination: The Rights of Native Americans under International Law'. *Buffalo Law Review* vol. 27 (1978): pp. 669–714.

Coakley, John. 'Approaches to the Resolution of Ethnic Conflict: The Strategy of Non-Territorial Autonomy'. *International Political Science Review* vol. 15, no. 3 (1994): pp. 297–314.

Daes, Erica-Irene A. 'An Overview of the History of Indigenous Peoples: Self-Determination and the United Nations'. *Cambridge Review of International Affairs* vol. 21, no. 1 (2008): pp. 7–26.

Dave, Bhavna. 'Management of Ethnic Relations in Kazakhstan: Stability without Success'. In *The Legacy of the Soviet Union*, edited by Wendy Slater and Andrew Wilson (Basingstoke: Palgrave Macmillan, 2004): pp. 83–100.

Decker, Christofer D. 'Contemporary Forms of Cultural Autonomy in Eastern Europe: Recurrent Problems and Prospects for Improving the Functioning of Elected Bodies of Cultural Autonomy'. In *The Participation of Minorities in Public Life* (Strasbourg: Council of Europe Publishing, 2008), pp. 101–12.

Decker, D. Christopher. 'The Use of Cultural Autonomy to Prevent Conflict and Meet the Copenhagen Criteria: The Case of Romania'. *Ethnopolitics* vol. 6, no. 3 (2007): pp. 437–50.

Deets, Stephen and Sherrill Stroschein. 'Dilemmas of Autonomy and Liberal Pluralism: Examples Involving Hungarians in Central Europe'. *Nations and Nationalism* vol. 11, no. 2 (2005): pp. 285–305.

Denis, Wilfrid. 'La complétude institutionnelle et la vitalité des communautés fransaskoises en 1992' [Institutional Completeness and Vitality of Fransaskoises Communities in 1992]. *Cahiers Franco-Canadiens de l'Ouest* vol. 5, no. 2 (1993): pp. 253–84.

Desrosiers, Marie-Eve. 'Reframing Frame Analysis: Key Contributions to Conflict Studies'. *Ethnopolitics* vol. 11, no. 1 (2012): pp. 1–23.

Dimitrijević, Vojin. 'Democracy versus Nation. The Post-Communist Hypernational State and the Position of its "Ethnically Different" Citizens'. *Helsinki Monitor* vol. 5 (1994): pp. 13–24.

Dobos, Balázs. 'The Development and Functioning of Cultural Autonomy in Hungary'. In *Cultural Autonomy in Contemporary Europe*, edited by David J. Smith and Karl Cordell (London/New York: Routledge, 2008): pp. 115–34.

Dolenc, Danilo. 'Priseljevanje v Slovenijo z območja nekdanje Jugoslavije po drugi svetovni vojni' [Immigration to Slovenia from the Former Yugoslavia after the Second World War]. In *Priseljenci. Študije o priseljevanju in vključevanju v slovensko družbo*, edited by Miran Komac (Ljubljana, INV: 2007), pp. 69–102.

Dragadze, Tamara. 'Ethnic Conflict as Political Smokescreen'. In *Ethnicity and Intra-State Conflict: Types, Causes and Peace Strategies*, edited by Hakan Wiberg and Christian Scherrer (Aldershot: Ashgate, 1999), pp. 262–79.

Đurđević, Nenad. 'Minority Policy in Serbia—Fostering Integration—Analyses and Recommendations for Improving Minority Policy and Integration Process in the Republic of Serbia', *Forum—Forum for Ethnic Relations, Policy Paper* vol. 4, no. 1 (2014): pp.1–54, accessed September 2014, <http://www.fer.org.rs/uploads/sr/dokumenti/publikacije/analiza-i-preporuke-za-unapredjenje-manjinske-politike-i-procesa-integracije-u-republici-srbiji/Forum-1-2014-ENG-web.pdf>.

Đurić, Vladimir. 'Javna ovlašćenja neteritorijalne autonomije u pravnom sistemu Republike Srbije' [Public Competences of Non-Territorial Autonomy in the Legal System of the Republic of Serbia]. *Pravna Riječ* vol. 10, no. 35 (2013): pp. 183–97.

Eide, Asbjørn. 'Cultural Autonomy: Concept, Content, History and Role in the World Order'. In *Autonomy: Applications and Implications*, edited by Markku Suksi (The Hague: Kluwer Law International, 1998), pp. 251–72.

Eide, Asbjørn. 'Legal and Normative Basis for Saami Claims to Land'. *International Journal on Minority and Group Rights* vol. 8, no. 2 (2001): pp. 127–49.

Eide, Asjbørn. 'The Council of Europe Framework Convention for the Protection of National Minorities'. In *Synergies in Minority Protection—European and International Law Perspective*, edited by Kristin Henrard and Robert Dunbar (Cambridge: Cambridge University Press, 2009), pp. 119–54.

Eidheim, Harald. 'Ethno-Political Development among Sami after World War II'. In *Sami Culture in a New Era. The Norwegian Sami Experience*, edited by Harald Gaski (Karasjohka: Davvi Giri, 1997), pp. 29–61.

Eiler, Ferenc and Nóra Kovács. 'Minority Self-Governments in Hungary'. In *Minority Governance—Concepts at the Threshold of the 21st Century*, edited by Kinga Gál (Budapest: Local Government and Public Service Reform Initiative, 2002): pp. 171–97.

Entman, Robert. 'Framing: Toward Clarification of a Fractured Paradigm'. *Journal of Communication* vol. 43, no. 4 (1993): pp. 51–8.

Erdmann, Gero and Ulf Engel. 'Neopatrimonialism Reconsidered: Critical Review and Elaboration of an Elusive Concept'. *Commonwealth & Comparative Politics* vol. 45, no. 1 (2007): pp. 95–119.

Fisher, Kim. 'Locating Frames in the Discursive Universe'. *Sociological Research Online* vol. 2, no. 3 (1997), accessed 19 March 2014, <http://www.socresonline.org.uk/2/3/4.html>.

Forrest, Scott. 'Indigenous Self-Determination in Finland: A Case Study in Normative Change'. *Polar Record* vol. 42 (2006): pp. 229–38.

Gel'man, Vladimir. 'Subversive Institutions, Informal Governance, and Contemporary Russian Politics'. *Communist and Post-Communist Studies* vol. 45, nos 3–4 (2012): pp. 295–303.

Gel'man, Vladimir. 'The Unrule of Law in the Making: The Politics of Informal Institutional Building in Russia'. *Europe-Asia Studies* vol. 56, no. 7 (2004): pp. 1021–58.

Gerencsér, Balázs Szabolcs. 'Gondolatok az új nemzetiségi törvényről' [Thoughts on the New Law on Nationalities]. *Pázmány Law Working Papers* no. 34 (2012), accessed 15 September 2014, <http://plwp.jak.ppke.hu/images/files/2012/2012-34-Gerencser.pdf>.

Ghai, Yash. 'Ethnicity and Autonomy: A Framework for Analysis'. In *Autonomy and Ethnicity: Negotiating Competing Claims in Multi-Ethnic States*, edited by Yash Ghai (Cambridge/New York: Cambridge University Press, 2000), pp. 1–25.

Giles, Howard, Richard Bourhis, and Donald Taylor. 'Towards a Theory of Language in Ethnic Group Relations'. In *Language, Ethnicity and Intergroup Relations*, edited by Howard Giles (London: Academic Press, 1977): pp. 307–48.

Goldenberg, Sheldon and Valerie Haines. 'Social Networks and Institutional Completeness: From Territory to Ties'. *Canadian Journal of Sociology* vol. 17, no. 3 (1992): pp. 301–12.

Gremsperger, Anna. 'On the Sámi Minority', *JURA* vol. I (2012): pp. 135–47.

Gretzinger, Susanne and Susanne Royer. 'Social kapital i regionale netværk skaber værdi—den sønderjyske mektronikklynge' [Social Capital in Regional Networks Create Added Value—the Southern Denmark Mekatronik Cluster], *Pluk* (May 2012): pp. 15–19.

Groenendijk, Kees. 'Nationality, Minorities and Statelessness: The Case of the Baltic States'. *Helsinki Monitor* vol. 4, no. 3 (1993).

Guboglo, Mikhail Nikolaevich. 'Assambleya narodov Rossii. Teoriya i praktika' [Peoples' Assembly of Russia: Theory and Practice]. In *Etnicheskaya mobilizatsiya i mezhetnicheskaya integratsiya* (Moscow: TsIMO, 1999), pp. 103–16.

Hale, Henry. 'Divided we Stand: Institutional Sources of Ethnofederal State Survival and Collapse'. *World Politics* vol. 56, no. 2 (2004): pp. 165–93.

Hallik, Klara. 'Rahvuspoliitilised seisukohad parteiprogrammides ja valimisplatvormides' [Parties' Programs and Electoral Platforms on Ethnic Issues]. In *Vene küsimus ja Eesti valikud* [The Russian Issues and Challenges for Estonia], edited by Mati Heidmets (Tallinn: Tallinna Pedagoogikaülikool, 1998), p. 95.

Heintze, Hans-Joachim. 'On the Legal Understanding of Autonomy'. In *Autonomy: Applications and Implications*, edited by Markku Suksi (The Hague/Boston: Kluwer Law International, 1998), pp. 7–32.

Helander-Renvall, Elina. 'A Marginalised Minority Remains Marginalized? On the Management of Fjord Resources'. In *Conflict and Cooperation in the North*, edited by Kristina Karppi and Johan Eriksson (Umeå: Norrlands Universitetsforlag i Umeå, 2002), pp. 214–15.

Helmke, Gretchen and Steve Levitsky. 'Informal Institutions and Comparative Politics: A Research Agenda'. *Perspectives on Politics* vol. 2, no. 4 (2004): pp. 725–40.

Henriksen, John B. 'The Continuous Process of Recognition and Implementation of the Sámi People's Right to Self-Determination'. *Cambridge Review of International Affairs* vol. 21, no. 1 (2008): pp. 27–40.

Henriksen, John B. ed. 'Sámi Self-Determination—Scope and Implementation', *Galdu Cala, Journal of Indigenous Peoples Rights* no. 2 (2008): pp. 1–48.

Henriksen, John B. 'Sámi Self-Determination: Autonomy and Self-Government: Education, Research and Culture', *Galdu Cala, Journal of Indigenous Peoples Rights* no. 2 (2009): pp. 1–48.

Henriksen, John B. ed. 'Sámi Self-Determination: Autonomy and Economy—The Authority and Autonomy of the Sámediggi in the Health and Social Services Sector', *Galdu Cala, Journal of Indigenous Peoples Rights* vol. 2 (2010): pp. 33–4.

Hicks, Christian Jakob Burmeister. 'Historical Synopsis of the Sámi/United Nations Relationship', accessed 21 September 2012, http://www.thearctic.is, pp. 1–8.

Hiden, John and David J. Smith. 'Looking beyond the Nation State: A Baltic Vision for National Minorities between the Wars'. *Journal of Contemporary History* vol. 41, no. 3 (2006).

Hiio, Toomas. 'Служба государственной пропаганды Эстонской Республики 1934-1940 гг' [The State Propaganda Service of the Republic of Estonia in 1934-1940]. In *Образ Другого. Страны Балтии и Советский Союз перед Второй мировой войной* [Images of the Other: Baltic States and the Soviet Union before the World War II], edited by Reinhard Krumm, Nikita Lomagin, and Denis Hanov (Moscow: Rosspen, 2012), p. 50.

Housden, Martyn. 'Cultural Autonomy in Estonia: One of History's "Curiosities"?'. In *The Baltic States and their Region: New Europe or Old?*, edited by David J. Smith (Amsterdam: Rodopi, 2005), pp. 251–73.

Imai, Shin. 'Indigenous Self-Determination and the State, Indigenous Peoples and the Law: Comparative and Critical Perspectives'. *CLPE Research Paper* no. 25 (2008).

Ipsen, Knut. 'Minderheitenschutz auf reziproker Basis: die deutsch-dänische Lösung in Heintze' [Minority Protection on a Reciprocal Basis: The German-Danish Solution in Heintze]. In *Selbstbestimmungsrecht der Völker-Herausforderung der Staatenwelt*, edited by Hans-Joachim Heintze (Bonn: Dietz, 1997), pp. 327–41.

Isin, Engin F. 'Theorizing Acts of Citizenship'. In *Acts of Citizenship*, edited by Engin F. Isin and Greg M. Nielsen (London: Zed Books, 2008), pp. 15–43.

Jacobs, Dirk and Marc Swyngedouw. 'Territorial and Non-Territorial Federalism in Belgium: Reform of the Brussels Capital Region, 2001'. *Regional and Federal Studies* vol. 13, no. 2 (2003): pp. 127–39.

Jernsletten, Regnor. 'The Development of a Saami Elite in Norden'. In *Conflict and Cooperation in the North*, edited by Kristina Karppi and Johan Eriksson (Umeå: Norrlands Universitetsforlag i Umeå, 2002), pp. 147–66.

Johnston, Darlene M. 'The Quest of the Six Nations Confederacy for Self-Determination'. *University of Toronto Faculty of Law Review* vol. 44 (1986): pp. 1–32.

Kállai, Ernő. 'The Hungarian Roma Population during the Last Half-Century'. In *The Gypsies/the Roma in Hungarian Society*, edited by Ernő Kállai (Budapest: Teleki László Foundation, 2002), pp. 35–51.

Kállai, Ernő. 'Működési tapasztalatok és változási igények a helyi cigány kisebbségi önkormányzatoknál' [Experiences and Claims for Changes among Local Roma Minority Self-Governments]. In *Tér és terep III* [Third Yearbook of the Institute for Minority Studies of the Hungarian Academy of Sciences], edited by L. Szarka et al. (Budapest: Akadémiai Kiadó, 2004), pp. 227–51.

Kaltenbach, Jenő. 'Esély vagy illúzió, a kisebbségi törvény a valóságban?' [Is the Minority Law a Chance or an Illusion in Reality?]. *Barátság* vol. 21, no. 1 (2014): pp. 7765–87.

Karlsbakk, Jonas. 'Sámi Parliament Wants Veto on Mineral Issues'. *Barents Observer*, accessed 20 December 2012, <http://barentsobserver.com>.

Katus, Kalev, Allan Puur, and Luule Sakkeus. 'The Demographic Characteristic of National Minorities in Estonia'. In *The Demographic Characteristics of National Minorities in Certain European States*, edited by Werner Haug, Youssef Courbage, and Paul Compton (Strasbourg: Council of Europe Publishing, 2000), pp. 29–86.

Kemény, István. 'Linguistic Groups and Usage among the Hungarian Gypsies/Roma'. In *The Gypsies/the Roma in Hungarian Society*, edited by Ernő Kállai (Budapest: Teleki László Foundation, 2002), pp. 28–34.

Kirzsán, Andrea. 'The Hungarian Minority Protection System: A Flexible Approach to the Adjudiction of Ethnic Claims'. *Journal of Ethnic and Migration Studies* vol. 26, no. 2 (2000): pp. 247–62.

Klatt, Martin. 'Genforening eller mindretal' [Unification or Minority]. In *Sydslesvigs danske historie*, edited by Lars N. Henningsen (Studieafdelingen: Dansk Centralbibliotek for Sydslesvig, 2009), pp. 177–236.

Koivurova, Timo. 'From High Hopes to Disillusionment: Indigenous Peoples' Struggle to (re)Gain Their Right to Self-Determination'. *International Journal on Minority and Group Rights* vol. 15, no. 1 (2008): pp. 1–26.

Koivurova, Timo. 'The Draft Nordic Sámi Convention: Nations Working Together'. *International Community Law Review* vol. 10 (2008): pp. 279–93.

Koivurova, Timo. 'Sovereign States and Self-Determining Peoples: Carving out a Place for Transnational Indigenous Peoples in a World of Sovereign States', *International Community Law Review* vol. 12 (2010): pp. 191–212.

Koivurova, Timo and Adam Stepien. 'How International Law Has Influenced the National Policy and Law Related to Indigenous Peoples in the Arctic'. *Waikato Law Review* vol. 19 (2011): pp. 123–43.

Kolláth, Anna, Judit Gasparics, Annamaria Gróf, and Livija Horvat. 'Hungarian in Slovenia: An Overview of a Language in Context'. *ELDIA Working Papers in European Language Diversity* no. 2 (2010): p. 10.

Komac, Miran. ed. 'Narodnost—manjšina ali skupnost. Urejanje,uresničevanje in varstvo pravic narodnosti (narodnih manjšin) v Republiki Sloveniji' [Nationality—A Minority or a Community. Managing, Implementation and Protection of the Rights of Nationalities (National Minorities) in the Republic of Slovenia]. *Razprave in gradivo/ Treatises and Documents*, no. 24 (1990): p. 133.

Komac, Miran. 'Minority Self-Government in Slovenia', *Südosteuropa* vol. 40, nos 7–8 (2000): pp. 358–74.

Komac, Miran. 'Varstvo "novih" narodnih skupnosti v Sloveniji' [Protection of the 'New' National Communities in Slovenia]. *Razprave in gradivo/Treatises and Documents* vol. 43 (2003): pp. 6–33.

Komac, Miran. 'Konstrukcija romskega političnega predstavništva' [The Construction of Roma Political Representation]. *Razprave in gradivo/Treatises and Documents* nos 53–4 (2007): pp. 6–26.

Korhecz, Tamás. 'Vojvodina—The Next Stage of the Dismantling Process?'. *Cambridge Review of International Affairs* vol. 12, no. 2 (1999): pp. 153–67.

Korhecz, Tamás. 'Democratic Legitimacy and Election Rules of National Ethnic Minority Bodies and Representatives—Reflections on Legal Solutions in Hungary and Slovenia'. *International Journal on Minority and Group Rights* vol. 9 no. 2 (2002): pp. 161–81.

Korhecz, Tamás. 'Non-Territorial Autonomy in Practice: The Hungarian National Council in Serbia'. In *Autonomies in Europe: Solutions and Challenges*, edited by Zoltán Kántor (Budapest: L'Harmattan, 2009): pp. 152–3.

Korhecz, Tamás. 'Nemzetiségi Autonómia Az Alkotmánybíróság Szorításában—A Szerbiai Alkotmánybíróság A Nemzeti Tanácsokat Szabályozó Törvénnyel Kapcsolatos Döntésének Kritikus Elemzése' [Ethnic Autonomy in the Wring [please check for sense]of the Constitutional Court—Critical Analyses of the Decision of the Serbian Constitutional Court on the Law Regulating the National Councils]. *JOG—ÁLLAM—POLITIKA* vol. 6, no. 3 (2014): pp. 3–32.

Kymlicka, Will. 'Estonia's Integration Policies in a Comparative Perspective'. In *Estonia's Integration Landscape: From Apathy to Harmony: Interviews with Estonian Leaders of Public Opinion, Materials of International Conference, Estonia's Integration Projects, Monitorings*, edited by Jaan Tõnissoni Instituut (Tallinn: Jaan Tõnissoni Instituut, 2000), pp. 29–57.

Lambertz, Karl Heinz. 'Die Verfassung Belgiens und ihre Institutionen' [The Belgian Constitution and its Institutions], *Nordrhein-Westfälische Verwaltungsblätter* vol. 9 (2003): pp. 329–33.

Lambertz, Karl Heinz. 'Drei Alleinstellungsmerkmale der Deutschsprachigen Gemeinschaft Belgiens' [Three Unique Features of the German-Speaking Community of Belgium]. In *La Communauté germanophone de Belgique. Die Deutschsprachige Gemeinschaft Belgiens*, edited by Katrin Stangherlin (Bruxelles: la Charte, 2005), pp. 8–13

Landry, Rodrigue, Réal Allard, and Kenneth Deveau. 'Bilingual Schooling of the Canadian Francophone Minority: A Cultural Autonomy Model'. *International Journal of the Sociology of Language* vol. 185 (2007): pp. 133–62.

Lantschner, Emma and Giovanni Poggeschi. 'Quota System, Census and Declaration of Affiliation to a Linguistic Group'. In *Tolerance through Law: Self-Governance and Group Rights in South Tyrol*, edited by Jens Woelk, Francesco Palermo, and Joseph Marko (Leiden: Martinus Nijhoff Publishers, 2008), pp. 219–33.

Lantto, Patrick and Ulf Mörkenstam. 'Sámi Rights and Sámi Challenges: The Modernization Process and the Swedish Sámi Movement, 1886-2006'. *Scandinavian Journal of History* vol. 33, no. 1 (2008): pp. 26–51.

Lawrence, Rebecca and Ulf Mörkenstam. 'Självbestämmande genom myndighetsutövning? Sametingets dubbla roller' [Self-Determining Parliament or Government Agency? The Curious Double Life of the Swedish Sámi Parliament], *Statsvetenskaplig tidskrift* vol. 114, no. 2 (2012): pp. 207–39.

Légaré, André and Markku Suksi. 'Introduction: Rethinking the Forms of Autonomy at the Dawn of the 21st Century'. *International Journal on Minority and Group Rights* vol. 15 (2008): pp. 195–225.

Lesnaja, Natalja. 'О сохранении преемственности в развитии русской культуры в Эстонии в XX веке' [On the Preservation of Continuity of the Russian Culture in Estonia in the Twentieth Century]. In *Русские в Эстонии. Сборник статей* [Russians in Estonia. The Compendium of Articles], edited by V. Boykov and H. Bassel (Tallinn: Russian Research Center in Estonia, 2000).

Lewis, Dave. 'Ethnic Mobilization: The Case of Indigenous Political Movements'. In *Conflict and Cooperation in the North*, edited by Kristina Karppi and Johan Eriksson (Umeå: Norrlands Universitetsforlag i Umeå, 2002), pp. 29–56.

Lubowitz, Frank. 'Oeversee 1864—Entstehung und Wandel eines Gedenktages' [Oeversee 1864—Formation and Transformation of Memorial Day], *Grenzfriedenshefte* vol. 4 (2005): pp. 301 ff.

Lustick, Ian. 'Stability in Deeply Divided Societies: Consociationalism versus Control'. *World Politics* vol. 31, no. 3 (1979): pp. 325–44.

Magga, Ole Henrik. 'Sámi Past and Present and the Sámi Picture of the World'. In *The Changing Circumpolar North: Opportunities for Academic Development*, edited by Lassi Heininen (Rovaniemi: Arctic Centre Publications, 1994).

Magga, Ole Henrik. 'The Sámi Parliament: Fulfilment of Self-Determination'. In *Conflict and Cooperation in The North*, edited by Kristina Karppi and Johan Eriksson (Umeå: Norrlands Universitetsforlag i Umeå, 2002).

Magnet, Joseph Eliot. 'Minority-Language Education Rights'. In *The New Constitution and the Charter of Rights*, edited by E. P. Belobaba and E. Gertner (Toronto: Butterworths, 1983), pp. 195–216.

Majtényi, Balázs. 'Nemzeti és etnikai kisebbségi jogok' [National and Ethnic Minority Rights]. In *Az Alkotmány kommentárja*, edited by András Jakab (Budapest: Századvég, 2009), p. 2400.

Majtényi, Balázs. 'Történelmünk hagyománya' [Tradition of our History]. *Fundamentum* no. 2 (2011), pp. 56–61.

Malakhov, Vladimir and Alexander Osipov. 'The Category of Minorities in the Russian Federation: A Reflection on Uses and Misuses'. In *International Obligations and National Debates: Minorities around the Baltic Sea*, edited by Sia Spiliopoulou Åkermark (Mariehamn: Åland Islands Peace Institute, 2006), pp. 497–544.

Malloy, Tove H. 'The Lund Recommendations and Non-Territorial Arrangements: Progressive De-Territorialization of Minority Politics'. *International Journal on Minority and Group Rights* vol. 16, no. 4 (2009), pp. 665–79.

Malloy, Tove H. 'Creating New Spaces for Politics? The Role of National Minorities in Building Capacity of Cross-Border Regions'. *Regional and Federal Studies* vol. 20, no. 3 (2010): pp. 335–52.

Malloy, Tove H. 'Denmark Adopts Unilateral Legislation in Favour of Kin-Minority'. *European Yearbook of Minority Issues* vol. 9 (2010): pp. 669–82.

Malloy, Tove H. 'Reflexive Minority Action: Minority Narratives and New European Discourses'. In *Globalization and 'Minority' Cultures. The Role of 'Minor' Cultural Groups in Shaping our Global Future*, edited by Sophie Croisy (Brill, 2014).

Mann, Michael. 'The Autonomous Power of the State: Its Origins, Mechanisms, and Results'. In *States in History*, edited by John A. Hall (Oxford: Blackwell, 1986), pp. 109–36.

McCombs, Maxwell and Salma Ghanem. 'The Convergence of Agenda Setting and Framing'. In *Framing Public Life: Perspectives on Media and our Understanding of the Social World*, edited by Stephen D. Reese, Oscar H. Gandy and August E. Grant (Mahwah, NJ: Lawrence Erlbaum Associates, 2001), pp. 67–81.

Meyer, Lukas H. 'Transnational Autonomy: Responding to Historical Injustice in the Case of the Sámi and Roma Peoples'. *International Journal on Minority and Group Rights* vol. 8 (2001): pp. 263–301.

Minde, Henry. 1996. 'The Making of and International Movement of Indigenous Peoples'. In *Minorities and their Rights of Political Participation*, edited by F. Horn (Rovaniemi: University of Lapland Press, 1996), pp. 90–128.

Mohr, Manfred. 'Abgrenzung von Selbstbestimmungsrecht und Minderheitenschutz' [Definition of Self-Determination and Minority Protection]. In *Selbstbestimmungsrecht der Völker—Herausforderung der Staatenwelt*, edited by Hans J. Heintze (Bonn: Dietz, 1997), p. 139.

Mozaffar, Shaheen and James Scarritt. 'Why Territorial Autonomy is not a Viable Option for Managing Ethnic Conflict in African Plural Societies'. *Nationalism and Ethnic Politics* vol. 5, nos. 3–4 (1999): pp. 230–53.

Musabaeva, Gulbakhsha Nurmukanovna. 'Aktual'nye voprosy mezhetnicheskih otnoshenii v Kazahstane i mezhdunarodnoe sotrudnichestvo' [Topical Issues of Interethnic Relations in Kazakhstan and International Cooperation]. *Vestnik Tverskogo gosudarstvennogo universiteta. Seriya: Pravo* no. 28 (2011), pp. 31–40.

Musaev, V. 'Kul'turnaya avtonomiya kak sredstvo razresheniya natsional'nyh problem: istoriya i perspektivy' [Cultural Autonomy as an Effective Means of Resolving National Problems: History and Perspectives]. In *Perekrestok kul'tur: mezhdisciplinarnye issledovaniya v oblasti gumanitarnyh nauk* (Moscow: Logos, 2004), pp. 83–107.

Myntti, Kristian. 'The Nordic Sámi Parliaments'. In *Operationalizing the Right of Indigenous Peoples to Self-Determination*, edited by Pekka Aikio and Martin Scheinin (Turku: Institute for Human Rights, 2000), pp. 85–130.

Nabiullina, A.V. 'Osobennosti natsional'noi politiki kak faktora mezhetnicheskogo vzaimodeistviya v Respublike Tatarstan' [Characteristics of National Policy as a Factor of Interethnic Cooperation in the Republic of Tatarstan]. *Kazanskaya nauka* no. 1 (2012): pp. 285–7.

Niemi, Einar. 'Saami History and the Frontier Myth'. In *Sami Culture in a New Era. The Norwegian Sami Experience*, edited by Harald Gaski (Karasjohka: Davvi Girji, 1997), pp. 62–85.

Nikiforov, Ilya. 'Национально-культурная автономия в Эстонии: повторение пройденного' [National Cultural Autonomy in Estonia: Repetition of the Past]. In *Natsional'no-kul'turnaya avtonomiya. Ideya i realizatsiya. Estonskii opyt*, edited by Alexander Osipov and Ilya Nikiforov (Tallinn: Tsentr informatsii po pravam cheloveka, 2008), pp. 43–55.

Nimni, Ephraim. 'Introduction: The National Cultural Autonomy Model Revisited'. In *National Cultural Autonomy and its Contemporary Critics*, edited by Ephriam Nimni (New York: Routledge, 2005), pp. 1–12.

Nimni, Ephraim. 'National-Cultural Autonomy as an Alternative to Minority Territorial Nationalism'. *Ethnopolitics* vol. 6, no. 3 (September 2007): pp. 345–64.

Oeter, Stefan. 'Minderheiten im institutionellen Staatsaufbau' [Minorities in the Institutional Structure of the State]. In *Das Minderheitenrecht europäischer Staaten, Teil II,* edited by Jochen A. Frowein, Rainer Hofmann, and Stefan Oeter (Berlin: Springer, 1994).

O'Leary, Brendan. 'The Logics of Power-Sharing, Consociation and Pluralist Federations'. In *Settling Self-Determination Disputes: Complex Power-Sharing in Theory and Practice*, edited by Barbara Metzger, Marc Weller, and Niall Johnson (Leiden: Martinus Nijhoff Publishers, 2008), pp. 47–58.

Olle, Vallo. 'Mõned vähemusrahvuse kultuuriomavalitsuse õiguslikud probleemid' [Some Legal Issues Regarding Cultural Autonomies for National Minorities]. *Juridica* vol. 2 (2009): pp. 86–97.

Osipov, Alexander. 'National Cultural Autonomy in Russia: A Case of Symbolic Law'. *Review of Central and East European Law* vol. 35, no. 1 (2010): pp. 27–57.

Osipov, Alexander. 'Non-Territorial Autonomy and International Law'. *International Community Law Review* vol. 13 (2011): pp. 393–411.

Osipov, Alexander. 'Non-Territorial Autonomy as a Way to Frame Diversity Policy: The Case of Russia'. In *The Challenge of Non-Territorial Autonomy: Theory and Practice*, edited by Ephraim Nimni, Alexander Osipov, and David J. Smith (Oxford: Peter Lang, 2013), pp. 133–48.

Osipov, Alexander. 'The "Peoples' Congresses" in Russia: Failure or Success? Authenticity and Efficiency of Minority Representation'. *ECMI Working Paper* no. 48 (2011), accessed 19 March 2014, <http://www.ecmi.de/uploads/tx_lfpubdb/Working_Paper_48_Final.pdf>.

Packer, John. 'Problems in Defining Minorities'. In *Minority and Group Rights towards the New Millennium*, edited by Deirdre Fottrell and Bill Bowring (The Hague: Martinus Nijhoff Publishers, 1999), pp. 223–74.

Palermo, Francesco. 'At the Heart of Participation and of its Dilemmas: Minorities in the Executive Structures'. In *Political Participation of Minorities: A Commentary on International Standards and Practice*, edited by Marc Weller and Katherine Nobbs (Oxford University Press, 2010), pp. 434–52.

Pan, Zhongdang and G. M. Kosicki. 'Framing as a Strategic Action in Public Deliberation'. In *Framing Public Life: Perspectives on Media and our Understanding of the Social World*, edited by Stephen D. Reese, Oscar H. Gandy, and August E. Grant (Mahwah, NJ: Lawrence Erlbaum Associates, 2001), pp. 34–66.

Parming, Tõnu. 'The Jewish Community and Inter-Ethnic Relations in Estonia, 1918-1940'. *Journal of Baltic Studies* vol. 10, no. 3 (1979): pp. 241–61.

Pernthaler, Peter. 'Gutachten über die Errichtung einer Körperschaft als öffentlich-rechtliche Vertretung der Sorben (Wenden)' [Opinion on the Establishment of a Corporation as a Public Representative of the Sorbs (Wends)]. In *Minderheiten als Mehrwert*, edited by Matthias Theodor Vogt, Jan Sokol, Dieter Bingen, Jurgen Neyer, and Albert Löhr (Frankfurt a. M.: Peter Lang, 2010), pp. 537–56.

Petričušić, Antonija. 'Croatian Constitutional Law on the Rights of National Minorities'. *European Yearbook of Minority Issues* vol. 2 (2004), pp. 607–29.

Petričušić, Antonija. 'Važnost sudjelovanja nacionalnih manjina u javnom životu: primjena međunarodnih standarda u Republici Hrvatskoj i Južnom Tirolu'. In *Manjine i europske integracije*, edited by Mitja Žagar et al. (Split, Stina, 2005), pp. 54–69.

Petričušić, Antonija. 'Širenje Europskeunije i zaštita nacionalnih manjina' [The Expansion of the European Union and the Protection of National Minorities]. *Međunarodne studije—časopis za međunarodne odnose, vanjsku politiku i diplomaciju* vol. 8, nos 3–4 (2008): pp. 5–32.

Petričušić, Antonija. 'Izbori za vijeća i predstavnike nacionalnih manjina—legalitet bez legitimiteta' [The Elections for the Councils and Representatives of National Minorities—Legality without Legitimacy], *Informator* vols. 6004–5 (2011): pp. 17–18.

Petričušić, Antonija. 'Vijeća nacionalnih manjina—institucija upitnog legitimiteta i uglavnom neostvarene nadležnosti' [National Minority Councils: Institution of Questionable Legitimacy and Predominantly Unachieved Competences]. *Revus—Revija za evropsko ustavnost* vol. 17 (2012): pp. 91–104.

Petričušić, Antonija. 'Lice i naličje brige o 'vlastitoj' manjini' [Both Sides of the Coin of the Care for 'Their Own' Minority]. *Nezavisni magazin Identitet* vol. 185 (2013): pp. 32–3.

Petričušić, Antonija. 'Ravnopravna službena uporaba jezika i pisma nacionalnih manjina: Izvori domaćeg i međunarodnog prava' [Equal Official Use of the Language and Script of National Minorities: Sources of National and International Law]. *Zagrebačka pravna revija* vol. 2, no. 1 (2013): pp. 11–39.

Poleshchuk, Vadim. 'The War of the Monuments in Estonia: The Challenges of History and the Minority Population', Report from the Åland Islands Peace Institute, no. 1 (2009).

Poleshchuk, Vadim. 'Вопросы об этничности, языке и религии в переписи населения Эстонии' [Issues of Ethnicity, Language and Religion in the Census in Estonia]. In Этнологический мониторинг переписи населения [Ethnological Monitoring of Population Census], edited by V. V. Stepanov (Moscow: Russian Academy of Sciences, Institute of Ethnology and Anthropology, 2011).

Poleshchuk, Vadim. 'Changes in the Concept of National Cultural Autonomy in Estonia'. In *The Challenge of Non-Territorial Autonomy: Theory and Practice*, edited by Ephraim Nimni, Alexander Osipov, and David J. Smith (Bern: Peter Lang, 2013), pp. 149–62.

Poleshchuk, Vadim and Jelena Helemäe. 'Estonia—In Quest of Minority Protection'. In *International Obligations and National Debates: Minorities around the Baltic Sea*, edited by Athanasia Spiliopoulou Akermark et al. (Mariehamn: The Aland Islands Peace Institute, 2006), pp. 109–70.

Proulx, Jean-Pierre. 'Le choc des Chartes: histoire des régimes juridiques québécois et canadien en matière de langue d'enseignement' [Clash of Charters: History of Quebec and Canadian Legal Systems in Language Education]. *Revue juridique Thémis* vol. 23 (1989).

Ra'anan, Uri. 'The Nation-State Fallacy'. In *Conflict and Peacemaking in Multiethnic Societies*, edited by Joseph Montville (New York: Lexington Books/Macmillan, 1991), pp. 5–20.

Rakowska-Harmstone, Teresa. 'The Dialectics of Nationalism in the USSR'. *Problems of Communism* vol. 23, no. 3 (1974): pp. 1–22.

Rátkai, Árpád. 'Az intézményesülő etnobiznisz' [The Institutionalization of Ethnobusiness]. 2003, accessed 15 September 2014, <http://www.nemzetisegek.hu/etnonet/ratbiz.htm>.

Rehman, Javaid. 'The Concept of Autonomy and Minority Rights in Europe'. In *Minority Rights in the 'New' Europe*, edited by Peter Cumper and Steven Wheatley (The Hague: Martinus Nijhoff Publishers, 1999), pp. 217–32.

Renner, Karl. 'State and Nation'. In *National Cultural Autonomy and its Contemporary Critics*, edited by Ephraim Nimni (New York: Routledge, 2005), pp.13–43.

Roach, Steven C. 'Minority Rights and an Emergent International Right to Autonomy: A Historical and Normative Assessment'. *International Journal on Minority and Group Rights* vol. 11 (2004): pp. 411–32.

Roeder, Philip. 'Soviet Federalism and Ethnic Mobilization'. *World Politics* vol. 43, no. 2 (1991): pp. 197–9.

Roter, Petra. 'Language Issues in the Context of "Slovenian Smallness"'. In *Nation-Building, Ethnicity and Language Politics in Transition Countries*, edited by Farimah Daftary and Francois Grin (Budapest: LGI/Open Society Institute, 2003), pp. 211–41.

Rothchild, Donald and Caroline Hartzell. 'Security in Deeply Divided Societies: The Role of Territorial Autonomy'. *Nationalism and Ethnic Politics* vol. 5, nos 3–4 (1999): pp. 254–71.

Ruutsoo, R. 'Eesti kodakondsuspoliitika ja rahvusriigi kujunemise piirjooned' [Estonian Citizenship Policies and a Sketch of an Emerging Nation State]. In *Vene küsimus ja Eesti valikud* [The Russian Issues and Challenges for Estonia], edited by Mati Heidmets (Tallinn: Tallinna Pedagoogikaülikool, 1998), p. 176.

Sagitova, Liliya Varisovna. 'Dom druzhby narodov kak ob'ekt i sub'ekt sotsial'nogo reformirovaniya: ot sovetskoi modeli k globalizatsionnoi?' [Home of the Commonwealth of Peoples as an Object and Subject of Social Reform: from the Soviet Model to Globalization]. *Zhurnal issledovanii social'noi politiki* vol. 9, no. 4 (2011): pp. 495–512.

Sándor, Erzsébet Szalayné. 'A 2014. évi választások a magyarországi nemzetiségekért felelős biztoshelyettes szemszögéből' [The 2014 Elections from the Perspective of the Deputy Commissioner Responsible for the Nationalities Living in Hungary]. *Kisebbségkutatás* no. 1 (2014), pp. 7–14.

Schaeffer-Rolffs, Adrian. 'Paternalistic versus Participation Oriented Minority Institutions in the Danish-German Border Region', *ECMI Working Paper* no. 67 (2013).

Scheufele, Dietram A. 'Framing as a Theory of Media Effects'. *Journal of Communication* vol. 49, no. 4 (1999): pp. 103–22.

Selle, Per and Kristin Strømsnes. 'Sámi Citizenship: Marginalisation or Integration?'. *Acta Borealia* vol. 27, no. 1 (2010): pp. 66–90.

Semb, Anne Julie. 'Sámi Self-Determination in the Making', *Nations and Nationalism* vol. 11, no. 4 (2005): pp. 531–49.

Semjonov, Aleksei. 'Estonia: Nation-Building and Integration—Political and Legal Aspects'. In *National Integration and Violent Conflict in Post-Soviet Societies: The Cases of Estonia and Moldova*, edited by Pål Kolstø (Lanham/Boulder/New York/Oxford: Rowman and Littlefield Publishers, 2002), p. 132.

Seurujärvi-Kari, Irja. '"We Are No Longer Prepared to be Silent": The Making of Sámi Indigenous Identity in an International Context'. *Suomen Antropologi: Journal of the Finnish Anthropologial Society* vol. 35, no. 4 (2010): pp. 5–25.

Shaimerdenova, L. 'Assambleya narodov Kazahstana—novyi institut obshestvenno-politicheskoi konsolidatsii' [Peoples' Assembly of Kazakhstan—New Institute of Sociopolitical Consolidation]. *Russkaya kul'tura vne granits* no. 6 (1997): pp. 16–18.

Shiryaev, Andrei. 'Eshe k voprosu ob avtonomizatsii' [More on Autonomy Issues]. *Vesti Dnya* (19 March 2009).

Shor, Tatjana. 'Культурная автономия евреев в Эстонии: подготовка и введение (1925-1927)' [Jewish Cultural Autonomy in Estonia: Preparations and Introduction (1925-1927)]. In *Евреи в меняющемся мире, Материалы 5-й международной к онференции, Рига, 16-17 сентября 2003 г.* [Jews in a Changing World. Materials of the 5th International Conference, Riga, 16–17 September 2003], edited by Г. Брановер and Р. Фербер (Riga: Latvian University, 2003).

Shor, Tatjana. 'Проблемы культурной автономии на страницах русской периодики в Эстонии 1925-1930 гг' [The Issue of Cultural Autonomy in the 1925-1930 Russian Periodicals of Estonia in 1925-1930]. In *На перекрестке культур: русские в Балтийском регионе. Часть 2* [At the Crossroad of Cultures: Russians in the Baltic Region. Part 2], edited by Andrei Klemeshev (Kaliningrad: Kaliningrad State University, 2004), p. 124.

Sillanpää. Lennard. 'A Comparative Analysis of Indigenous Rights in Fennoscandia'. *Scandinavian Political Studies* vol. 20, no. 3 (1997): pp. 197–216.

Sillanpää, Lennard. 'Government Responses to Saami Self-Determination'. In *Conflict and Cooperation in the North*, edited by Kristina Karppi and Johan Eriksson (Umeå: Norrlands Universitetsforlag i Umeå, 2002) pp. 83–112.

Smith, David J. and Karl Cordell. 'Introduction: The Theory and Practice of Cultural Autonomy in Central and Eastern Europe'. *Ethnopolitics* vol. 6, no. 3 (2007): p. 342.

Smith, David. J. 'Minority Territorial and Non-Territorial Autonomy in Europe: Theoretical Perspectives and Practical Challenges'. In *Autonomies in Europe: Solutions and Challenges*, edited by Zoltán Kántor (Budapest: L'Harmattan, 2009): pp. 15–25.

Smith, David J. 'Challenges of Non-Territorial Autonomy in Contemporary Central and Eastern Europe'. In *The Challenge of Non-Territorial Autonomy*, edited by Ephraim Nimni and Alexander Osipov (Oxford-Bern: Peter Land, 2013), pp. 117–32.

Smith, David James. 'Non-Territorial Cultural Autonomy as a Baltic Contribution to Europe between the Wars'. In *The Baltic States and their Region: New Europe or Old?*, edited by David J. Smith (Amsterdam: Rodopi, 2005), pp. 209–24.

Smith, David James. 'Non-Territorial Autonomy and Political Community in Contemporary Central and Eastern Europe'. *Journal on Ethnopolitics and Minority Issues in Europe* vol. 12, no. 1 (2013): pp. 27–55.

Stanovčić, Vojislav. 'Predgovor: Pregled istraživanja položaja manjina' [Introduction: Overview of Researches on the Situation of Minorities]. In *Položaj nacionalnih manjina u Srbiji*, edited by Vojislav Stanovčić (Beograd: Srpska akademija nauka i umetnosti, 2007): pp. 1–36.

Stroschein, Sherrill. 'What Belgium Can Teach Bosnia: The Uses of Autonomy in "Divided House" States'. *Journal on Ethnopolitics and Minority Issues in Europe* no. 3 (2003), accessed 5 October 2014, <http://www.ecmi.de/jemie/>.

Stroschein, Sherrill. 'Making or Breaking Kosovo: Applications of Dispersed State Control'. *Perspectives on Politics* vol. 6, no. 4 (2008): pp. 655–74.

Stroschein, Sherrill. 'Demography in Ethnic Party Fragmentation: Hungarian Local Voting in Romania'. *Party Politics* vol. 17, no. 2 (2011): pp. 189–204.

Suksi, Markku. 'Personal Autonomy as Institutional Form—Focus on Europe against the Background of Article 27 of the ICCPR'. *International Journal on Minority and Group Rights* vol. 15, nos 2–3 (2008): pp. 157–78.

Szabó, Orsolya. 'Reform vagy módosítás?' [Reform of Modification?]. In *Tér és terep III* [Third Yearbook of the Institute for Minority Studies of the Hungarian Academy of Sciences], edited by L. Szarka et al. (Budapest: Akadémiai Kiadó, 2004), pp. 191–208.

Tatalović, Siniša, Ružica Jakešević, and Tomislav Lacović. 'Funkcioniranje vijeća i predstavnika nacionalnih manjina u Republici Hrvatskoj' [The Functioning of the Councils and Representatives of National Minorities in the Republic of Croatia], *Medunarodne studije* vol. 10, nos 3–4 (2010): pp. 40–56.

Thacik, Michael. 'Characteristics of Forms of Autonomy', *International Journal on Minority and Group Rights* vol. 15 (2008): pp. 369–401.

Theobald, Robin. 'Patrimonialism'. *World Politics* vol. 34, no. 4 (1982): pp. 548–59.

Thiele, Carmen. 'Rechtsstellung der Sorben in Deutschland' [Status of Sorbs in Germany]. In *Selbstbestimmungsrecht der Völker—Herausforderung der Staatenwelt*, edited by Hans J. Heintze (Bonn: Dietz, 1997), pp. 342–78.

Thornberry, Patrick. 'On Some Implications of the UN Declaration on Minorities for Indigenous Peoples'. In *Indigenous and Tribal Peoples Rights—1993 and after*, edited by E. Gayim and K. Myntti (Rovaniemi: University of Lapland, 1994), pp. 46–91.

Thornberry, Patrick. 'Who is Indigenous?'. In *Economic, Social and Cultural Rights of the Sámi. International and National Aspects*, edited by Frank Horn (Rovaniemi: University of Lapland Press, 1998), pp. 1–40.

Tishkov, Valeriy Aleksandrovich. 'Kazanskie strasti' [Kazan Passions]. *Nezavisimaya gazeta* (4 October 2002).

Tomaselli, Alexandra. 'Research Results on Pre-Conditions in the Consultation Procedure of Well-Established Minority Consultative Bodies: Some Examples from the Sámi Parliaments' Experience', Office of High Commissioner for Human Rights/EURAC, 2009, <http://www2.ohchr.org/english/bodies/hrcouncil/minority/docs/Item%20IV%20 Conditions%20required%20for%20effective%20political%20participation/Participants/ Alexandra%20Tomaselli%20EURAC%20Sami%20political%20participation.pdf>.

Torode, Nicky. 'National Cultural Autonomy in the Russian Federation: Implementation and Impact'. *International Journal on Minority and Group Rights* vol. 15, nos 2–3 (2008): pp. 179–93.

Toso, Doncsev. 'A magyarországi kisebbségi törvény' [The Minority Law of Hungary]. *Kisebbségkutatás* vol. 1 (2004): pp. 94–101.

Tóth, Ágnes and János Vékás. 'Borders and Identity'. *Hungarian Statistical Review*, Special no. 13. (2009): pp. 3–31.

Turetskii, Nikolay Nikolaevich. 'Assambleya naroda Kazahstana—knou-how kazahstanskoi mezhetnicheskoi politiki' [Peoples' Assembly of Kazakhstan—Know-How of Kazakh Ethnopolitics]. *Yevraziiskaya integratsiya: ekonomika, pravo, politika* no. 5 (2009): pp. 118–21.

Tuulentie, Seija. 'National Rejection of Saami Claims in Finland'. In *Conflict and Cooperation in the North*, edited by Kristina Karppi and Johan Eriksson (Umeå: Norrlands Universitetsforlag i Umeå, 2002), pp. 343–60.

Ushakov, Alexander A. 'Zakonodatelnaya Tekhnika' [Legislative Technique], *Gosudarstvo, Pravo, Zakonnost: Uchenye Zapiski* vol. 2 (1970): pp. 214–25.

Van Parijs, Philippe. 'Power Sharing versus Border-Crossing in Ethnically Divided Societies'. In *Designing Democratic Institutions*, edited by Ian Shapiro and Steven Macedo (New York: New York University Press, 2000), pp. 296–320.

Várady, Tibor. 'Minorities, Majorities, Law, and Ethnicity: Reflections of the Yugoslav Case'. *Human Rights Quarterly* vol. 19 (1997): pp. 9–54.

Varady, Tibor. 'Mišljenje o ustavnopravnim pitanjima koja se postavljaju povodom osporenih odredaba zakona o nacionalnim savetima—Izneto na javnoj raspravi rred Ustavnim sudom 2. Jula 2013. Godine' [Opinion on Constitutional Law Issues Raised Regarding the Disputed Provisions of the Law on National Councils—A View Elaborated at the Public Hearing before the Constitutional Court on 2 July 2013], *Pravni Zapisi* vol. 4, no. 2 (2013): pp. 419–35.

Vékás, János. 'Serbia'. In *Minority Hungarian Communities in the Twentieth Century*, edited by Nándor Bárdi, Csilla Fedinec, and László Szarka (Boulder, CO: Atlantic Research and Publication Inc., 2011): pp. 538–45.

Vermeersch, Peter. 'EU Enlargement and Minority Rights Policies in Central Europe: Explaining Policy Shifts in the Czech Republic, Hungary and Poland'. *Journal on Ethnopolitics and Minority Issues in Europe* vol. 1 (2003): p. 12.

Vizi, Balázs. 'Does European Integration Support the Minority Quest for Autonomy? Minority Claims for Self-Government and Devolution Processes in Europe'. In *Autonomies in Europe: Solutions and Challenges*, edited by Zoltán Kántor (Budapest: L'Harmattan, 2009): pp. 25–37.

Vizi, Balázs. 'Protection without Definition—Notes on the Concept of "Minority Rights" in Europe'. *Minority Studies* no. 15 (2013): pp. 7–26.

Vogt, Matthias Theodor and Vladimir Kreck. 'Gesamtkonzept zur Förderung der sorbischen Sprache und Kultur, Teil II, Empfehlungen zur Stärkung der sorbischen Minderheit durch Schaffung eines abgestimmten Selbstverwaltungs-, Kooperations- Projekt- und Institutionenclusters. Im Auftrag der Stiftung für das sorbische Volk erarbeitet am Insititut für kulturelle Infrastruktur Sachsen' [Overall Concept for the Promotion of the Sorbian Language and Culture, Part II, Recommendations for the Strengthening of the Sorbian Minority by Creating a Coordinated Cluster of Self-Management, Cooperation, Projects and Institutions. Developed at the Institute for Cultural Infrastructure Saxony on Behalf of the Foundation for the Sorbian People], 2009, accessed September 2014, <http://stiftung.sorben.com/usf/IKS_Empfehlungen_Sorben_091205r.pdf>.

Walsh, Niamh. 'Minority Self-Government in Hungary: Legislation and Practice'. *Journal on Ethnopolitics and Minority Issues in Europe* vol. 4 (2000): pp. 1–73.

Waters, Timothy and Rachel Guglielmo. 'Two Souls to Struggle with'. In *State and Nation Building in East Central Europe*, edited by John Micgiel (New York: Columbia University, Institute on East Central Europe, 1996), pp. 177–97.

Watts, Ronald. 'Federalism, Federal Political Systems, and Federations'. *Annual Review of Political Science* vol. 1 (1998): pp. 117–37.

Weiss-Wendt, Anton. 'Thanks to the Germans! Jewish Cultural Autonomy in Interwar Estonia', *East European Jewish Affairs* vol. 38, no. 1 (2008), pp. 89–104.

Weller, Marc. 'A Critical Evaluation of the First Results of the Monitoring of the Framework Convention on the Issue of Effective Participation of Persons Belonging to National Minorities (1998-2003)'. In *Filling the Frame—Five Years of Monitoring the Framework Convention for the Protection of National Minorities* (Strasbourg: Council of Europe Publishing, 2004), pp. 69–94.

Young, Robert. 'The Programme of Equal Opportunity: An Overview'. In *The Robichaud Era, 1960-1970*, edited by Roger Ouellette (Moncton: Canadian Institute for Research on Regional Development, 2001), pp. 23–35.

Zabielska, Karina and Karl Kössler. 'Cultural Autonomy in Estonia—Before and after the Soviet Interregnum'. In *Solving Ethnic Conflict through Self-Government. A Short Guide to Autonomy in South Asia and Europe*, edited by Thomas Benedikter (Bozen/ Bolzano: EURAC, 2009).

Zaslavsky, Victor. 'Ethnic Group Divided: Social Stratification and Nationality Policy in the Soviet Union'. In *The Soviet Union. Party and Society*, edited by Peter J. Potichnyj (Cambridge: Cambridge University Press, 1988), pp. 218–28.

Zhakaeva, L. S. 'O proportsional'noi sisteme formirovaniya Mazhilisa parlamenta Kazahstana' [On Proportional Structuring of Mazhilis—Kazakh Parliament]. *Konstitucionnoe i munitsipal'noe pravo* no. 7 (2009): pp. 27–32.

WEBSITES AND OTHER SOURCES

Anaya, James. 'The Situation of the Sámi People in the Sápmi Region of Norway, Sweden and Finland', 6 June 2011, A/HRC/18/35/Add.2, accessed 21 September 2012, <http:// unsr.jamesanaya.org/country-reports/the-situation-of-the-sami-people-in-the-sapmi-region-of-norway-sweden-and-finland-2011>.

Bourgeois, Daniel. 'Acadians'. Symposium: 'Autonomy arrangements in the world', Flensburg, Germany: European Centre for Minority Issues, 14–15 September 2012.

Bourgeois, Daniel. 'Ensuring Cultural and Community Survival: How Canada's Official Language Minority School Boards and Schools Assume their Second Mandate', Paper presented at Commission scolaire de langue française de l'Île-du-Prince-Édouard, Mont-Carmel, 15 January 2015.

Bund Deutscher Nordschleswiger, accessed 26 March 2014, <http://www.bdn.dk/>.

Bund Deutscher Nordschleswiger, 'Vorgeschichte des Kopenhagener Sekretariats', accessed 16 March 2014, <http://www.bdn.dk/vorgeschichte.8635.aspx>.

Centar Za Regionalizam. 'Evaluacija Rada Pet Nacionalnih Saveta U Srbiji—Analize I Preporuke' [Evaluation of the Work of Five National Councils In Serbia—Analysis and Recommendations] (2012): pp. 1–137.

Centar za Regionalizam. 'Monitoring transparentnosti u radu nacionalnih saveta nacionalnih manjina—Analize i preporuke' [Monitoring Transparency in the Work of National Councils of National Minorities—Analysis and Recommendations] (2014): pp. 1–73, accessed September 2014, <http://www.centarzaregionalizam.org.rs/prilozi/monitoring/Monitoring_transparentnosti_u_radu_nacionalnih_saveta_nacionalnih_manjina.pdf>.

Cobo, Jose R. Martinez. 'Study of the Problem of Discrimination Against Indigenous Populations, Sub-Commission on the Promotion and Protection of Human Rights', (1982) E/CN.4/Sub.2/1986/7/Add.4, para 379.

'Competence Analysis: National Minorities as a Standortfaktor in the German-Danish Border Region', accessed 26 March 2014, <http://www.landtag.ltsh.de/export/sites/landtagsh/parlament/minderheitenpolitik/download/kompetenzanalyse_en.pdf>.

Dansk Skoleforening for Sydslesvig e.V., Vores Institutioner, accessed 26 March 2014, <http://www.skoleforeningen.org/institutioner>.

Danske Regioner, 'Statistik', accessed 26 March 2014, <http://www.regioner.dk/om+regionerne/statistik+ny>.

Deutschen Schul- und Sprachverein fur Nordschleswig, accessed 26 March 2014, <http://www.dssv.dk/>.

Đorđević, Mladen. 'Nacionalni saveti—Problem umesto rešenja' [National Councils—A Problem instead of a Solution]. *Nova Srpska Politička Misao* (2010), accessed September 2014, <http://www.nspm.rs/politicki-zivot/nacionalni-saveti---problem-umesto-resenja.html>.

Dobos, Balázs. 'The Hungarian Minority Policy—Ten Years after EU-enlargement'. Paper presented at the ASN Conference 'Nationalist Responses to Economic and Political Crisis', Central European University, Budapest, 12–14 June 2014.

Dom narodov Rossii. 2000-2005 (Moscow: Vserossiiskii Vystavochnyi tsentr, 2006).

Eide, Asbjorn. 'Cultural Autonomy and Territorial Democracy: A Recipe for Harmonious Group Accommodation?'. *Working Group on Minorities* (E/CN.4/Sub.2/AC.5/2001/WP.4), 2001.

Endbericht der Arbeitsgruppe. 'Körperschaft des öffentlichen Rechts' [Public Corporation] (2011), accessed September 2014, <http://stiftung.sorben.com/usf/110713_ENDFASSUNG_Gemeinsames_Papier_AG_KdoeR.pdf>.

Estonian Educational Database. 2011, available from the Ministry of Education and Research, accessed 24 January 2012.

Estonian Integration Strategy. 'Estonian Integration Strategy 2008-2013', 2008.

Fédération Nationale des Conseils Scolaires Francophones, accessed September 2014, <http://www.fncsf.ca/rndge>.

Government Office for National Minorities, accessed 15 June 2014, <http://www.un.gov.si/si/manjsine/madzarska_narodna_skupnost/vzgojno_izobrazevalna_kulturna_in_informativna_dejavnost/>.

Hine, David. 'Electoral Systems, Party Law and the Protection of Minorities', Report for the Committee of Experts on Issues Relating to the Protection of Minorities, Strasbourg, April 2009 (DH-MIN (2006)013final).

Hungarian Self-Governing Ethnic Community Association, 27 July 2014, <http://muravidek.si/?lang=sl>.

Jovanović, Tihomila, 'Kako nacionalne manjine troše proračunske kune' [How National Minorities Spend Budget Money], *T-Portal*, 12 October 2014, <http://www.tportal.hr/vijesti/hrvatska/354011/Kako-nacionalne-manjine-trose-proracunske-kune.html>.

Kabanen, Toivo. 'Soome vähemusrahvuse kultuuriautonoomiast' [About Cultural Autonomy of Finnish National Minority], presentation at the Follow-up Seminar on Implementation of the FCNM, 9 October 2006, Tallinn. On file with the author.

Kállai, Ernő. 'A nemzetiségi jogok helyzete Magyarországon a jogszabályváltozások tükrében' [The Situation of Nationality Rights in Hungary in the Light of Legislative Changes], accessed 15 September 2014, <http://www.uni-miskolc.hu/~wwwdeak/Collegium%20Doctorum%20Publikaciok/K%E1llai%20Ern%F5%20.pdf>.

Kállai, Ernő. 'Vélemény a készülő nemzetiségi törvény tervezetéről' [Opinion on the Draft Law on Nationalities], 14 November 2011, accessed 15 September 2014, <http://kisebb-segiombudsman.hu/hir-706-velemeny-keszulo-nemzetisegi-torveny.html>.

Karlsbakk, Jonas. 'Sámi Parliament Wants Veto on Mineral Issues'. *Barents Observer*, accessed 20 December 2012, <http://barentsobserver.com>.

Landry, Jonathan. 'Étude de représentations linguistiques de jeunes Acadiennes et Acadiens en milieu scolaire: Vers un éveil à sa propre langue?' [Study of Linguistic Representations of Young Acadians in Schools: Towards an Awakening to his (their) Own Language?] (Master's thesis, Moncton: Université de Moncton, Faculty of Graduate Studies and Research, September 2012).

Landwirtschaftlicher Hauptverein für Nordschleswig, accessed 26 March 2014, <http://www.lhn.dk/Forside.htm>.

Magyar Nemzeti Tanács, 'A Magyar Nemzeti Tanács Négy Éve—2010. Június 30.—2014 Június 30' [Four Years of the Hungarian National Council—30 June 2010–30 June 2014], *Subotica* (2014): pp. 1–204.

Ministry of Culture. Written communication of 5 July 2012 no. 7.15/907 (on file with the author). 2012.

Ministry of Justice and Police and the Ministry of Local Government and Regional Development (Norway), 'The Finnmark Act—A Guide' [Information brochure distributed in Finnmark] Zoom Grafisk AS, 2005, accessed 20 December 2012 <http://www.galdu.org/govat/doc/brochure_finnmark_act.pdf>.

Minority News, 'Intrvju Dr Suzana Paunović Direktorka Kancelarije za ljudska i manjinska prava' [Interview with Dr Suzana Paunovic, Director of the Office for Human and Minority Rights] (April/May 2013): pp. 4–10, accessed September 2014, <http://www.minoritynews.rs>.

Minority News, 'Ustavni sud o Nacionalnim savetima nacionalnih manjina' [The Constitutional Court of the National Councils of National Minorities] (July 2013): pp. 4–6, accessed September 2014, <http://www.minoritynews.rs>.

National Assembly of the Republic of Slovenia, accessed 24 May 2014, http://www.dz-<rs.si/wps/portal/en/Home>.

Nepujsag Newspaper, accessed 24 July 2014, <http://www.nepujsag.net/>.

Permanent Mission of Finland (Geneva) (8 July 2012) *Verbal Note* GEN7062-19, accessed 20 December 2012 <https://spdb.ohchr.org/hrdb/21st/Finland_09.07.12_%281.2012%29.pdf>.

Pokrajinski Ombudsman Autonomne pokrajine Vojvodine, *Dve godine nacionalnih saveta—Istraživanje Pokrajinskog Ombudsmana* [Two Years of National Councils—Research of the Provincial Ombudsman] (2011): pp. 1–31 accessed September 2014, <http://www.ombudsmanapv.org/riv/attachments/article/244/Izvestaj-dve%20godine%20primene%20Zakona%20o%20nac.savetima.pdf>.

Pokrajinski Ombudsman Autonomne pokrajine Vojvodine. 'Dve godine primene Zakona o nacionalnim savetima nacionalnih manjina—Izveštaj Pokrajinskog ombudsmana Autonomne Pokrajine Vojvodine' [Two Years of Implementation of the Law on National Minority Councils—Report of the Provincial Ombudsman of the Autonomous Province of Vojvodina] (2011): pp. 1–31, accessed September 2014, <http://www.ombudsman-apv.org/riv/index.php/istrazivanja/741-dve-godine-nacionalnih-sveta-ii-deo>.

Radio Free Europe/Radio Liberty (RFE/RL). 'Hungary Seeks Collective Rights in European Constitution'. *RFE/RL Newsline*, 30 September 2003, accessed 5 October 2014, <http://www.minelres.lv/mailing_archive/2003-October/002968.html>.

Region Sønderjylland-Schleswig, accessed 26 March 2014, <http://www.region.de/index.php?id=8&L=1%2Ftrainers.php%3Fid%3D%27__>.

'Responsum fra den dansk-slesvig-holstenske arbejdsgruppe til behandling af liges-tillingsspørgsmål ved finansieringen af det danske og det tyske mindretalsskoler', accessed 27 February 2014, <http://www.uvm.dk/Aktuelt/~/UVM-DK/Content/News/Int/2010/Nov/~/media/UVM/Filer/Om%20os/Int/PDF10/101112_Bericht_Minderheitenschulen_DK.ashxhttp://www.uvm.dk/Aktuelt/~/UVM-DK/Content/News/Int/2010/Nov/~/media/UVM/Filer/Om%20os/Int/PDF10/101112_Bericht_Minderheitenschulen_DK.ashx>.

Sámi Council, 'Observations by the Saami Council with regard to Finland's 20th, 21st, and 22nd Periodic Reports to the Committee for the Elimination of Racial Discrimination. To the Committee for the Elimination of Racial Discrimination', 12 August 2012, accessed 28 December 2012, <http://www2.ohchr.org/english/bodies/cerd/docs/.../SaamiCouncil_Finland81.doc>.

Sámediggi-Finland website, accessed 20 December 2012, <http://www.samediggi.fi.>.

Sámediggi-Norway website, accessed 20 December 2012, <http://www.samediggi.no>.

Sámediggi-Sweden website, accessed 20 December 2012, <http://www.sametinget.se>.

Sámi Council website, accessed 20 December 2012, <http://www.Sámicouncil.net>.

Sámi Parliament in Finland (Sámediggi), 'Statement of Finnish Sámi Parliament on the Realization of Sámi People's Right to Self-Determination in Finland', 15 April 2010. Meeting with the UN Special Rapporteur on the Rights of Indigenous Peoples, James Anaya.

Sámiskt Informationscentrum, accessed 20 December 2012, <http://www.eng.samer.se/GetDoc?meta_id=1228>.

Sara, J. M. 'Indigenous Governance of Self-Determination. The Saami Model and the Saami Parliament in Norway' (Speech by the Vice-President of the Saami Parliament in Norway during the Symposium on 'The Right to Self-Determination in International Law', organized by Unrepresented Nations and Peoples Organization (UNPO), Khmers Kampuchea-Krom Federation (KKF), Hawai'i Institute for Human Rights (HIHR)), 29 September–1 October 2006, The Hague, Netherlands.

Security Police of the Republic of Estonia, 'Annual Review 2011' (Tallinn: 2012), pp. 9–11.

Seurujärvi-Kari, Irja. 'Saamelaisten etnisyyden ja identiteetin rakentaminen saamelais- ja alkuperäiskansaliikkeen kontekstissa' [Sámi Ethnicity—and Identity-Building in the Context of the Sámi and Indigenous Movement] (Doctoral dissertation, University of Helsinki, 2012).

Slovenian Regional Development Fund, accessed 24 May 2014, <http://www.regionalnisklad.si/english>.

Smith, David John. 'Non-Territorial Autonomy and Political Community in Contemporary Central and Eastern Europe'. Paper presented at the panel Non-Territorial Autonomy and New Modalities for National Self-Determination, Political Studies Association Conference, Belfast, 3–5 April 2012.

State Programme 'Integration in Estonian Society 2000-2007', Tallinn, 2000.

Statistical Office of the Republic of Serbia, 'Population, Ethnicity, Data by Municipalities and Cities', *2011 Census of Population, Households and Dwellings in the Republic of Serbia* (2012): p. 15.

Statistische Ämter des Bundes und der Länder, 'Gebiet und Bevölkerung—Bevölkerung nach Altersgruppen', accessed 26 March 2014, <http://www.statistik-portal.de/Statistik-Portal/de_jb01_z2.asp>.

Toivo Kabanen, 'Soome vähemusrahvuse kultuuriautonoomiast' [About Cultural Autonomy of Finnish National Minority], presentation at the Follow-up Seminar on Implementation of the FCNM, 9 October 2006, Tallinn. On file with the author

United Nations Permanent Forum on Indigenous Issues, 'Who are indigenous peoples?' (UNPFII: n.d.).

UNDP Country Office in Serbia. *Human Development Report 2005—Serbia—Strength of Diversity* (Belgrade: UNDP, 2005), pp. 1–127.

Yakutsk: Assambleya Narodov Rossii; Assambleya Narodov Respubliki Sakha (Yakutiya), Pravitelstvo Respubliki Sakha (Yakutiya) [Yakutsk: Peoples' Assembly of Russia; Peoples' Assembly of the Sakha Republic (Yakutiya), The Government of the Sakha Republic (Yakutiya)].

'Обращение председателей правлений Союза русских просветительных и благотворительных обществ в Эстонии и Русского национального союза к президенту Эстонской Республики, февраль 1939 года' [Appeal to the President of the Republic of Estonia of the Chairmen of the Boards of the Union of Russian Educational and Charitable Societies in Estonia and the Russian National Union, February 1939], available from: Эстония (*Estonia Daily*), 3 July 1993.

Index

Index